Pauline Solidarity

Pauline Solidarity

Assembling the Gospel of Treasonous Life

PAUL AND THE
UPRISING OF THE DEAD,
VOLUME 3

Daniel Oudshoorn

Foreword by Ward Blanton

Postscript by Dave Diewert

CASCADE *Books* · Eugene, Oregon

PAULINE SOLIDARITY
Assembling the Gospel of Treasonous Life

Paul and the Uprising of the Dead, Volume 3

Copyright © 2020 Daniel Oudshoorn. All rights reserved. Except for brief quotations in critical publications or reviews, no part of this book may be reproduced in any manner without prior written permission from the publisher. Write: Permissions, Wipf and Stock Publishers, 199 W. 8th Ave., Suite 3, Eugene, OR 97401.

Cascade Books
An Imprint of Wipf and Stock Publishers
199 W. 8th Ave., Suite 3
Eugene, OR 97401

www.wipfandstock.com

PAPERBACK ISBN: 978-1-5326-7527-0
HARDCOVER ISBN: 978-1-5326-7528-7
EBOOK ISBN: 978-1-5326-7529-4

Cataloguing-in-Publication data:

Names: Oudshoorn, Daniel.

Title: Pauline solidarity : assembling the gospel of treasonous life. / Daniel Oudshoorn.

Description: Eugene, OR: Cascade Books, 2020. | Series: Paul and the Uprising of the Dead, Volume 3. | Includes bibliographical references.

Identifiers: ISBN 978-1-5326-7527-0 (paperback) | ISBN 978-1-5326-7528-7 (hardcover) | ISBN 978-1-5326-7529-4 (ebook)

Subjects: LCSH: Paul, the Apostle, Saint—Political and social views | Bible. Epistles of Paul—Criticism, interpretation, etc. | Christianity and politics | Church history—Primitive and early church, ca. 30–600. | Church—Biblical teaching

Classification: BS2655.C5 O93 2020 (print) | BS2655.C5 (ebook)

Manufactured in the U.S.A.   March 24, 2020

Unless otherwise specified, Scripture quotations are from the New Revised Standard Version Bible: Catholic Edition, copyright © 1989, 1993 National Council of the Churches of Christ in the United States of America. Used by permission. All rights reserved worldwide.

TABLE OF CONTENTS

Foreword by Ward Blanton vii
Preface xi
Acknowledgments xiii

1. Introduction: So What and Who Cares? 1

2. The Transnational Family of God 6
   Introduction: Deviating from Empire 6
   Uprooting Imperial Cornerstones: The Household Unit 8
   Summary and Conclusion 54

3. Embracing Shame in the Company of the Crucified 56
   Introduction 56
   Honor and Shame and Shame as Honor in the Household of God 57
   Cruciformity: Re-Presenting the Crucifixion of the Anointed 80
   Conclusion 96

4. Rejecting Patronage within a Sibling-Based Political Economy of Grace 99
   Introduction: Paul the Economist 99
   Laying the Foundation: Family, Marginality, and Eschatology 102
   Struggling to Create an Alternative to Patronage within the
      Assemblies of Jesus Loyalists 106
   The Collection as an Example of Sibling-Based Economic
      Mutualism 119
   Sharing against Private Property 134
   Other Economic Practices 142
   Conclusion: The Spread of the Jesus Movement and the Failure of the
      Pauline Faction 161

TABLE OF CONTENTS

Excursus: The Authority of Paul within the Early Assemblies of Jesus Loyalists 166
    Introduction 166
    Paul as an Authority Figure: Criticisms of the Apostle 167
    Paul as a Non-Domineering Charismatic Authority 170
    Subverting Authority and Equal Membership: Paul as
        Anti-Authority 173
    Conclusion: An Anarchist Parallel 174

5. The Lawlessness of Good News in the Making: Justice, Jesus Loyalty, and Lovingly Organizing Treasonous Life 177
    Introduction: What Do We Talk about When We Talk about the
        Pauline Gospel? 177
    The Foundation of the Gospel: Jesus and Why He Matters 202
    Implications Concerning Justice, the Law, Love, and Loyalty 231
    Assembling the Gospel: The Uprising of the Dead 247
    And, Finally, Romans 13:1–7 264
    Conclusion: The Fire This Time 281

Postscript by Dave Diewert 285
Bibliography 295

FOREWORD

ALL OF THE LIVING Pauline movements in existence today are known only by their miraculously energetic capacities to take up residence along the top of community fencing projects which were both manufactured and maintained in order to keep us out! To take a dictum like this seriously would itself be a Pauline event of some significance, one which would among other things afford a new canon for worthwhile interpretive labor on scriptural traditions.

Tell me, you who want to be Pauline interpreters—where are your evidently impossible friendships? Where is that awkwardly amorous or enthusiastic traffic between opposed camps? Where are the peculiarly shared agendas which should not be seeing eye to eye? When did you last engage that network of friends who nevertheless do not want to be seen together in public? And where then do you discover such furtive, almost unavowable meets, such that they yield new social space, a new public? Where, moreover, is the reaction, the righteous indignation, against your work because your interlocutors cringe and pull back in order not to be associated with them—those who are missing the point, those who are too intense, those who are too tied down (or not enough). Show me the Paulinist who simply belongs in her home institution, in her home community, in her own bibliographies even, and I will show you someone who is receding from the living energies of transformative un-fencing which constitute a Pauline taste for solidarity. Pauline scholarship is of value if you experience transgressive solidarity; otherwise your wordy commentary, however learned, is only the magician's misdirection above a predictably empty hat.

Daniel Oudshoorn unveils here a Pauline taste, nothing less than a Pauline style, which Oudshoorn sometimes articulates as a "deviant sense of kinship." This swerved kinship I understand as an intensive or "singular" solidarity which buzzes at, precisely, the borders it crosses. We must begin to take seriously something like this experience as a kind of spiritual test of Paulinist life, a life worth its salt of fidelity to this strange legacy. One cannot read Oudshoorn without feeling its call, its unique audacity, its vexing emancipations. If such a spiritual test should come, it would be a surprise to see who would endure it. Institutionally speaking, for example, in all seriousness I do not know whether many of our academic societies of Pauline interpreters would continue to stand. What a strange thought! But the judgment, or at least the wonder, would of course be here not merely theoretical or ideal. The question is whether these scholarly paradigms—and our paradigms are always strictly scripted by our social forms—are not themselves indices of a world order which is already beginning to pass away, just for the reason that they are no longer alive with that energetic form of living in emancipatory transgression. To change the paradigms, one must transform the social forms which produce them. Oudshoorn's book is, for the perceptive reader, a cookbook for such transformations, so many experiments with Paulinist life. That is perhaps what moves me most of all in these pages, the simple and honest experimentation in historical reconstruction which resonates with that vibrancy from which Oudshoorn's thinking is created and from which it finds its living form.

Diogenes Laertius tells us that the great Cynic philosophers would refuse to take on students who wanted wise and edifying words without a more awkward and demanding transformation of their social experiences. One does not live the life of the teaching unless words about truth become experiments in "defacing the currency" of the very cultural values which produced you. The Greco-Roman archive of spiritual exercises is worth remembering on these points. You want to learn philosophy? Here, take and eat—this is the food you will eat where you should not. This is your body which shall be excited where it must not. This is the loser who will be proud when she should hold her head in shame. And, above all, this is the divine work which happens where it must not, there where it is not owned or where it happens outside the proper systems of ownership that are (then as now) indistinguishable from religion or politics as such.

The "short-cut to virtue" on offer by these philosophical greats (where have they gone today!) was, immediately and directly, the scandalous refusal to be placed, to be made polite, by the inherited order of things. The Paulinist is perhaps sometimes more bookish than the Cynic, but she is nevertheless united with them in finding transformational energies in playing out truth where and how it should not happen. If we no longer buzz with the counterintuitive, countercultural energy of finding that we "are not ashamed" of our transgressive good news, then we have misunderstood our radical kinships, misrecognized our transformative solidarities, and failed to hold forth any truly Paulinist news at all. In that case, however, Oudshoorn's cookbook, or perhaps his Paulinist style guide, will be more important than ever.

Ward Blanton
University of Kent

PREFACE

IN *PAUL AND THE Uprising of the Dead*, I attempt a comprehensive study of the Pauline epistles, paying especial attention to socioeconomic and theopolitical matters. I survey a broad range of positions, and note how presuppositions related to the socioeconomic status of the early Jesus loyalists as well as presuppositions about Pauline eschatology heavily influence the conclusions that diverse parties draw in relation to these themes. I begin by surveying four prominent positions taken in relation to "Paul and politics," and then explore the socioeconomic and general eschatological arguments that are made to support these positions (volume 1: Pauline Politics). I then turn to examining Pauline apocalyptic eschatology in more detail and relate it to the realized eschatology of Rome, while studying the ideo-theology of Roman imperialism more generally (volume 2: Pauline Eschatology). This leads to a presentation of Paulinism that focuses especially upon the themes of living as members of the transnational family of God, embracing shame in solidarity with the crucified, engaging in sibling-based practices of economic mutuality, and loyally and lovingly gospeling the justice of God in treasonous, law-breaking, and law-fulfilling ways, within the newly assembled body of the Anointed (volume 3: Pauline Solidarity). This presentation is distinct, in many ways, from the most prominent conservative, liberal, and radical readings of the Pauline epistles. Ultimately, what is presented is an understanding of Paulinism as a faction within a movement that is actively working to organize the oppressed, abandoned, vanquished, and left-for-dead, into a body that experiences Life in all of its abundance and goodness. This body necessarily exists in conflict with dominant (imperial) death-dealing ways of organizing life in the service of Death. The Pauline faction, then, are those who help to organize this resistance to Death—and all the ways in which Death is structured into social, economic, political, and religious organizations—within assemblies where justice is understood to be that which is life-giving and life-affirming, especially for those who have been deprived of life and left for dead.

ACKNOWLEDGMENTS

I BEGIN BY ACKNOWLEDGING the various sovereign Indigenous peoples who have allowed me to live and work and play and complete this project on the lands to which they belong—from the Wendat, Petun, and Mississaugas, to the Musqueam, Squamish, and Tsleil-Waututh, to the Attawandaron, Wendat, Lenape, Haudenosaune, and Anishinaabe—I lift my hands to them and thank them for the care that they have shown the land and for allowing me and my children and other loved ones to live, work, and struggle alongside of them. In many ways, my ability to complete this project is related to my own status as a white, cishet, male settler of Christian European descent. It is precisely people like me who have benefited most from the ongoing and genocidal process of Canadian colonialism. Thus, when I acknowledge various sovereign Indigenous peoples, as I am doing now, I do so with a sense of my own interconnectedness, liability, accountability, and responsibility. I hope that this work contributes to the ongoing process of decolonization and the uprising of those whom my people have left for dead in these territories. Were I to begin this project again, I would be more interested in writing about Paulinism as it relates to militant Indigenous movements pursuing solidarity, resistance, and liberation within the overarching context of colonialism. The parallels, to me, are striking and I believe that kind of study could be very enriching and, perhaps, help bring together two groups of people who are often at odds with each other.

I acknowledge my children, Charlie and Ruby, and my partner, Jessica Marlatt. You each played central roles in my own *anastasis* from the dead. Thank you for giving me the gifts of wonder, gratitude, gentleness, love, joy, kindness, fatherhood, companionship, and life—new creation life, abundant life, resurrection life. You are all marvels and wonders, and I love you with all of my everything.

ACKNOWLEDGMENTS

I acknowledge those scholars who showed me that we have to figure these things out in the streets, on the barricades, in our homes, in squats, in physical altercations with riot police, and in the midst of the struggle. Thank you, Charles and Rita Ringma and Dave and Teresa Diewert. Nobody else whom I have known who bothers talking about Paul has ever come close to embodying Paulinism in the ways that you all have and do. Bob Eklad and Don Cowie also helped me a great deal in this regard. Thank you also to all those involved in the fight who may or may not have cared one bit about Paul but who helped teach me (personally or from a distance) what it means to serve Life and fight against Death—thank you, Jody Nichols, Nicky Dunlop, Andrea Earl, Jan Rothenburger, Anthony Schofield, Ivan Mulder, Stanislav Kupferschmidt, Alex Hundert, Ann Livingston, Harsha Walia, John Clarke, Mechele te Brake, Haley Broadbent, Richard Phillips, as well as all the people at Boy'R'Us (Vancouver) and SafeSpace London, everyone involved in creating overdose prevention sites across Canadian-occupied territories, and the old warrior from AIM who gave me his bandana late one night at a bar in Vancouver's downtown eastside. Indeed, it is Indigenous peoples who have spent generations organizing against colonialism, capitalism, patriarchy, and the devastation of Turtle Island—from the Wet'suwet'en camp, to Elsipogtog, to Amjiwnaang, to Kanehsatake, to Ts'peten, to Aazhoodena, to Esgenoopititj, to the Tiny House Warriors—who, to my mind, show us the closest example of what something akin to Paulinism might look like today. I lift my hands to them.

I acknowledge my brothers, Joshua, Judah, and Abram, who have shown me how wonderful, transformative, and good, sibling relationships can be. And my nephews and nieces—Evan and Wyatt, Emery and Selah, Ben and Chris and Daniella—who gave me life at a time when I was separated from my own children. Without their love, the joy they experienced playing silly games with me, and the ways that made me feel okay in the midst of a very not-okay time, this project would never have been completed.

I acknowledge all of those who encouraged me to complete this project at various times over these years. Apart from those already mentioned, thank you, Daniel Imburgia, Chris Graham, Nathan Colquhoun, Daniel Slade, Danielle Firholz, Chris Tilling, Nicole Luongo, Mark Van Steenwyk, John Stackhouse, Christian Amondson, Audrey Molina, Larry Welborn, Ward Blanton, Roland Boer, and my ever loving, ever gentle, ever patient, mother (I love you, mama!). Thank you, Neil Elliott,

ACKNOWLEDGMENTS

for agreeing to be the first reader of this project. It is a great joy to be able to work with you (it is like a dream come true for me after I first read *Liberating Paul* all those years ago). And thank you, Regent College (Vancouver), for allowing me to bring this project to completion after all this time and all these words. I appreciate the graciousness you have shown me. Thank you, also, to Steve Thomson (the Silver Fox) for making me read Paul in new and suddenly exciting ways when I was first an undergraduate student, and to Ms. Lane, my high school writing teacher, who believed I had a special gift for writing at a time when I had recently been deprived of housing (i.e., made homeless) by my parents and did not believe anything good about myself.

Finally, I also acknowledge the great multitude of those whom I have known who lost their homes, health, happiness, well-being, children, and, in many cases, their lives, because the Law of Sin and of Death continues to be enforced by the blind and corrupt rulers of this present evil age. I miss you and love you all. You are the song in my heart and the fire in my blood. And, since the system that killed you or left you for dead will not burn down by itself, I offer the following work as a spark.

1

INTRODUCTION: SO WHAT AND WHO CARES?

As I was concluding this project, I learned that a dear friend had died. Injecting opiates cut with fentanyl resulting in an accidental overdose is the suspected cause of death, but this is a dishonest conclusion. The actual cause of death was the law, which criminalizes certain kinds of drugs and certain ways of using drugs and then makes people who use those drugs or who use drugs in those ways the just targets of state-based violence. The so-called "opioid crisis" sweeping across the occupied territories of Turtle Island has killed several of my friends. Sometimes Death comes via an overdose. Sometimes it comes in other ways. For example, I recently had two other friends—two kind, gentle, loving men—die because they were discharged from the hospital even though they had very serious blood infections. The hospital would not provide them with pain relief because they were flagged as illicit drug users, and when they tried to find their own ways to medicate their pain, the hospital kicked them out—one to a rooming house, another to a homeless shelter. After these men died, the partner of one tried to sue the hospital for gross negligence, but once the hospital announced that the man was an intravenous drug user who was "red flagged" as a "drug seeking frequent flyer" and who was discharged from the hospital because he had been found injecting opiates into his PICC line (i.e., a peripherally inserted central catheter), she couldn't get a lawyer who would take the case. The law and the law-abiding are killers but, it seems, they are never guilty.

Along similar lines, just to the south of me, across a border Europeans carved through lands they stole and transformed into private property, representatives of a dying empire are once again quoting Rom 13:1–7 and urging people to continue to obey the law, even if the cries of children torn from their parents and caged in kennels built in an old Wal-Mart make sensitive oppressors feel uneasy. Some of these children are dying. Some of them are being sexually abused. Many of them have simply vanished. But the state tells us not to be afraid or worried. The state proclaims, "We have done nothing wrong. We are justified by the law. And you are too. Just keep paying your bills. Keep going to work. Keep shopping. Vote."

"And I, too, am justified by the law," the world's most famous pussy-grabber proclaims.

"I sleep the sleep of the just," declares the founder of the world's largest mercenary force.

"We did nothing wrong," declare the hospital administrators and social workers who sent my friends to their deaths.

And on this side of the border, in territories colonized by my people, a prime minister weeps and apologizes to Indigenous peoples and talks a pretty talk about reconciliation, but he still forces pipelines down their throats until they choke on oil, he still refuses to recognize their sovereignty, he still refuses to stop discriminating against Indigenous children living on reserves, he still refuses to provide reserves with clean drinking water, he still refuses to address matters related to Indigenous peoples being massively over-represented in foster care and in prisons, he still refuses to address the matter of the staggering suicide rates among Indigenous teens, and, even as a self-proclaimed feminist, he seems to not care about the thousands of missing and murdered Indigenous women and girls in Canadian-occupied territories, or about the fact that his government is facilitating the sale of billions of dollars worth of military hardware to the Saudis to assist with a genocide in Yemen. Everywhere, it seems, the rich get richer, the poor get poorer, those who are justified by the law continue to kill, and those who are not justified by the law continue to die or be left for dead. Even such sensitive colonizers as myself find ourselves in bondage to the law, and discover that we do not do the good we long to do but, instead, become complicit within and benefit from the very things that we hate. Wretched people that we are, how can we become liberated from this political economy, this body of Sin and of Death?

I have often asked myself these questions over the years. As a result, my interest in Paul and Paulinism (and this project) has waxed and waned. There was a time when it inspired me to wade into the struggle;

INTRODUCTION: SO WHAT AND WHO CARES?

there was a time when I viewed it like a ladder to be climbed and then kicked away; there was a time when I thought it was important; and there was a time when I viewed it as essentially meaningless. My friends are dying—my friends have always been dying ever since I joined the company of the abandoned and left for dead as a youth who was deprived of housing (i.e., made homeless) by his devout Christian parents—and here I am studying a few letters written by a self-proclaimed nobody almost two thousand years ago.[1] Why bother? Indeed, for a long time I didn't bother. I threw myself into the struggle—and when I was battered and broken and torn apart by conflicting allegiances (it took me some time to understand what loyalty to the crucified and left-for-dead looked like, and by then I was already enmeshed in various other commitments—which is precisely the kind of compromised and entangled situation imperialism tries to create in all its subjects), I threw myself into other things. I experienced the Spirit of Life and I experienced Death. I was filled with hope and I was filled with despair. All the while, Paulinism ebbed and flowed in and out of my life. Ultimately, it was only thanks to my children, Charlie and Ruby, my big love, Jessica, my brothers, nephews, and nieces, and the trees by the Deshkan Ziibiing that I found the strength, ability, and desire to return to this project and, after twelve long years, bring it to an end.

But why should anyone else care about this project? Well, I'm not sure that they should. In fact, the great majority of people whom I know who are gospeling in the ways I describe in this work have little or nothing to do with Paulinism or Jesus. In fact, a good many of them want nothing to do with anything associated with Christianity—which makes a lot of sense given the central role Christianity has played in the colonial history of genocide in these territories (a history that extends from the past up until the present day). I am not interested in converting these people to Paulinism, and I am also not interested in trying to redeem Paul (or Jesus) in their eyes. They do not need Paul or Jesus to do the amazing, difficult, inspiring, death-resisting, life-affirming, and life-giving work they are doing. The Spirit of Life is already their constant companion as they engage in an *anastasis* from the dead and assemble a body politic that is severed from and at war with the vampiric body of capitalism, colonialism, imperialism, and Death.

However, for those who care about Paul and his legacy, for those invested in these texts, I hope to offer a reading that inspires engagement

---

1. On "homelessness" understood as "housing deprivation," see Willse, *Value of Homelessness*.

in the war for Life and against Death. I hope to take texts that have been put in the service of Death and show that they are better suited to serve Life. After all, up until our present moment, the Pauline Epistles continue to be deployed in death-dealing ways. This needs to be changed, and I hope to contribute to that change. This does not mean that I think that the rulers and those who lick their boots will subsequently change their minds and repent and begin to serve Life. I believe that most of these people have already charted their courses. Regardless of devout professions of faith and virtue, their concern is not so much with what the texts say as with their own appetites (and so, as the Pauline factions says, their glory is their shame and their end is destruction). But I do hope that this text will help others to see how self-serving, violent, and inappropriate the readings imposed by the rulers and their servants are.

Furthermore, although this is a scholarly text, my primary audience is not the academy or scholars (who are probably not going to change any more than the rulers—they, too, have discovered the comfort that comes from saying pretty things while remaining almost universally uninvolved in any contemporary project that resembles Pauline gospeling). Instead, I write for students or those on the street, those already involved in the struggle, those who may be trying to create change but who are frustrated by the limits of their efforts, and those who are looking for other models of action. If this study of Paulinism is a useful contribution to the struggle to find Life in a Death-dominated context, use it. If it is not, discard it. After all, I am not urging loyalty to Paulinism per se—I am urging loyalty to the Spirit of Life and the left for dead in whose company the Spirit of Life moves like an *anastasis*. This loyalty is found not in the study of texts or the discussion of theories or in the logos itself, but it is found on the street, in the struggle, where one discovers one's siblings among the oppressed, where one pursues a mutually liberating solidarity with the humiliated and crucified, where one engages in concrete actions of mutual care, and where one breaks death-dealing laws in the service of Life. Anyone who gospels otherwise—regardless of how comforting or cautious or clever or radical their language may be—is betraying the body of the Anointed as understood by the Pauline faction. To imitate Paul and his coworkers today means this: start organizing yourselves in ways that the most oppressed, most vulnerable, most abandoned, and most betrayed experience as liberating, life-giving, and loving. Do this where you can, with what you can, however you can. If you have to lie, cheat, and steal to do this, then lie, cheat, and steal. There is no moral code, no law, no police

INTRODUCTION: SO WHAT AND WHO CARES?

force, no code of conduct, no security guard, no veneration of private property, and no policies or procedures that has authority to trump the service of Life. Not only this, but beware of the wisdom of the bosses, the rulers, and the academy. It is the wisdom of this age and it seeks to broker compromises with Death-dealers. If you do not compromise, you will be branded as a fool, but you should not be fooled—Death is uncompromising. To the best of your abilities and knowledge, do not compromise with it. Fight it. Fight foolishly, fight vigorously, fight collectively, fight laughingly, supporting one another and being united in love so that each can rest and heal and live to fight another day, but fight. Only do not always remain fixated upon that which you are fighting. Remember what you are fighting for. Create enclaves of new life now in one another's company. Abolish hierarchies of power between people. Let each give according to their ability and receive according to their need. Laugh. Play. Create. Be kind and gentle and tender with one another, and most especially with children.

And when my children are grown, I'll see you again on the barricades.
Xoxo
Dan
February 2019

2

THE TRANSNATIONAL FAMILY OF GOD

For freedom [the Anointed] has set us free. Stand firm, therefore, and do not submit again to a yoke of slavery.

—Galatians 5:1

So then you are no longer strangers and aliens, but you are citizens with the august ones and also members of the household of God, built upon the foundation of the diplomatic envoys and prophets, with the Anointed Jesus himself as the cornerstone.

—Ephesians 2:19–20 (my translation)

Introduction: Deviating from Empire

IN THE NEXT FOUR chapters, I will examine the ways in which the Pauline faction handles the themes raised in the exploration of the ideo-theology of Rome that took place in volume 2. How do Paul, his coworkers, and the early assemblies of Jesus loyalists addressed in their letters go about sharing life together? How do they engage with the four cornerstones of Roman imperialism and how do they engage the ubiquitous themes spread by the imperial propaganda communicated through the imperial cult(s)? In this chapter, I will cover Pauline material regarding household relationships. Chapter 3 will examine honor and shame, and chapter 4 will look at the practice of patronage and the economic issues it raises. I will then offer an excursus re-examining Paul to see how his personal practice of authority adheres to the themes developed in the letters he coauthored. In chapter 5, I will turn to a more detailed examination of the ways in which the early assemblies of Jesus loyalists related to traditional Roman religiosity and the gospel of the divine Caesars.

In what follows it will be demonstrated that the early Jesus loyalists, especially the Pauline faction and those associated with it, created a way of structuring life together that was not only an alternative to the socioeconomic and theopolitical structures of the Roman Empire but also directly deconstructed and rejected those imperial structures. It is here we will most fully begin to see how the Pauline faction was a part of what I have termed the *anastasis* (or uprising) of the dead. These are the concrete ways in which those who were left-for-dead by the rulers of their day—the poor and the slightly less poor, the vanquished and displaced, the oppressed and enslaved—began to resist Death, in all of its manifestations, and instead chose to formulate a way of sharing Life together in new and powerful ways.

The revaluation of values that occurred within the early assemblies of Jesus loyalists not only differed from the imperial vision of Rome, it also challenged and contradicted values that were deeply entrenched in the cultures that existed in the regions familiar to Paul and his coworkers. This further contributed to the persecutions experienced by the Jesus loyalists, as any who espoused alternative values would be branded as deviant. David deSilva summarizes this well:

> The early Christians [sic] proclaimed a message and stood for values that differed from, and indeed contradicted, core values within the dominant Greco-Roman culture as well as the Jewish subculture within which the church arose. Their non-Christian neighbors, therefore, subjected the early Christians to censure and shaming techniques, designed to bring these deviant people back in line with the values and behaviors held dear by the surrounding culture.[1]

Therefore, there was constant pressure to abandon the values of the movement and return to the more acceptable and publicly approved ways of being in society—pressure that, as we have seen, carried heavy material,

---

1. deSilva, *Honor, Patronage, Kinship, and Purity*, 43; see also 43–45. For others who have commented on this revaluation of values, see, for example, Dunn, *Beginning from Jerusalem*, 794–96; Kim, *Christ's Body in Corinth*, 39–54.

physical, and personal costs for any who persisted as deviant. This produced considerable tension and conflicts in the assemblies to which Paul and his coworkers wrote. This will become apparent in the following examination of the ways in which the early Jesus loyalists engaged with the cornerstones of Roman imperial society.

Uprooting Imperial Cornerstones: The Household Unit

Siblings Within the Transnational Family of God

Since at least the early 1990s, there has been a renewed popular and scholarly focus upon the role of the household unit within the communities associated with Paulinism. This focus upon "house churches" is well represented by Robert Banks's book, *Paul's Idea of Community: The Early House Churches in Their Cultural Settings*.[2] While trends in that direction may have faded in more recent years, the point remains well established that the household unit was fundamental to the rise, spread, and shape of the early Jesus movement. Unlike other cults, Judean religious groups, or Graeco-Roman political assemblies, those loyal to Jesus did not meet in spaces set apart for the purpose of those meetings. Rather, they were unique in choosing to meet and grow within homes and within the household unit.[3] However, given that the household unit was the basic unit of political and socioeconomic relationships, precisely how the early Jesus loyalists conceived of their relationships with one another within the household would have repercussions for all their social interactions.

Before examining the household unit as it is presented in the Pauline letters, it is worth recalling that the homes of those loyal to Jesus were nothing like the "house churches" or "cell groups" that are familiar to some North American Christians. The "house churches" the Pauline faction engaged were not groups of people meeting in a living room in somebody's suburban middle-class home. Rather, given what we concluded in volume 1, the abject poverty of the movement's members (with so-called "wealthier" members only being *relatively less poor*), it is worth remembering that the household unit in their communities is divorced from anything like home-ownership or houses. Rather, the early assemblies

---

2. See Banks, *Paul's Idea of Community*.

3. See Banks, *Paul's Idea of Community*, 49; Esler, *Conflict and Identity in Romans*, 102–6; deSilva, *Honor, Patronage, Kinship, and Purity*, 226–27; Meeks, *Moral World of the First Christians*, 110; Judge, *Social Distinctives of the Christians*, 24–27, 134.

of Jesus loyalists would gather in tiny, shared apartments, which often doubled as workshops. They would be rooted in slums and packed, dilapidated tenement buildings.[4] A better modern analogy would be to imagine a small group of people gathered together in a shanty in one of the favelas in Rio de Janeiro or a group of sweatshop laborers gathered together to meet in the cramped quarters assigned to them by the owners of the factory.

As I did in the examination of the importance of the household unit to the ideo-theology of Rome, I will explore the two primary elements of the household—kinship and slavery—and examine the ways in which the early assemblies of Jesus loyalists engaged these structures. I will begin by examining how the movement redefined kinship, radically altering the ways in which they were required to relate to one another—not only within their own household unit but also across the span of the Roman Empire. I will then turn to examining how this deviant sense of kinship impacted the biological family unit, paying special attention to gender issues. Finally, I will focus on how these altered relationships affected the status of slaves within the early assemblies of Jesus loyalists.

Kinship Redefined: The Family of God

One of the things that immediately becomes apparent when reading the Pauline letters is the abundant use of family language employed in order to refer to people who were not related by ties of blood, ethnicity, or nationality. By using this language, Paul and his coworkers reoriented the relationships (and therefore also the priorities and the activities) of those within the assemblies of Jesus loyalists in order to create a "fictive kinship" that superseded the bonds established by pre-existing kinship networks and obligations.[5] One's birth—along with the status and identity formed by that birth—was overruled and a new kinship was created

---

4. See Esler, *Conflict and Identity in Romans*, 107; Jewett, *Romans*, 65, 77–80. Jeffers suggests that the assemblies of Jesus loyalists would gather in the more deluxe first-floor apartments of the tenement buildings, but the socio-economic analysis of the early Jesus movement in volume 1 suggests to me that this is an overly optimistic assessment (see Jeffers, *Greco-Roman World*, 55–56).

5. Although I lack the space to fully develop the overlaps in this regard, it is worth noting that Paul and his coworkers were essentially following the trajectory established by Jesus and those who gathered with him, when they challenged kinship claims and overrode them in order to create an alternative community (see, for example, Mark 3:31–35; Matt 12:46–50; Luke 8:19–21; 9:59–62; 12:51–53).

through adoption (wherein one was born again), which completely reoriented one's identity, status, and the boundaries in which one lived.⁶

This reorientation as a new family was important for the resocialization of the Jesus loyalists who were being persecuted and who risked further alienating themselves from their neighbors and the surrounding cultural values. It helped them develop strong and positive self- and corporate-identities.⁷ At the same time, it heightened the persecutions and marginalization experienced by the Jesus loyalists. Those embedded within Graeco-Roman culture, especially those who benefited the most from it, would not welcome any reorientation of established relational networks and patterns. Roman law was constructed in such a way as to carefully guard kinship relationships (which, as we have seen, acted as one of the foundations of Roman power).⁸ Therefore, by imagining the early assemblies of Jesus loyalists as a fictive kinship transcending other biological or racialized kinship groups, Paul and his coworkers were both assisting the Jesus loyalists in finding ways to support one another in a marginal space, while simultaneously increasing the marginalization experienced therein.

What shape does this fictive kinship take? Succinctly stated, the assemblies of Jesus loyalists became the new transnational family of God. This family was composed of God the Father, Jesus the firstborn Son, and all others as siblings who are now identified as (adopted) children of God. It is these members who compose the *oikeious tes pisteos*—the household or family of the loyal (see Gal 6:10).

The primary person in this family is the God who is referred to as "father" in the Pauline letters. The Pauline faction regularly opens their letters by wishing the assemblies grace and peace, not just from God the Father, but from God *our* Father (see Rom 1:7; 1 Cor 1:3; 2 Cor 1:2; Gal 1:3; Phil 1:2; Phlm 3—the greeting is slightly different in 1 Thessalonians, where the Thessalonians are referred to as those who are "in God the

---

6. Many scholars have emphasized the importance of the creation of a fictive kinship within the Pauline communities. See, for example, deSilva, *Honor, Patronage, Kinship, and Purity*, 195–96, 209, 225–26; Elliott, "Strategies of Resistance," 102–5; Gorman, *Reading Paul*, 134–37; Kee, *Beginnings of Christianity*, 413; Malherbe, *Paul and the Popular Philosophers*, 62–63; "God's New Family in Thessalonica," 117–21; Malina and Pilch, *Social-Science Commentary*, 362–63; Moxnes, *Constructing Early Christian Families*, 1–2; Osiek, "Family Matters," 219; Crossan and Borg, *First Paul*, 187; Carter, "Vulnerable Power," 476.

7. See Matera, *New Testament Ethics*, 130–34; Remus, "Persecution," 439–40.

8. See Wright, *New Testament*, 448–51; Winter, "Roman Law and Society," 96–97.

THE TRANSNATIONAL FAMILY OF GOD

father"; 1 Thess 1:1). This Father God thus fulfills a similar role to that played by Jupiter in the Roman ideo-theology. And having God as "our Father" is a theme that then receives powerful expression elsewhere in Paul's letters. Prominently, Rom 8:14–17 states the following:

> For all who are led by the Spirit of God are children of God. For you did not receive a spirit of slavery to fall back into fear, but you have received a spirit of adoption. When we cry, "Abba! Father!" it is that very Spirit bearing witness with our spirit that we are children of God, and if children, then heirs, heirs of God and joint heirs with [the Anointed]—if, in fact, we suffer with him so that we may also be glorified with him.

As we already learned with the selection of Caesar's heirs, there is a close connection between adoption and inheritance, with adopted children also inheriting the family name, wealth, glory, and spirit of their adoptive father.[9] This is also what we discover with the Jesus loyalists who enter into the household of God. As Gal 4:4–7 states:

> But when the fullness of time had come, God sent his son, born of a woman, born under the Law, in order to redeem those who were under the law, so that we might receive adoption as children. And because you are children, God has sent the Spirit of his son into our hearts, crying, "Abba! Father!" So you are no longer a slave but a child, and if a child then also an heir, through God.

In a manner similar to coins, monuments, temples, and inscriptions all over the empire that proclaimed the divine sonship of the emperors adopted into heavenly kinship networks, the Jesus loyalists claimed to have been adopted as children of the most high God (an especially shocking claim given what we have learned about the socioeconomic and political status of the Jesus loyalists). Indeed, in the Pauline letters, "father" is the title employed for God more frequently than any other.[10] In this way, God becomes the new *paterfamilias*, full of both affection for his children and authority over the household of those loyal to him.[11]

---

9. See Peppard, *Son of God*, 30, 47, 136–40; Jennings, *Outlaw Justice*, 129.

10. For other references to God as father, see Rom 15:6; 1 Cor 8:6; 15:24; 2 Cor 1:3; 11:31; Gal 1:4; Phil 2:11; 4:20; 1 Thess 1:3; 3:11, 13.

11. See deSilva, *Honor, Patronage, Kinship, and Purity*, 196, 206–7; Meeks, *Origins of Christian Morality*, 170–72; Crossan and Borg, *First Paul*, 114. Jeffers asserts that Jesus is *the* single *paterfamilias* within the community of faith (with reference only to Eph 1:22; 2:19–20; Col 1:18—i.e., without reference to the non-contested Pauline

Pauline Solidarity

There are a few implications of understanding God as one's father in this context. First of all, being children of God offered the early Jesus loyalists a way of renegotiating their status and their self-understanding, despite the humiliation, low status, and violent persecutions they experienced.[12] Having been adopted by God, the movement's members could claim a superior lineage to that of their neighbors. Within the Roman Empire, only the Caesars made equally audacious claims. Which leads to a second point. Announcing God as "our father," within an empire wherein the Caesars claimed to be the universal fathers (and wherein Jupiter was most frequently called God the father), threw the assemblies of Jesus loyalists into conflict with Roman imperialism (we will see more of the significance of this conflict—and its inevitable seditious nature—momentarily).[13] The third implication, which will be explored in more detail in the next chapter, is that members of the household of God would be expected to emulate the character of their father.[14] However, it must also be emphasized that focusing upon God as the Father of the household removed any ultimate authority from all other members of the assemblies. For, just as we saw with Romans who adopted an heir, men who accepted a new father were required to give up their status of *paterfamilias* within their own families. God becomes the sole *paterfamilias*. Within gender-critical and feminist Pauline scholarship, the language of fatherhood has been sharply criticized for re/inscribing oppressive social arrangements into the early Jesus-movement and perhaps contributing to the stifling of the more egalitarian or radical impulses that the movement contained. While there is much that is important and appropriate about these criticisms, what is missed is that referring to God as the sole Father of the household of the faithful prevents any other person within the household from laying claim to that status. When God is the Father of the household, nobody else is. Within the Pauline ideology, the *paterfamilias* is made transcendent so that no human member of the assemblies of Jesus loyalists may claim this title or authority.

Yet, what of Paul himself? Does he not lay claim to fatherhood language on a few occasions? In 1 Cor 4:15, he states that he "became [the

---

Epistles) (Jeffers, *Greco-Roman World*, 84). However, it is better to understand these references to Christ as "the head" or "the cornerstone" as referring to Jesus's status as the eldest son.

12. See deSilva, *Honor, Patronage, Kinship, and Purity*, 209–11.
13. See Carter, "Vulnerable Power," 476.
14. See deSilva, *Honor, Patronage, Kinship, and Purity*, 211–12.

Corinthians'] father through the gospel," and in 1 Thess 2:11 he claims to have dealt with the Thessalonians "like a father with his children." However, as Beverly Gaventa has noted, more often than applying paternal imagery to himself, Paul refers to himself with maternal imagery—*as a mother*.[15] To mention some examples, slightly earlier in 1 Thessalonians, Paul refers to himself "like a nurse tenderly caring for her own children" (1 Thess 2:7), and in 1 Cor 3:1–2 he describes himself in a similar way, as one feeding milk to infants. Similarly, in Gal 4:19 he describes the Galatians as his children for whom he has personally experienced labor pains and in Phlm 10 he refers to Onesimus as his "child" to whom he "gave birth" (a point made more patriarchal and gender-normative in the NRSV, which mistranslates this as Paul saying he became the father of Onesimus). Thus, when he refers to the members of the assemblies of Jesus loyalists as his children, it is more likely that Paul is doing so while imagining himself as their mother.[16] Or, Paul may be claiming even less status and may be imagining himself as a wet nurse—a role fulfilled by slaves (another title Paul often applies to himself). In either case, by doing so, Paul is contradicting and challenging notions of gender status within his own society. It would be shameful for any man to identify as womanly in any way. Therefore, by doing so, he seems to demonstrate that he has no desire to be taken for any sort of *paterfamilias*. Or, at the very least, as he employs paternal language in 1 Thess 2, shortly after employing maternal language, he is significantly queering—altering and making strange—any prior conceptions of fatherhood.

Of course, by claiming to be like a mother to the members of the assemblies, by calling them his children (as well as children of God), Paul is claiming to have *some* authority over the assemblies (even if that is only the authority of a wet nurse over infants). This point will be explored later. For now, however, it should be emphasized that God was the living father of the household of Jesus loyalists and God was the *only* living father of the household of Jesus loyalists.

I emphasize that God is the only *living* father because at some points, Paul refers to Abraham as the father of the Jesus loyalists.[17] However, Abraham is neither understood as the most significant father nor

---

15. See Gaventa, "Our Mother St Paul," 86–90; *Our Mother Saint Paul*.

16. See also Gal 4:19; 1 Cor 4:14–15, 17; 2 Cor 6:13; 12:14; Phlm 10. This interpretation seems not to have occurred to earlier scholars, including Meeks (*First Urban Christians*, 87–88).

17. See Rom 4:1–17; 9:6–26; Gal 3:6–4:31.

is he understood as a father who currently exercises authority over the household (apart from being an example one is to emulate); rather, he is understood as an ancestor who grants the Jesus loyalists a prestigious lineage. Just as being able to claim God as one's father was a way of both employing and challenging cultural conceptions of honor and shame as they were brought to bear upon the assemblies of Jesus loyalists, so also being able to trace one's lineage back to Abraham provided the Jesus loyalists with an internal sense of high status. Additionally, employing this lineage and offering Abraham as a common ancestor and forefather of *all the nations* counters the story offered by the empire, wherein the Roman ancestry of Aeneas was praised and the Caesar was viewed as the father of a transnational family.[18] Over against the prestigious descent of the Romans from Aeneas, Paul posits the prestigious descent of the Jesus loyalists from Abraham. Over against the universal household of the imperial *pater patriae*, Paul posits the universal household of God the Father of Jesus.

Jesus is the firstborn Son of the Father who acts as the bridge between the Father and all the other (adopted) children.[19] Jesus is the eldest brother of the loyal.[20] Thus, in Rom 8:29, the Pauline faction refers to Jesus as "the firstborn" of all the siblings in the household of God. It is this status of the firstborn that the Pauline faction has in mind on the many occasions when they refer to Jesus as *the* son of God.[21] It is also why they refer to Jesus as *the* single seed of Abraham in Gal 3:16–19.[22] In this way, Jesus is assured the rank of the eldest son, with all the status and power that the firstborn was granted. Again, while gender-critical readings may (appropriately and importantly) highlight the androcentric nature of this familial structure, the point worth emphasizing is that, by viewing Jesus as the firstborn, no other person was capable of claiming the authority or status of that position. Jesus is the firstborn, and he alone is the firstborn. No other member of the assemblies may lay claim to the power

---

18. See Elliott, *Arrogance of Nations*, 121–38; Kahl, *Galatians Re-Imagined*, 261, 281–85; Lopez, *Apostle to the Conquered*, 154–56.

19. See deSilva, *Honor, Patronage, Kinship, and Purity*, 200–201.

20. Dunn observes that this focus upon Jesus as the eldest brother sets the Pauline assemblies apart from other Graeco-Roman associations that adopted familial language. See Dunn, *Beginning from Jerusalem*, 636.

21. See Rom 1:3–4, 9; 5:10; 8:3, 32; 1 Cor 1:9; 15:28; 2 Cor 1:19; Gal 1:16; 2:20; 4:4; 1 Thess 1:10.

22. See deSilva, *Honor, Patronage, Kinship, and Purity*, 203–4.

THE TRANSNATIONAL FAMILY OF GOD

and privilege granted to this position. Instead, all of the Jesus loyalists have become the adopted children of God and the (younger) siblings of Jesus. Apart from some passages wherein Paul claims others as his own children (passages which most often arise in his correspondence with the Corinthians, who were turning against the way of life affirmed by Paul and his coworkers... which makes the Pauline faction a little more desperate in their rhetoric, meaning that they probably recourse to some forms of appeal that may be inconsistent with what they write elsewhere), references to other Jesus loyalists as children of God play an important role in Paulinism.[23] All are now God's children, adopted by means of the advocacy of Jesus, confirmed by the coming of the Spirit, and symbolized in the rite of baptism. Here, hierarchies between peoples and nations are abolished as both Judeans and foreign nationals are adopted into God's family. Thus, for example, Rom 9:4 states that the Israelites received adoption from God and then shortly thereafter, in Rom 9:26, Hosea is quoted in order to assert that members of other nations and ethnicities have been adopted and are now called children of God. Therefore, all the members of the family of God, whether Judean or Greek, Roman or Gaul, have the same elevated and equal status within God's family.

The adoption of all into God's family as equal members both produces and reflects sibling relationships between Jesus loyalists. All are now siblings—and this includes Paul, who, far more than any other rank or title, is counted as a sibling among siblings. Hence, sibling-language is employed more than any other title or honorific when the Pauline faction refers to members of the assemblies. The term *adelphoi* appears sixty-five times in the non-contested epistles, the singular, *adelphos*, appears another twenty-five times, and references to individuals as a brother or sister appear another twelve times.[24] While the language here is androcentric—referring to a singular brother or to brothers in the plural—I believe that it is appropriate to translate this language with gender-neutral language and conclude that the Pauline faction is addressing siblings of all genders.[25] Within the household of God, as it existed within local and

---

23. See Rom 8:14-21; 9:8, 26; Gal 3:6-4:31; Phil 2:15; 1 Thess 5:5.

24. See Meeks, *First Urban Christians*, 86-87. According to Horrell's count, the term *adelphoi* and its cognates appear 112 times in the uncontested letters versus *hagios* appearing 25 times or *pisteuontes* appearing 15 times (Horrell, *Solidarity and Difference*, 111).

25. The point here is not to exonerate the Pauline faction by hiding their androcentric language; instead, it is to recognize the important presence of those who are not

international community networks, it is sibling relationships that are of the utmost importance.²⁶ By stressing this form of relationship, Paul and his coworkers are engaging in something innovative—nobody else in the Graeco-Roman context would refer to a person outside of their "natural" kinship networks as a sibling.²⁷ So the Pauline faction is quick to praise the Thessalonians in 1 Thess 4:9–10 for understanding this and actively loving one another in this way.

Contextually, this sibling-based love carried very concrete demands, responsibilities, and expectations. This was not some sort of romantic rhetoric devoid of material implications.²⁸ The transition to a fictive kinship was an active thing. First of all, relating to one another as siblings would require the abolition of any previously accepted cultural, social, or economic hierarchies within the assemblies. All Jesus loyalists were to be considered of equal status and value, just as siblings were equal in status and value.²⁹ Therefore, while the Graeco-Roman (and Judean) household was structured in a hierarchical manner, Paul and his coworkers remove the positions of unequal power and status—recognizing God as the Father and Jesus as the eldest son—from any other member of the assemblies. So, the formerly patriarchal household becomes modified and flattened in order to produce a sibling-based fellowship.³⁰ In this regard, Robert Jewett is absolutely correct to assert that the early assemblies of Jesus loyalists were to be defined by "agapaic-communalism"—a

---

identified as male within the assemblies of Jesus loyalists. Furthermore, while liberal scholars tend to use the translation "brothers and sisters" for the term "*adelphoi*," I do not ascribe to a binary conception of gender—and note that many Indigenous cultures, including some from the Pauline context, also refuse a binary way of thinking about gender—and so I prefer the gender-neutral form, "siblings."

26. See deSilva, *Honor, Patronage, Kinship, and Purity*, 213; Malina, "Social Levels, Morals, and Daily Life," 391–92; Yarbrough, *Not Like the Gentiles*, 80.

27. See Winter, *After Paul Left Corinth*, 70.

28. One gains a sense for the implications of this rhetoric when one thinks about the way sibling-based language was employed in other revolutionary movements—from the French Revolution and Haitian revolutions to the Black Panther movement (or, in a comparable manner, the comrade-based language that was employed in the communist revolutions).

29. See Malherbe, "God's New Family in Thessalonica," 121–22; Lassen, "Roman Family," 14–15.

30. See Sandnes, "Equality Within Patriarchal Structures," 150–63, esp. 151; Horrell, *Solidarity and Difference*, 112–15.

term he coins in opposition to Troeltsch and Theissen's emphasis upon "love-patriarchalism."[31]

Second, as siblings, the movement's members were to be mutually responsible for each other.[32] One of the primary ways that this was to be expressed was through the sharing of material goods and money. Culturally, siblings were expected to hold their goods in common with each other, and this form of sharing was one of the key components of the assemblies associated with Paulinism.[33] David deSilva captures the significance of the expectation that siblings were to put their inherited goods to common use:

> The believers are to pool their resources in every way so that each member of the family knows the love of this family at his or her point of need and so that all arrive safely at the heavenly [sic] goal. . . . What we witness in the early church [sic] is not an attempt to create a system of government and economics enforced through terror but rather an attitude that each believer has toward fellow believers—"love for the brothers and sisters"—and lives out without reservation.[34]

This form of material sharing was a central component of the sibling-based mutuality practiced by the early Jesus loyalists, but there were other expectations as well. Siblings were expected not to harm each other—even when that meant sacrificing one's own rights or well-being in order to protect someone else.[35] Thus, we see the Pauline faction engaging in precisely this sort of appeal to sacrifice in Rom 14:1–15:6, when they ask the "stronger" siblings not to despise their "weaker" siblings but instead request that "the stronger" refuse to please themselves and accept the "weakness of others," in order to prevent those others from stumbling. The same attitude is present in 1 Cor 12:20–26, when Paul and his coworkers urge the Corinthians to grant greater honor to the (purportedly) less honorable members of the body of the Anointed. Cooperation, not competition, is to define the ways in which the siblings

---

31. See Jewett, *Romans*, 66–68, 80–86.

32. See Malherbe, "God's New Family in Thessalonica," 123; Dodd, *Meaning of Paul for Today*, 153; Oakes, *Reading Romans in Pompeii*, 108–9.

33. See Crossan and Reed, *In Search of Paul*, 176; Banks, *Paul's Idea of Community*, 53–61. Hence the example of Acts 2:44 and 4:32 and the Collection for the poor in the Jerusalem explored in chapter 4 below.

34. deSilva, *Honor, Patronage, Kinship, and Purity*, 215–16.

35. See deSilva, *Honor, Patronage, Kinship, and Purity*, 213–15.

of the Anointed relate to one another.³⁶ If anything, they are to compete in elevating others above themselves. Thus, in Rom 12:10, the Romans are urged to "love one another with mutual affection; [and] outdo one another in showing honor."³⁷ Similarly, in Gal 5:13, Paul and his coworkers offer this exhortation: "You were called to freedom, [siblings]; only do not use your freedom as an opportunity for self-indulgence, but through love become slaves to one another. For the whole Law is summed up in a single commandment, 'You shall love your neighbor as yourself.'" They then urge the Galatians not to become conceited and compete with or envy each other (5:26) but instead to bear one another's burdens (6:2) and work for the good of all, especially those of the household of the loyal (6:10). All these actions are normative for sibling-based relationships.

As siblings, Jesus loyalists are to live together in unity, harmony, and concord.³⁸ Thus, in 1 Cor 1:10, the Pauline faction pleads in this way with the Corinthians: "Now I appeal to you, [siblings], by the name of our Lord Jesus [Anointed], [we pray] that all of you be in agreement and that there by no divisions among you, but that you be united in the same mind and purpose." They repeat this appeal in one way or another throughout their letters. This means that when conflicts or harmful activities arise within the household of God, the siblings are to actively seek reconciliation and should be quick to forgive. Even when more difficult corrective measures are deemed necessary, they are to be applied as one would act towards a sibling and not as one would act towards an enemy or an outsider or a stranger.³⁹ Thus, in Gal 6:1, Paul and his coworkers state that "if anyone is detected in a transgression, you who have received the Spirit should restore such a one in a spirit of gentleness" and in 1 Cor 6:1–11 they rebuke the Corinthians for engaging in lawsuits against each other.

By loving each other as siblings, the members of the early assemblies of Jesus loyalists were expected to: (a) relate to one another as equals; (b) take mutual responsibility for one another by materially pooling their financial resources; (c) take mutual responsibility for one another by honoring and protecting each other, especially more vulnerable members;

---

36. See deSilva, *Honor, Patronage, Kinship, and Purity*, 220–22.

37. That this perspective completely overturns culturally dominant conceptions of honor and shame will be demonstrated in chapter 3.

38. See deSilva, *Honor, Patronage, Kinship, and Purity*, 217–19.

39. deSilva, *Honor, Patronage, Kinship, and Purity*, 223–25. As I will argue in chapter 5, this is part of the strategy deployed by the Pauline faction to prevent lateral violence from occurring within the assemblies of Jesus loyalists.

(d) be united; (e) practice gentleness even in situations of conflict; and (f) place the self-identified needs of the other over the supposed rights of one's self.

The Universality of God's Family: Threatening Global Empire

What is most striking—and, to Rome, most obviously threatening—about this is the transnational nature of this God's household. The most obvious way in which the Pauline faction began to construct a transnational fictive kinship was by breaking down barriers between Judeans and other ethnicities or nationalities (who, despite their differences and antagonisms, all shared in the experience of being vanquished, colonized, dispossessed, and enslaved by Rome). Lengthy passages like Rom 9–11 and much of Gal 1–4 are devoted to this task, as are other prominent Pauline endeavors, such as the Collection. Some of the most famous passages from the Pauline letters powerfully express this theme. Thus, Gal 3:28 states that "there is no longer [Judean] or Greek, there is no longer slave or free, there is no longer male and female; for all of you are one in [the Anointed] Jesus" (Gal 3:28); again Rom 3:29–30 asks: "Is God the God of [Judeans] only? Is he not also the God of [people from other regions] also? Yes, of people from all nations also, since God is one" and Rom 10:12 states that "there is no distinction between [Judean] and Greek; the same Lord is Lord of all and is generous to all who call on him."[40] Therefore, although they originate from Second Temple Judaism(s), the Pauline faction sought to extend the boundaries of the family of God in such a way that others were grafted into the identity of Israel and, as we have seen, the lineage of Abraham. By doing so, they were essentially creating a *tertium genus*, a new category of people, and a new family, that was not strictly defined by categories of race and nationality.[41] As Lucian Cerfaux remarks, regarding Gal 3:28: "Every difference of race,

40. Apart from the lengthier passages already mentioned, see also Rom 15:17; 1 Cor 1:24; 10:32; 12:13.

41. See Cerfaux, *Church in the Theology of St. Paul*, 9–16, 66–67; Dunn, "Diversity in Paul," 111–12. The language of *"tertium genus"* applied to Jesus loyalists shows up first in Tertullian, and it is interesting to note that Tertullian states that this label was given to Jesus loyalists by their opponents (here, the opponents suggested that being third is inferior, in the same way that placing third in a competition denotes inferiority to those who placed first and second; they also suggest that the appearance of the third race is a monstrous apparition—and, in evaluating this *tertium genus* from the perspective of imperial values, they were not wrong).

country, and culture disappears. The equality that [Paulinism] brings into the world is not merely a metaphor, since the new people that comes into being is a political entity" and, it should be added, a family.[42]

Generally, recent scholarship has focused upon this issue not within discussions around the formation of sibling relationships within the new household of God, but (especially within the new perspective on Paul) in relation to liberal tolerance and an appreciation for diversity, especially given Christian anti-Semitism and the genocide of the Jewish people during the Second World War.[43] Thus, in the words of James Dunn, Paul becomes "the apostle of Christian diversity."[44] Others continue this emphasis, stressing that Paul desired racial-cultural equality, tolerated distinctions, rejected racial-cultural exclusiveness, and ultimately pursued racial and cultural reconciliation.[45] Of course, by engaging in this reading, scholars are also trying to understand the contemporary relevance of Paulinism. Philip Esler is especially explicit about this when writing his volume on Romans, which he reads in light of the (to his mind) definitive "ethnic" violence that marks our world (from the Balkans, to Rwanda, Northern Ireland, the Middle East, and Kashmir).[46]

---

42. Cerfaux, *Church in the Theology of St. Paul*, 71.

43. While this renewed focus upon Christian anti-Semitism and the desire to end violence against Jewish people is needed and commendable, one wishes that these scholars were equally sensitive to the other groups massacred by the Nazis and their only-too-willing allies during the Second World War—from ethnic groups like Roma, the Poles, and certain Slavic peoples, to groups of people who had physical and mental disabilities, to groups of people who did not fit hetero-normative gender and sexual categories, like homosexuals or transsexuals. When sensitized New Testament scholars choose to refer to the Holocaust by its Hebrew name (*Ha-Shoah*), they risk further marginalizing the other groups who were terminated and engage in a selective form of remembering that obliterates the forgotten. The same can be said of North American scholars who repeatedly stress the uniqueness of the Holocaust while overlooking the even greater number of Indigenous peoples exterminated in the territories forcibly colonized by the United States of America and Canada to say nothing of the contemporary genocide of Palestinians that is being accomplished by the Israeli state.

44. Dunn, "Diversity in Paul," 123.

45. See, for example, Longenecker, *New Testament Social Ethics*, 34, 37, 44–46; Richardson, *Paul's Ethic of Freedom*, 16–17, 28–39; Jewett, *Paul*, 32–44; Esler, *New Testament Theology*, 277–81; Elliott, *Liberating Paul*, 216; Crossan and Reed, *In Search of Paul*, 391–97.

46. Esler, *Conflict and Identity in Romans*, 10–12. Thus, in the epilogue of that volume he states: "For me, Romans reveals its connection with the taproot of human experience in relation to violent ethnic conflict in the world" (357).

While all of this is admirable and good and captures part of what the Pauline faction cares about, it is deficient on at least two counts. First of all, it is deficient in accounting for the root causes of many of our contemporary moments of violence—wherein attitudes related to race and culture are *exploited and manipulated* by elite groups in order to pursue the political economy of imperialism, colonialism, and capitalism—and thereby produces a somewhat superficial analysis of the problems that we face and the solutions we need to develop today.[47] The second criticism is very much related to the first—just as the socioeconomic and theopolitical analysis of our own context remains somewhat shallow within this scholarly trajectory, so also the truly political and counter-imperial intentions of the Pauline faction are overlooked. Neil Elliott is absolutely correct to assert that an overly emphatic focus upon issues of ethnocentricism and universalism (found especially within the new perspective on Paul) tends to eclipse Paul's critical interactions with the broader structures of the empire and the multi-ethnic, transnational household (or fleshy body) of Caesar.[48] Because the Pauline faction is, in fact, doing something very politically dangerous and subversive by creating a transnational network of siblings within the context of Roman imperialism. Think less of late twentieth-century culture wars and more of late eighteenth-century Haitian slaves meeting in the woods at night.

The boundary- and border-crossing nature of this has sometimes been neglected. For example, some New Testament scholars have argued that over against later developments related to the catholicity of "the church," Paul and his coworkers were only interested in local communities (Mark Strom, for example, asserts that "Paul knew nothing of a so-called universal church").[49] While it is true that the Pauline letters are (for obvious practical reasons) dominated by matters related to the very specific experiences of the recipients of each letter, and while it is good to not read later doctrinal or theological developments into the Pauline Epistles, it is unwarranted to conclude that the Pauline faction ever forgot the transnational nature of their work.[50] In fact, they understand local

---

47. For alternative analyses that do a better job of situating "ethnic" or "religious" struggles within political and economic structures, see Cavanaugh, *Myth of Religious Violence*; Federici, *Caliban and the Witch*; Klein, *Shock Doctrine*.

48. See Elliott, "Paul and the Politics of Empire," 20–22.

49. Strom, *Reframing Paul*, 172. For a more tempered view that still emphasizes the local over the universal, see Bird, "Early Christianity," 242.

50. For some who emphasize this, see deSilva, *Honor, Patronage, Kinship, and*

assemblies to be connected to one another internationally, or better stated, transnationally—a point powerfully made by the Collection. Thus, over against Strom's remark, Michael Gorman is correct to assert that Paul was working to "establish an international network of transformed, peaceable, multicultural communities worshiping and obeying the one true God by conformity to his Son in the power of the Spirit."[51]

Two further points are worth emphasizing. First, the early Jesus movement was unique in its aim and ability to forge such a transnational alliance without maintaining any sort of national base.[52] Second, Paul and his coworkers were taking a great risk by choosing to forge this sort of alliance among representatives of nations that had been defeated and colonized by Rome. As Davina Lopez has argued, this required a remapping of the world in which they lived—it was no longer Roman imperialism that united the various localities of the empire; instead, it was new life within the assemblies of Jesus loyalists that both united and liberated a multitude of defeated peoples.[53] Further, whereas the Romans tended to present the representatives of the nations as conquered women penetrated and dominated by powerful godlike Roman men, Paul presents the representatives of the nations as children and heirs of God.[54] Thus, as Brigitte Kahl observes, at the heart of the gospel is "a message of global reconciliation among the vanquished nations of the Roman Empire . . . the conquest-based alignment of the nations under Rome is now called by its proper name, *slavery*, opposed to the liberating unity of the nations in Christ, which is named *freedom* in a new, universal, exodus event."[55]

This is precisely what Paul is communicating when he refers to himself as God's apostle or diplomat to the nations. English translations of this term have tended to interpret him as the "Apostle to the Gentiles" but the Greek term, *ta ethnes*, also means "the nations" and is

---

Purity, 216; Esler, *New Testament Theology*, 172–73; Goguel, *Primitive Church*, 53–55; Meeks, *Moral World*, 121, 127; Kahl, *Galatians Re-Imagined*, 21; Dunn, *Beginning from Jerusalem*, 654–57.

51. Gorman, *Reading Paul*, 22. Gorman employs the term "international" whereas I prefer the term "transnational" because the Jesus movement abolishes and overrides national distinctions—the Jesus movement is without borders and boundaries, whereas the term "international" still implies a respect for borders and boundaries.

52. See Judge, *Social Distinctions of the Christians*, 31; Meeks, *First Urban Christians*, 75.

53. See Lopez, *Apostle to the Conquered*, 4–7, 17–25; Horsley, "Introduction," 9.

54. See Lopez, *Apostle to the Conquered*, 27–118.

55. Kahl, *Galatians Re-Imagined*, 11, 21.

more frequently intended in that sense when deployed in the literature of Paul's day.[56] Thus, Paul is God's apostle *to the nations*. That Paul favors the title "apostle" to describe his role is also telling. The Pauline faction applies it to Paul more frequently than any other title and regularly open their letters by referring to Paul as an *apostolos Christou*—an apostle of the Anointed.[57] While later Christian traditions have come up with various definitions of the word—usually in order to limit "apostles" to those who originally encountered the resurrected Jesus in the flesh, went on to see their vocation as the proclamation of the gospel, and performed miraculous acts (see 1 Cor 9:1–2; 15:3–11; 2 Cor 12:11–12)—it is worth recalling that the Pauline faction did not simply make up this title. They deployed a term that already carried certain cultural and political meanings. In their context, the word *apostolos* referred to "one sent out" a "delegate, envoy, messenger, [or] authorized emissary."[58] The idea, then, is that this political envoy or herald is invested with a unique status and shares in the authority of the party that has commissioned and sent out that representative.[59] This makes the political overtones of Paul's title more apparent. Paul is a "diplomatic herald" representing the political family of God within the nations subjected to the family of Caesar.[60] The other titles he employs also further this connection. In 2 Cor 5:20, Paul refers to himself as an "ambassador [*presbeuomen*] for [the] Anointed," and this term is also used for the ambassadors of Caesar.[61] Likewise, in 2 Cor 11:23, the Pauline faction speaks of the apostles as being "ministers" of the Anointed. This term, *diakonoi*, parallels the title given imperial ministers of Caesar and, like the term *apostolos*, the title *diakonos* contains the missional, military, and political overtones of being a messenger, herald, or envoy.[62]

Now, if Paul was simply coming as a diplomat to offer allegiance to Rome on the Anointed's behalf, there would be nothing troubling about him employing this language (until, that is, it was realized that the Anointed was a man crucified by Rome for seditious activities).

56. See Lopez, *Apostle to the Conquered*, 4–7, 17–25.
57. See Rom 1:1; 1 Cor 1:1; 2 Cor 1:1; Gal 1:1.
58. Dunn, *Beginning from Jerusalem*, 531.
59. Dunn, *Beginning from Jerusalem*, 531–32, 536–39. See also Schnabel, *Paul and the Early Church*, 967–69, 1355.
60. A term taken from Elliott, "Apostle Paul and Empire," 98.
61. See Deissmann, *Light From the Ancient East*, 374.
62. Deissmann, *Light from the Ancient East*, 376; Georgi, *Theocracy*, 27–32.

Pauline Solidarity

If anything, it would be a source of amusement that, if carried too far (and, if anything, the oppressed knew well that even joking at all might be going too far), could get a person killed. However, as we have seen, the Pauline faction is very clearly remapping the domain of the Roman Empire. They were going into Roman-occupied territory—to nations and cities vanquished by Rome—and establishing the household of God, *over against* the household of Caesar.

This, then, is what it meant for Paul to be God's apostle *to the nations*.[63] As made apparent in Rom 1:5, the Pauline faction believed they had been commissioned by Jesus Anointed to "bring about the submissively obedient loyalty *en pasin tois ethnesin*" (my translation). Many have tended to understand this work "*among all the Gentiles*" to be an overcoming of the exclusive ethnocentricism of Judaism. But this misses the broader point (and stinks of anti-Semitism). Rom 1:5 is more accurately translated as saying that the Pauline faction was commissioned by Jesus to "bring about the submissively obedient loyalty *among all the nations*" (again, my translation).

Within this transnational network of the vanquished, the poor, and the oppressed, newly constituted and assembled as siblings, the Pauline faction speaks about submissively obedient loyalty.[64] However, as Neil Elliott notes, requiring obedience and loyalty from the nations, newly constituted into a single body, was the privilege of the emperor; and to create an alternate network, embodying and enacting a different loyalty, was to usurp an imperial prerogative.[65] This is genuinely seditious activity. As Kahl observes in her volume about Galatians:

> The Galatians had banded together with Jews in ways completely antithetical to the terms and conditions under which the empire allowed the vanquished nations under its rule to associate . . . what constitutes "lawful" relations between Jews and Galatians can vary greatly, but it is always dictated from above, never on the basis of an "illegal" peacemaking from below . . . the divine Caesar *alone* was allowed to set the terms and conditions for licit interactions between Jews and Galatians.[66]

---

63. See Rom 3:29; 11:13; 15:9–11; Gal 1:16; 2:8; 3:7–8.

64. See Lopez, *Apostle to the Conquered*, 129–37; Kahl, *Galatians Re-Imagined*, 23, 269–70; Smith, "'Unmasking the Powers,'" 54; Elliott, *Arrogance of Nations*, 50–51; Horsley, "General Introduction," 8.

65. Elliott, *Arrogance of Nations*, 25, 44–50.

66. Kahl, *Galatians Re-Imagined*, 228, 235, 242.

Therefore, she concludes:

> The entire letter [to the Galatians] is a "coded" theological manifesto of the nations under Roman rule pledging allegiance to the one God who is other than Caesar; this "semi-hidden transcript" contradicting and resisting the dominant order is embodied in a new horizontal and international community practice of mutual support.[67]

With this in mind, it becomes clear just how much the household of God existed as a dangerous unification and an ideological threat to the household of Caesar.[68] Essentially, Paulinism is creating an alternative empire—which is an *anti-empire* given that the ways of empire are antithetical to the ways in which life was shared within the assemblies of Jesus loyalists. Within this transnational anti-empire, Paul and his coworkers are helping birth an intimately bonded family of siblings in and of the Anointed who are, collectively, rising up from the dead.[69]

New Relationships between Men and Women

This is a noble vision, but how does this new fictive kinship impact the more immediate relationships that existed between the members of the assemblies of Jesus loyalists? In this section I will examine how it impacted relationships between men and women. In the next section I will examine how it impacted relationships between slaves and freedpeople.

As explored in volume 1, there continues to be both scholars and communities who maintain that the Pauline faction was essentially

---

67. Kahl, *Galatians Re-Imagined*, 287.

68. That it was also far more than a *merely* ideological threat will become apparent in what follows.

69. Two points: (1) in this regard, I would suggest the Pauline faction is faithfully following the trajectory established by Jesus; and (2) some think that Paul and his coworkers do posit a more imperial form of being-in-communion than I have argued. For example, Neil Elliott, following in the footsteps of Elizabeth Schüssler-Fiorenza, argues that Paul replaces the Imperium Romanum with the Kyriarchy of Christ (see Elliott, *Arrogance of Nations*, 52–57). While this is true in some ways—Jesus is very much a (vastly superior) alternative to the emperor, as we shall see below—the completely different character of the Anointed (versus the August) must be emphasized and we should recall the way in which any sort of imperial power positions are removed from the relationships that are to exist between siblings (as I noted when describing the ways in which God and Jesus are the only ones granted the title of father and firstborn).

socially conservative when it came to the actual lived relationships between men and women within the assemblies of Jesus loyalists. Some insist that Paulinism was thoroughly and aggressively patriarchal while others take a slightly more nuanced approach but come to the same practical conclusions. Thus, for example, L. Michael White argues that Paulinism has a somewhat ambiguous relationship to patriarchy within biological kinship units but concludes that Paulinism, although mildly deviating from the norm, rarely challenged the patriarchal hierarchy in any overt manner.[70] Similarly, Dunn argues that the fictive kinship of the family of God did not replace normal family structures, thereby conforming to social norms while simultaneously engaging in a "deep (but little apparent on the surface) subversiveness" of the household by subordinating all relationships to the lordship of Anointed Jesus.[71] Essentially, for what it's worth (and cis-gendered male-identified scholars tend to emphasize its worth more than other scholars do), the liberating element of Paulinism is said to be that it granted women the same ontological or spiritual value as men, while continuing to subordinate woman to men in matters of social rank and function.[72] Hence, we see the "love-patriarchalism" identified by Troeltsch and Thiessen and described by Daniel Boyarin as "a moderate 'benevolent' domination of women by men, or rather wives by husbands."[73]

Before examining how well this view aligns with the content of the Pauline letters, it is important to begin by observing that there was a strong female presence within the assemblies of Jesus loyalists associated with the Pauline faction. From the Pauline letters, we learn that women often served as prominent members who were not only recognized in their local assemblies but also renowned within the movement more broadly. Thus, of the twenty-seven people named in Rom 16, ten are women, and of the eleven people specifically praised, five are women; furthermore, the only people the Pauline faction praises for working hard in dedicated vocations comparable to Paul's are the women Mary,

---

70. White, "Paul and the *Pater Familias*," 472.

71. Dunn, *Beginning from Jerusalem*, 637; see also 810–13.

72. See, for example, Cadoux, *Early Church and the World*, 122–23; Jeffers, *Greco-Roman World*, 85–86; Malina, "Social Levels, Morals, and Daily Life," 391; Boyarin, *Radical Jew*, 187–91; Ladd, *Theology of the New Testament*, 573; Lietzmann, *Beginnings of the Christian Church*, 147; Richardson, *Paul's Ethic of Freedom*, 59, 69, 75–78.

73. See Troeltsch, *Social Teachings*, 81; Theissen, *Social Setting of Pauline Christianity*, 107–8; Boyarin, *Radical Jew*, 191.

THE TRANSNATIONAL FAMILY OF GOD

Tryphaena, Tryphosa, and Persis.[74] Additionally, Junia, one of Paul's female coworkers, is praised as an apostle, Phoebe as a patron (and she is also the letter-carrier to the Romans, thereby acting as the authorized representative of the Pauline faction), and Prisca as a "leading figure within the assemblies."[75] In the assembly of Jesus loyalists at Philippi, we also observe the prominent status of two women—Euodia and Syntyche—who are viewed as equal to the central leaders of the Pauline faction. They likely had the same status as Paul within the local assembly (or assemblies)—as the Pauline faction writes: "They have struggled beside me in the work of the gospel."[76] Similarly, in Corinth, we can observe the prominent role played by female prophets.[77] It is therefore safe to conclude that women were actively involved alongside of Paul and within the assemblies of Jesus loyalists associated with the Pauline faction, both as prominent members of their local assemblies and of the movement more broadly, and as equals of Paul.[78] Indeed, it is probable that this elevation of the status of women was a significant part of the reason why the Jesus movement spread so rapidly in its early days.[79]

However, that there was a prominent presence of influential women within the assemblies of Jesus loyalists does not mean that the Pauline faction supported this. It could be that their undeniably vocal approval of

---

74. See Crossan and Borg, *First Paul*, 51–52.

75. See Dunn, *Beginning from Jerusalem*, 634–35; Clarke, "Jew and Greek," 115–19; Crossan and Borg, *First Paul*, 51. Although some conservative scholars have tried to argue that Junia was a male (based upon their presupposition that women could not be apostles), the historical record makes it quite clear that Junia was a name reserved for women. Of the more than 250 times when the name Junia appears in antiquity, it was always used for a woman and never used, for example, as an abbreviation for the male name Junianus. See Crossan and Borg, *First Paul*, 52–53; Clarke, "Jew and Greek," 119; Sanders, *Paul: The Apostle's Life*, 139; and especially Epp, *Junia*.

76. Phil 4:3. See Dahl, "Euodia and Syntyche," 3–15; Dunn, *Beginning from Jerusalem*, 634–35.

77. See 1 Cor 11:2–16; 14:29–32.

78. This prominent liberated presence of powerful women has been observed by many. See Elliott, *Liberating Paul*, 203; Jeffers, *Greco-Roman World*, 249–52; Schüssler-Fiorenza, *In Memory of Her*, 161–84.

79. See Kee, *Christian Origins*, 89. Of course, as I observed earlier, the Roman imperial cult had begun to grant higher status and broader authoritative functions to the women within the imperial family, and women also had more prominence in other religious associations, but the amount of status and authority granted to ordinary—not just high status—women within the Jesus movement is striking. See Scheid, "Augustus and Roman Religion," 179–80; Dunn, *Beginning from Jerusalem*, 633–34; Longenecker, *New Testament Social Ethics for Today*, 70–75.

a number of these women was only granted reluctantly when "the facts" became "stronger than [their] prejudices."[80] Or it could be that Paul paid little attention to the prominence of women because, despite being a "complementarian," matters of gender were less important to him than other more "spiritual issues."[81] Or perhaps he was "theologically radical ... but socially conservative."[82] Or it could be that Paul was inconsistent or politically manipulative—being both androcentric and patriarchal while also supporting women leaders and arguing that baptism erased gender divisions.[83] Or it could be that Paul and the female leaders represented different factions that actually conflicted with each other.[84] Or perhaps Paul was more egalitarian in his approach but decided to make some concessions to social conservatives out of a sense of missional pragmatism that sought to not confuse or alienate others.[85] Or perhaps Paul actually was an egalitarian and fully committed to women and men being equal in all ways as siblings within the household of God.[86]

In order to try and determine the plausibility of these alternatives, it is necessary to engage the texts in which the Pauline faction most explicitly addresses issues related to gender (apart from the texts already mentioned, wherein they speak approvingly of prominent women within the movement). Unfortunately, we do not have a lot of material in the

80. A stance taken in Goguel, *Primitive Church*, 553.

81. A stance taken in Judge, *Social Distinctives of the Christians*, 114–15.

82. Sanders, *Paul: The Apostle's Life*, 285; see also 284–86.

83. A stance described in Boyarin, "Paul and the Genealogy of Gender," 13–41; also taken in Jewett, *Paul*, 46–52. One of the possible ways of explaining this inconsistency or tension is by observing that women generally had a more prominent leadership within a household—running the domestic space, having authority over children and slaves, and also controlling some matters of business. Therefore, given that the Jesus movement developed within household spaces, it is possible that women gained greater prominence within the movement, while also operating in what was fundamentally a patriarchal social network (see Jeffers, *Greco-Roman World*, 80–82; Cousar, *Letters of Paul*, 8–69; Schüssler-Fiorenza, *In Memory of Her*, 181–82). I think this hypothesis is of limited value given what has already been observed about the role and significance of the Roman *paterfamilias* and patriarchs more broadly in Graeco-Roman and Judean cultures.

84. This stance is taken by, for example, Schüssler-Fiorenza, *In Memory of Her*; Wire, *Corinthian Women Prophets*.

85. Richard N. Longenecker makes this suggestion in Longenecker, *New Testament Social Ethics*, 85–87.

86. This stance is taken by Cousar, *Letters of Paul*, 137–38; Longenecker, *New Testament Social Ethics*, 75, 83–85; Scroggs, *Text and the Times*, 70; Remus, "Persecution," 437–38.

non-contested Pauline Epistles. Three passages will be examined: 1 Cor 7:1–40; 11:2–16; and Gal 3:28.[87]

In 1 Cor 7, Paul and his coworkers explore themes related to marriage, slavery, circumcision, and celibacy. It is primarily the verses related to marriage and celibacy—vv. 1–16 and 25–39—that are of interest here. Regarding marriage, we should note their considerable emphasis on the total equality that they want to exist between marriage partners.[88] The Pauline faction builds an argument intended to overthrow male-dominated Graeco-Roman (and Judean) conceptions of marriage.[89] But they ease into it. Initially, they argue that "the husband should give to his wife her conjugal rights, and likewise the wife to her husband" (7:3) and they add that "the wife does not have authority over her own body; but the husband does" (7:4a). This is all well and good (from the perspective of dominant social values), but this injunction is immediately followed by a shocking statement: "Likewise the husband does not have authority over his own body, but the wife does" (7:4b). This, then, results in a principle of mutual reciprocity and self-giving: "Do not deprive one another except perhaps by agreement for a set time" (7:5a). This is related to the matter of sexual contact, but Paul and his coworkers also counsel the same reciprocity when it comes to divorce: "The wife should not separate from her husband . . . the husband should not divorce his wife" (7:10b–11). This levels the playing field within a culture wherein the institution of divorce was structured in order to favor the desires and interests of men. But Paul and his coworkers continue to emphasize the need for men to check their privilege. Thus, later in the chapter: "Are you bound to a wife? Do not seek to be free" (7:27a—although they return to the theme of reciprocity when, in 7:39a, they assert that a wife is also bound to her husband for as long as the husband lives). Furthermore, they are keen to guard against any male-initiated violence directed at women during courtship prior to marriage. Given that women would be shamed and stigmatized for engaging in sexual relationships prior to marriage, the Pauline faction's suggestion that those who "burn with passion" should marry (see 7:9, 36)

---

87. I have decided not to include a discussion of 1 Cor 14:33b–34 because I believe it to be a later interpolation and not a part of the original letter.

88. See Crossan and Borg, *First Paul*, 50; Winter, *After Paul Left Corinth*, 226–30; Judge, *Social Distinctives of the Christians*, 113–14.

89. This goes against the perspective of those (like Yarbrough) who argue that Paul was not really proposing a marriage ethic that differed from Graeco-Roman morality in any substantive manner (Yarbrough, *Not Like the Gentiles*, 67, 77).

Pauline Solidarity

can be read as part of their commitment to the equality and importance of women.[90] Therefore, far from affirming the well-entrenched patriarchy of its context, Paulinism envisions marriage to be a relationship between equals who mutually give themselves to each other.[91]

Second, one finds some significant counter-cultural and counter-imperial themes in Pauline advice related to (temporary) times of celibacy within marriage, or to the decision to remain celibate instead of marrying. Several times, the Pauline faction suggest that their opinion is that it is best to remain unmarried, especially in light of some impending crisis (see 7:6–8, 25–35, 39b–40). It is possible that the crisis referred to is a grain shortage and general famine that was impacting Corinth and the surrounding area at this time.[92] However, the Pauline faction also employs apocalyptic language when describing this crisis, and it is equally possible that they saw it as one of the signs of the inauguration of the new age of the Anointed's reign and the collapse of the prior age of imperialism, Sin, and Death.[93] Indeed, it is likely this apocalyptic perspective that prompted the Corinthians to ask if "it is well for a man not to touch a woman" (7:1).[94] The Pauline faction rejected this androcentric asceticism and advised that Jesus loyalists engage in mutual self-giving. However, the faction's preference for people to remain unmarried is still significant,

---

90. Note that these passages suggest that some sort of sexual contact may have *already* occurred. If that is the case, then Paul is advising men to marry women in a manner that would prevent the women from being left in a shameful position. While this may appear admirable, it should be noted that, taken by itself, this position risks pressuring young women (or girls) who have been assaulted by men to marry their assailants—something that has, in fact, all too often occurred in the history of patriarchal Christian ethics.

91. Although this doesn't confront cultural notions related to sex and purity and honor. It is a potentially harm-reducing measure, not a revolutionary overhaul. Generally, although they do seem to be a part of a faction that pushes strongly for revolutionary measures in some situations, Paul and his coworkers seem to lack any interest in applying that same lens to matters related to sexual activity (sometimes a blindspot in the early stages of revolutionary uprisings that occur within patriarchal contexts).

92. See Winter, *After Paul Left Corinth*, 215–23, 241–68.

93. Winter, *After Paul Left Corinth*, 253, 260–61; Yarbrough, *Not Like the Gentiles*, 103–5. As we saw in the chapter above on eschatology, this view of the current age passing away was one that contradicted the Roman ideo-theology, which saw the empire as eternal. For more on that in relation to this passage, see Winter, *After Paul Left Corinth*, 253–60.

94. See Winter, *After Paul Left Corinth*, 224–26.

especially in light of Graeco-Roman conceptions about the importance of marriage and childbearing.

As we saw in the last volume, Augustus and the Roman imperial ideo-theology highly valued marriage and the bearing of children. Even outside of Roman imperialism, it was considered the duty of all members of Greek societies to bear children in order to support the city or state in which they lived. Therefore, when we combine Pauline advice to remain unmarried with the marked absence of any sort of suggestion that married people should bear children, we see how this advice transgresses and fails to fulfill imperial and cultural expectations.[95] Furthermore, by presuming to speak in this way, Paul and his coworkers interfere with the legal rights of the *paterfamilias*, who was the only person authorized to determine when and to whom his children should marry.[96] Indeed, that the Pauline faction even speaks about marriage when, according to Roman law, marriage was legally restricted to citizens and Junian Latins (former slaves freed under the age of thirty, except for women who have been freed in order to be married by a citizen) suggests a general disregard for Roman law (a disregard that, in this case, was common among the lower classes).[97]

Therefore, we can conclude that in 1 Cor 7 Paul and his coworkers are suggesting that men and women relate to one another as equals within relationships constructed in a counter-imperial and counter-cultural manner (even if the institution of marriage itself is not questioned). Here, then, the new relationships that are to exist within the household of God do not support existing household codes but rather override and replace them with a new way of being together within the biological family unit.[98] Thus, while people continue to marry and have families, not only are new

---

95. See Schüssler-Fiorenza, *In Memory of Her*, 225. Yarbrough notes Paul's silence on any reference to the duty people had to bear children but suggests that this is more related to Pauline spirituality and his expectation of an imminent end—a perspective we have already rejected earlier (Yarbrough, *Not Like the Gentiles*, 107–8).

96. See Schüssler-Fiorenza, *In Memory of Her*, 225.

97. On the legal limitations related to marriage, see Osiek, "Family Matters," 211.

98. This contradicts the conclusion of Malherbe, who follows Theissen (see Malherbe, *Social Aspects of Early Christianity*, 71–72). It is also a stronger stance than that taken by others who feel more ambiguous about the relationship of the household of the Jesus loyalists to the biological household. See Barclay, "Family as the Bearer," 72–79.

motivations present but also "startling modifications of old behaviors" become necessary.[99]

The second significant passage regarding the relationships that existed between men and women within the assemblies of Jesus loyalists is 1 Cor 11:2–16. In this passage, Paul and his coworkers move beyond the context of marriage and comment on gender relationships within the local assemblies. Initially, it seems as though they are annulling some of the more egalitarian implications of what they wrote in 1 Cor 7. Thus, they assert that "the husband is the head of his wife" (11:3b) and that "man was not made from woman, but woman from man" and that woman was created "for the sake of man" (11:8–9). This certainly posits a hierarchical relationship, with men being superior to women and women being subordinated to men. Therefore, in light of prior remarks about the importance of prominent women within the early Jesus movement, coupled with earlier Pauline remarks about mutuality within marriage in 1 Cor 7, how are we to understand this passage?

Antoinette Clark Wire has studied this passage extensively in her book, *The Corinthian Women Prophets*.[100] She argues that there was a prominent faction of women within the Corinthian assembly who were, in many ways (notably because of their prophetic gifting), leaders within that assembly. However, the Pauline faction and these women understood the assemblies of Jesus loyalists—and especially the role of prominent members within those assemblies—in contradictory ways. According to Wire, the Pauline faction was concerned that the free gifts of the Spirit—like prophecy—would be co-opted for human gain and would be employed by individual members to serve their own interests and boost their individual status.[101] Therefore, the Pauline faction wanted to impose a series of checks and balances that helped maintain a focus upon the community as a whole, paying especial attention to solidarity with the crucified.[102] On the other hand, Wire suggests that the women prophets were less worried about the need for such checks and balances or any form of regulation and restriction; instead, they claimed to experience direct access to the resurrection life of the Anointed in the Spirit

---

99. See deSilva, *Honor, Patronage, Kinship, and Purity*, 226–29.
100. Wire, *Corinthian Women Prophets*.
101. Wire, *Corinthian Women Prophets*, 182.
102. Wire, *Corinthian Women Prophets*, 186–87.

here-and-now.[103] Thus, 1 Cor 11:2–16 is a response to the Corinthian conflict, wherein the status of these women prophets was rising and the status of the Pauline faction was falling.[104]

This conflict fits within the broader context of Paul's time, wherein prophecy tended to be dominated by two major streams, both well populated by women. Prophecy could be employed by people seeking personal empowerment and transcendence in order to advance their own status or it could be employed in a more broadly subversive manner to assist communities in creating resistant alternatives.[105] Both approaches are subversive and liberating in their own way—the former approach would permit otherwise marginalized women to gain status within the oppressive social structures of the empire, and the latter approach permitted this possibility while also emphasizing that personal empowerment should not come at a cost to the rest of the community of the oppressed.[106] These two approaches to prophecy are likely what is at stake in this passage and in the Pauline conflict with the women prophets.[107] The Pauline faction is not opposed to women being equal members of the family of God represented in the assemblies of Jesus loyalists—they clearly support this elsewhere—but it is opposed to any member, male or female, seeking to advance their personal status at the expense of others.

Concerns about some members seeking to advance their own personal status at the expense of others ties in with the remarks about head-covering found in this passage. Specifically, the Pauline faction writes that men should pray and prophesy with their heads uncovered and women should do so with their heads covered (11:4–6, 10, 13–16). In relation to the men, it is likely that the Pauline faction is trying to prevent men at Corinth from mimicking the pious actions of Roman elites. Within Roman piety, the elite males would cover their heads with their togas when

---

103. Wire, *Corinthian Women Prophets*, 182–87.

104. Wire, *Corinthian Women Prophets*, 62–71.

105. Pickett, "Conflicts at Corinth," 129; Rossing, "Prophets, Prophetic Movements," 261–63. Tacitus provides a great example of women prophets who speak in strange tongues and prophesy destruction in his *Annals* 14.32.

106. Rossing, "Prophets, Prophetic Movements," 273–74.

107. This fits with the conclusions of Wire, but see also Rossing, "Prophets, Prophetic Movements," 270–72. Roughly speaking, one can compare these two strands to the contemporary differences between mainstream White feminism and Black feminism, radical feminism, and feminisms that arise from the two-thirds world (see, for example, Eisenstein, *Feminism Seduced*).

engaged in public prayers or libations.[108] Hence, the instructions given to Aeneas in Virgil's *Aeneid*: "For offerings, veil your head in a red robe. . . . You and your company retain this ritual veiling in the future, let your progeny hold to religious purity thereby."[109] In Corinth itself a famous sculpture of the emperor was erected between 12 CE and 14 CE and the sculpture shows Augustus as a pious figure with his head veiled (and statues like this were erected throughout the empire, often working from prototypes sent out from Rome).[110] Others from lower social strata who were seeking to claim higher status among their peers would mimic this action in order to try and assert their superiority over their peers.[111] Consequently, by urging men to pray and prophesy with their heads uncovered, the Pauline faction was likely trying to prevent the same hierarchies and the same self-focused exhibitions of personal piety from infecting the assembly (or assemblies) of Jesus loyalists at Corinth. Thus, they are keen to prevent both men and women from shifting the communal focus of the assemblies of Jesus loyalists to one of personal advancement.[112] Indeed, as they assert, anyone who seeks to do this by imitating the emperor and the piety of the elite, ends up dishonoring the Anointed (i.e., "the head") by doing so (11:3–4); for the Anointed himself was crucified under imperial law and at the behest of the paragons of imperial piety.

If this explains the matter of the unveiling of the male head, what of the assertion that women should have their heads veiled? If, with the men, the Pauline faction is trying to distance the practices of the assemblies of Jesus loyalists from the practices of the imperial cult, with the women, they are more concerned to distance the practices of Jesus loyalists from those of the mystery cults that were flourishing in Corinth and elsewhere in the empire at this time. Women with loose hair who

---

108. See Jeffers, *Greco-Roman World*, 42; Winter, *After Paul Left Corinth*, 121–23; Elliott, *Liberating Paul*, 209–10.

109. Virgil, *Aeneid* 3.547, 550–51 (text modified from poetry to prose).

110. See Pickett, "Conflicts at Corinth," 118; Fig. 5.3.

111. See Meggitt, *Paul, Poverty and Survival*, 125–26.

112. Winter argues that some of the men and women involved in Corinth were already people of high status and so he suggests that Paul is trying to prevent these people from drawing attention to their (already present) high social status while praying and prophesying in the assemble of Jesus loyalists (Winter, *After Paul Left Corinth*, 131). However, given the socioeconomic analysis of those assemblies offered in volume 1 of this series, I think it is better to imagine a community of poor people who are at risk of imitating and re-inscribing the habits and hierarchies of their elite counterparts.

THE TRANSNATIONAL FAMILY OF GOD

spoke in ecstatic tongues tended to be associated with adultery, sexual promiscuity, and the orgies of cults like those devoted to Priapus.¹¹³ The Pauline faction urged women to cover their heads so that they would not be associated with those other cults and their activities.¹¹⁴ Furthermore, given that it was likely only married women who wore veils on their head, the removing of that veil would lead outsiders to draw questionable conclusions about the sexual conduct that occurred within the assemblies.¹¹⁵ In this regard, Bruce Winter makes an interesting argument about Paul's assertion that women should cover their heads "because of the angels" (11:10). Noting that the word translated as "angels" simply means "messengers," Winter argues that the Pauline faction may have been worried that some outsiders had come into the assembly in order to spy on them—a cause for concern, given that the weekly meetings of the Jesus loyalists were illegal and would provoke considerable suspicion from the local authorities (and this suspicion could have dire consequences for the Jesus loyalists).¹¹⁶

Be that as it may, there is still also a status-elevation component to this as the women who tended to associate with the mystery cults were often those who had high status and were able to flaunt that status in some ways (by, for example, ignoring some of the moral codes binding other members of society). Therefore, according to the Pauline faction, the focus must remain on what is in the best interest of the community as a whole. In this regard, they seem to think it is in the best interest of the community to not be associated with the mystery cults and their practices.¹¹⁷

113. Although writing somewhat later than Paul, Juvenal captures these stereotypes in *Satires* 6.313–16; 9.21–26.

114. See Schüssler-Fiorenza, *In Memory of Her*, 227–28.

115. See Winter, *After Paul Left Corinth*, 126–29; Crossan and Borg, *First Paul*, 50.

116. See Winter, *After Paul Left Corinth*, 134–38.

117. Of course, by doing this, the Pauline faction is still aligned with some of the more dominant cultural notions related to sexual distinctions and practices. Hence, their remarks about men have short hair and women having long hair, which are rooted in uncharacteristic appeals to "nature" and "tradition" in 1 Cor 11:14–16. See Heen, "Role of Symbolic Inversion," 157, 164; Knust, "Paul and the Politics," 166–69; Horrell, *Social Ethos*, 168–76. Indeed, although I lack the space to engage this in detail, there seems to be a larger theme of hetero-normativity running through the Pauline writings (for example, despite the various ways in which scholars have tried to engage passages like Rom 1:26–27, the conclusion that Paul supported hetero-normativity seems hard to shake). However, rather than using this to support ongoing hetero-normative practices, this suggests to me that even the Pauline faction—with all their

Pauline Solidarity

With all this in mind, we can reevaluate the quotation from 1 Cor 11:2–16. If the Pauline faction is concerned that a quest for personal status would reinstate oppressive hierarchical relationships into mutualistic communities, why do they express their argument in such a broad theological or ontological manner that seems to subordinate women to men? I would suggest that this occurs because, in the heat of the conflict (which, as we see throughout the letters to the Corinthians, was a conflict that affected Paul and his coworkers in deeply personal ways), the Pauline faction gets carried away. This is something *they themselves acknowledge* immediately after their frustrated hyperbolic explosion. Thus, after speaking about how woman was created from man and how man is the head of woman, they immediately return to the theme of reciprocity developed in 1 Cor 7. In 1 Cor 11:11–12, they write: "Nevertheless, in the Lord, woman is not independent of man or man independent of woman. For just as woman came from man, so man comes through woman; but all things come from God." That is an important "nevertheless." They have overstated their case and they know it (even though, in the heat of the moment, they choose to allow their words to stand as written).[118] Therefore, in 11:11–12, they clarify that their argument does not hinge upon the subordination of women to men.[119] Rather, the point is to prioritize the collective good over one's own personal status.

Therefore, having moved from the context of marriage to the context of the gatherings of the assembly of Jesus loyalists, the Pauline faction once again stressed the importance of mutual self-giving in a way that countered other imperial, counter-cultural, and cultural ways of gathering together. This is why, despite the tension that is apparent in this passage, they never once suggest that women should not pray or prophesy within the assemblies. Women are to continue to function in

---

creative insights and radical commitments—still had an imagination disciplined in some less-than-ideal ways by the culture in which Paul lived (the heteronormativity that infected the Black Panther Party and even the Zapatistas in earlier days—but which were also quickly uprooted by those movements—is instructive in this regard).

118. Not that this makes the Pauline faction any less of a jerk for making this statement in the first place. Patriarchy enables and quickly forgives these kinds of outbursts when they come from men, so we should not be quick to excuse these words and their subsequent impact.

119. Just as the argument in Galatians does not hinge upon the Pauline faction wanting their opponents to castrate themselves (as they say in an outburst in Gal 5:12). This sort of rhetoric shows that the Pauline faction, like anybody else, sometimes gets heated and says regrettable things.

this prominent and visible way. It is simply their hope that the women prophets—along with the men who engage in similar status seeking activities—will act in such a way that builds up the assembly so that a gain for one is a gain for all (and a gain for all is a gain for each).

Finally, this leaves us with Gal 3:28: "There is no longer [Judean] or Greek, there is no longer slave or free, there is no longer male and female; for all of you are one in the Anointed." Although it is quite possible that this was a pre-Pauline baptismal formula common to the broader Jesus movement, the Pauline faction clearly cite it in an approving manner.[120] While some have taken this passage to refer to the "spiritual" status women had in the assemblies of Jesus, the evidence we have accumulated up until now would suggest that there are no grounds for reading this verse in such a limited way. It seems clear that Paul and his coworkers, both male and female, were committed to enacting and realizing this formula in concrete ways within the assemblies of Jesus loyalists. There are no longer to be any gaps of status, role, or function between men and women, because all are one in the Anointed. Men and women (and, it is reasonable to conclude, people of all genders) are united as equals in every way as siblings within the household of God.[121]

---

120. Schüssler-Fiorenza thinks that Paul rearranges this formula in order to demote the male/female status to the third and less significant position (Schüssler-Fiorenza, *In Memory of Her*). It seems to me that the order of the partnerships Judean/Greek, slave/free, male/female does not imply any sort of ranking. In this regard, it is closer to the non-hierarchical list of the fruit of the Spirit found in Gal 5:22 than it is to the clearly marked hierarchy involved in some gifts of the Spirit found in 1 Cor 14:1-5 (although, even within the broader context of 1 Cor 12-14, Paul makes it clear that all members, regardless of their gifting, should be equally valued and that those with less honor should be treated with greater honor). Alternatively, Wayne Meeks suggests that Gal 3:28 is connected to a Jewish myth about the original androgynous state of humanity. Meeks asserts that this appeal to a primal androgyny is employed by Paul in order to rebel against stratified gender roles and produce equality in the functions granted to women and men within the assemblies of Jesus loyalists (Meeks, "Image of the Androgyne," 11-27). I am unconvinced that this is the case, but it should be noted that the same conclusion results, regardless of whether or not the Pauline faction has this androgynous state in mind.

121. Unfortunately, with the spread of the Jesus movement and its growth into more influential and powerful segments of the population, it seems that accommodation to the more culturally accepted but oppressive norms occurred. This trend is already visible within the New Testament in what John Dominic Crossan and others refer to as the shift from the original "radical" Paul to the "liberal" Paul of Ephesians and Colossians, to the "conservative" or "reactionary" Paul of the Pastorals (see Crossan and Reed, *In Search of Paul*, 116-20; Crossan, *God and Empire*, 172-78; Meeks, *Moral World*, 111-13; Elliott, *Liberating Paul*, 53. See also, in their own way, Dunn,

Pauline Solidarity

Slavery within the Household of God

So far, it appears that the Pauline faction followed through fairly consistently on the concrete relational implications concerning mutuality between siblings within the household of God. This newly constituted kinship abolished racial, national, and gender-based status distinctions. Did Paul and his coworkers also advocate for a similar abolition of status and function between slaves, freedpeople, and freeborn citizens?

As we saw in the previous volumes of this series, both slaves and freedpeople (including the freeborn descendants of former slaves) made up a significant percentage of the population of cities familiar to Paul and his coworkers. Furthermore, in some of the Judean communities they visited, slaves and freedpeople would be an even larger percentage of the population. For example, the bulk of the Judean community in Rome was composed of the descendants of the thousands of Judeans who were brought to Rome as slaves after Pompey's conquest in 64 BCE.[122] Therefore, although conclusions about socioeconomic status and places of origin based solely upon the analysis of names are not always entirely reliable, Clarke's suggestion that two-thirds of the names mentioned in Rom 16 point toward a slave origin is highly likely.[123] Paul and his coworkers interacted primarily with slaves and the immediate descendants of freed slaves. Not only that, but when we recall the subsistence level at which most of the Jesus loyalists lived, it is likely that slaves and freedpeople made up almost the entire population of their assemblies.[124]

"Diversity in Paul," 116; Malherbe, *Social Aspects of Early Christianity*, 51–53).

122. See Jewett, *Romans*, 55.

123. Clarke, "Jew and Greek," 113–14. Peter Lampe also engages in a detailed analysis of these names based upon Roman inscriptions and arrives at a slightly lower number that still contains a significant slave-based representation. He concludes that four names are definitely not slave names, ten are, and twelve cannot be determined (Lampe, "Roman Christians of Romans 16," 44–52). This is contra Banks, *Paul's Idea of Community*, 155–56. Jennings also argues that almost all those named in Rom 16 possessed slave names with some groups seeming to be made exclusively of slaves (Jennings, *Outlaw Justice*, 225–26).

124. In this regard it is telling that the Pauline faction talks about and to slaves and freedpeople but never once refers to citizens (except in Phil 3:21 which mentions a "citizenship in heaven" which is likely very different than their current status—i.e., as non-citizens of any city—given that this "citizenship" is said to reside in "the body of our humiliation" [Phil 3:21]). This suggests that there may have been no citizens of Corinth, Philippi, Rome, or elsewhere in the assemblies of Jesus loyalists.

This is not surprising given what we have seen of Pauline rhetoric thus far. The themes they write about and the values they laud would appeal to slaves and former slaves. Thus, for example, Paul and his coworkers place considerable emphasis upon the freedom that one gains in the Anointed.[125] In fact, of the forty-eight uses of the words "freedom," "free," and "to free," in the New Testament, twenty-eight occur in the Pauline letters.[126] To pick a few examples: "For freedom [the Anointed] has set us free. Stand firm, therefore, and do not submit again to a yoke of slavery. . . . For you were called to freedom" (Gal 5:1, 13); and "Now the Lord is the Spirit, and where the Spirit of the Lord is, there is freedom" (2 Cor 3:17). Similarly, the Pauline faction warns against those who "spy on the freedom we have in [the Anointed] Jesus, so that they might enslave us" (Gal 2:4). This is the sort of rhetoric that would have readily attracted slaves and former slaves—and other members of oppressed and colonized populations—to the assemblies.[127]

The same is true of the Pauline usage of "redemption" language. As Adolf Deissmann has shown, the language of redemption—*apolytrosis*—is language that refers to the manumission or liberation of slaves.[128] One of the ways in which slaves could be manumitted was by being purchased by a divinity.[129] Hence, on multiple occasions, the Pauline faction speaks of the Jesus loyalists as those who were "bought at a price" in order to be set free from their prior slavery to various other lords (both human and non-human).[130] Thus, as Richard Longenecker notes, the Pauline message of redemption "stresses reconciliation between [people] and God spiritually. But it also includes the reconciliation of [people] with [other people] socially."[131] The appeal of this to slaves should be fairly obvious.

However, the Pauline approach to slavery is not always and immediately obvious. There are other elements of Pauline rhetoric that can be

---

125. On this point, see, for example, Banks, *Paul's Idea of Community*, 23–25; Beker, *Paul the Apostle*, 270; Weiss, *Paul and Jesus*, 123–24.

126. See Richardson, *Paul's Ethic of Freedom*, 164–65. He includes the deutero-Pauline epistles as Pauline in this count.

127. See Pickett, "Conflicts at Corinth," 124; Martin, "Spirit in 2 Corinthians," 229–30. Although, as we have already seen, the rhetoric of freedom was also frequently deployed by the Romans.

128. Deissmann, *Light from the Ancient East*, 319–21.

129. Deissmann, *Light from the Ancient East*, 322; *Paul*, 214–17.

130. Deissmann, *Light from the Ancient East*, 326–29. See 1 Cor 6:20; 7:23.

131. Longenecker, *New Testament Social Ethics for Today*, 43.

taken as proof of what is, at best, an acritical acceptance of slavery or, at worst, the positive affirmation of slavery. Primarily, this point is made in relation to assertions that the members of the assemblies of Jesus are, in fact, *douloi Christou*—slaves of (the) Anointed.[132] Thus, in Rom 6:15–22, they write:

> What then? Should we sin because we are not under Law but under grace? By no means! Do you not know that if you present yourselves to anyone as obedient slaves, you are slaves of the one whom you obey, either sin, which leads to death, or of obedience, which leads to justice? But thanks be to God that you, having once been slaves of sin, have become obedient from the heart to the form of teaching to which you were entrusted, and that you, having been set free from sin have become slaves of [justice]. I am speaking in human terms because of your natural limitations. For just as you once presented your member as slaves of impurity and to greater and greater iniquity, so now present your members as slaves to [justice] for sanctification.
>
> When you were slaves of sin, you were free in regard to [justice]. So what advantage did you then get from the things of which you are now ashamed? The end of those things is death. But now that you have been freed from sin and enslaved to God, the advantage you get is sanctification. The end is eternal life. For the wages of sin is death, but the free gift of God is eternal life in [Anointed] Jesus our Lord.

Already a century ago, Johannes Weiss cited this passage in order to suggest that Paul has nothing like a "modern" attitude towards slavery but, instead, viewed it as a respectable profession.[133] Others then suggest that this language reveals how deeply Paul was focused on the spiritual realm—issues of actual slavery or material freedom are deemed inconsequential.[134] Some, however, are less comfortable with this approach and its implications for Paulinism (and Christianity), so they hasten to add that Graeco-Roman slavery was rather different than more recent practices of slavery and that slaves of people with high status were actually

---

132. A term that the Pauline faction is especially keen to apply to themselves. See 1 Cor 4:1; 2 Cor 11:23; Phil 1:1.

133. Weiss, *Earliest Christianity*, 1:176; 2:587–88. Of course, the role of slavery within the rise of modernity has been well documented by others (see, for example, the exceptional Williams, *Capitalism and Slavery*), so Weiss may have been right, but for all the wrong reasons!

134. See, for example, Richardson, *Paul's Ethic of Freedom*, 54.

THE TRANSNATIONAL FAMILY OF GOD

situated in positions of considerable prestige and power (thus, to be a slave of [the] Anointed would be prestigious, like being a presumably high-ranking slave of Augustus [rather than being one of the slaves stuck working in an Augustan salt mine]).[135] While there is certainly some truth in this, the absolute brutality of slavery, as highlighted in the last volume of this series, should not be forgotten. Here it is worth quoting a character in Plautus's *Amphityron*:

> The wealthy make bad masters; don't envy a rich man's slaves— "Do that!" "Say this!"—never a bit of rest. And that spoiled master who never worked a day thinks you must satisfy his lightest whim—this he expects and who cares how you work? Oh, slavery's the mother of injustice: *Take up your load and carry it*—That's life.[136]

Thus, in the Pauline context, many believe that it is better to be free and poor than to be a rich man's slave. Given this and the brutality that was a part of the daily lives of slaves already examined in our last volume, we cannot so easily whitewash slavery.

J. Albert Harrill explores the implications of Pauline rhetoric about slavery in detail. He argues that the Pauline faction's rhetorical use of the motif of slavery is one that (consciously or not) ends up colluding with and supporting the Roman ideology and practice of mastery.[137] Thus, for example, Harrill argues that in the letter to the Jesus loyalists at Rome, Paul finds slaves to be good thing to think with—a useful trope—but one that is employed in a manner that serves the Roman slave-holding ideology.[138] Not surprisingly, then, Harrill argues that this ideology influences Paul's own actions in relation to slaves. In the letter to Philemon, Harrill asserts that Onesimus is treated as a thing transferred from one person to another to be owned and used, regardless of what Onesimus thinks or wants.[139] Therefore, Harrill asserts that "the evidence cannot support readings that purport to find early Christianity's moral unease

---

135. See Meeks, *Origins of Christian Morality*, 169; Osiek, "Family Matters," 209.

136. Plautus quoted in Martin, "Spirit in 2 Corinthians," 227.

137. Harrill, *Slaves in the New Testament*, 1–3.

138. Harrill, *Slaves in the New Testament*, 23–26. Knust also notes how Paul further perpetuates this ideology when he associates being driven by one's desires with "slavishness" (Knust, "Paul and the Politics," 170).

139. Harrill, *Slaves in the New Testament*, 6–16.

with slavery . . . we cannot correct New Testament passages that appear immoral, even when the interest to do so serves the noblest aims."[140]

One way of approaching this Pauline rhetoric is to view it as rooted in the tensions found in colonized populations that are trying to overcome colonial power dynamics even though they (sometimes inadvertently) end up replicating those very dynamics in their efforts to be free. Thus, Michael Gorman notes, the early Jesus loyalists appear to experience both liberation and enslavement—they are transferred from malevolent masters to a benevolent master.[141] However, two further comments are in order here. First, references to themes that appear favorable and appealing to slaves and former slaves—freedom and redemption, for example—significantly outweigh any seemingly acritical deployment of slavery as a useful thing with which to think. Second, in the passage quoted from Rom 6, it should be observed that the Pauline faction may be aware that the analogy they are making is problematical. Thus, just as we see them stepping back from the assertions that they made about gender in 1 Cor 11, so also they step back from speaking in an overly positive manner about slavery and they hedge their remarks by saying: "I am speaking in human terms" (Rom 6:19). Obviously, they think this rhetoric is far from perfect.

Having made those observations—and before we turn to the three passages in the letters Paul co-authored that directly address slavery (1 Cor 7:20-24; Philemon; Gal 3:28)—it is worth observing that, just as differing opinions emerge from the analysis of Pauline rhetoric, so also differing opinions are taken about actual Pauline practices in relation to slavery. What we find are a continuum of three views that fall roughly into the categories of conservative, liberal, and emancipatory readings.

First, the conservative position holds that the Pauline faction did not have a problem with slavery but instead developed a spiritual focus that held such material or earthly matters to be adiaphora. This position has already been explored in some detail in volume 1 of this series, but it is primarily based upon two assertions: that Pauline eschatology led the Pauline faction to believe in the imminent end of the world (a view we have already rejected) and that their spirit-focused ontology led them to believe that all were equal in (the) Anointed regardless of

---

140. Harrill, *Slaves in the New Testament*, 6.
141. Gorman, *Cruciformity*, 126–29.

their social status—making real or material differences in status inconsequential.[142] Thus, for example, writing in the mid-twentieth century, Hans Conzelmann argues that it is "dangerous" to focus too much upon Pauline assertions that social distinctions are done away with in the body of the Anointed because the Pauline faction is not offering a "Christian programme for changing the world" as all social distinctions are "neutral in relation to salvation."[143] Similarly, demonstrating the degree to which this trajectory of thought has endured among conservative Christians, Thomas Schreiner writes in 2008 that Paul's focus is not on a person's social status but on whether a person is in Adam or in the Anointed, so all social barriers are "immaterial" because they constitute "no advantage relative to salvation."[144] Coming to the same conclusion from a different direction, Peter Richardson hypothesizes that part of the reason for this was that Paul was not personally engaged with the issue to the same extent as he was with matters related to race and ethnicity, and he also suggests that Judaism's scriptural acceptance of slavery further added to Paul's lack of engagement on the matter.[145] Frequently, it should be repeated, these assertions are made by scholars who make no distinction between the epistles universally recognized as Pauline and those that are contested are considered by many to be deutero-Pauline. Thus, material found in Colossians, Ephesians, and the Pastorals is granted far more significance than material found in the uncontested Pauline Epistles.[146]

---

142. On slavery in relation to this proposed eschatological outlook, see Cadoux, *Early Church and the World*, 132–33; Goguel, *Primitive Church*, 554–55; Sampley, *Walking Between the Times*, 78; Richardson, *Paul's Ethic of Freedom*, 40–41. On slavery being inconsequential to the one's spiritual or ontological status in the Anointed, see Ladd, *Theology of the New Testament*, 574–75; Sampley, *Walking between the Times*, 77–80; Banks, *Paul's Idea of Community*, 113–18; Longenecker, *Paul, Apostle of Liberty*, 109–11; Conzelmann, *History of Primitive Christianity*, 107; Richardson, *Paul's Ethic of Freedom*, 41.

143. Conzelmann, *Outline of the Theology*, 263–64.

144. Schreiner, *Paul*, 31.

145. See Richardson, *Paul's Ethic of Freedom*, 42–47. In my opinion, both of these arguments seem particularly weak. First of all, to hypothesize that Paul did not care about slavery simply because he was not a slave posits Paul as overwhelmingly cold-hearted in light of the large presence of slaves and freedpeople within the early assemblies of Jesus loyalists. Secondly, Richardson's understanding of the Judean Scriptures is questionable and does not recognize just how critical those writings can be of slavery.

146. See Schnabel, *Paul and the Early Church*, 1345; Crossan, *God and Empire*, 164–65; Lampe, "Paul, Patrons, and Clients," 489; Martin, "Spirit in 2 Corinthians," 231–32, 236–37. It is also worth noting that some outside of the conservative camp

Second, the more liberal view holds that it was beyond Paul's scope and range of thinking (given that he was a product of his own time) to imagine a total overthrow or reversal of the system of slavery but that Paul did encourage a way of relating to others within the assemblies of Jesus loyalists that would lead to the abolition of slavery over time.[147] The benefits of this position are threefold. First, it is more nuanced than the conservative position and makes better sense of the seemingly contradictory material we find in the Pauline letters. Second, it remains focused upon the uncontested letters. Third, it helps contemporary readers who find slavery to be problematical to make peace with the content of their sacred texts. Richard Longenecker has argued strongly for this position in his book *New Testament Social Ethics for Today*. Over against those who suggest that the issue of slavery was "immaterial" to Paul, he states that it is striking that matters related to social relations between slaves and free people, paired with questions about the status of slaves, are a matter of great concern for the early assemblies of Jesus loyalists (given how deeply ingrained the institution of slavery was in the Graeco-Roman world).[148] Turning then to the content of Paul's letters (and incorporating the *Haustafeln* in Colossians and Ephesians into his reflections), Longenecker argues that the Pauline faction emphasizes freedom without directly assaulting the institution of slavery. Instead, they elevate the status of slaves in relation to free people and establish the principles of reciprocity, mutual obligation to each other, and mutual obligation to God.[149] Consequently Longenecker concludes that:

> Rather than engaging in a head-on confrontation with slavery, Paul sought to elevate the quality of personal relationships within the existing structures of society. His insistence on mutual acceptance among Christians [sic], while disparaged by some, was

---

have sometimes felt it was necessary to grudgingly concede this point. Kautsky, for example, argues that early Christianity never sought to abolish slavery but instead, saw slaves as property that was shared as part of the injunction to hold all things in common (Kautsky, *Foundations of Christianity*, 121–24).

147. See Dodd, *Meaning of Paul for Today*, 153; Dunn, *Theology of Paul the Apostle*, 698–701; Theissen, *Fortress Introduction to the New Testament*, 70; Coggan, *Paul*, 158–60; Weiss, *Earliest Christianity*, 2:586. Jeffers extends this same conclusion to the *Haustafeln* found in Colossians and Ephesians (Jeffers, *Greco-Roman World*, 229).

148. Longenecker, *New Testament Social Ethics*, 51.

149. Longenecker, *New Testament Social Ethics*, 54–58.

in reality an explosive concept which ultimately could have its full impact only in the abolition of the institution of slavery.[150]

Edwin Judge develops a slightly more tempered argument, straddling more than one of the interpretative camps laid out here. Judge argues that the Pauline faction engaged in a "head-on personal assault on the status system which supplied the ideology of the established order" but that they still ended up affirming slave ranks—while simultaneously denying slaves the (low) status they received from society.[151] Although this suggests that Judge may lean towards the conservatives (which views a spiritualized ontology as "radical"), he quickly distances himself from that position by asserting that the Pauline faction repudiated "status conventions which permitted people to exploit the system to private advantage."[152] Slavery persists, but new ways of being in relationship occur which are opposed to exploitation and which overturn conventional notions of status.[153] Therefore, Judge holds that this view led to the invalidation of slavery within the early assemblies of Jesus loyalists even though some appearances of slavery persisted in order to assist the Jesus loyalists in maintaining the illusion of social conformity (Judge views this as a survival strategy although he also imagines that Paul himself probably owned slaves).[154]

---

150. Longenecker, *New Testament Social Ethics*, 59. The implication for today, then, is that the personhood, dignity, and freedom of all people should be affirmed (69).

151. Judge, *Social Distinctives of the Christians*, 159–62.

152. Judge, *Social Distinctives of the Christians*, 163.

153. Neil Elliott mirrors Judge when he argues that Paul is not urging "quietism" on this matter but is, instead, encouraging "withdrawal from the public frenzy of exploitation" (Elliott, *Liberating Paul*, 202).

154. Judge, *Social Distinctives*, 55–56, 108–9. David Horrell also struggles to develop a carefully nuanced position on this matter and concludes that there are "egalitarian impulses" in Paul but that they remain impulses, even though corporate solidarity is a "basic metanorm" in Pauline ethics and an "essential foundation" for other aspects of Paul's ethical instructions (Horrell, *Solidarity and Difference*, 130–31). David deSilva adopts a similarly nuanced approach and argues that Paul calls for a reversal of values related to masters and slaves—in that Jesus loyalists are urged to relate to one another as equals—but suggests that this is to take place *only* within the assemblies of Jesus loyalists (deSilva, *Honor, Patronage, Kinship, and Purity*, 235). DeSilva's position relies upon a reading of Eph 5:21 and does not rely upon the uncontested Pauline material. That said, deSilva also agrees with Judge in seeing this as a survival strategy as being associated in the public eye with slave revolts would have doomed the early Jesus loyalists to annihilation (235–36). He therefore concludes: "These texts say less than liberationists would wish, but they also say far more than the supporters of hierarchies

Pauline Solidarity

Third, emancipatory readings of Paulinism suggest that it was entirely opposed to slavery both at personal and structural levels. While those who argue for acritical or explicit acceptance of slavery within the early assemblies of Jesus loyalists tend to rely upon contested or deutero-Pauline epistles, scholars in this camp point to the practice of ecclesial manumission that is mentioned in writings dated to the early second century (but which reference a practice that predates the writing of those epistles). Thus, already in 1 Clem. 55:2, we see Jesus loyalists emancipating others from slavery with some members going so far as to sell themselves into slavery so that others could be free![155] Furthermore, communities of Jesus loyalists would also pool resources in order to purchase the freedom of slaves.[156] However, we see the recently institutionalized hierarchy of power that developed in the assemblies, trying to control this practice. Thus, Ignatius of Antioch writes to Polycarp of Smyrna and urges him not to allow slaves to "desire to be made free from the common fund."[157] That this is occurring, and occurring at a rate that alarms those trying to control the Jesus movement in order to advance their personal status and well-being at the expense of others, reminds us that there was a high number of slaves in the early Jesus movement and that the early Jesus movement was concerned with the material and physical well-being and freedom of slaves in the here-and-now. It suggests a practice that may date back to the time of the Pauline faction. This is also supported by another early second-century document, the Shepherd of Hermas, which urges Jesus loyalists to use their resources to "purchase afflicted souls as each one is able, and look after widows and orphans"[158] and "to redeem [i.e., emancipate] from distress the slaves of God."[159] Furthermore, despite the efforts of the nascent conservative hierarchy, this practice continued to persist for some time, suggesting it was deeply engrained in the practices of local assemblies of Jesus loyalists. Hence, in a fourth-century

---

(like patriarchy) would wish" (236).

155. See Jeffers, *Greco-Roman World*, 222–23.

156. See Jeffers, *Greco-Roman World*, 235.

157. Letter to Polycarp, 4.3, quoted in Martin, "Spirit in 2 Corinthians," 231. See Pickett, "Conflicts at Corinth," 125.

158. Herm. Sim. 1:8, quoted in Harrill, *Manumission of Slaves*, 178–79. See Pickett, "Conflicts at Corinth," 135.

159. Herm. Mand. 8:10, quoted in Harrill, *Manumission of Slaves*, 179. Recalling, of course, that "redemption" literally refers to the emancipation of slaves (more on this in chapter 5).

text entitled *Apostolic Constitutions*, we find the following injunctions directed at Christians: "Maintain and clothe those who are in want.... And such sums of money as are collected... appoint to be laid out in the redemption [again, emancipation] of the saints, the deliverance of slaves and of captives, and of prisoners."[160] The same text also urges Christians to avoid attending public meetings unless the purpose of their attendance was "to purchase a slave and save a life."[161]

Therefore, what we see in the early Jesus movement is the rapid development of two conflicting trajectories—one that incorporates and affirms dominant cultural practices related to slave-based hierarchies and one that disrupts and rejects those practices (the rapid development of these two increasingly divergent strands—one that is accommodationist and one that doubles down on the revolutionary potential of the founders—is common to revolutionary movements that attract large numbers of people and persist over time). The question, then, is if either tradition arises from practices supported by Paul and his coworkers (or if, perhaps, both do). Those who hold to an emancipatory reading of Paulinism suggest that it is this practice of ecclesial manumission that most faithfully adheres to the Pauline vision of the household of the loyal. Thus, for example, Robert Jewett asserts that Paul should be seen as a "revolutionary who struggled for the freedom of early church members in profound and successful ways," and Peter Oakes states that Paul assaults all hierarchical boundaries and calls for householders and slaves to be "members of one another" (see Rom 12:4–5)—mutually interdependent in a manner that abolishes previously existing hierarchies.[162] Andrew Clarke then argues that the high number of names suggesting a slave-origin found in Rom 16 is a strong affirmation of Gal 3:28, understood as a creed affirming the manumission of slaves in the here-and-now.[163] Therefore, against the assumptions made by those like Judge, some argue that the absence of any reference to Paul and his coworkers owning slaves suggests that they are deliberately trying to set an example of what it means to assert that there

---

160. Apostolic Constitutions 4.92.2, quoted in Martin, "Spirit in 2 Corinthians," 231.

161. Apostolic Constitutions, 2.62.4, quoted in Martin, "Spirit in 2 Corinthians," 231.

162. Jewett, *Paul*, 60; Oakes, *Reading Romans in Pompeii*, 102–3. See also Jewett, *Paul*, 59–69.

163. Clarke, "Jew and Greek," 103–25.

is no difference between slaves and free people—owning slaves is simply out of the question.[164]

Rating the relative plausibility of these three perspectives requires an examination of the passages in which the Pauline faction address the matter of slavery. We will examine three: 1 Cor 7:20–24, the epistle to Philemon, and Gal 3:28. Beginning in 1 Cor 7:20–24, we have already seen how within this chapter the Pauline faction explains the counter-cultural and egalitarian implications of what it means to live as the household of God in matters related to intimate relationships between men and women. Do they also follow through consistently on these implications when the matter addressed is that of slavery? How this passage is translated is crucial for a proper understanding. I will begin by quoting it as it appears in the NRSV:

> Let each of you remain in the condition in which you were called. Were you a slave when called? Do not be concerned about it. Even if you can gain your freedom, make use of your present condition now more than ever. For whoever was called in the Lord as a slave is a freed person belonging to the Lord, just as whoever was free when called is a slave of [the Anointed]. You were bought with a price; do not become slaves of human masters. In whatever condition you were called, [siblings], there remain with God.

This translation seems to favor the position that the Pauline faction believed that being a slave is of little significance. Thus, they urged people to "remain in the condition" in which they find themselves, and may even have suggested that there is no need to avail one's self of freedom, even if that opportunity arises. Certainly, this is how conservative Christian scholarship has interpreted it. In (the) Anointed, one receives a form of spiritual elevation and detachment that makes the concrete experience of slavery irrelevant, especially since Pauline eschatology is also taken (by these scholars) to herald the imminent end of the world.[165] However, this

---

164. See Jeffers, *Greco-Roman World*, 235.

165. See Lietzmann, *Beginnings of the Christian Church*, 134–35; Fitzpatrick, *Paul*, 52–53; Vos, *Pauline Eschatology*, 85–87; Pate, *End of the Age has Come*, 200; Schrage, *Ethics of the New Testament*, 232–33; Sampley, *Walking Between the Times*, 101; Sanders, *Paul: The Apostle's Life*, 295. Some scholars have tried to argue that this position is actually a radical position to take—making certain things meaningless even if others say they are meaningful—in order to live within certain structures without being determined by them (see Jennings, *Outlaw Justice*, 126–27, who follows Agamben, *Time That Remains*, 22–23, 35). I am unconvinced.

understanding of 1 Cor 7:20–24 faces some problems. Notably, it seems odd that the Pauline faction would counsel some not to avail themselves of opportunities to attain freedom while simultaneously counseling others not to "become slaves of human masters" precisely because God has bought them (and not because such things are irrelevant—in fact, this suggests that such things continue to matter a great deal). Furthermore, what is the present condition which they call slaves to make use of in verse 21? Is the present condition that of slavery or is it a reference to an opportunity for freedom? The Greek here is fairly ambiguous—the Pauline faction could be arguing that slaves should choose to remain as slaves (as conservative scholars have asserted), or they could be saying the following: "Were you a slave when called? Never mind; but if you can gain freedom, take the opportunity."[166]

This interpretation seems to make better sense of the context of the passage—and adheres well with the injunction for people not to become slaves to human masters—and is, indeed, how the majority of scholars now translate the passage.[167] This translation also fits well with the observation that Paul and his coworkers are addressing this passage to those who are actually slaves—something completely unheard of among writers in antiquity.[168] By writing in this way, they are addressing slaves as equal members of the assemblies at Corinth. This is then affirmed by the explicit status-reversing and -leveling injunction that, within the assemblies of Jesus loyalists, slaves must be viewed as freedpeople (since they have been "bought with a price," that is, redeemed or manumitted by the Anointed), and freedpeople are viewed as slaves (of the Anointed, who

---

166. See Elliott, *Liberating Paul*, 32–34.

167. See Cadoux, *Early Church and the World*, 133–34; Scroggs, *Paul for a New Day*, 44–45; Ralph Martin, "Spirit in 2 Corinthians," 230–31; Grant, *Early Christianity and Society*, 90; Horrell, *Social Ethos*, 161–62; *Solidarity and Difference*, 126–27; Dunn, *Beginning from Jerusalem*, 800–801; Elliott, "Apostle Paul and Empire," 107; Witherington, *Paul Quest*, 196–97; Winter, *Seek the Welfare of the City*, 152; Harrill, "Paul and Slavery," 586–88. Of course, as we already observed, Harrill holds this position despite thinking that the Pauline faction supports slavery as a trope and useful tool by which one can conceptualize various relationships. Winter also seems somewhat hesitant to draw this conclusion about the Pauline affirmation that slaves should take the opportunity to be free. Instead, noting that the remarks here are paired with advice regarding circumcision, Winter argues that the Pauline faction is opposing those who would seek to elevate their status in different ways (by trying to undo circumcision, or by trying to advance one's status by becoming a slave in a wealthy or high-status household) (Winter, *Seek the Welfare of the City*, 146–62).

168. See Judge, *Social Distinctives*, 108–9.

also "bought" them).[169] Thus, they minimize the significance of a person's status as a slave *only* in order to assist slaves to attain material equality within the assemblies of Jesus loyalists, while simultaneously encouraging those slaves to gain their freedom if they get the opportunity (a practice supported by assemblies who pooled their resources together in order to redeem members who were slaves). After all, it should be remembered that freedom was not something slaves could choose for themselves—it was something granted to them based upon the choice of their masters. This also suggests that the masters of the slaves being addressed were not members of the assemblies of Jesus loyalists at Corinth and did not share the revaluation of values for which Paul and his coworkers advocated. Therefore, given that the freedom of these slaves is something that cannot be produced by the assemblies of Jesus loyalists (at this time), the Pauline faction seeks to ensure that all members of the household of God relate to one another as equals and are equally valued—whether they be slaves or freedpeople. Hence, in 1 Cor 7:20–24 we find that Paul consistently applies the same emancipatory and practical understanding of what it means to be siblings within the transnational family of God, male and female, slave and free.

But what of a situation where a slave-owner is a member of an assembly of Jesus loyalists? What might the Pauline faction say about this sort of situation? This is what we find in the epistle to Philemon.[170] The traditional reading of this letter has viewed the Pauline faction as unopposed to slavery.[171] Instead, Paul is seen as trying to give Onesimus a new sense of personal dignity while he remains a slave to Philemon.[172] Thus, it

169. Notably absent here or anywhere else in any of the Pauline Epistles is any reference to freeborn *citizens*. See Witherington, *Jesus, Paul and the End of the World*, 197–98; Horrell, *Social Ethos*, 160; Harrill, "Paul and Slavery," 596–97.

170. Although some have suggested that Onesimus was not a slave—since Paul only urges Philemon to treat Onesimus not "*as* a slave," which is not the same thing as saying that Onesimus *was* a slave (see Martin, "Spirit in 2 Corinthians," 230; Winter, "Philemon and the Patriarchal Paul," 122)—I favor the majority reading that understands Onesimus as a runaway slave. I think this makes the best sense of the language and the letter as a whole. The name itself means "Useful" which was a common slave name (see Crossan and Borg, *First Paul*, 40). Furthermore, within Graeco-Roman society, slaves could flee to temples or to influential friends of their masters in order to beg for intercession or mercy, which is likely what has occurred with Onesimus, Philemon, and Paul (see Crossan and Borg, *First Paul*, 38; Crossan and Reed, *In Search of Paul*, 107–8).

171. Elliott, *Liberating Paul*, 41–44.

172. See Fitzpatrick, *Paul*, 35–36; Richardson, *Paul's Ethic of Freedom*, 49.

THE TRANSNATIONAL FAMILY OF GOD

is no wonder, as Charles Cousar observes, that many contemporary readers of this letter are left "disappointed and puzzled as to why [Paul] did not attack the institutionalized social evils of his day more than he did."[173]

However, there may be more occurring in this letter than first meets the eye of the twenty-first-century reader. Of central importance is the injunction that Philemon receive Onesimus as "a beloved brother" (v. 16) and in the same way that Philemon would receive Paul (v. 17). As we have already observed, this is not flowery rhetoric devoid of practical implications. The Pauline faction is not trying to put a humanizing gloss over a dehumanizing practice. Rather, if Philemon was to receive Onesimus as a brother, he would be required to relate to him in all the ways in which sibling relationships were expected to be practiced. If Philemon receives Onesimus as a brother, then Onesimus can no longer be his slave.[174] In this context, to be equal before God means to exist as social equals in relationship with one another.[175] Thus, although the Pauline faction does not say "free Onesimus!" they leave Philemon no other option but to do so. Indeed, that the Pauline faction may have been known to hold this position on slavery (as already evidenced by the letter to the Corinthians) may have been why Onesimus chose to flee to Paul in the first place![176]

Why, then, do they not simply say: "Free Onesimus"? Clearly the Pauline faction sees this as Philemon's "duty" (v. 8), which in itself is an interesting reversal of duty. Significantly, the Pauline faction never mentions the duty of a slave to a master but instead argues that a master has a duty to their slaves and that this duty is fulfilled by manumitting them.[177] The Pauline faction appeals to Philemon to make this choice himself

---

173. Cousar, *Introduction to the New Testament*, 69. Cousar makes this point even after observing that manumission could sometimes make the lives of slaves harder rather than easier (as they would be required to provide for themselves everything they had previously received from their masters).

174. See Longenecker, *New Testament Social Ethics for Today*, 58–59; Witherington, *Paul Quest*, 198; Martin, "Spirit in 2 Corinthians," 230; Winter, "Philemon and the Patriarchal Paul," 123. Horrell falls short of stating this. He argues that establishing a sibling bond between Philemon and Onesimus "requires a more radical change than would manumission per se" (Horrell, *Solidarity and Difference*, 127). This is the kind of use of the word "radical" about which one should be very suspicious.

175. See Crossan and Reed, *In Search of Paul*, 108–10; Crossan, *God and Empire*, 160–64; Crossan and Borg, *First Paul*, 40.

176. A suggestion made by Elliott, *Liberating Paul*, 51.

177. See Elliott, *Liberating Paul*, 49, 51; Crossan and Borg, *First Paul*, 36–37, 40. See also Harrill, "Paul and Slavery," 592–93, as Harrill argues that Paul treats Onesimus as a thing to be freed to be of further use.

without being told to do so, on the basis of love (v. 9) and in hope that Philemon may "become effective when [he] perceive[s] all the good that we may do for [the Anointed]" (v. 6; good that it presumably includes manumitting Onesimus). Although they claim Paul can make demands, the Pauline faction appeals to Philemon as a brother (v. 20) and treats him as an equal, just as they hope that Philemon will treat Onesimus as an equal. In this way, they model the form of equality they desire to see within the assemblies where Paul, too, is simply one sibling among many.[178] No one, they argue, should be enslaved—not to them, not to Philemon, not to anyone apart from the Anointed who sets them free.

However, the Pauline faction is also trying to tip the scales in their favor. They spend a fair bit of time in a short letter "buttering up" Philemon and reminding Philemon of how loving he has already been "to all the holy ones" (v. 5; again, this presumably includes Onesimus), which would make it harder for Philemon to reject their request.[179] They also make this request publicly in a letter written not only to Philemon but to Apphia, Archippus, and all those who meet together with them (v. 2). This, then, would create a communal pressure for Philemon to publicly demonstrate his character and values.[180] That the letter mentions that Paul himself would like to visit Philemon soon (v. 22) only heightens this pressure.

In light of this analysis it seems clear that the advice to Philemon is consistent with the position on slavery that the Pauline faction takes in 1 Cor 7:20–24. Slaves are not only equal with others "before God." They are also equal with other members in the community in tangible, practical ways that make a difference in their day-to-day lives. This equality requires any members of the assemblies of Jesus loyalists who own slaves—exceedingly rare members like Philemon (he is the only member we can be sure owned a slave of all those mentioned in the Pauline Epistles)—to set them free so that they may truly know and love each other as siblings.

This leaves us with our final passage in the uncontested Pauline material: Gal 3:28, which states that "there is no longer slave or free" because all are one in the Anointed (a formula echoed in 1 Cor 12:13). This

---

178. Even if he sometimes tries to tip the scales by claiming to be the mother of them all . . . a claim that folx may not have been inclined to take seriously.

179. The practice of *captatio benevolentiae*, what Crossan and Borg describe as capturing benevolence by laying it on thick (Crossan and Borg, *First Paul*, 36).

180. See Elliott, *Liberating Paul*, 44–46; Theissen, *Fortress Introduction to the New Testament*, 69–70.

passage demonstrates how central a meaningfully experienced unity is to the conception of the body of the Anointed developed by Paul and his coworkers.[181] However, how ideal or practical this unity is taken to be has been contested. Those within or closer to the conservative position have tended to see this as an ideal devoid of social implications.[182] From this perspective the point is that the differences Paul mentions—such as differences between slaves and free people—are not abolished (just as many [socially constructed] gender differences, especially as they relate to biology and sexual activity, are not abolished by the Pauline faction), but they are no longer grounds for any kind of feeling of separation or division within the assemblies themselves.[183]

This may well be true in situations like the one mentioned in 1 Cor 7:20–24, wherein freedom was not an option for some, but this reading tends to fall short of what is intended here. Instead, as the bulk of contemporary scholars that fall into the more "liberal" or "radical" positions argue, this passage is fraught with implications and calls for the abolition of slavery.[184] This is the interpretation that makes the best sense of what we have seen in other Pauline passages. The Pauline faction demonstrates the proper interpretation of Gal 3:28 in 1 Cor 7:20–24 and in the epistle to Philemon. The meaning of the statement that there is "no longer slave or free" means that those who own slaves in the body of the Anointed should set them free and those who are slaves of masters outside of the body of the Anointed are to avail themselves of freedom when they get the opportunity (often with the financial assistance of their new siblings in the Anointed).

That Paul and his coworkers are possibly quoting a previously existing baptismal formula that was employed by the earliest Jesus loyalists, demonstrates just how essential this kind of practical liberating and unifying action was to the early Jesus movement.[185] By understanding that

---

181. See Cerfaux, *Church in the Theology of St. Paul*, 224–29; Davies, *Jewish and Pauline Studies*, 207, 211–12; Kee, *Christian Origins*, 88 (a key component of sibling relationships, as mentioned above).

182. See Harrill, "Paul and Slavery," 594.

183. See Fitzpatrick, *Paul*, 25; although Fitzpatrick does still suggest that this ideal should have some practical outworkings in the body of the Anointed (26).

184. See Longenecker, *New Testament Social Ethics*, 30, 51–52; Crossan and Reed, *In Search of Paul*, 74–75; Crossan, *God and Empire*, 160; Gorman, *Apostle of the Crucified Lord*, 126–28; Gorman, *Reading Paul*, 19–20.

185. See especially Schüssler-Fiorenza, *In Memory of Her*, 162, 199, 213; *Rhetoric and Ethic*, 154–57.

loyalty to Jesus required one to oppose slavery—at personal and ideological levels—the Pauline faction followed the trajectory established by Jesus and those who first gathered with him.[186] No wonder, then, that Elizabeth Schüssler-Fiorenza concludes that the early Jesus movement, as an "association of equals," was "especially attractive to those who had little stake in the rewards of religion based either on class stratification or on male dominance."[187]

In light of these three passages, it appears that the emancipatory understanding of Paulinism offers us the most plausible perspective on the position Paul and his coworkers took when faced with slavery, not as a rhetorical device but as the lived experience of many of the members of the household of God. Although the Pauline faction is, in some ways, still bound by their own context, they are clearly dedicated to an emancipatory practice.[188] When freedom is not an option, because masters are not members of the assembly in question, then slaves and freepeople are to relate to one another as equals within that assembly, and when freedom becomes possible for any slave (whether by chance or by pooling funds), it is to be taken. This means that it is to be taken from masters who are not members of the assemblies when it is offered, but it also means that masters who are already members of the assemblies ought to manumit their slaves since all members are now siblings in the Anointed.

Summary and Conclusion

Throughout this chapter, we have seen the ways in which the Pauline faction engaged in a thorough deconstruction and reorientation of the household unit, one of the cornerstones of Graeco-Roman society and the ideo-theology of Rome. Within their understanding of the Jesus movement, all members of the assemblies of Jesus loyalists exist as co-equal siblings within the household of God where the positions of elevated power and authority have been assigned to God (the Father) and Jesus (the firstborn). Furthermore, this is a transnational household that

---

186. Jesus and Paul, in turn, are possibly following an emancipatory stream of apocalyptic Judean eschatology that pre-existed them. See Crossan and Reed, *In Search of Paul*, 233–34.

187. Schüssler-Fiorenza, *In Memory of Her*, 181.

188. Of course, probably the most notable way in which the Pauline faction remains blinded by their context is the hetero-normativity that they appear to take for granted as an expression of worship within the assemblies associated with them.

crosses barriers of race, ethnicity, class, and gender as it encroaches upon and invades territories and bodies claimed by the household and body of Caesar. Within the household of God and the body of the Anointed, all were considered equals, communally and materially responsible to and for one another. Previously accepted barriers to status, authority, and functions that existed between men and women were abolished. Just as slaves were treated as equal to free people, free people were treated as equal to slaves, and, whenever possible, slaves were redeemed as a part of the material demonstration of this commitment. No wonder, then, that we find such a prominent presence of women and slaves in the assemblies of Jesus loyalists that formed within the urban slums visited by Paul and his coworkers. This was a movement created by and for the lowest members of society, over against everything that was valued by the social, political, economic, and religious elites.

By engaging in the embodied proclamation of this innovative and seditious approach, the Pauline faction knowingly deepened the perceptible deviance of the early assemblies of Jesus loyalists. This would both heighten the marginalization and socioeconomic and political persecutions experienced by those assemblies while also establishing an embodied ideology that would strengthen and unite the assemblies within that experience. It is interesting to observe that the Pauline faction does this on a regular basis (as we saw with the matter of circumcision in volume 1 of this series and see now in relation to the household unit). This suggests that those who continually suggest that Paul and his coworkers chose to follow this-or-that situational ethics as a "survival strategy" are offering an explanation that is out of character with actions taken and supported by Paulinism. The Pauline faction seemed to be very willing to jeopardize their survival on several points, refusing to take the easier way out many times over. Living the abundant life promised by Jesus and experienced in the fellowship of the Spirit of Life—a life so abundant that it triumphed over Death in all its manifestations, from the household of Caesar to the structures of patriarchy or slavery—was what mattered more than questions of whether or not the small body of insurgents would survive under the ever-watchful gaze of the empire. After all, their inspiration, Jesus, had been killed by the representatives and laws of Caesar. But they also knew that God their father had raised this Jesus from the dead and would do the same for them.

3

EMBRACING SHAME IN THE COMPANY OF THE CRUCIFIED

> The very word "cross" should be far removed not only from the person of a Roman citizen but from his thoughts, his eyes and his ears. For it is not only the actual occurrence of these things or the endurance of them, but liability to them, nay, the mere mention of them, that is unworthy of a Roman citizen.
>
> —Cicero, *pro Rabirio Postumo* 5.16

> I decided to know nothing among you except Jesus [Anointed], and him crucified.
>
> —1 Corinthians 2:2

Introduction

HAVING EXAMINED THE WAYS in which Paul and his coworkers deconstructed and reconfigured the household unit in a life-giving manner that sought to counter the death-dealing ways in which that unit operated as a central component of the ideo-theology of the Roman Empire and the dominant culture of their day, I will now turn to an examination of how the Pauline faction and the early assemblies of Jesus loyalists engaged with cultural notions of honor and shame that were also used by the empire in order to further a death-dealing status quo. In this chapter, I will argue that the Pauline faction created an alternative system of honor, an anti-honor system, based upon a reevaluation of what it means to honor God in light of Jesus's experience of crucifixion. For the Pauline faction, the embrace of a self-debasing trajectory that culminated in a death on a cross was, itself, the fullest revelation of the character of God. Consequently, this alternative conceptualization led the household of God to a cruciform way of living that expressed itself in the shameless embrace of one's own shamefulness, including shameful practices of love—such as love of enemies. Given the upheaval this causes in relation to the embodiment of Roman standards of honor and shame, it is entirely accurate to state that those who embraced the views and practices held by the early assemblies of Jesus loyalists would be viewed not only as deviants but also as traitors, rebels, and terrorists.

Honor and Shame and Shame as Honor in the Household of God

An Alternative Court of Reputation

Honor and shame operated as elements of an ideology that preserved and strengthened the status quo of the empire within cultures wherein the identity and value of an individual was formed by the place that individual had within the collective group. Honor was "one's own sense of worth and the corroboration of that understanding by a relevant group."[1] Similarly, shame was understood positively as a sensitivity to one's reputation as determined by the group and, negatively, as acting in a way that contradicts the value of the group.[2] Because there were various groups to which any given person would be related, some competition for honor took place with the understanding that honor was a limited good—a person could not gain or lose honor without that costing or profiting another person. However, for any person, one's sense of honor was especially connected to the place one had in the family unit. Departing from that place and the practices of one's family was considered especially shameful.

---

1. Esler, "Mediterranean Context of Early Christianity," 16.
2. deSilva, *Honor, Patronage, Kinship, and Purity*, 25; Malina, "Social Levels, Morals, and Daily Life," 49.

Pauline Solidarity

As we saw in the last chapter, this departure from the structures and values of one's bio-family was precisely what Paul and his coworkers were urging the Jesus loyalists to do as they formulated the fictive kinship of the household of God. Other factors contribute to the shamefulness of this endeavor. The prominent presence of slaves, the observation that others who were free were to be considered as slaves (of the Anointed) and that slaves and free were to relate to one another as equals, the elevation of women and the lowering of men, along with the observation that at least one prominent man—Paul—sometimes speaks of himself as a woman, all point to the formation of a group that would be considered disgraceful. Additionally, this group formed in and among peoples who were already considered to be without honor—vanquished peoples living at or near the subsistence level, primarily surviving by means of manual labor or slavery—and so the values, allegiances, and practices that came from these experiences would only heighten their shamefulness and the degree to which they would be ostracized and persecuted, not only by the more respected and powerful members of society but also by their own peers and colleagues. Indeed, persecution itself, which we have already observed was experienced widely by the assemblies of Jesus loyalists associated with the Pauline faction, would be seen as a mark of dishonor. Persecution was something of a vicious cycle in relation to honor: people were persecuted because they were dishonorable and would be considered dishonorable because they were persecuted.

However, as with other areas wherein some might be tempted to take an easier way out in order to survive, Paul and his coworkers did not advise the assemblies of Jesus loyalists to try to regain honor and reduce their shame in the eyes of their neighbors or those who exercised disciplinary force over their lives. Instead, following in the footsteps of some of the resistance movements that existed within Second Temple Judaism(s), they urged those loyal to Jesus to adhere to an alternative "court of reputation" and an alternative system of honor which, in the eyes of the elites and the dominant culture, would be considered a system of dishonor. For this reason, they would be considered "fools," for, as we have seen, the fool is a person who attempts to lay claim to a degree of honor which is not granted to him or her by the larger group. Thus, the Pauline faction writes in 1 Cor 1:18–25:

> For the message about the cross is foolishness to those who are perishing, but to us who are being saved it is the power of God.

> For it is written, "I will destroy the wisdom of the wise, and the discernment of the discerning I will thwart."
>
> Where is the one who is wise? Where is the scribe? Where is the debater of this age? Has not God made foolish the wisdom of the world? For since, in the wisdom of God, the world did not know God through wisdom, God decided, through the foolishness of our proclamation, to save those who believe. For [Judeans] demand signs and Greeks desire wisdom, but we proclaim [the Anointed] crucified, a stumbling-block to [Judeans] and foolishness to [people from other regions], but to those who are the called, both [Judeans] and Greeks, [the Anointed] the power of God and the wisdom of God. For God's foolishness is wiser than human wisdom, and God's weakness is stronger than human strength.

This language, which both recognizes that those in the assemblies are considered "fools," while simultaneously reversing the charge to assert that those who claim to be wise (and who, therefore, know what is properly honorable or shameful) are actually fools, is repeated on multiple occasions throughout the letters to the Corinthians (see 1 Cor 2:14; 3:18–19; 4:10; 2 Cor 11:1–33). Similarly, in Rom 1:18–24, the tables are turned and the Pauline faction assert that those who claim to be wise are, in fact, the fools. Consequently, persecution itself actually becomes a mark of honor as it demonstrates that people are following the example of Jesus and have embraced the "folly" of God over against the "wisdom" of the rulers of their age.[3] The same is true even of persecutions that leads to death for, as is revealed in the raising up of the Anointed, God will vindicate and honor those who die as a part of their loyal allegiance to Jesus, to one another, and to all who suffer under and against Caesar's reign (see 1 Thess 4:13–18; 1 Cor 4:3–5; 15:1–58; 2 Cor 5:9–10; Rom 6:5; Phil 3:10–11).

Therefore, an alternative system of honor is constructed wherein God the Father of Jesus the Anointed and of all the Jesus loyalists is now considered the most prominent person in this new "court of reputation" and it is God's opinion, not the opinions of others, which matters.[4] Receiving honor from God is what is important. As Gal 1:10 asserts: "Am I now seeking human approval, or God's approval? Or am I trying to

---

3. See deSilva, *Honor, Patronage, Kinship, and Purity*, 65–67; 1 Thess 2:2, 14; 3:2–4, 7; 1 Cor 1:3–7; Phil 1:29–30.

4. See deSilva, *Honor, Patronage, Kinship, and Purity*, 55–57; Meeks, *Origins of Christian Morality*, 41; Oakes, *Reading Romans in Pompeii*, 111.

please people? If I were still pleasing people, I would not be a slave of [the Anointed]." Similarly, 1 Thess 2:4b–6 says: "We speak not to please people, but to please God who tests our hearts. As you know and as God is our witness, we never came with words of flattery or with a pretext for greed; nor did we seek praise from people, whether from you or from others." Furthermore, God grants an incredible degree of honor to the members of the household of the loyal—indeed, there is no greater honor than being adopted into the household of God—and so, from this perspective, it is only understandable that all other standards are demoted.[5]

At this point, it is important to emphasize that this is still an *honor* system, even if it radically reworks and reverses the ways in which honor and shame are recognized. Consequently, because God is the new adjudicator of honor and the new father of the members of the assemblies of Jesus loyalists, members are expected to avoid anything that would dishonor God.[6] As David deSilva remarks: "Any course of action that would show dishonor toward God or bring the name of Christ into disrepute must be avoided at all costs since the Christian [sic] who affronts God would then become the target of God's anger and satisfaction of God's honor."[7] Or, as 1 Cor 6:20 bluntly states: "You were bought with a price. Therefore, honor God with your bodies" (see also 1 Thess 4:4; Rom 12:1).

One of the primary ways in which the Jesus loyalists were expected to do this was by avoiding anything that would dishonor the group or create factions and dissension within the group—just as it would shame any human father to have his children splitting into feuds and factions, so also any divisions or acts of shaming one another would bring dishonor upon God.[8] To maintain this unity, the judgments made by the assemblies must be given precedence over the judgments made by the dominant culture so that "intense in-group reinforcement and mutual commitment" could be produced.[9] Thus, for example, the Pauline faction urges the Corinthians not to be concerned with judging outsiders but to instead judge one another (1 Cor 5:13), while also refusing to submit

---

5. See deSilva, *Honor, Patronage, Kinship, and Purity*, 73.

6. See Malina, "Social Levels, Morals, and Daily Life," 389; deSilva, *Honor, Patronage, Kinship, and Purity*, 58.

7. deSilva, *Honor, Patronage, Kinship, and Purity*, 83.

8. See Malina, "Social Levels, Morals, and Daily Life," 389; deSilva, *Honor, Patronage, Kinship, and Purity*, 58, 74.

9. deSilva, *Honor, Patronage, Kinship, and Purity*, 60; see also 78–81.

themselves to any outside judgment—which is explicitly seen as a shameful practice (1 Cor 6:1-6).

Therefore, there are some ways in which this system of honor mirrors the system of honor of the dominant culture and of Roman imperialism. Honor and shame are important. How one is perceived by the group is important, and one is to submit one's self to the group. There is still a superior (male) authority (God the Father) who assigns honor to the members of the household of those who pledge and practice allegiance to Jesus (the firstborn son) and whose honor the members of the household are duty-bound to maintain. However, this is where the similarities end. The content of that which is honorable and that which is shameful is dramatically reversed when God the Father of Jesus the Anointed is taken as the judge of honor and shame.

In fact, that Paul and his coworkers must spend so much time emphasizing the things mentioned above demonstrates that something unusual is occurring within the assemblies associated with them. Rather than continuing to adopt the values of the dominant culture and the empire, the Jesus loyalists are proposing the embrace of shame-as-honor. Essentially, as Gerd Theissen asserts, things that would have been considered moral defects were being elevated as virtues.[10] Because this is such a strange endeavor, the Pauline faction is constantly on guard to prevent the values, definitions, and standards of the death-dealing status quo from slowly working their way back into the assemblies and eroding the new, life-giving practices that were occurring there.[11] One of the results of this is caution regarding other highly respected charismatic figures in the assemblies—for the temptation of any leader would be to turn a local assembly into a body of clients, and then using that body as a means of boosting one's own status and honor in society.[12] Thus, in 1 Cor 3:21-23, the Pauline faction urges the Corinthians not to boast in any human leaders, for the assembly does not belong to any so-called leaders but, instead, the leaders belong to the assembly, just as all belong to the Anointed (who belongs to God). Hence, also, the language Paul and his

---

10. Theissen, *Religion of the Earliest Churches*, 71-72. See also deSilva, *Honor, Patronage, Kinship, and Purity*, 70-72; Jewett, "Paul, Shame, and Honor," 551; Meeks, *Origins of Christian Morality*, 41, 63-65.

11. See deSilva, *Honor, Patronage, Kinship, and Purity*, 50, 74.

12. Theissen draws some attention to this in his *Religion of the Earliest Churches*, 77. The erosive influence of the dominant values of the empire are already evident in the Pastoral epistles.

coworkers apply to themselves in 1 Cor 4:10: "We are fools for the sake of [the Anointed], but you are wise in [the Anointed]. We are weak, but you are strong. You are held in honor, but we in disrepute" (see also 2 Cor 11:7). Clearly, then, a very different understanding of honor and shame is operative in the Pauline faction, one that was opposed to and challenged by dominant conceptions of honor and shame from the very beginning.

The Crucifixion of Jesus Anointed and the Revaluation of Values

The cause of this reversal is the affirmation that Jesus, who was crucified, has, in fact, been raised and vindicated as the Anointed son of God. Here we should note how often Paul and his coworkers refer to Jesus's death on a cross in conjunction with the application of the title Anointed ("Christ" or "Messiah") to Jesus. In 1 Cor 2:2, they state that they "decided to know nothing among [the Corinthians] except Jesus the Anointed, and him crucified," and in Gal 6:14, they hope that they may never boast in anything except "the cross of our Lord Jesus the Anointed" (see also 1 Cor 1:17, 23; Gal 3:1; Phil 3:18). Thus, Jesus of Nazareth, crucified at the behest of both the imperial and local elites in Jerusalem, is said to be the Anointed of God.

Not only this but, as the Anointed, Paul and his coworkers believed that Jesus apocalypsed the character of God (just as the Caesars, as loyal and faithful children, would also reveal the character of their divine forefathers). Michael Gorman expresses this especially well: "The Son's act on the cross was an act of 'family resemblance,' of conformity to God" and so we discover a "cruciform God" and affirm that "cruciformity is the character of God."[13] As a result of this, the cross of the Anointed becomes the new standard for honor and shame within the household of God.[14] Therefore, just as it is emphasized that it is *the Anointed* who is crucified it must also be emphasized that the Anointed is, in fact, *crucified*. Hence, while loyally gospeling the *anastasis* of Jesus is that which permits one to

---

13. Gorman, *Cruciformity*, 16–18 (and throughout); *Apostle of the Crucified Lord*, 78–79 (and throughout). Crossan and Borg pick up on this in less detail (*First Paul*, 131).

14. See Jewett, "Paul, Shame, and Honor," 557–59. Gorman offers the best material in relation to this (see especially *Cruciformity*; *Apostle of the Crucified Lord*). Also Harink, *Paul Among the Postliberals*, 110; Meeks, *Origins of Christian Morality*, 196–97; Judge, *Social Distinctives of the Christians*, 115; Theissen, *Religion of the Earliest Churches*, 78.

embrace all the sufferings associated with bearing a family resemblance to the Anointed and guarantees the outcomes of one's endeavors—"if the Anointed has not been raised, then our gospeling is in vain and your loyalty is in vain" (1 Cor 15:14; my translation)—the focus remains primarily upon *the cross* rather than any glorious *telos*. As Ernst Käsemann writes: "The theology of the resurrection is a chapter in the theology of the cross, not the excelling of it."[15]

In order to understand just how dramatically this reverses all dominant conceptions of honor, it is necessary to spend some time explaining what crucifixion was and how it operated in the social imaginary of the Roman Empire. Traditional readings of the New Testament have tended to spiritualize the crucifixion (for example, Johannes Weiss argues that Paul tried to picture the cross in detail for personal pietistic reasons).[16] However, this sort of reading—often sustained today by conservative Christians—fails to acknowledge the significance of crucifixion within the Roman Empire. Here two things must be emphasized: the scandal and shame associated with crucifixion and the entirely political nature of the cross.

---

15. Käsemann, *Perspectives on Paul*, 59. See also Roetzel, *Paul*, 40–42. As has been widely noted, this is part of what is at stake in the Pauline faction's struggles with the Corinthians as evidenced in 2 Cor. The Corinthians appear to have embraced an overrealized eschatology and a "theology of glory" that neglects the centrality of the cross for the life of Jesus loyalists.

16. Weiss, *Earliest Christianity*, 2:491—as if Paul needed to try to imagine what a crucifixion was like (in all likelihood, he had already witnessed more than one such event). Like other pietistic visions (for example, Mel Gibson's cinematic rendition of Jesus's passion), Weiss also shifts the blame off of Pilate or any sort of political understanding of the event and, instead, focuses upon the spiritual powers that are responsible (494). Others have tried to suggest that Paul lived his life suffering from a chronic form of illness and it is this experience of illness that leads him to focus so heavily upon a theology of the cross. See Lietzmann, *Beginnings of the Christian Church*, 113. Passages such as 1 Cor 9:27; 2 Cor 4:10; 12:7; Gal 6:17 are used to support this. While it is possible that Paul did suffer from some sort of chronic illness or pain (which seems altogether likely given the multiple ways in which he was tortured by various civic ruler, authorities, and mobs), it entirely misses the point of the centrality of the cross for Paul's understanding of life in the Anointed to make it the exclusive source of this focus and this (rather difficult to substantiate) hypothesis should not be deployed in order to make the cross less significant for Jesus loyalists. Thus, Crossan and Borg do a fine job of recognizing the possibility of this hypothesis—postulating both that Paul may have contracted malaria in Tarsus when young (malaria was common there due to its geography) and suffered ongoing health issues because of this—and that the cross remains central to Paul and to others regardless of this possible experience (Crossan and Borg, *First Paul*, 62–65).

PAULINE SOLIDARITY

Mors Turpissima Crucis: The Utterly Vile Death of the Cross[17]

Within a culture and empire structured around performing honor and avoiding shame, there was nothing more shameful than crucifixion. One could go no lower than this. Crucifixion was an "horrendous, ignominious happening reserved for the scum of society, that is traitors and runaway slaves."[18] Every Greek-speaking Easterner would have known that a crucified person had "suffered a particularly cruel and shameful death, which as a rule was reserved for hardened criminals, rebellious slaves, and rebels against the Roman state."[19] Even mentioning crucifixion was avoided in polite Roman society and the term "cross" became a vulgar taunt among the lower classes.[20] To be crucified was to lose all honor, dignity, and respect. It was to lose one's place not only in the civic community but also within the community of humanity. This is why it was particularly appropriate as a means of punishing foreigners (whose humanity was questioned) and slaves (whose humanity was denied). The following exchange in one of Juvenal's satires makes this apparent:

> "Crucify that slave!"
> "But what is the slave's offence to merit such punishment? Who has brought charges against him? Where are the witnesses? You must hear his defence: no delay can be too long when a man's life is at stake."
> "So a slave's a man now, is he, you crackpot? All right, perhaps he didn't do anything. This is still my wish, my command: warrant enough that I will it."[21]

In his survey of pre-Christian literature that mention crucifixion and crosses, Larry Welborn observes that they are called terrible, infamous, barren, criminal, an evil instrument, cruel and disgusting, shameful, the supreme penalty, and the most wretched of deaths.[22] It is hard to convey

---

17. The quotation is from Origen, the translation from Hengel, *Crucifixion*, xi.

18. Beker, *Paul the Apostle*, 206. See also Elias, *Remember the Future*, 89–91; Gorman, *Apostle of the Crucified Lord*, 79–90; Cullmann, *Christ and Time*, 125; Davies, *Paul and Rabbinic Judaism*, 227–29; Hengel, *Crucifixion*, 24 (and throughout). This degree of shame is why, as Jeffers notes, crosses did not appear in Christian art for the first two centuries of Christianity (Jeffers, *Greco-Roman World*, 158).

19. Hengel, *Crucifixion*, 83.

20. Hengel, *Crucifixion*, 9–10.

21. Juvenal, *Satires* 4.219–22 (text modified from poetry to prose).

22. Welborn, *Paul, the Fool of Christ*, 21.

the depths of this shame to contemporary readers. Perhaps the best point of comparison would be to consider contemporary attitudes about people who sexually abuse children. People who are identified as engaging in this kind of violence are driven from the community and—even in jails—are rejected and face a constant threat of violence from others. Indeed, violence against such people is considered to be both desirable and admirable; essentially, the opinion seems to be that such people are no longer people, they are *pedophiles* ("goofs" in local street and prison slang) and, as such, we are all be better off if they were dead.

This is the same attitude that Roman society—and those who sought to adopt the values and standards of Rome—held towards those who were crucified. Consequently, we may understand how the proclamation that a crucified person was God's Anointed would appear as "folly" or "madness" or a "sick delusion."[23] Describing a crucified person as the supremely anointed one is positing a paradox that would strike people as both "utterly unique" and utterly "stupefying."[24] No wonder, then, that it appears to be folly to the rulers of the age and to those who are keen to advance their status by the same means used by those rulers. To proclaim a crucified Anointed would, today, feel the same as proclaiming that a person convicted of sexually abusing children was, in fact, acting as God's true representative.[25] It was entirely shocking, absurd, offensive, and shameful to make this proclamation. It was like a sick joke that a few perverse deviants had decided to take literally.[26] No wonder, then, that those

---

23. Quotations are from Hengel, *Crucifixion*, 1–5. See also, Beker, *Paul the Apostle*, 183; Dunn, *Theology of Paul the Apostle*, 209; Cousar, *Introduction to the New Testament*, 100; Gorman, *Apostle of the Crucified Lord*, 12. Schnabel, despite his desire to read the Pauline corpus in an apolitical (i.e., conservative) manner is forced to concede that the cross would be considered as an unavoidable "scandal" (Schnabel, *Paul and the Early Church*, 1362–63).

24. Welborn, *Paul, the Fool of Christ*, 23; see also 18–19.

25. Just to be clear: I am using this point of comparison not because I support any form of violence against children—I do not, and I am unequivocally against any kind of child abuse or sexual violence. Instead, I am using this point of comparison because of the *feelings* of revulsion and shock that it is likely to evoke in contemporary readers. The observation that I feel compelled to be very clear about this only further affirms the appropriateness of the analogy.

26. In terms of this being a "sick joke," see Welborn's analysis of mentions of crucifixion in gallows humor deployed by mimes, and popular among the lower classes who often used this kind of humor to mask their fear of joining the company of the crucified (Welborn, *Paul, the Fool of Christ*, 2, 99–101, 144–45). The rich also deploy gallows humor to further contribute to their mocking and degradation of those whom they

like the Corinthians were trying to replace a "theology of the cross" with a "theology of glory!"[27] Adhering to such a foolish proclamation carried a heavy cost. To proclaim such an Anointed as one's Lord was to immediately identify one's self with a crucified person, and was to then have one's previous status and honor replaced with the lack of status and the shame of the crucified. To continue our point of comparison: imagine speaking approvingly of a notorious pedophile to the regulars at the neighborhood bar, to your coworkers, to other parents at your child's soccer game, or *any* other group and see how you end up being viewed and treated. It is *this* that is the folly of the cross, not, as those like Weiss have suggested, that the cross is foolishness because it fails to convince through "reason" or a "rational argument."[28] No, in the Pauline context, the language of "folly" is *status* language, and the folly of the cross is that, regardless of any arguments one makes on the matter, it would be considered total madness to proclaim a crucified person as Lord and as the Anointed. But this is precisely what the Pauline faction does. Consequently, this leads to a revaluation of all values related to honor and shame.

The Cross and the Empire: State-Executed Terrorist—Risen Lord

This is not the only element that is scandalous about the Pauline proclamation of a crucified Anointed. Such a proclamation was also scandalous because it was treasonous. Two things should be emphasized here: first, that the title "Anointed" was a title that was inescapably political and, second, that the practice of crucifixion was also a political practice.

Beginning with references to the Anointed, we should emphasize that Second Temple Judean messianic expectations were just as deeply social, political, and economic as they were religious, spiritual, and metaphysical. Messianic expectations were deeply marked by a longing for liberation from the colonizing imperial power of Rome (and her predecessors) and from the compromised local elites who were also intimately involved in oppressing the people. Thus, the Anointed was expected to be the one whose power, authority, and anointing exceeded the power,

---

crucified, even crucifying people in positions they, the rich, found comical (137–42). Thus, Ward Blanton, following Welborn's lead, refers to the affirmation of the resurrection of the crucified and the elevation of those who are daily left-for-dead within the empire as "a peculiar kind of piss-take" (Blanton, *Materialism for the Masses*, 159).

27. See Hengel, *Crucifixion*, 18–19.

28. See Weiss, *Earliest Christianity*, 1:335.

authority, and anointing of the most august Caesar, his allies, and the *Imperium Romanum*. Consequently, when Paul and his coworkers employ messianic rhetoric, they do so in a way that would trigger those expectations and bring the contrast between Rome and the anti-empire of God, between the August and the Anointed, to the attention of their readers.[29] Thus, in the words of Adolf Deissmann, the Pauline faction is drawing attention to a "polemical parallelism" between Jesus Anointed and the deified emperors.[30] Those who belong to the Anointed parallel those who belong to Caesar (in the same way that the title *Christianoi*, which is first applied to Jesus loyalists at Antioch, parallels the title *Kaisarionoi*).[31]

The temptation for contemporary readers is to think that the Pauline faction is significantly redefining previous Judean messianic expectations in order to exclude the political overtones. After all, Jesus did not fulfill a number of messianic expectations—he did not lead anything resembling an armed overthrow of the Roman colonization of Judea, and the Romans continued to dominate Judea after Jesus had come and gone. In light of this, Paul and his coworkers do revise some messianic expectations in order to arrive at an Anointed who is killed by the Roman authorities and who, instead of expelling the Romans from Palestine, wins a broader victory over the cosmic Powers of Sin and Death. But this shift neither drains crucifixion of its political content nor makes the Pauline faction apolitical.

To draw this out, we need to understand why and how the Romans practiced crucifixion. For the Romans, the cross was a political tool used to inspire public terror and maintain large-scale socioeconomic and political control.[32] As such, as we observed, its use tended to be the supreme penalty deployed against slaves, violent criminals, and, most especially,

---

29. See Carter, *John and Empire*, 178, 182; Wright, *Paul*, 5.

30. Deissmann, *Light from the Ancient East*, 342. For more on this see the exploration of Phil 2 below.

31. See Deissmann, *Light from the Ancient East*, 377; Ziesler, *Pauline Christianity*, 61. These titles, and others like them—"Christians," "Caesarians," "Herodians," and so forth—all denote various political factions defined by their allegiances to different Lords (the Anointed, Caesar, Herod, and so forth). We tend to miss this in our current context but the word ending here (*-ianoi* in Greek or *-ianus* in Latin) was not used for followers of a god—it was used to classify people as partisans of a political or military leader. See Judge, "Did the Churches Compete with Cult Groups?" 515–17; Malina, "Social Levels, Morals, and Daily Life," 269; Winter, "Roman Law and Society," 70–71, 82–98.

32. See Elliott, *Liberating Paul*, 95, 99; Hengel, *Crucifixion*, 86–90.

rebellious foreigners.³³ Crucifixion also tended to be practiced in very public places (hence, for example, along the road to Tibur, archaeologists discovered several businesses specializing in torture and execution, serving both public authorities and private citizens, flogging and crucifying slaves for four sesterces each).³⁴ As such, crucifixion was something to be feared and escaped, not embraced.³⁵

Furthermore, crucifixion was deeply integrated into the imperial way of viewing the world. From the Roman perspective, the cross of Jesus was salvific, but for precisely the opposite reasons than it was for the Pauline faction. From the perspective of the ideo-theology of the empire, some people—the "evil other" who threatened the stability of the world (Jesus in this case)—had to be violently eradicated by the representatives of the firstborn son of God the Father (i.e., Caesar) so that world peace and stability could be maintained or restored.³⁶ The cross sets the world aright by removing any who would destabilize it by challenging Rome (after all, according to the Romans, the entire world was created and always intended to be the world of Roman *imperium*). Tom Thatcher makes this point especially well: "Every cross told a story; every story has a moral; the moral of the cross story was calculated to rationalize and maintain the imperial status quo."³⁷ Drawing on the work of Yael Zerubavel, Thatcher then argues that crucifixion was a ritual of commemoration that was employed in order to create a social memory that both generated and reinforced the values of the empire.³⁸ Hence, crucifixion becomes a dramatic reenactment of Rome's world conquest and makes the following points:

> Many years ago, the gods elevated Rome to a special place of power and authority. The Romans used this privileged position to bring peace and order to the whole world. This thing you see hanging here was once a man, who rose up within an insolent race and dared to threaten the natural order of things by rebelling against Rome. Of course, his insolence inevitably earned

---

33. See Hengel, *Crucifixion*, 33–34, 46, 50–51.
34. See Welborn, *Paul's Summons to Messianic Life*, 25.
35. Welborn, *Paul's Summons to Messianic Life*, 61–62.
36. See Kahl, *Galatians Re-Imagined*, 205, 245.
37. Thatcher, "'I Have Conquered the World,'" 143.
38. Thatcher, "'I Have Conquered the World,'" 144.

him the most extreme form of pain and shame imaginable. Don't try it.[39]

Quintilian, a Roman contemporary of Paul, is quite clear that this is the objective of crucifixion: "Every punishment has less to do with the offense than with the example" and so "when we [Romans] crucify criminals the most frequented roads are chosen, where the greatest number of people can look and be seized by this fear."[40] This is also why, as Thatcher notes, Roman citizens were not to be crucified: "It would be illogical to crucify Romans, for such an act would symbolize Rome's self-destruction, an empire conquering itself."[41]

Gaining this contextual awareness permits us to see how the proclamation of a crucified (and risen) Anointed is scandalous, not only because of the shame involved but because one is actually proclaiming that a state-executed terrorist is the true Lord and firstborn son of God. This proclamation contradicts the values of the empire and the "normalcy" of its control over others.[42] Brigitte Kahl makes this point especially well:

> The image of the crucified not as the image of an evil other to be lawfully destroyed but as the image of the world savior and divine life-giver, shatters all the images of power that were the embodiment of imperial ideology. . . . To exhibit the messiah and God-self as crucified and dying like one of the Dying Gauls, and to do so "publically," is the most fundamental attack on the normative way of seeing.[43]

Again:

> Paul's exclusive allegiance to God "the father" and Christ crucified implied the ridicule of the images of power so carefully set up and staged everywhere. . . . In a ground-shaking act of divine iconoclasm, the God of Paul has broken the imperial world image and world rule of the Olympic gods, and most notably of the divine Jupiter/Caesar.[44]

---

39. Thatcher, "'I Have Conquered the World,'" 145.
40. *Decl.* 274, quoted in Thatcher, "I Have Conquered the World," 147.
41. Thatcher, "I Have Conquered the World," 146.
42. See Gorman, *Cruciformity*, 5; Crossan and Reed, *In Search of Paul*, 242; Crossan and Borg, *First Paul*, 27, 131; Martyn, *Theological Issues*, 289; deSilva, *Honor, Patronage, Kinship, and Purity*, 45–46.
43. Kahl, *Galatians Re-Imagined*, 205.
44. Kahl, *Galatians Re-Imagined*, 245.

Pauline Solidarity

And once more:

> Though the Hellenistic and Roman world had no difficulty imagining how Caesars, divine sons, or victorious demi-gods like Heracles could be raised from the dead to heavenly glory and power . . . neither could ever contemplate a *crucified* man representing the vanquished nations being raised to life—and lordship . . . the resurrection of Jesus could only be an abominable, blasphemous act of insurgence by the God of a subject people.[45]

This means that any such proclamation—let alone a proclamation coupled with a desire to follow the example and trajectory of Jesus, asserting that "I have been crucified with [the Anointed]" and now that crucified Anointed "lives in me" (see Gal 2:19–20)—is inevitably seditious and treasonous. Proclaiming the Lordship of a crucified person in Roman-occupied territory would comparable to going to Texas and proclaiming that Osama bin Laden had risen from the dead and was, in fact, the true son and representative of God, bringing freedom, democracy, and peace to the world. If one then went so far as to suggest that one should emulate Osama bin Laden (claiming to have been summarily executed in a compound with bin Laden and now having bin Laden live in oneself), and if one tried to assemble communities of bin Laden loyalists throughout the United States, well, it should be obvious how that would end. The communities would be targeted as terror cells and eliminated—which, of course, is precisely what the Romans began doing to the assemblies of Jesus loyalists as the movement built momentum and gained the attention of increasingly higher echelons of imperial powers.

To make this proclamation is not to say that the crucifixion of Jesus was a miscarriage or misstep of Roman justice—the sedition runs much deeper than that. This proclamation reveals that Roman justice is, itself, fundamentally unjust.[46] *No mistakes were made.* This is Roman justice operating consistently with itself and its own principles. But it is contradicted by the justice of the God who raises the crucified to new life. Therefore, by condemning Roman justice in this way, the Pauline faction also condemns the rulers who are operating within the empire

---

45. Kahl, *Galatians Re-Imagined*, 260. See also Maier, *Picturing Paul in Empire*, 47.

46. A point well made by Elliott, *Liberating Paul*, 113, 124. Of course, some of the Roman satirists could also point out the unjust nature of Roman justice. Hence, Juvenal writes: "The same crime often produces quite different results: one man / Ends on the cross, but another wearing a royal crown" (Juvenal, *Satires* 13.104–15).

and proclaims that they are unrighteous and unjust judges (1 Cor 6:1). The "rulers of this age" who "crucified the Lord of glory" (2 Cor 2:8) are revealed for what they truly are. Instead of being who they claim to be, the socioeconomic and theopolitical leaders of the empire are revealed to be on the side of Sin and of Death.[47] Indeed, as Warren Carter suggests, to say that Jesus takes away the sin of the world "does not necessarily mean that he must die, let alone be crucified by Rome—unless Rome has something to do with the 'sin of the world.'"[48] The empire is, in fact, the structural embodiment of Sin within the world. This is why Paul and his coworkers state that "the world" of the Roman Empire is now "crucified" to them (Gal 6:14). Ted Jennings summarizes this well:

> The verdict of the empire, executed through the crucifixion of a messianic pretender who threatened the "peace" is, however, overturned through the power of life-giving spirit through the return to life of the executed. The resurrection of the dead is first and foremost the return of the executed.[49]

A final implication of this, which will be explored in more detail in the next chapter, is that the crucifixion also speaks of God's scandalous and seditious solidarity with all the victims of the empire. It demonstrates that God is on the side of those who are oppressed by the socioeconomic and theopolitical rulers.[50] Thus, the cross of Jesus, while remaining a symbol of Roman violence, also comes to represent the loyalty of those who dare to resist that violence.[51]

All of this, then, demonstrates just how far removed the conception of honor and shame held by the Pauline faction were from the dominant conception. Not only do Paul and other Jesus loyalists embrace shame as honor, they embrace a treasonous form of shame as honor. By doing this, they willingly embrace the status of *homo sacer*—those who experience "bare life" and who can be "killed but not sacrificed" by the sovereign, who can "kill without committing homicide."[52] They reject the form of honor that operated as a cornerstone of the empire, even though this moves them into the "place of no place," wherein they have the status of

47. See Carter, *Roman Empire and the New Testament*, 88.
48. Carter, *John and Empire*, 11.
49. Jennings, *Outlaw Justice*, 19.
50. See Elliott, *Liberation Paul*, 138–39; Horsley, "Introduction," 19.
51. See Horsley and Silberman, *Message and the Kingdom*, 161.
52. As explored by Giorgio Agamben in *Homo Sacer*, 83 (and throughout).

"nothings" or the left for dead. This is one part of a holistic assault upon and invasion into the empire.

Exegesis: Philippians 2:5–11

Phil 2:5–11 demonstrates how all of the themes explored so far were interwoven within Paulinism. As Michael Gorman demonstrates, this passage summarizes key narrative elements of Paulinism.[53] Although it is quite possible that this passage is a hymn employed by the movement prior to Paul—which simply highlights its importance to the Jesus movement as a whole—it very clearly summarizes much that is central to the Pauline faction. It is, to use Gorman's term, a "master story."[54] I will begin by quoting the passage in full and then highlight how it: (a) develops an alternate conception of honor and shame; (b) shows how this conception is rooted in the character of God the Father of Jesus; (c) offers Jesus as the paradigmatic example to be emulated by Jesus loyalists; and (d) posits all of this in a manner that is markedly counter-imperial. The passage runs as follows:

> Let the same mind be in you that was in [the Anointed] Jesus,
> who, though he was in the form of God,
> did not regard [being equal] with God
> as something to be exploited
> but emptied himself,
> taking the form of a slave,
> being born in human likeness.
> And being found in human form
> He humbled himself
> and became obedient to the point of death—
> even death on a cross.
>
> Therefore God also highly exalted him
> and gave him the name
> that is above every name,

---

53. See Gorman, *Cruciformity*.

54. Gorman, *Cruciformity*, 88–92; *Apostle of the Crucified Lord*, 102–5. Meeks also refers to this as Paul's "master model" (Meeks, *In Search of the Early Christians*, 111). However, in chapter 5, I will push back against any understanding of Paulinism that puts either narrative or theses or the logos at the core of Paulinism.

> so that at the name of Jesus,
> every knee should bend,
> in heaven and on earth and under the earth,
> and every tongue should confess
> that Jesus [Anointed] is Lord,
> to the glory of God the father.

First, in this passage we clearly see an alternate court of reputation operating with God the Father of Jesus acting as the supreme judge of all matters related to a person's honor or shame. Notably, God chooses to exalt Jesus precisely because he embraced humility and took on the form of a slave who died on a cross. By, quite literally, becoming the lowest of the low—by not only becoming human (being "born in human likeness" and "being found in human form") but also then having that humanity stripped from him and by choosing to be treated as less-than-human or no-longer-even-human (experiencing "death on a cross")—Jesus is vindicated by God who then exalts him above all others. One of the implications of this is that those who are "in the Anointed" and loyally follow Jesus will also be vindicated and elevated by God, even if they are also shamed and killed by contemporaries who possess wealth and power and who are elevated based upon dominant conceptions of honor and shame.[55]

Second, part of the reason why God chooses to exalt Jesus is because Jesus is acting as a faithful son and revealing the character of his family and father. This cruciform trajectory is one that betrays a familial resemblance. This is what is revealed in the assertion that "though he existed in the form of God" he "did not regard being equal with God as something to be exploited, but emptied himself." The crucial point here is that this passage is asserting that Jesus did, in fact, possess an intimate, familial resemblance to God (his father) and that this can be described as "being equal with God" is demonstrated not by seeking to wield power over others but, instead, is demonstrated by his movement into a cruciform trajectory. N. T. Wright summarizes this well: "[Jesus] regarded equality with God not as excusing him from the task of (redemptive) suffering and death, but actually as uniquely qualifying him for that vocation."[56]

---

55. See Theissen, *Social Reality*, 190–96.
56. Wright, *Climax of the Covenant*, 83–84. Much of Wright's efforts here are devoted to also demonstrating the pre-existence of Jesus, although Heen challenges this by pointing out how Jesus's status seems higher at the end of the passage than at the

Pauline Solidarity

Third, as the vindicated Anointed and Lord and as the one who reveals the character of God the Father and judge, Jesus then becomes the model for the lives of all those loyal to him. This is why the passage begins by saying, "Let the same mind be in you that was also in Jesus the Anointed." Once again, Wright summarizes this well: "As God endorsed Jesus' interpretation of what equality with God meant in practice, so he [sic] will recognize [the embodiment of similar attributes] in his people as the true mark of the life of the Spirit."[57] Essentially, Paul and his co-workers are offering this model of Jesus to the Jesus loyalists at Philippi with the hope that they will then imitate Jesus and endanger their own status and well-being (which, although very low, may have been higher than some other members of the assembly or assemblies found there, and which may have been at risk of bottoming out altogether) to maintain solidarity with the crucified.[58]

Finally, and not surprisingly, given the status reversal that is occurring here and given who crucified Jesus, this passage is also markedly counter-imperial. The ideo-theology of the Roman Empire was prominent within Philippi.[59] It was the location of the victory of Octavian (Augustus) and Antony over Brutus and Cassius in 42 BCE. After the Battle of Actium in 31 BCE, veterans were sent to settle there, it was refounded as a Roman colony (with approximately 3,000 Roman citizens in residence), and it was given the status of *ius Italicum*, meaning that it was considered Italian soil—the highest privilege possible for a Roman

---

beginning and so resolves the matter as follows: (1) while humbly serving, Jesus shared (in a hidden way) the glory and honor of God; (2) in return for his paradigmatic service to humanity; (3) he was rewarded with an *apotheosis*—which all fits a common Graeco-Roman pattern (Heen, "Role of Symbolic Inversion," 139-40).

57. Wright, *Climax of the Covenant*, 87. Wright describes these attributes as "self-giving love" but, as we will see, this is something of a bleached-out presentation of what Paul and his coworkers were on about.

58. See Oakes, *Philippians*, 175-210; Hays, *Moral Vision*, 27-31. Stephen Fowl pushes back against this interpretation and argues that Jesus, as described here, is not being offered as a universal model to be imitated in general ethics for all Jesus loyalists but as a model strictly relevant to the Philippians and their experiences of persecution (see Fowl, *Story of Christ*, 79-81, 101, 199). I find this argument unconvincing, not only because immediately after this passage, in Phil 3, Paul clearly demonstrates that this understanding of Jesus is the model for his own life but because the sustained work of Michael Gorman demonstrates how crucial this understanding of Jesus is for Paulinism (see especially, Gorman, *Cruciformity*).

59. For what follows, see Heen, "Role of Symbolic Inversion," 133-36; Tellbe, *Paul Between Synagogue and State*, 212-19.

provincial colony. After Octavian was renamed Augustus in 27 BCE, the colony had its name changed to Colonia Julia Augusta Philippensis. Consequently, the city was very Roman in ethos and population and, at the time of Paul, paid cultic honors to Augustus, his wife Livia, their adopted sons (Gaius and Lucius Caesar), and probably Claudius. There were multiple temples in the forum with statues of the imperial family, and other cults incorporated the imperial cult into their spaces and practices. At the same time, priesthoods were established and dedicated to the Divine Julius, the Divine Augustus, and the Divine Claudius, and the head of the administration of the colony was a high priest in the cult of Augustus.

In light of this, the parallels between the divine Caesar and Jesus as he is described within Phil 2:5–11 would surely have been striking to the readers of this letter. Turning again to the verses that mention Jesus "being equal with God," we should note how the Greek term for this (*isa theo*) is one that has a long history within ruler cults and was also applied to the emperor—so much so that by the end of the reign of Augustus this term was reserved *exclusively* for the emperor and his family.[60] Indeed, some members of the imperial family were hesitant to accept such a title for, as Germanicus writes in 19 CE: "[Such titles] are appropriate only to him who is actually the savior and benefactor of the whole human race, my father [Augustus]."[61] What is at stake here is a dramatic contrast between two people who are said to be the exclusive savior of the world: Caesar, who views equality with God as "something to be exploited" and so constantly seeks to advance his wealth, honor, privileges, and power over others, the honor he receives, and the privileges afforded to him, and Jesus, who does not see equality with God as "something to be exploited" but instead embraces humility, slavishness, and crucifixion (by the representatives of Caesar).[62] In fact, the Pauline faction considerably emphasizes this difference. While Rome emphasized and advertised the divine form and likeness of the Caesars, the Pauline faction stresses not Jesus's equality with God, but his human likeness and his human form. And the vindication of this all-too-human Jesus—who lived and died in solidarity with the most exploited and abandoned groups of people—is

---

60. See Heen, "Role of Symbolic Inversion," 125, 133–34.

61. Germanicus quoted in Heen, "Role of Symbolic Inversion," 145; that said, other emperors and members of the imperial family were not nearly so hesitant to accept this honor after Augustus (142–46).

62. See Heen, "Role of Symbolic Inversion," 138–39; Tellbe, *Paul Between Synagogue and State*, 255–56; Oakes, *Philippians*, 138–47.

the condemnation of the all-too-divine Caesar. Thus, to a Roman colony populated by veterans, Paul and his coworkers present an "apotheosis... of the crucified."[63]

Peter Oakes describes eight other elements in the text that provide additional parallels between Jesus and Caesar: (1) each has universal authority; (2) given to them; (3) by a competent body; (4) for a reason—usually for establishing peace in a situation of chaos; (5) and is also selected for possessing certain characteristics—the ability to save through victory, being connected to the gods, maintaining a standard of moral excellence in care for others and disregard for self; (6) accomplishes universal submission as a part of salvation; (7) is granted a high name—like the title "Lord"; (8) and then goes on to provide an example to be followed by the ethics of their peoples.[64] Therefore, as Oakes observes, the situation is "deeply ironic" for "Christ's self-lowering makes his accession to power fit a prominent pattern of legitimation of Imperial authority. Yet Christ's self-lowering led to crucifixion, the fate furthest from the career of a candidate for the Imperial throne."[65] This is why Crossan and Reed describe this passage as a "lampoon" of Roman imperial theology.[66] But this lampoon is far from harmless. It is one that requires those who agree with it to reject the claims made by the empire and its rulers. This would include a rejection of the claims made by the local members of the elite, in Philippi or beyond, as they would be implicated in following Caesar's model of "exploiting" or "grasping after."[67]

Now, it should be noted that this reading goes against the reading offered by several scholars who prefer to see Adam as the person being contrasted with Jesus. Much of this can be explained by the observation that a reading of the New Testament which explicitly engages the themes of Roman culture and religion was not considered by earlier scholarship.[68] However, even in light of more recent developments, there

---

63. Maier, *Picturing Paul in Empire*, 51.
64. See Oakes, *Philippians*, 129-74.
65. Oakes, *Philippians*, 159-60.
66. See Crossan and Reed, *In Search of Paul*, 289-91.
67. See Heen, "Role of Symbolic Inversion," 148-52.
68. Even Wright in his 1993 essay focuses almost exclusively upon the contrast with Adam. The political analysis is very limited and he only gets as far as noting that "oriental despots" saw status as something to exploit (see Wright, *Climax of the Covenant*, 83; British lords pointing the finger at "oriental despots," calls Edward Said to mind...).

still remains a group of scholars who will concede elements of a political reading, while also seeking to remove any supposedly radical or subversive political implications from the text. Thus, for example, Christopher Bryan argues that the primary contrast is with Adam and, while this does not exclude the emperor entirely from the picture, the point is not to focus upon the claims of either Adam or the emperor but to think about Jesus's humility.[69] Similarly, Seyoon Kim argues that while the passage is "evoking a comparison between Christ and the emperor and affirming the superiority of Christ and his salvation" it is "not meant to lead the Philippian Christians [sic] to counter the imperial claims politically."[70] How can this be? Because, Kim asserts, the Pauline faction is essentially moving from the historical realm of politics to a supposedly apolitical realm of eschatology in asserting the lordship of Jesus, so the reigns of Jesus and Caesar are not in the "same category."[71] Thus, Seyoon Kim concludes that, in Phil 2:5–11, Paul is not "calling believers to resist Caesar's authority and regime."[72]

What are we to make of these interpretations? First of all, there is nothing wrong with also noting a contrast between Jesus and Adam in this passage. As Crossan and Borg observe, the contrast between Jesus and Caesar need not be exclusive.[73] Second, I can't help but feel that Bryan's reading is an exercise in missing the point and, intentionally or not, is disingenuous. To focus upon the person and work of Jesus need not require that we neglect all the other implications and parallels that are drawn from the text and stressed within the text itself. Furthermore, Bryan operates with an understanding of humility that is rooted in hundreds of years of Christian virtue ethics rather than understanding its associations with shame and little or no socioeconomic and political status. Third, we should observe how Seyoon Kim is imposing a modern de-historicized and spiritualized eschatology into his reading. This then permits him to construct a (false) categorical distinction between the lordship of Jesus and the lordship of Caesar (or of any contemporary imperial rulers). Once this error is rectified and Pauline eschatology is properly understood and the passage is read as it stands (without the

---

69. See Bryan, *Render to Caesar*, 85–87.
70. Kim, *Christ and Caesar*, 16.
71. Kim, *Christ and Caesar*, 16–17.
72. Kim, *Christ and Caesar*, 16–17.
73. Crossan and Borg, *First Paul*, 208–13.

imposition of absent category distinctions), we see that his reading is a kind of "grasping after" that seeks to exploit the passage to fit it within the ideo-theology of contemporary forms of imperialism.

Up until this point, I have mostly refrained from commenting on those who view such passages as "hidden transcripts" or as "coded" material. I have also refrained from using that language myself. This is primarily because this terminology—intended in a technical sense—seems to be too open to misunderstanding or manipulation even by experts, like Seyoon Kim, who either cannot grasp what is intended by the deployment of that language or chooses to exploit it to feed into popular beliefs that any reference to a "code" is an exhibition of paranoia or desperation. However, it is worth mentioning this theme here, because the language of "hidden transcripts" and of a "coded" message are deployed by some in reference to the contrast that the passage exhibits between Jesus and Caesar. Essentially, then, a "hidden transcript" is a way in which a group of people deploys ambiguous or guarded language in order to try and communicate a subversive message in a way that does not draw undesired attention or punishment onto those involved in this communication. Hence, a message is crafted that may appear one way to the uninitiated but another way to those who are "in the know." Oppressed people, not to mention traitors and rebels, have been engaging in this sort of activity for millennia. Seyoon Kim seems incapable of understanding this.[74] Instead, he mocks the idea that there was a counter-imperial message in Phil 2:5–11 that was so subtle that nobody was able to discover it until those like N. T. Wright came along.[75] Of course, this neglects the long history of those who have always existed—often at the margins of (or entirely at odds with) institutional or orthodox Christianity, and certainly far from the conservative, empire-affirming kind of Christianity promoted by Seyoon Kim—who have understood the New Testament and the example of Jesus to be a call to resist the death-dealing rulers (of any day or age) in order to pursue abundant life with people experiencing colonization, dispossession, and oppression. Additionally, Kim's suggestion also neglects the obvious point that the Jesus loyalists at Philippi were being persecuted—suggesting that the seditious nature of the early Jesus movement

---

74. See Kim, *Christ and Caesar*, 14. Essentially, he asks: "If this meaning is hidden, how do you find it, and if you can find it, how is it hidden?" Thereby suggesting that anything found can never have been hidden, and anything hidden can never be found.

75. Kim, *Christ and Caesar*, 14.

was not as "hidden" as some may have desired.[76] What Kim seems to miss is that the conservative, empire-affirming Christianity for which he advocates is, itself, full of filters and blinders and external controls that help to dictate which readings of the New Testament are more or less plausible or desirable. Therefore, regardless of any rhetorical, historical, or contextual strengths, counter-imperial readings are written off and, instead, appeals to any kind of "code"—i.e., any kind of understanding of how oppressed minorities tend to communicate—are taken by Kim to be admissions that these readings are not possible under the conditions of "normal exegesis."[77] The reader should not be led astray here: "normal exegesis" is simply the sort of interpretation that is considered acceptable by the empire and its advocates.[78] Any other interpretation is automatically discounted and seen as desperate, self-contradictory, and implausible, not because it lacks substance or strength, but because its conclusions are opposed to the empire and those who seek to benefit from it.

By way of conclusion, it is worth highlighting one further contrast between Jesus and Caesar which, although not made explicit here, comes to light in other passages. Returning to the kinship language studied in the previous chapter, Rom 8:28 refers to Jesus as the "firstborn among many." Or, in other words, as the "first among equals." However, this title—the "first among equals" (in Latin, *princeps*)—was a title preferred by the emperors from Augustus onwards.[79] As we saw in volume 2 of this series, when Augustus consolidated his imperial authority over the senate and republic he took this title, which was given to the leading member of the senate (the first among equals there), in order to support his claim that he was restoring the republic rather than creating a dictatorship or monarchy. Relating this back to Phil 2:5–11, we see Jesus as a very strange sort of *princeps*—he is the first among the slaves, the humiliated, the crucified, and the enemies of the empire. Yet, precisely because he represents this company, Jesus is vindicated by God and becomes what the *princeps* claimed to be: the "representative of humanity, reconciler and ruler of the world."[80] It is this representative who will ultimately vanquish all rulers

76. A suggestion made in Heen, "Role of Symbolic Inversion," 150.

77. See Kim, *Christ and Caesar*, 14–15.

78. Once again, a theme well explored by Foucault. See, for example, Foucault, *Archaeology of Knowledge*; *Abnormal*.

79. For this and what follows see Georgi, *Theocracy*, 74, 96–99; Ando, *Imperial Ideology*, 41–46.

80. Georgi, *Theocracy*, 99.

on the day when even Caesar's knee will bow and even Caesar's tongue will confess that a slave—a slave crucified at his command, according to his laws—is the true Lord of all.

Cruciformity: Re-Presenting the Crucifixion of the Anointed

As has been mentioned, the crucified Anointed is not held up as a stand-alone anomaly within the fictive kinship that has been formed on the basis of his work; rather, Jesus is upheld as the model for the lives of those who are loyal to him. Those who are loyal to Jesus are to follow him into this shame and sedition with the expectation that they will, for that reason, be vindicated with Jesus by God (their father). Hence, to use language popularized by Michael Gorman, Jesus loyalists are to be marked by "cruciformity"—"conformity to the crucified Christ," which is "a dynamic correspondence in daily life to the strange story of Christ crucified as the primary way of experiencing the love and grace of God."[81] This has both individual and collective implications: "The narrative of the crucified and exalted Messiah is the normative life-narrative within which the community's own life-narrative takes place and by which it is shaped."[82] In this way, the communities influenced by Paul and his coworkers "become living commentaries on their master story [Phil 2:5–11]. . . . This people . . . lives the story, embodies the story, tells the story. It is the living exegesis of God's master story of faith, love, power, and hope."[83] Others make similar statements. According to Calvin Roetzel, Paul views Jesus's death as a model for action in the world and this is experienced not only in the cultic setting but in daily life.[84] According to Richard Hays's Paul, "Jesus' death on a cross is the paradigm for faithfulness to God in this world."[85] According to I. Howard Marshall, the shape of "Christian" [sic] living is oriented around Jesus's cruciform life, death and resurrection.[86] According to Gerd Theissen, the death of Jesus serves

---

81. Gorman, *Cruciformity*, 4–5. See also Gorman, *Reading Paul*, 22n2, where he defines "conformity" as "a similar life-pattern."

82. Gorman, *Cruciformity*, 44; emphasis removed.

83. Gorman, *Cruciformity*, 366–67; see also 92.

84. Roetzel, *Letters of Paul*, 125–26.

85. Hays, *Moral Vision*, 197; emphasis removed.

86. Marshall, *Concise New Testament Theology*, 178.

as an exemplum, "a model of divine and human conduct."[87] According to David Horrell, the imitation of the Anointed in regards to the cross is a paradigmatic metanorm that overrules any specific ethical rule if there is ever a clash between the two.[88] According to Jacob Elias, Phil 2:5–11 is the story within which the Pauline faction wants the assemblies to live, and which should be replicated in the lives of individual believers and the community as a whole.[89] And according to Wayne Meeks, this is the "dramatic plot structure" of the lives of believers, which should be analogous to the life of (the) Anointed as described in Phil 2:5–11.[90]

To further demonstrate this, I will first examine how the shameful and seditious example of Jesus was the model upon which Paul based his own life (which, in turn, he holds up as an example to be imitated by other Jesus loyalists). I will then emphasize the call to embrace shame, before exploring how the understanding of love offered by Paul and his coworkers—love as expressed not only in mutuality but also in the love of enemies—is sustained by this reversal of dominant conceptions related to honor and shame.

The Example of Paul

When highlighting the manner in which Paul personally tried to live into the shameful and seditious cruciform trajectory, it is significant to observe that Phil 2:5–11 is immediately followed by the (auto)biographical remarks about Paul in Phil 3. The Pauline faction begins by warning the Jesus loyalists at Philippi not to fall into the trap of imitating those who propose circumcision as a means of escaping persecution and pursuing a relatively higher and safer status (3:2), given that such a trajectory would be a betrayal of the pattern established in Phil 2:5–11.[91] Instead, Paul is offered as an example that fits the pattern set in Phil 2:5–11 and others are urged to imitate him instead of living as "enemies of the cross of [the Anointed]" (3:17–18). The Pauline faction claims that Paul could boast

---

87. Theissen, *Religion of the Earliest Churches*, 144.
88. Horrell, *Solidarity and Difference*, 221–22.
89. Elias, *Remember the Future*, 76, 79.
90. Meeks, *In Search of the Early Christians*, 109.
91. This reason for pursuing circumcision has already been explored in volume 1 of this series. In relation to this passage, see Tellbe, *Paul Between Synagogue and State*, 159–67.

according to dominant constructions of honor and shame—being a "Hebrew born of Hebrews," a zealous Pharisee, and just and blameless under the Law (3:4–6). However, like Jesus, the Pauline faction does not view these traditional status markers as things to be exploited. Instead, they consider them to be rubbish and refuse (literally: "shit") and highlight that Paul has now "suffered the loss of all things," including and especially those things just mentioned, in coming to know Jesus as the Anointed and Lord (3:7–9). Hence, in total contradiction to the dominant system of honor and shame, Paul actually *wants* to share in the sufferings of the Anointed so that he may also attain *anastasis* (3:10–11). For those who continue to ascribe to the dominant conception of honor will discover that "their glory is their shame," but those who are following the example set by Jesus will see that "the body of our humiliation" is conformed to "the body of glory" (3:18–21). This humiliation is certainly something well-known to Paul's body. This was already explored in volume 1 of this series when we studied the nature of Pauline sufferings, but the Pauline faction also highlighted Paul's bodily sufferings at the beginning of this letter, when they remind the Philippians that Paul writes while imprisoned and facing the possibility of execution as he follows in the footsteps of the shameful and seditious Anointed Jesus (1:7, 13–14, 19–21).

While the Pauline faction clearly rejects the dominant imperial understanding of honor in this passage, they openly mock imperial conceptions of honor in 2 Cor 10–11. In 2 Cor 10, the Pauline faction responds to some who have questioned their place within the assemblies and who have suggested that they—the questioners and not the Pauline faction—should be treated as authorities. Initially, Paul and his coworkers play along with the dominant conception of honor employed by their opponents. They admit that perhaps Paul does "boast a little too much" about his authority and the authority of his coworkers (10:8), and state that they "do not dare to compare ourselves with some of those who commend themselves" (10:12). Not, it should be noted, because those people are more honorable than Paul and his coworkers but rather because those people "boast beyond limits" and hence act in a manner that the Pauline faction considers dishonorable (10:12–16). Now all this seems within the established rules of the dominant, agonistic honor game—even though Paul has already warned the Corinthians that he and his coworkers "do not wage war according to human standards" (10:3)—but the end of chapter 10 begins to build pressure in another direction. "Let the one who boasts," Paul and his coworkers write, "boast in the Lord. For it is not those who commend themselves that are approved, but those whom the Lord commends."

However, it has been made apparent that the Lord—crucified like a rebellious slave—reverses all expectations related to boasting, honor, and shame, and so it is no surprise that 2 Cor 11 opens with the Pauline faction stating that "I wish you would bear with me in a little foolishness" (remembering, once again, that folly is related to honor, and that the fool is one who posits a different degree of honor than that which the group assigns). Having just stated that they would not compare Paul and his coworkers with their opponents, they do just that using Paul as the prime example and speaking in his voice. Thus, Paul states: "I think I am not in the least inferior to these super-apostles," even if he is "untrained in speech" (suggesting that the "super-apostles," a title that is surely applied mockingly, had some rhetorical abilities that Paul did not have) and, even if he humiliates himself by gospeling "free of charge" out of his love for the Corinthians and his desire not to burden them (11:5–11). However, Paul then reverses the charges and states that those who oppose him and his coworkers are the ones engaging in an inappropriate form of boasting—having just called them "super-apostles" he now suggests that they are actually state-representatives (i.e., ambassadors) of Satan (11:12–15). Thus, it is they who are wrong to claim equal status to Paul and his coworkers, not Paul and his coworkers who should be asked to compare themselves to their opponents.

By speaking in this way and making these claims, Paul knows he risks being understood as a low-class buffoon—and from the dominant perspective, he *is* a low-class buffoon—but he wants to have his folly reinterpreted in the tradition of the "wise fool."[92] Perhaps the Corinthians find this hard to believe—the other faction has, after all, clearly had a dramatic impact upon the Jesus loyalists gathered there and established ways of viewing others that are hard to shake—and so the Pauline faction continues their rejection of dominant conceptions of honor and shame that still linger in the beginning of 2 Cor 11. Continuing in the voice of Paul, they write:

> I repeat, let no one think that I am a fool; but if you do, then accept me as a fool, so that I too may boast a little. What I am saying in regard to this boastful confidence, I am saying not with the Lord's authority, but as a fool; since many boast according to

---

92. See Welborn, *Paul, the Fool of Christ*, 12–13, 149–56.

> human standards, I will also boast. For you gladly put up with fools, being wise yourselves! (11:16–19)

Why is Paul not speaking with the Lord's authority here? Because he is going to boast according to human standards—the same standards he just rejected. Of course, the final line is sarcastic and it leads to further sarcasm: "For you put up with it when someone makes slaves of you, or takes advantage of you, or puts on airs, or gives you a slap in the face. To my shame, I must say, we were too weak for that" (11:20–21a). Clearly, the Pauline faction is referring to those who oppose them here (and mocking the Corinthians' willingness to allow others to re-impose oppressive hierarchies within communities of people who were assembled to be free from such things). Furthermore, even though the Pauline faction is being sarcastic from start to finish (they do not actually find the Corinthians particularly wise, nor do they find it shameful to refuse to be enslaved by anybody apart from Jesus the Anointed), they are not being overly hyperbolic. Recalling the remarks I made when examining the social status of the Corinthians, it is clear that some members were very much trying to take advantage of others by increasing their own honor at the expense of those others, and that Paul and his coworkers opposed this. Thus, the voice of Paul continues talking "folly" and boasts "according to human standards":

> But whatever anyone dares to boast of—I am speaking as a fool—I also dare to boast of that. Are they Hebrews? So am I. Are they Israelites? So am I. Are they descendants of Abraham? So am I. Are they ministers of [the Anointed]? I am talking like a madman—I am a better one. (11:21b–23a)

At this point, the Pauline faction pulls out all the stops, stops measuring Paul according to human standards, and mocks the dominant imperial standards of honor and shame. Because when Paul then explains why he is a better minister of the Anointed, he ends up being "better" for precisely all the wrong reasons. Hence the crashing litany of experiences and deeds that demonstrate his acceptance of shame-as-honor:

> I am a better [minister of the Anointed]: with far greater labours, far more imprisonments, with countless floggings, and often near death.
> Five times I have received from the [Judeans] the forty lashes minus one. Three times I was beaten with rods. Once I received a stoning. Three times I was shipwrecked; for a night

and a day I was adrift at sea; on frequent journeys, in danger from rivers, danger from bandits, danger from my own people, danger from [foreign nationals], danger in the city, danger in the wilderness, danger at sea, danger from false [siblings]; in toil and hardship, through many a sleepless night, hungry and thirsty, often without food, cold and naked. And, besides other things, I am under daily pressure because of my anxiety for the [assemblies]. Who is weak, and I am not weak? Who is caused to sin and I do not burn?

If I must boast, I will boast of the things that show my weakness. The God and father of the Lord Jesus (blessed by he forever) knows that I do not lie. In Damascus, the governor under King Aretas guarded the city of Damascus in order to seize me, but I was let down in a basket through the wall and escaped from his hands. (11:23b–33)

All of these things were causes of shame. Manual labor, public punishment at the hands of both synagogue authorities and civic authorities, extreme poverty and weakness—nobody would boast in these things. Furthermore, almost all of these things are representative characteristics of the lower-class buffoon, who was considered intellectually, physically, and morally weak and who was driven by poverty and dire need, through hunger, homelessness, and nakedness, required to perform hard physical labor or was harassed, beaten, and driven away like a parasite.[93] Thus, Paul must truly be a full-fledged "madman" or "fool" to boast in any of this. Indeed, such a person must be the very worst kind of refuse and scum—the kind that needs to be exterminated in order to purify a city (and this is precisely the term used by the Pauline faction earlier in the Corinthian correspondence [1 Cor 4:13]).[94] However, because the Pauline faction views things from the perspective of a crucified and vindicated Anointed, they think it is madness to boast in anything but these things. The reference to Paul's flight from Damascus is a beautiful crashing finale to the crescendo that has been building since 2 Cor 10. Within Greek and Roman societies, one of the highest marks of honor that a person could receive was a medal given to the first soldier over the

---

93. See Welborn, *Paul, the Fool of Christ*, 32, 49–50, 58, 60–79. As Welborn also observes, even the earliest images we have of Paul depict Paul with physical characteristics—baldness, a lack of physical attractiveness—that were commonly assigned to fools (39, 59).

94. For this interpretation of "refuse and scum," see Welborn, *Paul, the Fool of Christ*, 79–80.

wall when assaulting an enemy city. It took considerable strength and bravery to accomplish this. Yet Paul boasts about doing the opposite of this—when his life was threatened, he was the first to retreat and escape over the city wall on his way out! Thus, Paul provides "the antithesis of an 'achievements-list' or a *cursus honorum*: a catalogue of what mainstream society would regard as catastrophes, of repeated physical punishment, of suffering and danger."[95] By doing so, he would have shocked people by making a mockery of the entire system of honor and shame as it was established in the dominant culture and encouraged by the ideo-theology of Rome.[96] Although, as Neil Elliott notes, such talk would surely have excited others who were "humiliated, ritually mistreated, and expelled in public events that represented the prevailing order of power, and distinguished citizens from subjects."[97]

This boasting in shame in a manner that would resonate with others who had been shamed, conquered, and enslaved also appears in an earlier passage in this letter. In 2 Cor 2:14–16, Paul and his coworkers describe themselves in these terms:

> But thanks be to God, who in [the Anointed] always leads us in triumphal procession, and through us spreads in every place the fragrance that comes from knowing him. For we are the aroma of [the Anointed] to God among those who are being saved and among those who are perishing; to the one a fragrance from death to death, to the other a fragrance from life to life.

Here, Paul and his coworkers are describing themselves with the imagery of an imperial triumph.[98] When a Roman general received a triumph, they paraded notable captives through the city before executing them and offering burnt offerings to the gods. The aroma of those offerings—offered as an appropriately pious response to divinely-granted victory over their enemies—would smell to the Roman citizens like "a fragrance

---

95. See Dunn, *Beginning from Jerusalem*, 855.

96. See Crossan and Reed, *In Search of Paul*, 337; Strom, *Reframing Paul*, 159–67. The minstrel who sings the praises of Brave Sir Robin in *Monty Python's Quest for the Holy Grail* provides an excellent illustration of the Pauline variety of boasting: "Brave Sir Robin ran away / Bravely ran away away / When danger reared its ugly head / He bravely turned his tail and fled / Yes, Brave Sir Robin turned about / And gallantly he chickened out / Bravely taking to his feet / He beat a very brave retreat / Bravest of the Brave, Sir Robin!"

97. Elliott, "Apostle Paul's Self-Presentation," 79.

98. See, for example, Schnabel, *Paul and the Early Church*, 962–63.

from life to life" (for it meant that they were, once again, victorious and could continue to live in divinely-sanctioned peace and security) but would smell to any enemies of Roman like a "fragrance from death to death" (for it signified the deaths of some who rose against Rome and foreshadowed the deaths of any others who would dare to do this). What is interesting, in light of this, is that Paul and his coworkers do not describe themselves as victorious generals celebrating a triumph. Far from it—they have been defeated by God through the Anointed and now they are being paraded as a sign of God's victory. In this way, the Pauline faction identifies not with the conquerors, but with the conquered—the vulnerable, the penetrated, the enslaved, and the humiliated.[99] Nobody with any sense of honor would voluntarily do this. It is also a risky move because it contains a seditious implication: just as God defeated Paul, the formerly zealous persecutor of those loyal to Jesus, so God stands to defeat the local elites and the empire itself, which persecutes the Jesus movement and adheres to contradictory values (like those gospeled by the opposition at Corinth). This is the warning contained in the description of Paul and his coworkers as "a fragrance from death to death."

Other passages that we have explored confirm this cruciform trajectory in Paul's own life. For example, when the Pauline faction refers to Paul as a suffering woman they continue this reversal of honor and shame.[100] Other passages that speak of Paul's weakness, manual labor, poverty, suffering, folly, and disrepute—notably, in the correspondence with the Corinthians (e.g., 1 Cor 4:8–13; 2 Cor 4:7–12; 4:16–5:4; 6:4–10; 12:7)—further confirm this.[101] All of this makes this conclusion unavoidable: Phil 2:5–11 provided the model imitated by Paul and his coworkers. Just as God is revealed in the crucified Anointed so now, Paul and his coworkers believe, God will be revealed in their humiliation. This is a central part of what it means to be "crucified with the Anointed" (Gal 2:20). As Elliott says, "The body [of Jesus] exhibited by the empire as tortured and crucified has been decisively counter-exhibited by God's act in raising Jesus from the dead; and that counter-display continues to be re-presented by apostolic and ecclesial performance as the locus of God's

---

99. See Lopez, *Apostle to the Conquered*, 137–41; Elliott, "Apostle Paul's Self-Presentation," 75–77.

100. See Lopez, *Apostle to the Conquered*, 141–46.

101. See Horrell, *Social Ethos*, 200–204; Malina and Neyrey, *Portraits of Paul*, 207–10.

life-giving power."[102] It is precisely this litany of suffering, shame, political persecution, and economic exclusion that make Paul such an appropriate ambassador of Jesus to the nations.

Valorizing Shame: Making Humility into a Virtue

The Pauline faction offers Paul as a prime example to be emulated in the imitation of the Anointed revealed in Phil 2:5–11. This is explicitly stated in Phil 3:17 ("[Siblings], join in imitating me [Paul], and observe those who live according to the example you have in us [the Pauline faction]") but similar appeals are made elsewhere. Hence, the comparably shameful litany of Paul's shame, suffering, weakness, and folly found in 1 Cor 4:8–12 is followed by this injunction: "I appeal to you, then, be imitators of me." Similarly, in 1 Cor 11:1, the chapter just examined, Paul states: "Be imitators of me as I am of [the Anointed]." Calls to imitate Paul always come after descriptions of Paul's shame and humiliation. Cruciformity is to be the model for the lives of all the Jesus loyalists. Shame, suffering, sedition, and solidarity with those who are left for dead by the rulers are all to be markers of Jesus loyalists who will, for those reasons, also be vindicated by God through Jesus. This is what prompts Paul and his coworkers to use the language of crucifixion in relation to the transformation of their lives (language, it should be noted, which was even more offensive to the original recipients of the letters than the language of "slavery" that he also applies to this transformation). For example, in the letter to the assemblies of Jesus loyalists at Rome, Rom 6:3–11, the Pauline faction writes the following:

> Do you not know that all of us who have been baptized in [the Anointed] Jesus were *baptized into his death*? Therefore we have been buried with him by baptism into death, so that, just as [the Anointed] was raised from the dead by the glory of the father, so we too might walk in newness of life.
> For if we have been *united with him in a death like his*, we will certainly be united with him in a[n *anastasis*] like his. We know that *our old self was crucified with him* so that the body of sin might be destroyed and we might *no longer be enslaved to sin*. For whoever has died is freed from sin. But if we have died with [the Anointed], we believe that we will also live with him. We know that [the Anointed], being raised from the dead,

---

102. Elliott, "Apostle Paul's Self-Presentation," 84.

will never die again; *death no longer has dominion over him.* The death he died, he died to sin, once for all; but the life he lives, he lives to God. So you must consider yourselves dead to sin and alive to God in [the Anointed] Jesus. (Rom 6:3–11; emphasis added)

To be baptized into the death of Jesus is to share in his crucifixion, which is also what it means to be united with Jesus in "a death like his." This is appalling, but following the now well-established pattern of status reversal, it is also said to be that which leads to liberation. Liberation from Sin and Death and, therefore, liberation also from the Roman Empire (which, as chapter 5 will show, is what the Pauline faction is talking about when they refer to "the body of sin"), which wields death as its ultimate weapon.

In this regard, it is worth recalling Suetonius's account of one of Nero's nightmares.[103] In this nightmare, Nero is standing in the theater of Pompey, which is lined with statues representing all the peoples conquered by Rome. Suddenly, the statues come to life and surround him. They press closer and closer to him, until he is completely trapped, terrified, and unable to move. Nero's nightmare—the fear of the ruler of the free world at the time of Paul—finds some startling resonance with the words of Gal 2:19–21:

For through the law I died to the law, so that I might live to God. I have been crucified with [the Anointed]; and it is no longer I who live, but it is [the Anointed] who lives in me. And the life I now live in the flesh I live by faith in the Son of God, who loved me and gave himself for me. I do not nullify the grace of God; for if the process of making things just comes through the Law, then [the Anointed] died for nothing.

I will have more to say about this in chapter 5 when I address the Pauline understanding of the law, but it is important to think of the law here as the Roman law—the same law that condemned Jesus to death. Jesus died to this law through the law in order to live to God. This is why Jesus died for nothing if justification—that is, the bringing of justice, and the making right of all things—came through the implementation of the rule of law. Hence, instead of following unjust legal and social arrangements, Jesus lives to the God of Life and is crucified but vindicated as the Anointed and the rightful "Son of God." The Pauline faction, then,

---

103. See Kahl, *Galatians Re-Imagined*, 1–2.

follows Jesus along the same trajectory and has been crucified with the Anointed (which is why, in Gal 3:1, Paul can state that Jesus was "publicly displayed as crucified" before the very eyes of the Galatians), and now the crucified Anointed lives in him. Hence, Paul and the other Jesus loyalists become the living embodiment of Nero's dream—they are the statues of vanquished people who have come back to life. They are the nightmare of the empire.

All of this leads to the embrace of humility as a virtue. This humility should not be read in light of hundreds of years of Christian pietism—it is, perhaps, better understood as debasement and degradation.[104] Hence, immediately prior to relating Phil 2:5-11, Paul and his coworkers write: "Do nothing from selfish ambition or conceit, but in humility regard others as better than yourselves" (Phil 2:3). As Klaus Wengst observes, nobody in Graeco-Roman culture placed any value on humility—it was the disposition of insignificant people, who either tried to escape it or learned to resign themselves to it, and so anybody of any importance was seen as (appropriately, justly, and morally) free from humility.[105] However, the apocalypse of a God in solidarity with the humiliated, leads the Pauline faction to embrace humiliation as something good and, in what would be considered a foolish, subversive, and possibly even suicidal trajectory, something to aspire to possess.[106]

Humility Expressed in Mutuality and the Love of Enemies

One of the primary ways in which this humiliating embrace of shame was expressed was through the mutuality that was to be practiced between Jesus loyalists. As we have seen, this was to be the comprehensive mutuality of siblings within the household of God, wherein previously existing hierarchies between slaves and free people, men and women, and various nationalities, were no longer recognized. Furthermore, it was a mutuality practiced among the conquered, the vanquished, the penetrated, and the crucified. Precisely for this reason, the Pauline faction is adamant that those who belonged to the household of God but who were scorned

---

104. Words used by Horrell (*Solidarity and Difference*, 118) and Sanders (*Paul: The Apostle's Life*, 599), respectively.

105. Wengst, *Humility*, 4-15. See also Horrell, *Solidarity and Difference*, 210-11.

106. Wengst, *Humility*, 36-57.

within the dominant culture of the empire were to be treated with higher honor. They dwell on this in detail in 1 Cor 12–13.

In this passage, Paul and his coworkers first make it clear that all members of the household of God are equal because, although people have different gifts, serve in different ways, and engage in different activities, all have the same Spirit within them, and this Spirit inspires all to work towards the common good (1 Cor 12:4–11). Second, they then turn to the analogy of members of the assemblies of Jesus loyalists acting as members of the body of the Anointed (12:12–27). "In the one Spirit we were all baptized into one body—[Judeans] or Greeks, slaves or free—and we were all made to drink of one Spirit" (12:13). For this reason, no single member can look down upon any other member and treat them as superfluous, nor can any single member suppose that they could exist independently of the others:

> If the foot would say, "Because I am not a hand, I do not belong to the body," that would not make it any less a part of the body. And if the ear would say, "Because I am not an eye, I do not belong to the body," that would not make it any less a part of the body. If the whole body were an eye, where would the hearing be? If the whole body were hearing, where would the sense of smell be? But, as it is, God arranged the members of the body each one of them, as he chose. If all were a single member, where would the body be? As it is, there are many members, yet one body. The eye cannot say to the hand, "I have no need of you," nor again the head to the feet, "I have no need of you." (12:14–21)

Therefore, precisely because all possess the same Spirit and participate in unique ways within the same body, hierarchies of conquest or any expression of inequality—which could easily find its way into the assemblies of Jesus loyalists (and which was already finding its way in at Corinth) must be explicitly countered and rejected:

> On the contrary, the members of the body that seem to be weaker are indispensable, and those members of the body that we think less honorable we clothe with greater honor, and our less respectable members are treated with greater respect; whereas our most respectable members do not need this. But God has so arranged the body, giving the greater honor to the inferior member, that there may be no dissension within the body, but the members may have the same care for one another. If one

member suffers all suffer together with it; if one member is honored, all rejoice together with it. Now you are the body of [the Anointed] and individually members of it. (12:22–27)

Hence, we see a body wherein diversity is affirmed and expressed in solidarity with the humiliated.[107] In this body, we see a rejection of the dominant system of honor and shame—a rejection that would have led to a loss of honor (in the eyes of one's neighbors) and an increase of shame (in the eyes of one's neighbors). A freed Greek man who earned slightly more than that which was needed for subsistence who treated women, slaves, Gauls, and those below the subsistence level as his equals—and who was treated in return as their equals—would quickly lose the (admittedly little) respect or honor granted to him by his peers. He would be considered a fool. To be the body of the Anointed is to be the crucified body of the crucified Anointed.[108] It is to be cut out of the body politic of Caesar.

But it gets worse. Any individual or collectivity embracing this trajectory would be viewed as a threat since their way of living and acting threatened one of the cornerstones needed to sustain the smooth functioning of the status quo. Because of this, they would be shunned and find their well-being in jeopardy unless they were associated with another body which could help provide for their immediate material needs. Hence, the use of a body metaphor in this passage. Using a body as a metaphor for a larger group was a familiar political metaphor in Graeco-Roman society.[109] The diverse but united constituents of the empire were understood as members of a body—the "body politic"—and the emperor was understood to be the head or mind of the body.[110] It is common to mention this parallel while then stressing that nothing subversive or threatening (to the empire) is occurring in the passage. According to some, Paul and his coworkers simply find this to be an easily recognizable metaphor for the (apolitical) embrace of diversity within

---

107. See Kim, *Christ's Body in Corinth*, 1–5, 11–21, 97–102. This is argued over against those who see the deployment of "body" language here as a means of imposing sharp boundaries between outsiders and uniformity within the assemblies of Jesus loyalists.

108. Kim, *Christ's Body in Corinth*, 62, 65–66, 70–71; Horrell, *Social Ethos*, 180–84.

109. See Horrell, *Social Ethos*, 178–80; Banks, *Paul's Idea of Community*, 62–65, 70;

110. See, for example, Livy, *Histories* 2.32; Seneca, *De clementia* 1.3–5. For this reason, Seneca urges Nero to deploy mercy, since harming other members of the "body politic" would end up being a form of self-harm.

unity.¹¹¹ However, it is quite possible that those who affirm this position are not paying sufficient attention to (or are simply ignoring) what is at play here. As we have seen, Paul and his coworkers are affirming an approach to honor that reverses values that are central to the smooth functioning of imperialism. Furthermore, previously in 1 Cor 11:3, they stated that the Anointed (and not emperor) is "the head" of every person. This Anointed, who was crucified in order to maintain the health of the imperial body politic, is now proclaimed as the Lord of all by an alternate body which continues to embody, embrace, and ennoble the crucifixion of their Lord. I will have more to say about this in chapter 5. For now, however, everything we have pointed out thus far suggests that there is more going on here than a politically irrelevant model of maintaining diversity in unity.¹¹²

Yet, as the text continues, something surprising happens: after having stated that all are equal, we find a hierarchy of the various gifts given to Jesus loyalists by the Spirit (2 Cor 12:28–30). However, the Pauline faction quickly realizes that this sounds anachronistic and so they write: "I will show you a still more excellent way" (12:31) and offer the well-known passage on love (1 Cor 13:1–13). This then permits them to return to their hierarchy of gifts and explain that some gifts are considered more valuable because they are of greater service to the assemblies (1 Cor 14:1–25). They are more valuable, not because they bring greater honor to those who possess them but because they bring greater benefits to the whole body. Note, also, how the discussion of love contributes to a transformation in one's understanding of what is valuable. A number of things that would be considered as honorable or granting a person a special degree of status—speaking in mysterious tongues, having prophetic powers and all knowledge of mysteries, the ability to move mountains, or the manifestation of a great degree of charity—are all considered worthless without love (13:1–3). "Love" is then defined in this way: "Love is patient; love is kind; love is not envious or boastful or arrogant or rude. It does not insist on its own way; it is not irritable or resentful . . . it bears all things, believes all things, hopes all things, endures all things. Love never ends" (13:4–8a). Love is what occurs when one embraces shame in solidarity

---

111. See, for example, Dunn, *Beginning from Jerusalem*, 621, 819, 920; Pate, *End of the Age has Come*, 170.

112. Oakes is sympathetic to this reading but does not think that the radical reworking of relationships within the assemblies of Jesus loyalists would be "unambiguously visible to outsiders" (Oakes, *Reading Romans in Pompeii*, 111).

Pauline Solidarity

with the humiliated and commits one's self to mutual care with one's siblings in the Anointed.[113] Love, for Paul and his coworkers, is cruciform.[114]

As proper siblings, love becomes the means by which cooperation and mutuality replace competition and antagonisms.[115] Instead of competing with one another for honor, the Jesus loyalists are instructed to "love one another with mutual affection" and "outdo one another in *showing honor*" to each other (Rom 12:10; emphasis added; see also Gal 5:13–14). In doing so, they should refuse to be "haughty" and should, instead, "associate with the lowly" (Rom 12:16). Recalling that slaves and freedpeople of all genders, composed economically of the desperately poor and the slightly less poor, were all in these assemblies together, this is a radical injunction—it is foolish enough for a free Greek male to treat a foreign female slave as his associate, it's beyond foolish for him to try and treat her as though she is *more* honorable than him.[116] Yet this is the anti-honor, anti-competitive mutuality that the Pauline faction desired to see in the assemblies of Jesus.

In order to arrive at this mutuality the Pauline faction stresses that Romans, Judeans, Greeks, and all people are equal in relation to God. As Robert Jewett demonstrates, this is a prominent theme in the letter to the Romans (especially in Rom 1–3 and 5)—no group may claim superior honor before God, all are saved by grace and no group has any grounds for boasting in relation to any other group.[117] Furthermore, as Jewett also observes, while this was a universally challenging statement, it was especially challenging to Roman imperialism, which possessed the power and hegemony needed to impose its faith in its own superior piety and honor onto other groups.[118]

---

113. On this conclusion, see Theissen, *Religion of the Earliest Churches*, 76; Dunn, *Beginning from Jerusalem*, 821–24. Hence, Crossan and Borg assert that the cross leads to "at-one-ment" through participation in (the) Anointed in political and other ways (Crossan and Borg, *First Paul*, 137–40).

114. See Gorman, *Cruciformity*, 63–74, 155–267.

115. A point that those who opposed Paul and his coworkers at Corinth seem to have missed (see, for example, Georgi, *Opponents of Paul*, 164–74, 234–37). Although those who were within the assemblies of Jesus loyalists at this time tended to be excluded from the Roman conception of honor—slaves and barbarians and so forth—they were frequently eager to compete for it among themselves (see Jewett, *Romans*, 49–53).

116. See Oakes, *Reading Romans in Pompeii*, 110–11.

117. Jewett, *Romans*, xv, 1, 48–49, 559–64.

118. In a much earlier writing Jewett proposed that this should result in a Christian

The final extent of the shameless folly of Paul and his coworkers is revealed in the injunction that love should extend *even to one's enemies*. The contrast between this and the imperial values is highlighted in the following quotation from the Roman historian Dionysius of Halicarnassus: "We love those who do us good and hate those who do us harm, and renounce our friends when they injure us, which is just, honorable, and holy."[119] It is honorable to hate and harm one's enemies. It is shameful to love them and shameful to refuse to retaliate when harmed. Furthermore, in an economy that affirmed honor and blessing as a limited good—meaning that one could not gain something without others losing something—it was madness to bless your enemies, for that would mean that you would be deprived of blessing.[120] Yet the Pauline faction urges those loyal to Jesus at Rome to do this:

> Bless those who persecute you; bless and do not curse them.... Do not repay anyone evil for evil but take thought for what is noble in the sight of all.... Beloved, never avenge yourselves, but leave room for the wrath of God; for it is written, "Vengeance is mine, I will repay, says the Lord." No, "if your enemies are hungry, feed them; if they are thirsty, give them something to drink." (Rom 12:14, 17–20a)

Similarly, in 1 Cor 12:2–3, they argue that the name of Jesus should not be employed as a means of cursing others—which then leads immediately into the passage we examined in detail regarding living in solidarity with one another and showing especial honor (within the assemblies of Jesus loyalists) to any who might be considered to be less honorable (outside of the assemblies of Jesus loyalists).[121] The basis for this foolish and shameful expression of love is, once again, found in the apocalypse of God in the crucifixion of the Anointed. As Paul and his coworkers explain in Rom 5:8–10:

---

ethics of "tolerance." (Jewett, *Christian Tolerance*, 10–13, 36–42). This approach does not have the same depth as the mutualism being proposed here or, it should be noted, by the agapaic-communalism that Jewett proposes in his later writing (e.g., Jewett, *Romans*, 66–68, 80–86).

119. *Roman Antiquities* 34.1-2, quoted in Winter, "Roman Law and Society," 80.

120. See Oakes, *Reading Romans in Pompeii*, 118–19.

121. Bruce Winter helps shed light on this somewhat puzzling passage by examining curse tablets there were common within religious practices at Corinth at this time. See Winter, *After Paul Left Corinth*, 164–83.

> But God proves his love for us in that while we still were sinners [the Anointed] died for us. Much more surely then, now that we have been made just by his blood, will we be saved through him from the wrath of God. For if while we were enemies, we were reconciled to God through the death of his Son, much more surely, having been reconciled, will we be saved by his life.

Those loyal to Jesus choose to love their enemies because they themselves were once the enemies of God. However, God demonstrates his love—the foolish shameful love we examined above—by dying for his enemies in order to save them and give them abundant life. Therefore, as Kahl observes, "God's appearance on the side of the *other* . . . destroys the image of the enemy."[122] Henceforth, those who attempt to model themselves after Jesus are to also love their enemies.

However, this love of enemies is not, as we will see in more detail in chapter 5, a universal call to love all enemies in the same way. Some enemies are to be embraced, while others (like the blind and foolish rulers of this present evil age) are set aside for future annihilation. Indeed, any discussion of enmity and the love of enemies, in the Pauline context, must reckon with the observation that Rome held onto colonized territories by exacerbating, exploiting, and then mediating various conflicts and enmities that existed between various foreign nationalities. Consequently, it is best to view the Pauline call to love enemies as a tactic used to address and overcome the lateral violence that oppression and colonization fostered within the oppressed and colonized. It is these people who are called to be united, loving one another as members of the crucified (but resurrected) body of the Anointed, over against the crucifying (but doomed) body of Caesar.

Conclusion

As we saw with matters related to the household, family, and kinship, Paul and his coworkers redeploy some central themes—in this case, honor and shame, a court of repute, an ultimate (fatherly) judge of one's status—but completely rework those themes in order to posit an order that not only subverts and challenges the dominant imperial order but also eagerly pushes toward the collapse of the empire. Not surprisingly, then, is our discovery that seditious counter-imperial themes, motifs, and

---

122. Kahl, *Galatians Re-Imagined*, 260.

EMBRACING SHAME IN THE COMPANY OF THE CRUCIFIED

implications are interwoven throughout material that we, as twenty-first-century readers, might be inclined to see as more "cultural" than "political." This is what happens when a state-executed terrorist is elevated as the new standard for honor. Shame is embraced as honor, judgments made by any outside the household of God are rejected, mutuality is practiced within the assemblies, and even enemies are treated with love.

All of this is "subversive" and "counter-cultural" in a manner that is rather different than the ways in which we tend to think of those things. The early Jesus loyalists who embraced the perspective of the Pauline faction would be perceived either as utter fools—completely mad and suffering the loss of whatever little honor or status they originally had—as terrorists—terrifying threats to the order and well-being of the entire civic community—or both. Today, however, much of what passes for "subversive" or "counter-cultural" is a kind of impotent posturing or a simulacrum of action that accomplishes nothing—other than boosting a person's brand status as an "activist" or an "aware" or "woke" or "passionate" person. As such, it has precisely the opposite result of the sort of sedition proclaimed and embodied by Paul and his coworkers. It is easy (as opposed to costly), it is impotent (as opposed to threatening), and it increases a person's honor (instead of making that person humiliated when measured by the standards of the wealthy and powerful). Furthermore, contemporary notions of "subversive" or "counter-cultural" action are too often employed outside of any kind of lived solidarity and mutuality with those who both suffer and die because of contemporary forms of imperialism. They are far removed from any kind of lived solidarity and mutuality with those who resist contemporary forms of imperialism. Yet lived solidarity and mutuality with those people are essential to the discovery of honor in the shameful cruciformity that is proposed by Paul and his coworkers as they seek to live like the Jesus they describe in Phil 2:5–11.

In conclusion, we should return once again to the observation that honor and shame operated within an economy of limited good—wherein there was not enough for everybody and any gain made by some would require a loss on behalf of others. Part of what makes it possible for the early Jesus loyalists to break with the dominant imperial conception of honor is their rejection of this belief via the affirmation of God's unlimited grace and God as the giver of abundant gifts.[123] Within God's economy

---

123. See Oakes, *Reading Romans in Pompeii*, 100–102.

of abundant grace, there is enough for everybody. All the members of the assemblies may be highly honored without any member suffering a loss. It is this affirmation of an economy of abundant grace that establishes the foundation for the counter-imperial economics that will be explored in the next chapter.

4

REJECTING PATRONAGE WITHIN A SIBLING-BASED POLITICAL ECONOMY OF GRACE

> Whatever it is, even when Greeks bring gifts,
> I fear them gifts and all.
>
> —Virgil, *Aeneid* 2.49

> They asked only one thing, that we continue to remember the poor, which was actually what I was eager to do.
>
> —Galatians 2:10

Introduction: Paul the Economist

WITHIN THIS CHAPTER, I will explore how the Pauline faction responded to the third cornerstone of Roman imperialism—the practice of patronage—and will use this as a way of entering into a discussion of the broader economic practices of the assemblies to which they wrote. It is here that we will begin to see precisely *how* the fictive kinship established by entry into the household of God and the embrace of cruciformity as honor in solidarity with the degraded impacted the material practices of the Jesus loyalists. What becomes apparent, particularly in this area, is that Paul and his coworkers are acting as "organic intellectuals"—people who formulated their thoughts within a specific, experimental communal praxis defined by the pursuit of a specific way of sharing their material life together.[1] It demonstrates how, to quote the Zapatistas, they made the road by walking.[2]

In this first section, I will explore some of the core beliefs that founded the economics proposed by the Pauline faction. In section 2, I will examine the ways in which the Pauline faction and other Jesus loyalists responded to the widespread and ultimately oppressive practices of patronage (a Graeco-Roman precursor to philanthrocapitalism). In section 3, I will then examine the so-called Pauline "Collection" as a particularly powerful and significant demonstration of the alternative economics practiced by the assemblies of Jesus loyalists. This will then lead, in section 4, to an exploration of how the economics proposed by Paul and his coworkers is a form of sharing that is against private property. To explore this further, section 5 will examine some of the other material and economic practices related to hospitality, table fellowship, benefaction, and care for those who are experiencing material poverty. Through all of this, we will discover the quiet yet steady work of those dedicated to creating an alternative transnational economic network, over against the general economic structure of the empire. Finally, I will conclude with some remarks about how this was a fundamental and absolutely central part of the appeal and spread of the early Jesus movement—even though the success of that spread also resulted in the betrayal of the values and practices of the Pauline faction (which, itself, was a diverse faction making some members—especially those most likely to personally benefit from re-adopting dominant cultural values and economic practices—more willing to also shift their allegiances when given the opportunity).

For some, it may be strange to speak of Paul as an economist.[3] All sorts of other titles have been applied (apostle, missionary, pastor,

---

1. Calvin Roetzel applies this title to Paul drawing from Antonio Gramsci—who coined the term—and Cornel West (Roetzel, *Paul*, 20; Gramsci, *Selections from the Prison Notebooks*, 3–23). I think the use is appropriate not only technically but also because of the overtones it carries. Antonio Gramsci was (like Paul) imprisoned by a despotic national leader for trying to participate in the formation of communities of solidarity, liberation, and resistance (see Gramsci, *Selections from the Prison Notebooks*). Recognizing Paul and his peers as organic intellectuals also carries significant implications (in my opinion) for any who would claim to be interpreters of Paul and, most especially, to any who would claim to have some sort of influence upon the legacy of Paulinism today.

2. See, for example, Neumann, "We Make the Road by Walking."

3. Here I am drawing on Barton's observations about how many people find it odd

radical) and the significance of economics in and to Paulinism has often been overlooked. Not only overlooked, but some have explicitly denied that economic matters matter at all. For example, Nils Dahl and Paul Donahue argue that, in comparison to other New Testament writers, Paul seems "unusually silent" on the topic of wealth, and they conclude that economics is not a "pressing question" for Paul.[4] Not surprisingly, from what we have seen up until this point in our study, this conclusion is drawn, in part, from the belief that Pauline eschatology expected the imminent end of the world and this makes economic affairs "trivial" but "not totally insignificant."[5] Martin Hengel came to the same conclusion in an earlier study—the Pauline belief in an imminent end "makes the possession of property a relative matter."[6] Furthermore, given what Hengel takes to be the failure of the "love communism" practiced by the Jesus loyalists in Jerusalem (described in Acts 2 and 4), he concludes that the Pauline faction pushed aside the entire question of property and riches and gives greater emphasis to spiritual "detachment."[7] However, given what we have already explored regarding Pauline eschatology and ethics, it would seem odd to find such a lack of attention to matters related to economics—especially since everything from the experience of oppression to the reformulation of Jesus loyalists as siblings within the household of God had concrete material ramifications and implications. Consequently, on the other end of the spectrum, we find scholars asserting that economics, money, and material things were very important to Paulinism. Thus, Dieter Georgi asserts that the Pauline faction speaks freely and confidently in some of the most elaborate reflections found in the ancient world about money, and Stephen Friesen observes that they speak more about money than other issues which have drawn far more attention—for example, the Pauline faction writes more about money than they do about the Lord's Supper, baptism, or matters related to gendered relationships within the assemblies of Jesus loyalists.[8] These are

---

to speak of "Paul the accountant" (see Barton, "Money Matters," 37–38). I believe the term "economist" is more appropriate than "accountant."

4. Dahl and Donahue, *Studies in Paul*, 22, 28.
5. Dahl and Donahue, *Studies in Paul*, 24–25.
6. Hengel, *Property and Riches*, 39.
7. Hengel, *Property and Riches*, 35–36, 40.
8. See Georgi, *Remembering the Poor*, 141, 149; Friesen, "Paul and Economics," 27–28.

important observations. As we will see, money matters mattered a great deal to Paul and his coworkers.

Laying the Foundation: Family, Marginality, and Eschatology

In order to enter into an understanding of the ways in which the early assemblies of Jesus loyalists associated with the Pauline faction negotiated the economic dynamics of the Graeco-Roman world, it is necessary to briefly recall four central features related to their practices, context, and beliefs. First, we should recall the ways in which Paul and his coworkers urged the assembled Jesus loyalists to relate to one another as a family and as siblings. As we saw above, living as siblings carried very concrete demands in terms of how one's finances were utilized and to whom one's material goods belonged. Specifically, siblings were financially responsible for one another and they were to consider what they owned to be collective property. Material goods were to be used for the common good of all within the family. Consequently, if Paul and his coworkers are consistent and thoroughgoing in their application of this kinship language to the assemblies of Jesus loyalists, we should expect a certain kind of economics—"*active and effective* [sibling-based] love"[9]—to develop within those assemblies.

Second, as we have also seen, the experience of poverty, persecution, colonization, and marginalization was common to the Jesus loyalists associated with Paul and his coworkers. I have already argued that Paul and his coworkers urged those loyal to Jesus not to flee from the experience of persecution—even though that may have dire consequences and might push them from living at or slightly above the subsistence level to living at or below the subsistence level. Instead, Jesus loyalists were called to move into deeper solidarity with one another and find ways to care for one another without compromising their lived commitment to establishing local footholds for the Jesus movement (in otherwise hostile territories). If this solidarity is to sustain the assemblies over time, it would require certain kinds of economic practices to be developed and consistently practiced—otherwise members would starve, or be forced to sell themselves (or their children) into slavery, or they could simply drop

---

9. Hengel, *Property and Riches*, 39; emphasis added. I substituted the word "sibling-based" for his more androcentric use of the term "brotherly."

out of the assemblies in order to be reincorporated into the networks they had previously participated within as a part of the body of Caesar at their location. At this point, we should also recall Gerd Theissen's observation that *active* "love of neighbor" tended to be more of a lower-class ideal.[10] Indeed, Karl Kautsky asserts that this was the case: the early assemblies of Jesus loyalists were more charitable, not because they were more noble but because they were more poor.[11] And, as those experiencing poverty and oppression who now experienced themselves as the newly assembled household of God, it is reasonable to expect their economics to look different than those of the rich.

The pressing need for a more liberating economics is only heightened when one recalls the double-marginality of the assemblies. They were marginalized within the broader society they inhabited because of their poverty, and they were also marginalized because they were ostracized by other support networks that existed among those who lived at or near the subsistence level because their ideo-theology was considered a sick joke that, if taken seriously, was actually a dangerous threat to everyone's well-being. Therefore, members of other subsistence-level networks would cut Jesus loyalists out in order to protect their own (already exceedingly precarious) safety and well-being.[12] Surviving within this experience of double-marginality required the development of a strong sense of unity and mutuality in order to facilitate more life-giving economic practices.

Third, we have already observed the eschatological tension that operated within Paulinism. There was a strong anticipatory element to this: those who were possessed by the eschatological Spirit of Life and who now made up the body of the Anointed began to proleptically live into the kinds of life-giving, life-affirming relationships and dynamics that were to be fully unveiled when the Anointed returned. This has concrete economic implications. As Bruce W. Longenecker asserts: "[Paul and his coworkers] imagined urban Jesus-groups to be miniature oases

---

10. Theissen, *Religion of the Earliest Churches*, 87.

11. Kautsky, *Foundations of Christianity*, 118. This leads Kautsky to refer to early "Christian" economics as "communistic hospitality," which I will remark upon in more detail below. Such economic practices still flourish in many communities of people experiencing poverty today (often under our very noses), as I have personally witnessed, and as documented, for example, in Bourgois and Schonberg, *Righteous Dopefiend*.

12. Oakes develops this theme in detail in his reading of Philippians. See Oakes, *Philippians*, 77–96.

of eschatological refreshment amid the harsh economic conditions of the Greco-Roman world."[13] Jacob Taubes makes an even stronger assertion: "There is a clear connection between enthusiasm for the Kingdom and communism. By adopting a life of communism, the early Christian [sic] community seeks to anticipate the divine economy of God's Kingdom."[14] Now, we have yet to see if Paul and his coworkers were advocates of a kind of economics that could be called "communist" (although taken at its most basic level—with all people sharing according to their ability and receiving according to their need—we should note that this seems to be a fairly appropriate contemporary parallel for the sibling-based relationships described previously). Instead, at this point, we should merely observe that their eschatological vision *should* have economic implications and lead into an economic arrangement different than that of the status quo of empire.

Finally, in relation to this eschatological vision and its economic implications, we should note the importance of an emphasis upon God's grace and generosity. As we saw above, the Graeco-Roman world believed in a political economy rooted in scarcity and the notion of a limited good. No person could hope to rise above their lot in life without that creating a loss for others (and so any one person experiencing a change in their situation threatened the stability of the whole community). Over against this, Paul and his coworkers affirm "the immense generosity of God" and an (over)abundance of grace.[15] As they write in 2 Cor 9:8–9:

> And God is able to provide you with every blessing in abundance, so that by always having enough of everything, you may share abundantly in every good work. As it is written, "He scatters abroad, he gives to the poor; his [justice] endures forever."

In other words, God, the Father of Jesus, gives generously and so the adopted children of God and siblings of Jesus are enabled and required to give in the same way.[16] Over against an economics of scarcity, this vision leads to an economics of excess.[17] This then leads to what Brian Walsh and Sylvia Keesmaat refer to as "an ethic in which the generosity of God

---

13. Longenecker, *Remember the Poor*, 300.
14. Taubes, *Occidental Eschatology*, 67.
15. Cousar, *Introduction to the New Testament*, 45.
16. Thompson, "Paul's Collection," 94.
17. See Jennings, *Reading Derrida/Thinking Paul*, 89–91.

overcomes the violence and economic exploitation of the empire."[18] As Giorgio Agamben puts it, grace "essentially signifies a gratuitous service, freed from contractual obligations of counterservice and command. . . . Faith and law now fracture and give way to the space of gratuitousness."[19] This leads to an embodied *prosperity gospel*—but a prosperity gospel that does not result in the hoarding of personal wealth and goods. It moves in exactly the opposite direction. The prosperity of God leads those who worship this God to share *everything* they have with others who are in need of it because the abundant grace of God will continue to provide for all who do so.

These four elements—sibling relationships within the assemblies of Jesus loyalists, the experience of double-marginality, the eschatological vision propagated by Paul and his coworkers, and their vision of God's abundant grace, which sets the standard for the behavior of those in God's household—should lead the contemporary reader to suspect that an alternative economics is operative among the Jesus loyalists. Rather than assuming that the economics of the imperial status quo sets the agenda for the Pauline faction an awareness of these various elements (not to mention the other themes already addressed in this work) should create an informed initial hypothesis which posits that something different is happening within the political economy of the early assemblies of Jesus loyalists.

I want to emphasize this point because contemporary Western Christians tend to assume that any kind of economic vision proposed by Paulinism would be one that affirms the practices of (charitable) liberal democracies and would be opposed to any sort of economic vision proposed by (what they understand to be) "communism," "anarchism," or "socialism." There is a need to break away from this, not in order to push for some kind of proof-texting that then affirms one of these supposedly taboo socioeconomic and political visions, but in order for us to be able to more fully encounter and comprehend what exactly was occurring within the early assemblies of Jesus loyalists associated with Paul and his coworkers.[20] It is likely that something very different was occurring with-

---

18. Walsh and Keesmaat, *Colossians Remixed*, 74.

19. Agamben, *Time That Remains*, 119.

20. Although, full disclosure, I should note that the European political philosophy that I believe fits best with the early Jesus movement is anarchism—especially of the variety proposed by Kropotkin, Bakunin, Malatesta, and Makhno (see, for example, Kropotkin, *Fugitive Writings*; Bakunin, *Bakunin on Anarchism*; Guérin, *No Gods No*

in this movement—something different than the imperial economics of the Roman Empire and something different than the imperial economics practiced by contemporary Western nations (and affirmed by most Western Christians). In fact, as we will see, the charitable economics developed by Western liberal Christians is extraordinarily similar to the kind of patronage practiced by the super apostles in Corinth and vigorously resisted by the Pauline faction.

Struggling to Create an Alternative to Patronage within the Assemblies of Jesus Loyalists

In volume 2 of this series, we saw the role that patronage played in structuring the status quo of the Roman Empire. We saw how asymmetrical, vertical relationships of exchange and dependency were created between those who had more and those who had less, and we saw how those who had nothing at all were excluded from this process altogether. We also saw how central and all-pervasive this practice was and how it operated as a soft form of power that produced a self-disciplining populace who acted in a way that supported social, political, and economic arrangements that were intended to meet the interests of the elite and wealthy few over against the interests of the multitudes of people who were impoverished. As such, and given the agonistic understanding of honor that was also prominent within Graeco-Roman culture, we also observed how patronage interfered with the development of anything that looked like "solidarity" or "class consciousness" even though the language of friendship and family was used to mask these oppressive and colonizing dynamics.

Because of the ubiquity and influence of patronage, we will begin our examination of the economics proposed and practiced by Paul and his coworkers with an examination of how the Pauline faction engaged with patronage. Did they affirm patronage as good? Did they engage patronage critically, accepting some elements of it while refusing other

---

Masters, 2:1–39, 123–62). I came to the study of anarchism rather later than some of my peers but, heavily influenced by the study of the early Jesus movement, I had always struggled to articulate where that left me in terms of the contemporary political terrain. When I first read Kropotkin on anarchism, I realized, "this is it! This is the political philosophy that fits with the early Jesus movement!" Having realized this, I have also learned that European or post-European anarchist movements must also partner with and learn from (and follow the lead of) Indigenous liberation movements (at least here on Turtle Island).

elements? Or did they reject it in order to participate within a more liberating alternative? New Testament scholars have proposed and debated all these alternatives and I will summarize the various positions taken before arguing that the Pauline faction was thoroughly opposed to the system of patronage. I will then look at the "Collection" as an example of a significant economic effort performed by the Pauline faction, demonstrating a sibling-based economic mutualism, which operated over against patronage.

Patronage and the Ideology of the Early Jesus Loyalists: An Alternative Pyramid of Power?

A number of the scholars who have produced excellent work in sociological and social-scientific readings of the New Testament have argued that Paul and his coworkers developed an alternative patronage pyramid. Peter Lampe sees this as a part of the "explosive" communal alternative being created by the early Jesus loyalists—while the dominant patronage system proclaimed Caesar as the ultimate patron, the Jesus loyalists proclaimed God, the Father of Jesus, as the one who dethroned Caesar and occupied this central place of importance.[21] Hence, from Lampe's perspective, the incorporation of the language and structures of patronage in the early assemblies of Jesus loyalists was an act of subversive mimicry. I believe that we should be cautious about rushing to accept this conclusion. After all, shifts in rhetoric—indeed the deployment of more radical and subversive rhetoric—can still be attached to practices that are just as deeply implicated in the violence of the status quo. One would need to see if a rhetorical shift—and a shift from Caesar as the ultimate patron, to God the Father of Jesus as the ultimate patron—also resulted in new practices and new relational dynamics, opening a way for patronage to be utilized in a way that no longer prevented the development of things like class consciousness or the lived practices of solidarity and sibling-based equality.

David deSilva spends more time providing the details of what this alternative patronage system may have looked like. God, the Father of Jesus, is seen as the ultimate patron and benefactor in that he creates and sustains all life. All people are, therefore, indebted to God and must act in a way that honors God (in order to be assured of ongoing favor) or risk

---

21. Lampe, "Paul, Patrons, and Clients," 494.

experiencing God's wrath and being cut-off from favor.[22] Prayer, then, is the means by which clients bring their petitions to God, their patron.[23] Furthermore, as particularly privileged clients, due to their proximity to God's firstborn son, the early Jesus loyalists were also the recipients of many other gifts from this patron—primarily the results produced by the sacrifice made by Jesus (which also shows God acting as a faithful patron to his earlier, more exclusive clientele, the Israelites).[24] They received from this divine patron all the various gifts needed to build up the transnational body of the Anointed at both personal and collective levels.[25] Because of this, they are expected to act as good and faithful clients. As this cycle of grace plays out, the Jesus loyalists are to show gratitude to God and are to seek to increase the recognition of God's honor.[26] They are also to show loyalty to their patron, no matter what the cost, so they must avoid courting God's enemies as potential patrons—which means not participating in rites that would proclaim one's indebtedness to other gods.[27] Furthermore, as clients of this patron, the Jesus loyalists are to honor this God not just with words but with works.[28] They are to serve this God by putting the gifts received to their good and proper use—which is whatever is in the best interest of the community as a whole.[29] This is also why "faith," or "loyalty," and "faithfulness" are so important to Paul and his coworkers. Faithfulness (i.e., loyalty), as we have seen, is the proper response of an honorable client to an honorable patron.

---

22. deSilva, *Honor, Patronage, Kinship, and Purity*, 126–29, 149. See Rom 1:21; 2:4–5; Gal 1:6; 2:21; 5:2–4.

23. deSilva, *Honor, Patronage, Kinship, and Purity*, 132. Hence the various remarks about the efficacy of prayer. See, for example, 1 Cor 1:10–11; Phil 1:19; 4:6–7, and the appeals for prayer as in 1 Thess 5:17, 25.

24. See deSilva, *Honor, Patronage, Kinship, and Purity*, 128–29; Rom 5:5; 15:8; Gal 3:1–5, 28–4:7; 2 Cor 1:22; 5:5.

25. deSilva, *Honor, Patronage, Kinship, and Purity*, 132–33; 1 Cor 1:5–7; 12:1–11, 18; 14:12; 1 Thess 1:2.

26. deSilva, *Honor, Patronage, Kinship, and Purity*, 141–42; 1 Thess 3:9; 5:18; 1 Cor 1:4–7; 2 Cor 1:9–11; 2:14.

27. deSilva, *Honor, Patronage, Kinship, and Purity*, 144–45; Phil 1:29–30; 1 Cor 10:14–21.

28. deSilva, *Honor, Patronage, Kinship, and Purity*, 143, 146; 2 Cor 5:14–15; Gal 2:20.

29. deSilva, *Honor, Patronage, Kinship, and Purity*, 147; 1 Cor 4; 12:4–11; Rom 12:3–8;

DeSilva's presentation of this perspective is initially quite compelling, but the more details one adds, the more cracks begin to appear. For example, it is not quite clear if God the Father of Jesus is the patron of the early Jesus loyalists or if Jesus is the patron of those loyal to him. Probably, to make the model work, it is best to see Jesus as a broker between God—the patron—and the Jesus loyalists—the clients, which is what deSilva proposes.[30] However, Lampe proposes that Jesus is actually the patron of those loyal to him.[31] Jesus, as the corporate representative of those loyal to him, could fit with this understanding, as would the language around the faithfulness one is to exhibit towards Jesus.[32] Could it be that both Jesus and God the Father of Jesus are patrons of the early assemblies of Jesus loyalists? How would having multiple patrons fit with the standard model of patronage presented above? Is not a faithful client to be loyal to one patron and is not a faithful client to try and advance the honor of that patron over all others? How can this be done when one has multiple patrons? Or perhaps these patrons do not exist within the structures of competition that were definitive of patronage? If that is the case, if people can be clients of multiple patrons who are not in competition with one another, should we even be speaking of this as "patronage" and with patronage language?

Now it is true that civic assemblies would try to cultivate the patronage of all the members of the imperial family—there would be no problem with erecting multiple shrines to the traditional gods alongside of shrines dedicated to Caesars. Hence, veneration of God the Father of Jesus, Jesus the Anointed, and the Spirit of Life could be a parallel to the veneration of, for example, Zeus (the father of the gods), Augustus the savior, and the spirit of Roma (indeed, this imperial Roman vision strikes me as something of a prototype for the development of trinitarian theology). So, when it comes to divine figures and members of the imperial family, it was possible to move beyond the attachment to a single patron in a non-competitive manner.

Speaking of moving outside of the sphere of competition, deSilva notes that what is surprising about the patronage and benefaction

---

30. deSilva, *Honor, Patronage, Kinship, and Purity*, 122, 133, 137. Maier, on the other hand, asserts that Jesus is the "chief patron" in assemblies that otherwise rejected external patrons and benefactors (Maier, *Picturing Paul in Empire*, 12).

31. Lampe, "Paul, Patrons, and Clients," 505. See Rom 1:4; 7:4; 8:34; 10:9, 12; 14:6–9, 14; 1 Cor 1:3; 3:23; 2 Cor 5:15.

32. Lampe, "Paul, Patrons, and Clients," 506.

exhibited by God the Father of Jesus is that it is freely given to enemies.[33] Here is it worth quoting Rom 5:6–10:

> For while we were still weak, at the right time [the Anointed] died for the ungodly. Indeed, rarely will anyone die for a [just] person—though perhaps for a good person someone might actually dare to die. But God proves his love for us in that while we still were sinners [the Anointed] died for us. Much more surely then, now that we have been made [just] by his blood, will we be saved through him from the wrath of God. For if while we were enemies, we were reconciled to God through the death of his Son, much more surely, having been reconciled, will we be saved by his life.

While the ultimate patrons of the empire could give some gifts to their enemies—notably showing mercy to the vanquished who were properly subdued and who recognized their all-encompassing supremacy—the difference here is that gifts are given to enemies *while they are still enemies*, and *the* single most precious gift (the life of the eldest son) is given, not to a close friend or a family member or a just person but to these enemies *qua* enemies. Certainly, the emperors could be merciful to those whom they conquered and they were happy to elevate compliant high-status members of colonized populations—but all of this occurred after the enemies were subdued. The giving of gifts to enemies *qua* enemies would be obscene and unheard-of, and to give one's firstborn son and heir as that gift would be taken as a sign of utter moral depravity and folly. This leads one to wonder if this is an example of the subversion of a patronage system or if it is an example of something altogether different happening. Is it useful to see patronage as a model of something that would be unconscionable within the patronage system?

Furthermore, what is the role of Paul in this? Malina and Neyrey argue that Paul claims a special status within the assemblies because God is his patron and has repeatedly vindicated Paul.[34] From this perspective, which deSilva supports, Paul, as an apostle, would be a mediator or broker of divine favor to the assemblies.[35] White goes so far as to suggest that, in the letter to Philemon, Paul claims to be a "spiritual patron" to Philemon in order to supersede the authority Philemon has over

---

33. See deSilva, *Honor, Patronage, Kinship, and Purity*, 129; Rom 5:6–10.

34. Malina and Neyrey, *Portraits of Paul*, 211.

35. deSilva, *Honor, Patronage, Kinship, and Purity*, 139. See 2 Cor 1:3–7, 24; 4:7–15; 6:4–10; 1 Thess 2:8–9; Phlm 18–19.

REJECTING PATRONAGE

Onesimus.³⁶ So is Paul a patron . . . along with God the Father of Jesus (and maybe also Jesus himself)? Or is Paul a broker . . . along with Jesus? How would this fit with all the other assertions that God and (maybe) Jesus are the patrons of the assemblies of Jesus loyalists or with the assertion that Jesus is the broker for these assemblies? Wouldn't that make Paul somewhat superfluous—why use Paul as a broker to Jesus, when one may have direct access to Jesus through the Spirit? Furthermore, how does this all fit with Paul's own assertion that he is in a symmetrical relationship with other Jesus loyalists—that they are his siblings?³⁷ Perhaps, as Lampe suggests, Paul employs patronal references to himself in the letter to Philemon in order to "abolish the relevance of such vertical hierarchies in inner-Christian [sic] social life"?³⁸ But, if that is the case, one wonders if it is best to describe what is occurring by means of another paradigm.

Furthermore, although certain themes related to patronage are prominent in the letters written by Paul and his coworkers—themes related to grace and loyalty (i.e., faith), for example—the specific language of patronage is markedly absent. The only mention of any "patron" in the early assemblies comes when the Pauline faction recommends Phoebe to the Jesus loyalists at Rome in Rom 16:1-2.³⁹ Otherwise, patronal terms are missing even though they would have been very familiar to Paul and his coworkers and even though the context—particularly when our reading is determined by the perspective taken by those already mentioned in this section—would seem to incline or even require the reader to find the terms. But they are just not there. Even the language of friendship, so frequently deployed by patrons to try and make power imbalances more palatable to the dispossessed is swallowed up in sibling-based language. So, if Paul is a patron, why does he not refer to himself as such? If Jesus is a patron or if God the Father of Jesus is a patron, why not refer to them as such? The absence of this obvious terminology may lead the reader to wonder if Paul and his coworkers were deliberately avoiding patronage language.

Given the inconsistencies and gaps highlighted above, David Downs argues that the patronage model is one that is inappropriate to apply to the understanding that the Jesus loyalists had regarding their

---

36. White, "Paul and *Pater Families*," 469-70.
37. See Lampe, "Paul, Patrons, and Clients," 500-501.
38. Lampe, "Paul, Patrons, and Clients," 502.
39. I will have more to say about Phoebe below.

relationships with God the Father of Jesus, Jesus himself, and other members of the assemblies in which they participated.[40] Instead, Downs argues that the embodiment of a fictive kinship and of familial language is far more dominant (as we have already explored above), and that this adequately explains and shapes the dynamics of the relationships that existed within the early assemblies of Jesus loyalists. Hence, God is the Father of Jesus and the adoptive Father of Paul and the other Jesus loyalists. Jesus is the firstborn and this explains his special status. One may account for the privileged position of both Jesus and God the Father of Jesus without appealing to patronage. This also accounts for the absence of competition, the absence of scarcity (at the ideological level), and the practices of mutuality that we will observe in more detail. Consequently, I believe that Downs has drawn the best conclusions. Malina, Neyrey, deSilva, and Lampe's conclusions are not as compelling (even though, in many ways, this whole debate is indebted to them and their excellent work). In many ways, the patronage system was modeled after traditional familial hierarchies, but the opposite is not the case. The family exists independent of patronage, and the kinds of relationships that existed within the family were different than the kinds of relationships that existed within patronage.

The Presence of Patronage within the Assemblies of Jesus Loyalists

How, then, does all of this play out in the practices of the assemblies of Jesus loyalists associated with Paul and his coworkers? In a culture inundated by patronage, with all other Graeco-Roman associations utilizing patronage as one of their central structures, were the assemblies of Jesus loyalists able to put this sibling-based ideology into practice or was patronage still practiced among them? Granted, as Philip Harland observes, the Jesus loyalists likely could not help but participate within networks of patronage that existed in their civic environments (for example, the many members who were slaves would be inescapably caught within it), but the question is the extent to which these networks impacted and shaped the relationships that were internal to their assemblies.[41]

---

40. Downs, "Is God Paul's Patron?," 130–56.
41. See Harland, "Connections with Elites," 404.

REJECTING PATRONAGE

Some, like Wayne Meeks and Mark Strom, assume that patronage was present based upon the argument that those who resided in the "private households" used to host the assemblies would function as patrons.[42] Similarly, albeit from a Marxist perspective, Karl Kautsky argues that the practice of charity within the assemblies of Jesus loyalists would have created a "dictatorship of benefactors."[43] However, what we have already observed about the gathering places of Jesus loyalists should cause us to question this conclusion. Given that the meetings were likely held in small apartments in rundown tenement buildings located in poor neighborhoods—apartments rented by poverty-stricken tenants and not purchased by home owners—one might question the extent to which the host could be considered a patron.[44]

The experiences of the Jesus loyalists at Corinth is instructive. At Corinth it seems very clear that some members of the assembly (or assemblies) that gathered there were seeking to become patrons of the Jesus loyalists and even of Paul himself. This is probably one of the primary causes of the tension Paul feels in his relationship with the Corinthians.[45] In Corinth some people are acting in ways that were recognized as rightful and appropriate ways for patrons to act—yet the Pauline faction vociferously condemns these actions as inappropriate within the assemblies of Jesus loyalists. Thus, for example, in 1 Cor 11:18-23, we read the following:

> Now in the following instructions I do not commend you, because when you come together it is not for the better but for the worse. For, to begin with, when you come together as [an assembly], I hear that there are divisions among you; and to some extent I believe it. Indeed, there have to be factions among you, for only so will it become clear who among you are genuine. When you come together, it is not really to eat the Lord's supper. For when the time comes to eat, each of you goes ahead with your own supper, and one goes hungry and another becomes drunk. What! Do you not have homes to eat and drink in? Or do you show contempt for the assembly of God and humiliate

---

42. See Meeks, *In Search of the Early Christians*, 125; Strom, *Reframing Paul*, 175.
43. Kautsky, *Foundations of Christianity*, 15-17, 323, 331, 345, 347, 422, 464, 467.
44. See Jewett, *Romans*, 53-55, 63.
45. As observed by Chow, "Patronage in Roman Corinth," 125. Chow spends a fair bit of time detailing the significant presence of patronage within Corinth during Paul's day (see 105-10, 117). On this, see also Crossan and Reed, *In Search of Paul*, 329, 333; Crossan, *God and Empire*, 166.

> those who have nothing? What should I say to you? Should I commend you? In this matter I do not commend you!

Practicing table fellowship in this way was the socially-expected and morally-defended norm. The patrons ate more courses and ate better food. This was right and good, according to the dominant way of thinking. However, Paul and his coworkers argue that this is a way of coming together that is "for the worse." They also call this a "division" within the assembly and condemn it as an unacceptable form of (socioeconomic) factionalism. Indeed, they argue that it "humiliates" others—which is a practice that, as we have seen, should be completely absent from sibling-based relationships—and that it shows contempt for the assembly of God.[46] Paul and his coworkers then go on to conclude with the following words in 11:27–34:

> Whoever, therefore, eats the bread or drinks the cup of the Lord in an unworthy manner will be answerable for the body and blood of the Lord. Examine yourselves, and only then eat of the bread and drink of the cup. For all who eat and drink without discerning the body, eat and drink judgment against themselves. For this reason many of you are weak and ill, and some have died. But if we judged ourselves, we would not be judged. But when we are judged by the Lord, we are disciplined so that we may not be condemned along with the world.
>
> So then, my [siblings], when you come together to eat, wait for one another. If you are hungry, eat at home, so that when you come together, it will not be for your condemnation.

Note the final reminder that the members of the assemblies are siblings—they are not to be patrons and clients to and with one another. They are family. To act otherwise may (literally) have deadly consequences as it places a person on the side of those who are responsible for the crucifixion of Jesus—suggesting that this person is now doing something akin to repeating that act of crucifixion by treating their siblings in this way—and associates that person with the condemnation that belongs to the world of the empire. It also has deadly consequences for those on the receiving end as they are, once again, consigned to the status of the left-for-dead.

---

46. Note: as we saw in the last chapters, their embrace of humiliation comes about as people pursue a *mutually liberating solidarity* from the oppressive and violent dynamics of the status quo. Thus, the embrace of humiliation has nothing to do with resigning oneself to accepting abuse of any kind from others (despite the ways in which abusive Christians have tried to make this argument over the last two millennia).

REJECTING PATRONAGE

We also see Paul himself actively taking steps to prevent himself from being incorporated into any patronage network in Corinth, even though his refusal to participate in this opened him to the charge of being a bad friend to some of the Corinthians (given, as we have seen, the ways in which the ideology of patronage co-opted the motif of friendship).[47] Hence, in contrast to the "Super Apostles" he criticizes—and who likely desired to be seen and treated as patrons—he writes the following in 2 Cor 11:7–15:

> Did I commit a sin by humbling myself so that you might be exalted, because I [gospeled] to you free of charge? I robbed other [assemblies] by accepting support from them in order to serve you. And when I was with you and was in need, I did not burden anyone, for my needs were supplied by the friends who came from Macedonia. So I refrained and will continue to refrain from burdening you in any way. As the [disclosure (*aletheia*)] of [the Anointed] is in me, this boast of mine will not be silenced in the regions of Achaia. And why? Because I do not love you? God knows I do!
>
> And what I do I will also continue to do, in order to deny an opportunity to those who want an opportunity to be recognized as our equals in what they boast about. For such boasters are false [ambassadors], deceitful workers, disguising themselves as [ambassadors] of [the Anointed]. And no wonder! Even Satan disguises himself as a [messenger] of light. So it is not strange if his ministers also disguise themselves as ministers of [justice]. Their end will match their deeds.

Note the passionate rhetoric—those "Super Apostles" who want to be patrons are comparable to Satan disguising himself as a messenger (or angel) of light. These are those who would participate within the assemblies of Jesus loyalists (wholly or in part) "in order to acquire their own loyal clients and enhance their social status."[48] In contrast to such people, Paul states that he refused any support from the Corinthians because he did not want to "burden" them. He has no desire to be a bad friend or to

---

47. See Dunn, *Beginning from Jerusalem*, 840.

48. Horsley and Silberman, *Message and the Kingdom*, 172. Here, Horsley and Silberman are more skeptical about the motives of the Super Apostles, arguing that their allegiance to the gospel of the Anointed is "nominal" and arguing that their primary intention was personal gain. This may be the case but it's hard to know. All too often, people have mixed motives and can, with the best of intentions (and the cleanest of consciences), import the worst of practices into a community (see, for example, Barry-Shaw and Jay, *Paved with Good Intentions*).

sin; rather, he argues that he is motivated to do this out of his love for the Corinthians.

Yet the Pauline faction accepted support from other (poorer) assemblies in Macedonia. Why? Because that support was provided within a context of mutuality—the kind of sharing that is to exist among siblings—and was not tainted by overtures of patronage.[49] A similar argument is made in 1 Cor 9:1–23. While observing that those who gospel the gospel to people experiencing poverty, oppression, and violence have a right to be supported by those being assembled (support that is made possible within a transnational network of sibling-based economic mutuality), the Pauline faction states that they want to ensure that they gospel "free of charge" (v. 17) so as not to put any obstacle in the way of "the gospel" (v. 12). The "obstacle," in this case, would be incorporating patronal relationships into the work of the gospel.[50] Therefore, in direct opposition to any possible understanding of Paul through the lenses of patronage, the Pauline faction repeatedly refers to Paul as a "*slave*." Hence, also, their repeated focus within these passages upon Paul's need to perform menial and strenuous manual labor in order to earn money, so as not to be reliant upon others (as much as that was possible for a person earning a near subsistence level income, who also traveled throughout the eastern part of the empire—after all, as Meeks observes, "The radical separation of Jesus' messengers from the ordinary person's rootage in place, family, and livelihood requires for its fulfillment unqualified dependence upon the charity of strangers").[51] Manual labor was one of the ways in which the Pauline faction works towards maintaining independence from the patronage system.[52] Thus, as Larry Welborn notes, the injunction to "owe no one anything" in Rom 13:8 is, in fact, a call to "unplug from the patronage system" and is intended to be taken completely seriously.[53]

---

49. See Georgi, *Opponents of Paul*, 240.

50. See Elliott, *Liberating Paul*, 201; Horrell, *Social Ethos*, 204–8; Pickett, "Conflicts at Corinth," 132; Dunn, *Beginning from Jerusalem*, 806; Horsley and Silberman, *Message and the Kingdom*, 163–64; Lampe, "Paul, Patrons, and Clients," 503.

51. Meeks, *Moral World*, 105. Meeks is overstating the case a bit since Paul and others would be dependent not upon "strangers" per se but rather the members of the assemblies of Jesus loyalists with whom they interacted. These people would not be considered strangers but siblings in the Anointed.

52. See Horrell, *Social Ethos*, 210–16; Downs, "Is God Paul's Patron?," 147–51; Dunn, *Beginning from Jerusalem*, 563–65; Gorman, *Cruciformity*, 290–91.

53. Welborn, *Paul's Summons to Messianic Life*, 55–56; see also 79–80.

REJECTING PATRONAGE

But perhaps I am jumping ahead of myself by arguing that the support the Pauline faction received from Macedonia (and elsewhere) was an example of sibling-based economic mutuality practiced over against patronage. After all, E. A. Judge recognizes Paul's discomfort with the ways in which money was being manipulated at Corinth to create forms of subordination that the Pauline faction saw as opposed to the good news of Jesus, but Judge goes on to argue that they still recognized other patrons—notably, Phoebe, who is described as Paul's patron in Rom 16:1–2.[54] This is the only time in the Pauline writings that we see this term used for any person involved with the assemblies of Jesus loyalists. However, we should note that having a client (Paul) recommend a patron (Phoebe) is an inappropriate reversal of the protocol related to patronage.[55] Patrons were to recommend clients, not vice versa. Add to this that Paul also refers to Phoebe as a "sister" and a "servant"—one who is commended not for being a benefactor but for the *service she has performed*—and that she is being recommended in order to *receive* material support, and one begins to think that Phoebe is a very strange kind of "patron" indeed. Judge resolves this by arguing that the Pauline faction recognizes Phoebe as a patron while placing no value on patronage as such, as their focus is upon the mutual subordination of all to one another and to the Anointed.[56] Lampe draws a similar conclusion and argues that, while there may be times when the form (but not function) of patronage appears within the early assemblies of Jesus loyalists, any effort to impose "vertical" or hierarchical power dynamics and relationships into those assemblies was resisted by an "egalitarian maxim" which was rooted in the desire for horizontal symmetry to govern the assemblies as all were now equal before God and should possess the same equality with one another.[57]

---

54. Judge, *Social Distinctives of the Christians*, 171–72. See also White who thinks Paul received patronal support from other assemblies, although White recognizes that Paul's language could be friendship language devoid of patronal implications (see White, "Paul and *Pater Families*," 468).

55. See Lampe, "Paul, Patrons, and Clients," 498–99; Agosto, "Patronage and Commendation," 123.

56. See Judge, *Social Distinctives of the Christians*, 106–8. Strom follows the lead of Judge here (Strom, *Reframing Paul*, 174–77).

57. See Lampe, "Paul, Patrons, and Clients," 495–98, 505. Hence, Jeffers also concludes that there was "no connection between financial patronage and congregational authority" (Jeffers, *Greco-Roman World*, 83).

Gerd Theissen is more skeptical of this. He argues for a greater degree of tension within the assemblies associated with the Pauline faction—and he argues that this tension is found in Paul himself. Just as the Greek *polis* affirmed the equal rights of all, while actually embracing a firm hierarchy of rights, Theissen argues that Paul could hold that all were equal, while affirming the practice of inequality between "the strong" and "the weak."[58] Theissen argues that this inequality is rooted in a "compassion ethic"—i.e., inequality is accepted through the language of care for others.[59] Hence, he concludes that:

> On the one hand, early Christianity [sic] was a "revolution of values" through which groups outside the ruling class acquired a chance in life. . . . On the other hand, there are unmistakable signs of repression. . . . Paradoxically enough, "revolutionary" and "repressive" tendencies can be found in close proximity to each other.[60]

In a later work, Theissen rephrases this somewhat: the practice of solidarity prevents the assemblies from simply becoming the social clientele of some rich patrons, even though rich patrons were a key component of those assemblies.[61]

While I agree with Theissen that both "revolutionary" and "repressive" tendencies were found in close proximity in the early Jesus movement—especially at Corinth—I think it is wrong (in this case) to posit that those tendencies are found in the Pauline faction.[62] I also question the value of finding the "form" but not the "function" of patronage in the Pauline letters, especially when it comes to economic practices. True, this seems to be occurring in one isolated and very unusual case—in the reference to Phoebe—but it is quite possible that a focus upon this exceptional case may distract us from the very different way of sharing life together that may be occurring within the early assemblies of Jesus loyalists.[63] Granted, one could make a comparison to the patronage sys-

---

58. Theissen, *Social Reality and the Early Christians*, 276–77.
59. Theissen, *Social Reality and the Early Christians*, 276–77.
60. Theissen, *Social Reality and the Early Christians*, 279.
61. Theissen, *Religion of the Earliest Christians*, 93. I've already discussed the reasons why I think this conclusion about the supposed wealth of these so-called patrons is misguided in volume 1.
62. I say "in this case" because I think both those tendencies are found in Paulinism in some other cases—for example, in its affirmation of heteronormativity.
63. It seems to me that we know too little about the situation of the assembly or

tem any time money is given from one party to another, but one should wonder if another economic model is more appropriate as a descriptor of what is happening. In order to explore this further, we should look at some of the actual economic and material practices of the assemblies of Jesus loyalists associated with the Pauline faction. We will begin with the most significant effort, the "Collection" gathered from throughout the eastern part of the empire on behalf of the poor members of the assembly (or assemblies) of Jesus loyalists in Jerusalem.

The Collection as an Example of Sibling-Based Economic Mutualism

The Significance of the Collection

The Collection is a central and definitive example of the economic practices that the Pauline faction encouraged among the early assemblies of Jesus loyalists. This is true not only because of the geographical span of the project—from Macedonia, to Corinth, to Rome, to Jerusalem—but also because of the temporal span of the project. The Collection is initiated as early as Paul's meeting with other apostles in Jerusalem and continues up until his return to Jerusalem (when, according to Luke, Paul was arrested and imprisoned for a lengthy period of time).[64] Hence, we find reference to this endeavor in four different letters written by Paul and

---

assemblies of Jesus loyalists at Rome, including Paul and Phoebe, to know why the Pauline faction chose to employ the word "patron" on this one occasion. Some have suggested that this word is used to boost her support and status within an environment unknown to Paul himself, but that would seem to go against other titles applied to Phoebe, and the Pauline faction's general way of relating to dominant imperial themes and cultural motifs within the rest of the letter (this is explored in Elliott, *Arrogance of Nations*). On another note, Agosto's "Patronage and Commendation, Imperial and Anti-Imperial," suggests that some of this mimicry and subversion of "form" but not "function" may be occurring at multiple sites. Agosto's study is quite fascinating as he looks at the ways in which Pauline words of commendation (in 1 Thess 5:12–13; 1 Cor 16:15–18; Phil 2:25–30; 4:2–3; Rom 16:1–2) are borrowed from the patronage system. He concludes that the parallel exists only in form and not in function, as the ways in which the form is employed generally contradicts the values of the patronage system (Agosto, "Patronage and Commendation," 110–23).

64. See Georgi, *Remember the Poor*, 15; Nickle, *Collection*, 100. Thompson questions some of this and notes that a proper chronology is "notoriously difficult" to construct and would be "highly speculative" (Thompson, "Paul's Collection," 11). However, he concludes that the significance of the Collection for Paul—regardless of the exact chronological details—cannot be contested (15).

PAULINE SOLIDARITY

his coworkers (Gal 2:10; 6:6–10; 1 Cor 16:1–4; 2 Cor 8:1–9:15; 12:14–18; Rom 15:25–32) and, in the case of the letters to the Corinthians, a sizeable amount of material is focused on it.[65] Consequently, several scholars appropriately conclude that the Collection was a "central preoccupation" of the "utmost importance" to the Pauline faction, with Paul himself being willing to "risk his own life" to bring the initiative to fruition.[66]

In particular, the way in which the Collection is taken to be *the* paradigmatic tangible embodiment of much of the ideo-theology affirmed by Paul and his coworkers should be emphasized. As James Dunn writes: "Most important of all, the Collection sums up to a unique degree the way in which Paul's theology, missionary work, and pastoral concern held together as a single whole."[67] It is this form of economic sharing that makes present (and demonstrates the unity of) the body of (the) Anointed.[68] It is *this* which demonstrates what "love" is.[69] The Collection is the "practical agape" which defines the new family of God (see 2 Cor 8:7–8, 24; Rom 15:30).[70] The same applies to notions of "ministry" that are expressed in the Pauline letters. The Collection as *diakonia* is an "essential act of Christian [sic] fellowship fulfilled in the service of the Lord" (see 2 Cor 8:4; 9:1, 12; Rom 15:31).[71] Such financial ministry made good

---

65. Of course, it is possible that some of the references—notably Gal 2:10—refer to earlier efforts to raise famine relief money for the poor in Jerusalem (see Nickle, *Collection*, 59). However, concluding this would not undermine the significance of this economic practice within the early assemblies of Jesus loyalists. Far from it, it would show that collections were taking place in multiple places on multiple occasions which would only further affirm the centrality of this practice of transnational economic mutuality. As Oakes argues, Rom 12:6–8 also makes a case for this as a general practice as "sharing" (and "showing mercy" in this context should be understood as related to economic practices; see Oakes, *Reading Romans in Pompeii*, 106).

66. See, in order, Thompson, "Paul's Collection," 15; Downs, "Is God Paul's Patron?," 151, Longenecker, *Remember the Poor*, 312; Horrell, *Solidarity and Difference*, 231.

67. Dunn, *Theology of Paul the Apostle*, 707; see also 706–7. See Elliott, "Strategies of Resistance," 109–10. Sadly, as one works through the thousands of pages Dunn has written about Paul, one quickly discovers that the Collection does not have anything close to the same significance in his own theology, scholarly work, and pastoral concern.

68. See Georgi, *Remember the Poor*, 153; Cousar, *Introduction to the New Testament*, 46; Tenney, *New Testament Times*, 300; Longenecker, *Ministry and Message of Paul*, 100; Scroggs, *Paul for a New Day*, 42–44.

69. See Nickle, *Collection*, 102–3; Schrage, *Ethics of the New Testament*, 231–32.

70. See Wright, *Paul*, 165–67.

71. Nickle, *Collection*, 109; see also 106–9. Thompson takes *diakonia* to mean

sense in a context where other political-appointed ministers (*diakonia*) in civic assemblies were tasked with engaging in financial projects like famine relief. Similarly, the only time that the Pauline faction actually uses the word "equality" (*isothes*) is in 2 Cor 8:13–14 when the Collection is being discussed (although this does resonant with Phil 2:5–11, when the Pauline faction talks about Jesus's "being equal with God" due to his cruciform life):

> I do not mean that there should be relief for others and distress on you, but it is a question of equality between your present abundance and their need, so that [at some future time] their abundance may be for your need, in order that there may be equality.

Here, Paul and his coworkers are possibly alluding to the exodus tradition of gathering manna (see Exod 16:18).[72] Each family was to gather enough to meet their daily needs. No one had too little and no one had too much. Each had enough. Paul and his coworkers take this exodus tradition as representative of what equality looks like in the material distribution of goods within the assemblies of Jesus loyalists. "Equality" is demonstrated by following the exodus tradition and implementing a form of "mutuality and reciprocity that is responsive to need."[73] In other words, this sharing does not create equality; rather, equality is expressed in this kind of sharing.[74] Beyond the exodus tradition, in the Graeco-Roman context, equality was understood as the basis of democratic relationships between diverse groups and, here, the Pauline faction are requiring that this claim to equality is fulfilled in a tangible, material manner.[75] Furthermore, in some Hellenistic Judean traditions, this equality was seen as fundamental to preserving concord in the cosmos and so the Pauline faction urges a material redistribution of (admittedly very limited) wealth in order to achieve this.[76] Another term for this equality, then, is economic mutualism. Given the universal financial precarity of the individual assemblies,

---

"providing the necessities of life" (Thompson, "Paul's Collection," 136).

72. See Georgi, *Remember the Poor*, 1965, 84–85; Thompson, "Paul's Collection," 83–86. Also, briefly, Horsley, "Building An Alternative Society," 213.

73. Sampley, *Walking Between the Times*, 40.

74. Thompson, "Paul's Collection," 83–84.

75. See Welborn, "That There May Be Equality," 83–85.

76. Welborn, "That There May Be Equality," 86–87.

Pauline Solidarity

support would flow in different directions at different times.[77] It is in this practice of corporate solidarity that David Horrell finds a "metanorm" of the ethics proposed by the Pauline faction.[78]

Consequently, one cannot claim to understand let alone practice what Paul and his coworkers mean when they speak about unity, love, kinship, ministry, and equality apart from this kind of economic mutuality. Unity, love, kinship, and equality were not transcendental attributes that were solely related to the status one had before God or to *feelings* one had about a sibling with a different socioeconomic status level—nor was ministry understood to be a strictly spiritual matter. There is no room here for "mystical introversion."[79] Unity, love, kinship, ministry, and equality were found in the practice of economic mutuality, wherein those who experienced a (relatively small) surplus distributed it to those who were unable to generate even enough to feed themselves on any given day.

Likewise, we should emphasize that this is how one tangibly demonstrated one's faith in (and loyalty to!) the abundant grace of God, which was able to bring abundance out of poverty.[80] This is made clear in 2 Cor 8:7–8: "Each of you must vie as you have made up your mind, not reluctantly or under compulsion, for God loves a cheerful giver. And God is able to provide you with every blessing in abundance, so that by always having enough of everything you may share abundantly in every good work." Hence, while some have experienced the "surpassing grace of God" (1 Cor 9:14), participating in the Collection becomes a means of "sowing and increasing the harvest of their [justice]" (1 Cor 9:10). In other words, as Georgi argues, this is justification in praxis.[81] This is what the process of making things just looks like. It is by means of this kind of

---

77. See Horrell, *Solidarity and Difference*, 239.

78. Horrell, *Solidarity and Difference*, 99; see also 99–132.

79. Georgi, *Remember the Poor*, 52.

80. See Cousar, *Introduction to the New Testament*, 46. Here it is important to remember that "faith" is not just a belief but the act by which all the benefits of the work of the Anointed are taken into a person's life. See Davies, *Jewish and Pauline Studies*, 215–17; Oscar, *Salvation in History*, 12; Deissmann, *Paul*, 161–64; Kahl, *Galatians Re-Imagined*, 281; Crossan and Borg, *First Paul*, 168. This is the basic stance of one's existence in the Anointed and it counters the form of faithfulness required by the Roman ideo-theology (see Deissmann, *Paul*, 164; Scroggs, *Paul for a New Day*, 26–33; Howard-Brook and Gwyther, *Unveiling Empire*, 182, 231; Carter, *John and Empire*, 266–73).

81. Georgi, *Remember the Poor*, 158–60.

economic mutuality that one participates in the cycle of grace initiated by God the father of Jesus the Anointed. This is why Paul and his coworkers regularly refer to the Collection as a "gift" (2 Cor 8:12, 20; 9:5, 7, 15).[82] Grace gives birth to grace—the self-giving of the Anointed leads to sharing all one has within the household of God.[83]

Therefore, notions of loyalty (faithfulness), divine abundance, justice, the making just of the structures of one's community, and grace are all connected to the Collection. This is also related to Pauline eschatology, and it is surely related to matters concerning the unification of Judeans and other ethnicities or nationalities within the body of the Anointed. Therefore, we cannot avoid the conclusion that Dunn is perfectly on point when he argues that this economic practice uniquely summarizes the theology, work, and concern of the Pauline faction.

Prominent Interpretations: Minimizing the Economic Relevance of the Collection

Having highlighted the significance of the Collection to Paul and his coworkers—and to the assemblies of Jesus loyalists more broadly—it is interesting to observe how the history of Christian interpretations related to the Collection has sought to minimize its economic relevance. Given that this practice is about *sharing money* with those who are said to be *poor* within a newly constituted transnational household—wherein all the members are encouraged to relate to one another as siblings—one may think that this is a difficult move to sustain. Yet one finds a long history of reading the Collection as being significant for anything but economic reasons. I suspect that the relatively high level of status and class privilege experienced by prominent interpreters of these passages has a lot to do with this—those who enjoy a comfortable position within the status quo tend to (consciously or not) have trouble affirming or even identifying that which may unsettle their comfort and material wealth.[84]

---

82. See Nickle, *Collection*, 109–10; Bockmuehl, *Jewish Law in Gentile Churches*, 140; Crossan and Reed, *In Search of Paul*, 385–87.

83. Georgi, *Remember the Poor*, 152–53.

84. So, when Paul and his coworkers talk about radical acts of economic mutuality as being a definitive practice among those who claim to follow Jesus, they must really be talking about, well, as we will see, any number of other things, so long as the implication is not that contemporary people who claim to follow Jesus should also engage in this kind of economic mutuality! Of course, this is a bit of a caricatured position to

Consequently, a great deal of emphasis has been laid upon the purported eschatological significance of the Collection and, concomitantly, upon its significance for establishing good relations between Judeans and foreign nationals within the body of the Anointed.

Beginning with a rather extreme example, Horsley and Silberman postulate that Paul believed that his personal deliverance of the Collection to Jerusalem would trigger the dawning of the kingdom of God.[85] In a related but less extreme way, Georgi and Nickle argue that the Collection is made for the poor at Jerusalem because Jerusalem was an eschatologically prominent location, and so the assembly (or assemblies) of Jesus loyalists there needed to be maintained as an "eschatological outpost."[86] Georgi then pushes this in the same direction, followed by Horsley and Silberman: the Collection becomes the eschatological pilgrimage of the nations to pay tribute to the God of Israel in Jerusalem and, as such, it becomes a sign of the "last times."[87] Nickle agrees and sees Paul's party as the delegates nominated to bring the firstfruit of the nations to Zion to worship in the end times.[88]

In this regard, the reference to those who benefited from the Collection as "the poor" could also be drawing upon the language employed within some apocalyptic Judean groups, which referred to the eschatological remnant as "the poor."[89] Georgi is careful to maintain this as a both/and scenario—wherein those in Jerusalem are both an eschatological remnant and those who are experiencing material poverty—but not all subsequent interpreters have been keen to hold onto the material poverty side of this equation.

---

take—and it certainly does not apply to Georgi's study of the Collection, or the broader counter-imperial work done by Horsley—but it is all too often the result of scholarly studies of these matters.

85. Horsley and Silberman, *Message and the Kingdom*, 186. Sanders essentially agrees in his *Paul: The Apostle's Life*, 437.

86. Georgi, *Remember the Poor*, 38–42; Nickle, *Collection*, 60.

87. Georgi, *Remember the Poor*, 100. Georgi falls short of saying what Horsley and Silberman say—i.e., that the Collection will actually trigger the final dawning of the kingdom—although he does say that the Jesus loyalists were experiencing a general sense of "impending eschatology completion" after the resurrection appearances of Jesus (Georgi, *Remember the Poor*, 36–38). That said, he also reads this eschatological interpretation in a more positive materialist light as he believes that Paul has succeeded in "fully historicizing the mystical theme of spiritual worship" in the Collection (107).

88. Nickle, *Collection*, 138.

89. See Georgi, *Remember the Poor*, 33–35; Nickle, *Collection*, 138.

Holmberg follows Georgi's view but nuances it in two ways: first, he believes that the material poverty experienced by those in Jerusalem is due to failed efforts at "communism" (as described in Acts 2:44–47; 4:32–37) exacerbated by an influx of Galilean Jesus loyalists and an increase in persecution.[90] The irony, not observed by Holmberg, would be that the Pauline faction, in conjunction with the Jesus loyalists in Jerusalem, would be advocating for the reproduction of the exact same economic practice within other assemblies that led to the impoverishment of the assembly at Jerusalem.

Holmberg's second nuance is that the Collection is made in order to demonstrate the subordination of all other local assemblies to the central assembly in Jerusalem.[91] Georgi and Nickle explicitly disagree with this suggestion. They believe that the Collection was provocative for precisely the opposite reason—it was the manifestation of an eschatological reversal, wherein delegates from the nations arrive at Jerusalem as the true Israel, after the Judeans rejected God's Anointed.[92] Thus, the Pauline faction's hope would be to prompt the Judeans to jealousy and to a new acceptance of "the gospel."[93] However, both Georgi and Nickle emphasize that, despite this provocation, Paul and his coworkers are motivated by a desire to bring unity to the broader Jesus movement and, in particular, to demonstrate the unity of Judean and non-Judean elements.[94] This tends to be the perspective that has gained the most traction among scholars—the primary goal of the Collection is to demonstrate and foster the unity-in-diversity of Judeans and foreign nationals, to repair relationships that have fractured (as, for example, occurred in the split between Paul and Cephas in Antioch [see Gal 2:11–14]), and to recognize the legitimacy of both the faction associated with Paul and the faction(s) associated with Jerusalem.[95]

90. Holmberg, *Paul and Power*, 35–37.

91. See Holmberg, *Paul and Power*, 15–43. Holmberg argues that Paul originally agrees to this sign of subordination but, as Paul's thinking develops, his view of the Collection broadens. Sandra Hack Polaski argues for more ambiguity in relation to this, observing that giving money could be a sign of patronage just as much as it could be a sign of subordination (Polaski, *Paul*, 85–89).

92. See Georgi, *Remember the Poor*, 117–19; Nickle, *Collection*, 68–70, 139.

93. Nickle, *Collection*, 136. See also Esler, *Conflict and Identity in Romans*, 359.

94. See Georgi, *Remember the Poor*, 55; Nickle, *Collection*, 9, 115–17, 125–27.

95. See Holmberg, *Paul and Power*, 38; Thompson, "Paul's Collection," 143–45; Dunn, *Beginning from Jerusalem*, 755; Polaski, *Paul*, 96–99; Longenecker, *Remember the Poor*, 313; Dumbrell, *Search for Order*, 259, 263, 268–80.

What, then, are we to make of these theoretical readings of a thoroughly material practice? First, it is likely that there is an eschatological element to the Collection as it was related to the recognition and incorporation of foreigners *as foreigners* (i.e., foreigners who were not circumcised and did not follow Sabbath and food laws) into the people of God.[96] However, it likely does not have the eschatological significance to the Pauline faction that Georgi and Nickle—not to mention Horsley and Silberman—suggest. The union of Judeans and other peoples within the people of God *was* an eschatological event, but it seems a stretch to posit that Paul and his coworkers thought the Collection would prompt any sort of dramatic "end times" event.[97] After all, why would Paul make plans to continue his travels by going to Rome (and then onwards to Spain?) after he delivers the Collection to Jerusalem?[98] More probably, while the deliverance of the Collection to Jerusalem was a manifestation of the general eschatological moment in which Paul and his coworkers believed they lived, its primary importance was not eschatological. Rather, its primary importance was economic.[99] That this economic practice also had eschatological relevance simply furthers the point made by Dunn earlier—the Collection, in many ways, sums up central elements of Paulinism. Consequently, a focus upon the eschatological element—whether related to some form of imminent expectation or to the general eschatological union of Judeans and people from other regions—should never distract us from the importance of the economic practice. Unfortunately, this happens all too frequently and for understandable reasons—if this is simply the manifestation of an eschatological belief (and perhaps even a mistaken eschatological belief?), then contemporary Christians are liberated from any need to emulate this kind of concrete practice of

---

96. Here the reference to "zeal" in relation to the Collection in 2 Cor 9:2 is significant. Within the Judean tradition, zeal is that which marks out those who are particularly committed to serving God in courageous ways, regardless of the consequences for self or others.

97. I believe that this fits with the general scholarly consensus on this matter. For more, see Thompson, "Paul's Collection," 1–2, 6, 96–98, 140–43.

98. One of the better points made by Thompson, "Paul's Collection," 142. Also Horrell, *Solidarity and Difference*, 234.

99. Of course, economics and eschatology need to be understood as thoroughly intertwined at this point. Here Friesen's observation is especially important. He remarks that "study of Paul's Collection has focused primarily on the ideological level and needs to be complemented by attention to the real exchange of goods and services brought about by Paul's economic practice" (Friesen, "Paul and Economics," 47).

love, unity, faith, justice, and grace. A more Pauline eschatology would be one that continues to see the present moment as "'the now time' . . . Messianic time, which is charged to the bursting point with hope" thereby encouraging people in the present to engage in "the equalization of resources between persons of *different* social classes through voluntary redistribution."[100] Pauline eschatology is shot through with this kind of economic materialism. After all, as Rom 12:1–2 states, religious sacrifices are still made, but these are now embodied, economic, collective sacrifices made in solidarity with others who are also suffering under Roman imperialism.[101]

Indeed, even those who have highlighted the economic aspect of the Collection have tended to shy away from this conclusion and have reduced it from a practice of economic *mutuality* to a practice of *charity*, or they have reiterated the subordination motif mentioned above. For example, Nickle notes parallels that exist between the Collection and charitable provisions that existed on behalf of the poor within Second Temple Judaism(s)—even though he ultimately finds those parallels to be unconvincing.[102] Elliot also points out how the ways in which the Judeans at Rome were known to participate in acts of charity or assistance to Judean communities located in other cities in the empire.[103] However, this element is rarely emphasized by interpreters and, when it is mentioned or supported, the assumption tends to be that the Collection is then simply a kind of alms-giving or charitable donation. This does not approach the kind of economic mutuality and solidarity being expressed in the Collection (even if the charitable practices of Second Temple Judaism were an important jumping-off point for the Jesus movement).[104]

An economic practice that has gained more attention is a comparison of the Collection to the half-shekel temple tax collected from diasporic Judeans (with imperial permission because, in part, this tax paid for daily sacrifices made for the health and well-being of the emperor)

---

100. Welborn, "That There May Be Equality," 89–90. Welborn makes an important contemporary point even if, for reasons provided above, I feel he overstates the level of economic stratification that existed between the members of the assemblies associated with Paul and his coworkers.

101. See Oakes, *Reading Romans in Pompeii*, 99–100; Jennings, *Outlaw Justice*, 180, 187.

102. Nickle, *Collection*, 93–95.

103. Elliott, "Disciplining the Hope," 182. He cites Cicero, *Flac.* 28.66–69.

104. More on this below.

that existed during Paul's day (up until the Judean revolt that resulted in the destruction of Jerusalem in 70 CE, after which the temple tax was collected on behalf of the imperial cult[s]). Nickle notes several parallels: (1) both were delivered to Jerusalem; (2) Pentecost was an important date for delivery; (3) men were appointed from each local community to accompany the funds; (4) central reception points were established; (5) advantageous use was made of official protections; (6) prudently setting aside money was encouraged; (7) special care was taken to ensure that people associated with the money could not be vilified; and (8) the action was taken as a tangible manifestation of unity and solidarity.[105] However, Nickle also notes the following differences: (1) the tax was collected for the purchase of sacrifices (including those made for the emperor), whereas the Pauline Collection was made on behalf of the poor; (2) the tax claims to belong to a tradition dating back to Moses, whereas Paul and his coworkers lay claim to no prior tradition; (3) the Pauline faction had far less detailed regulations about the gathering of the Collection; (4) the tax was annual, but the Collection was related to particular events occurring at a particular time and place; (5) the tax amount was legislated but the amount for the Collection was not; and (6) the payment of the tax was compulsory, whereas participation in the Collection was voluntary.[106] Consequently, it seems best to conclude that while Paul and his coworkers may have imitated or been inspired by the temple tax, it is likely that they understood the Collection to be something rather different.

This then leaves us with Georgi's tentative suggestion that Jubilee-based principles may have been in mind when Paul and his coworkers began to formulate and enact the Collection.[107] That may be a better angle to begin to approach what was, as far as I can tell, an historically

---

105. Nickle, *Collection*, 87–89.

106. Nickle, *Collection*, 90–93. Deissmann's observation that Pauline reference to the Collection as a *logia*, which derives from terms primarily used for religious collections for the gods could support this reading, although it is not necessarily the case that it does so given the Pauline emphasis that everything a person does should be an act of worship (Deissmann, *Light from the Ancient East*, 104–5). Thompson agrees with Nickle that there are methodological parallels to the temple tax, but thinks that Nickle stretches the case a fair bit—he argues that the location is incidental, that Paul may have already planned on being in Jerusalem for Passover regardless of the Collection, that we don't know if Paul took advantage of any official concessions, and that taking care against vilification is just common sense (Thompson, "Paul's Collection," 61n53).

107. Georgi, *Remember the Poor*, 156.

unprecedented action of economic mutuality practiced by poor communities across national, ethnic, gendered, religious, and social divides.

The Collection as the Practice of Sibling-Based Economic Mutuality

> [The "Collection"] was a symbol of resistance and subversion, and it was at the heart of an anti-imperial and anti-hegemonic protest. At the same time, it was also a daring proposal to reorder economic life.
>
> —Sze-kar Wan[108]

It is by means of the Collection that Paul and his coworkers demonstrate the material nature of what later theologians have referred to as the "catholicity" and unity of the various assemblies of Jesus loyalists who gathered in cities far removed from one another.[109] Observing this point leads us to a different conclusion than those drawn by scholars who have argued that Paul only cared about local communities and was not concerned with participating in the formation of any kind of "universal" body. This is truly an international or, better yet, transnational undertaking. Geographical, national, and cultural boundaries are not only transcended but violated and abolished by the economic mutuality practiced by the members of the household of God.[110] This means that the Collection is a genuinely revolutionary act. It is revolutionary because it goes against the conventions the empire had established for relationships between conquered peoples. The vanquished are not to establish solidarity networks with one another that are devoid of Roman mediation and control, and they are especially not to establish networks that are emancipatory and challenge the values and practices of the imperial status quo.[111] The Judeans gained a special exemption from the emperor

---

108. Wan, "Collection for the Saints," 196.

109. See Georgi, *Remember the Poor*, 51.

110. See Theissen, *Religion of the Earliest Churches*, 88, 94; Sampley, *Walking Between the Times*, 40; Thompson, "Paul's Collection," 153; Oakes, *Reading Romans in Pompeii*, 116.

111. See Wright, *Paul*, 170; Wan, "Collection for the Saints," 191–215; Lopez, *Apostle to the Conquered*, 150. In this regard, despite the strengths of their argument, Horsley and Silberman miss the point to a certain extent. They assert that, by the time

in order to make the gathering of the temple tax both legal and possible (and, apart from many other acts of loyalty, the daily sacrifices made for the emperor that this funded helped maintain imperial approval of this practice). However, the Jesus loyalists had no such exemption and, in the absence of that, collecting funds in this way would be considered deeply troubling and treasonous. Further, as far as I can tell, the Collection is revolutionary because it is new. For the first time, we see a *transnational network of poor people finding a way to connect with one another and care for one another*.[112] To quote Horsley and Silberman, this is "an unprecedented act of cooperation and sharing of resources that could help overcome the subjugation of *all* peoples."[113] Thus, while something like this kind of economic mutuality was regularly practiced in local communities of poor people within the Roman Empire, the extension of this practice to the transnational level is striking and unique.[114] Yet this, according to Paul and his coworkers, is what the in-breaking of the justice of God looks like. It is, quite literally, the kingdom of the poor. Again, Horsley and Silberman express this well: "Paul was beginning to forge an empire-wide movement of suffering and disenfranchised people who dreamed of being the beneficiaries, not the victims, of an all-powerful emperor."[115] Efrain Agosto summarizes things in this way: "Paul's collection 'for the poor among the saints at Jerusalem' constituted a kind of

---

of his imprisonment in Ephesus, when the letter is written to the Philippians, Paul has become aware that monetary sharing and spiritual selflessness do more than political agitation, class warfare, or nationalistic zeal (Horsley and Silberman, *Message and the Kingdom*, 182). While they may be correct to see Paul (and his coworkers) as seeking to overcome nationalistic zeal, the Collection is very much an agitating political act that is rooted in a conflict between the rich and poor, the colonizers and the colonized, and the empire and those it leaves for dead.

112. See Horsley, "1 Corinthians," 245–51; Callahan, "Paul, Ekklesia," 221; Lopez, *Apostle to the Conquered*, 146–50; Horrell, *Solidarity and Difference*, 115, 234–38.

113. Horsley and Silberman, *Message and the Kingdom*, 170.

114. In terms of local examples, Fitzpatrick sees the Collection as an example of the generosity that exists among people who are experiencing poverty. Horsley and Silberman explicitly link this moral economy of sharing that existed among people who experience poverty to the broader scope of the Collection (see Fitzpatrick, *Paul*, 56–57; Horsley and Silberman, *Message and the Kingdom*, 186). Such sharing proliferates among dispossessed and oppressed communities of people, in part because it is hard to survive without it and in part because people who are not sold out to imperial power structures tend to incline more towards life-giving ways of sharing life together (see, for example, Scott, *Art of Not Being Governed*; Kropotkin, *Mutual Aid*; Crow, *Black Flags and Windmills*).

115. Horsley and Silberman, *Message and the Kingdom*, 158.

underground economy in the international anti-imperial movement that Paul was building."[116] Consequently, Davina Lopez is right to recognize a clash of two universalisms: the universalism through patriarchal domination enforced by the Roman Empire, and the universalism created by establishing solidarity among those who were defeated by the empire.[117] This is, in a very material and tangible way, "reconciliatory justice-making through solidarity."[118] As an anti-imperial form of justice-making, it is also a concrete expression of resistance. The elite rulers would interpret this as a threatening act of "economic defiance."[119]

However, participation in this was voluntary. Paul and his coworkers may attempt to pressure or cajole various local assemblies to participate within this endeavor—and, as Thompson notes, go so far as to employ the rhetoric of honor and shame in order to challenge the Corinthians to match the Macedonians—but they never say that it is required.[120] Some, like Johannes Weiss, have taken this as evidence that what is asked for is a more standard form of "charity" or "sacrifice" and has nothing to do with "communistic demands or ideals."[121] However, Weiss's observation misses the point on at least two counts. First, Paul and his coworkers lived in a context far removed from Eastern-Bloc communism. They were developing an economic way of sharing life together that was rooted within sibling-based relationships that extended, with material ramifications, throughout the transnational household of God. Second, the voluntary nature of the project does not diminish its centrality. As we observed above, the Collection was intimately and inextricably related to many central themes developed by Paul and his coworker and it was of pivotal significance to their work. Participation should not need to be mandated.

---

116. Agosto, "Patronage and Commendation," 122.

117. Lopez, *Apostle to the Conquered*, 166–68. See also Wan, "Collection for the Saints," 191–215, esp. 196.

118. Lopez, *Apostle to the Conquered*, 168; emphasis removed.

119. Horsley and Silberman, *Message and the Kingdom*, 185. See also Wright, *Paul*, 170.

120. Thompson; "Paul's Collection," 74–78. See also Goguel, *Primitive Church*, 252. Thompson also notes that, despite this rhetorical power-play, Paul and his coworkers are still trying to establish an economic arrangement that contravenes and goes outside of conventions related to honor and shame (Thompson, "Paul's Collection," 87, 152).

121. Weiss, *Earliest Christianity*, 2:593–94. Kautsky, from an opposing end of the political spectrum, makes the same mistakes as Weiss when discussing communism in relation to the economics of the assemblies associated with the Pauline faction (see Kautsky, *Foundations of Christianity*, 280–84, 292–93).

Pauline Solidarity

Here, one finds a rejection of the Roman tactic of deploying lethal force in order to fabricate a "voluntary" consensus among the vanquished. Within the assemblies associated with the Pauline faction, if one refused to engage in this form of economic mutuality, then one was simply demonstrating that one had understood little or nothing about what it means to be a member of the body of the Anointed and a representative citizen within assemblies that functioned as outposts of the justice of God.[122]

That said, part of the reason to emphasize the voluntary nature of this participation is to ensure that the form of economic sharing being practiced is not incorporated into previously existing models of patronage. This is to be an economic practice detached from any sense of enforced duty, lest cycles of debt and obligation enter into the household of God or, even worse, lest the power hierarchies that exist within the empire start to enter into and disrupt the egalitarian relationships within the body of the Anointed. The Collection is "mutualism against patronage" and, as such, it is a critical strategy.[123] To avoid patronage, we see the following factors implemented: (a) all praise is to go to God; (b) the one making the contribution was not to be this or that individual but an entire community; (c) Paul distances himself from being perceived of as a benefactor; and (d) an essentially horizontal, rather than vertical, form of economic mutuality is established.[124] Money is now shared between equals and peers—siblings—and not between creditors and debtors, or patrons and clients.[125] In this way the patronage system is avoided. Not only this but also the successful spread of this kind of practice would destroy patron-client networks as they existed throughout the empire.[126] As people who lived in poor communities were increasingly able to rely upon one another, they would not need to seek the patronage of the powerful and would be liberated from their (spiritual, moral, social, and material) obligations to the elites. This, in turn, would foster an environment

---

122. Banks comes to a similar conclusion when discussing the voluntary nature of the Collection. However, he moves the conversation in an unhelpful direction by stressing that what is important is the *attitude* one takes to one's possessions (Banks, *Paul's Idea of Community*, 89–90).

123. Welborn, *Paul's Summons to Messianic Life*, 56–57.

124. Friesen, "Paul and Economic," 49–50; Downs, "Is God Paul's Patron?," 153; Pickett, "Conflicts at Corinth," 143.

125. See Georgi, *Remember the Poor*, 155–56.

126. See Howard-Brook and Gwyther, *Unveiling Empire*, 193; Friesen, "Paul and Economics," 49; Elliott, "Strategies of Resistance" 99–101; Jewett, *Romans*, 64–65.

that led assemblies to question the existence of such hierarchical arrangements in the first place (i.e., it would give rise to something like "class-consciousness"). Welborn is not wrong to then describe members of the newly constituted household of God as "militants of the messianic event, capable of unplugging themselves from the patronage system and devoting themselves entirely to mutual love, expressed concretely in the practice of economic mutualism."[127] No wonder, then, that Rome would not abide this sort of development. That the persecution of the early Jesus movement rapidly spread from local leaders to the highest imperial levels of authority after the state-sanctioned executions of Jesus and Paul should surprise nobody tracing this development.

This also helps to explain why those at Corinth who were seeking to benefit from importing or encouraging the patronage model sought to undercut the Collection by attacking Pauline efforts in that regard. The Super Apostles had charged the Pauline faction with robbing assemblies and pocketing money they had claimed was intended for the Collection.[128] By doing so, the Super Apostles hoped to discredit an effort that—if successful—would demolish the hierarchical power arrangements in which they were invested (and which they hoped to exploit to their own advantage). Their strategy is instructive. Rather than addressing the imbalance of power that existed within the status quo of the empire, rather than looking at the motivation for the Collection, and rather than engaging the underlying issues, the Super Apostles simply sought to vilify those who represented it and accused Paul and his coworkers of being thieves, bad friends (and here we do see friendship deployed in that less-than-honest patronal manner) and all-around social ingrates (see 2 Cor 12:14–18). Is this not the way that those with (relatively) more power than others always respond to challenges that arise from below? The passionate stance the Pauline faction then takes against the Super Apostles—while simultaneously trying to refocus the debate on the matters that they believe are priorities—is not surprising.

Finally, it should also be observed how this reformulates understandings of the call to "sacrifice" found within the Pauline writings. Some have charged Paul and, by implication, his coworkers with deepening

---

127. Welborn, *Paul's Summons to Messianic Life*, 69. The materialism of this really deserves to be emphasized given Christianity's history of spiritualizing all of this. Ward Blanton does a good job of developing this thesis in Blanton, *Materialism for the Masses*.

128. See Thompson, "Paul's Collection," 109–11; Horrell, *Social Ethos*, 224–25.

the ways in which people are enmeshed and held in bondage to oppressive relationships and socioeconomic dynamics because of their call to sacrifice (especially when paired with the valorization of humility). This criticism cuts to the core of many interpreters of Paul and the way in which Paulinism has been incorporated into patriarchal and imperial forms of Christianity—but something different is occurring with Paul and his coworkers. In relation to the practice of economic mutuality they sought to develop, the notion of "sacrifice" refers to the sharing of the little surplus one has with those who are below the subsistence level, with the understanding that this action would be reciprocated when the tables are turned (see 2 Cor 8:13–15). This is actually something that fosters liberation (just as solidarity with the humiliated is valorized not in order to enable abusers but to foster justice and freedom from abuse). Theissen summarizes it well: "Surrender does not lead to disadvantage, but to a real distribution of the commodities of life for all."[129] Hence, as Engberg-Pedersen emphasizes, the call to altruism is not to be equated with "abject self-surrender" but, instead, means that one comes to see one's self not primarily as an "I" but, first and foremost, as part of a "we."[130] Therefore, when Paul and his coworkers urge the Philippians to not look to their own interests but to the interests of others (Phil 2:4), all of this is understood in light of the body metaphor offered in 1 Cor 12:12–27 (or, more immediately, the citizenship mentioned in Phil 3:20). All are members of one body—each member helps care for that body, and each member is cared for by that body. This, then, is what it means to be united with the Anointed. This is new creation, for, as Crossan and Reed ask: "What better deserves the title of a new creation than the abnormalcy of a share-world replacing the normalcy of a greed-world?"[131]

Sharing against Private Property

Before exploring some of the other ways in which sibling-based economics impacted the material practices of the early Jesus loyalists, it should be emphasized how this kind of mutuality requires those who participate

---

129. Theissen, *Religion of the Earliest Churches*, 159. Theissen observes that precisely this understanding of surrender—or sacrifice—is symbolically depicted in the Eucharist.

130. Engberg-Pedersen, *Paul and the Stoics*, 198, 202–3, 207, 210–11.

131. Crossan and Reed, *In Search of Paul*, 176; emphasis removed.

within it to reexamine their understanding of private property. As the Collection makes clear, and as Dieter Georgi observes: "The concepts of private property and private ownership find in Paul no place at all."[132] To defend private property is to tear down the nature of the relationships that Jesus loyalists are to have with one another as siblings (indeed, Paul and his coworkers go so far as to state that one's body does not even belong to one's self but actually belongs to God [see 1 Cor 6:19–20]).[133]

By seeking to establish this kind of sibling-based economy of sharing against private property, Paul and his coworkers are simply following in the trajectory established by the earlier assemblies of Jesus loyalists in Jerusalem, who, in turn, followed the practices modeled by Jesus and those who gathered with him.[134] Similarly, Jesus himself was developing the Torah-based tradition which understood that any claim to private property was always subordinated to the obligation to care for the more vulnerable members of society.[135] Indeed, the Torah actually focuses more on matters related to wealth and poverty than any other issue when it came to the structuring of communal life together.[136] Consequently, it is no surprise that Judeans were known throughout the empire for their care of people experiencing material poverty within their communities.[137] It is also no surprise to see this kind of sibling-based sharing carry over into the early assemblies of Jesus loyalists and some subsequent factions of Christianity.[138] What we discover here is a consistent tradition that subordinates the surplus of those who have a little more to the needs of those who do not have enough to get by. From the Torah, to Jesus, to the early Jesus movement, the goal was the creation of a household—an extended

---

132. Georgi, *Remember the Poor*, 160–61. The sentence concludes: "Nor do the accompanying notions of credit, debt, obligation, interest, dividend, profit, market, temple, or bank."

133. Georgi, *Remember the Poor*, 149.

134. See Hengel, *Property and Riches*, 23–33. Hengel refers to this as a form of "love communism," which, while being a fairly accurate descriptor imports a foreign political ideology into a practice that was really rooted in the reorientation of one's kinship.

135. See Hengel, *Property and Riches*, 12–22.

136. See Barton, "Money Matter," 39.

137. Countryman, *Rich Christians in the Church*, 103–5; Hengel, *Property and Riches*, 1.

138. See Countryman, *Rich Christians in the Church*, 103; and González's study on this topic, *Faith and Wealth*. Wes Howard-Brook, however, convincingly tempers much of this in his more critical work, *Empire Baptized*.

family—wherein all things are shared so that everyone has enough. Paul and his coworkers are simply rooting themselves within this tradition. It is a tradition that believes Life—and the abundant flourishing of life within each person—is of greater importance than the surplus material wealth of any.

However, while the Pauline faction is following practices that defined the Jesus movement while Jesus was still alive, this practice completely contradicted the Roman legal tradition regarding private property.[139] As David Graeber explains, the Romans defined property, or *dominium*, as a relation between a person and a thing, characterized by the absolute power of that person over that thing—private property is the most fundamental kind of property (as opposed to communal property, for example), and private property encapsulates the notion of the owner's absolute power to do anything whatsoever with their property.[140] Essentially, Graeber explains, the Romans developed this view of private property because their empire was premised upon slavery—which is a relation between two people, wherein one person is actually treated as a thing owned by another person, to be used in any way that owner sees fit.[141] This is why the term *dominium* first appears in Latin in the Late Republic when hundreds of thousands of slaves were transforming Italy into a slave-based society. In light of these structural changes the authority of the *paterfamilias*, the head of the *domus*, was extended to *dominium* over property.[142] The father had the right to do whatever he pleased with his slaves—even execute them at times (just as he could also execute his children at times—a uniquely Roman power), and so a relation of conquest and absolute power became essential to the household.[143] Consequently, when the Roman emperors, like Augustus or Nero, claimed *dominium* over the territories and people vanquished and controlled by Rome, they

---

139. It is important to note here that the Roman legal tradition provided the foundation for current Western views and laws related to private property.

140. See Graeber, *Debt*, 198–99. Graeber also notes that this extreme view on private property is not found in other early legal traditions.

141. Graeber, *Debt*, 199–200. Drawing on Orlando Patterson.

142. Graeber, *Debt*, 200–201. Again, Graeber notes how the harshness of this was unique to the Romans, and notes that creditors were even permitted to execute insolvent debtors!

143. Graeber, *Debt*, 201–3.

gained the absolute freedom to do whatever this wished with their property.¹⁴⁴ Graeber summarizes things in this way:

> In creating a notion of *dominium*, then, and thus creating the modern principle of absolute private property, what Roman jurists were doing first of all was taking a principle of domestic authority, of absolute power over people, defining some of those people (slaves) as things, and then extending the logic that originally applied to slaves to geese, to chariots, barns, jewelry boxes, and so forth—that is, to every other sort of thing that the law had anything to do with.¹⁴⁵

In other words, for the Romans, private property is not formulated in relation to the possession of things and then extended to the possession of people who have been transformed into things. Quite the opposite. It begins with the latter and extends to the former. Consequently, we can see how the approach taken by Jesus and the Pauline faction within the Jesus movement—a community of people intimately familiar with the lived experience of slavery—proposes a completely different and contrary understanding of property (and people). As the Pauline faction states in 1 Cor 15:24, the return of Jesus will bring about the destruction of all authority and power and all *dominion*—i.e., all private property.¹⁴⁶ Furthermore, given that the Roman view of private property was so deeply and inextricably connected with the basic building blocks of the economy and of Roman power in general, we are also equipped to see how any who espoused the views held by the Pauline faction would be seen as threats to national security.

Later interpreters of the Pauline letters—primarily White men rooted in places of relatively high status, wealth (property), and privilege—have not always agreed with this understanding of Paulinism and have sought to expunge any hint of "communism" or of "sharing against private property" from the legacy of the early Jesus movement. On this point, yet again, one finds a great deal of (anxious? desperate?) emphasis upon the *voluntary* nature of the Collection. For example, Banks (following Weiss) emphasizes that Paul never *required* believers to share all things in common.¹⁴⁷ Consequently, while it is commendable to be charitable, Dahl

---

144. Graeber, *Debt*, 204.
145. Graeber, *Debt*, 201.
146. See also Eph 1:21; Col 1:13.
147. Banks, *Paul's Idea of Community*, 89; Weiss, *Earliest Christianity*, 1:68–71.

and Donahue further argue that one should avoid "extremes" (after all, as 1 Cor 13:3 says, "If I give away all my possessions, and if I hand over my body so that I may boast, but do not have love, I gain nothing").[148] In light of this, Dahl and Donahue conclude that the Pauline faction demanded nothing but "solid middle-class respectability."[149] Paired with this "middle-class respectability" are two concomitant attitudes: first, the need to be responsible with one's finances and, second, the importance of one's attitude—what matters is not how much one hoards for one's self as private property; what matters is one's attitude towards one's property.

In terms of exercising financial responsibility—which is simply assumed to be the opposite of anything that looks like sharing against private property—Dahl and Donahue point to the injunctions found in the epistles that are opposed to covetousness and greed (Rom 1:29; 1 Cor 5:10–11; 6:10 as well as passages from the deutero-Pauline epistles) and to passages that seem to urge people to live financially independent of others.[150] 1 Thess 4:11–12, for example, states that those loyal to Jesus should "aspire to live quietly, to mind your own affairs, and to work with your hands, as we directed you, so that you may behave properly towards outsiders and be dependent on no one."[151] Consequently, urging others not to covet the property of those with more wealth is taken as an implicit acceptance of the moral goodness of private property as such, and this is further affirmed by what is taken to be as the first appearance of a Protestant work ethic, which (conveniently for most of these interpreters) fits well with the approach that capitalism takes to private property, wherein the bourgeois are taught to both internalize this belief and then preach it to the proletariat.[152] Consequently, one's *attitude* towards one's property becomes what is important. What one needs is "an inner freedom from material things."[153] Therefore, there can be "no trace of a communistic

---

148. Dahl and Donahue, *Studies in Paul*, 23.

149. Dahl and Donahue, *Studies in Paul*, 24. Indeed, these authors argue that those involved with Paul and his coworkers were middle-class (27), a point that we have already refuted above.

150. Dahl and Donahue, *Studies in Paul*, 22–23. Cadoux comes to similar conclusions while also suggesting that the early Jesus movement was prejudiced against wealth and glorified poverty (Cadoux, *Early Church and the World*, 127–30).

151. Rom 13:1–7 is also mentioned here, as the payment of taxes and respect for authorities is seen as a sign of the validity of private property (see Dahl and Donahue, *Studies in Paul*, 23). I will address this passage at length in chapter 5.

152. As per Weber, of course. See Weber, *Protestant Work Ethic*.

153. Dahl and Donahue, *Studies in Paul*, 26, 31.

ideal in Paul's letters, not even a voluntary consumer's communism as an expression of love."[154]

Robert Grant comes to the same conclusion and argues that Paul replaces the communalism of the Jerusalem church with spiritual equality practiced in hierarchical relationships: "To put it simply, the Christian [sic] attitude towards property tended to be an aristocratic one, and the criticism of avarice was an important aspect of it."[155] Sampley concurs:

> Believers' relationship to possessions is analogous to their relationship to authorities. Just as there are authorities in the world with whom one must come to terms without granting them power at the center of one's life, so there are possessions and goods in the world that one can deal with, use, and even enjoy as long as one's involvement with them is an eschatological engagement.[156]

This eschatological element is important. Those who have argued for this perspective have often stressed that this attitude towards private property is a part of either: (a) a general Pauline shift of attention to that which is spiritual and otherworldly; or (b) the expectation of the imminent return of Jesus (even if some are quick to add that this sense of imminence should not lead to financial irresponsibility!).[157] This is well-captured in the view of Schrage, who argues that Pauline eschatology only throws into question the *future control* of one's private property and it is this that makes one's *present ownership* provisional.[158]

I have already addressed a number of these points in preceding chapters: (a) I believe that this eschatological perspective and its hyper-spirituality are misrepresentations of the beliefs and practices of Paul and his coworkers; (b) the early Jesus loyalists were not "middle-class";

---

154. Dahl and Donahue, *Studies in Paul*, 30.

155. Grant, *Early Christianity and Society*, 123; see also 102-4. Weiss also argues for this shift between the Pauline faction and the group in Jerusalem mentioned in Acts 2 and 4. Indeed, he argues that the Collection was necessary because of the ways in which this kind of sharing impoverished the Jesus loyalists at Jerusalem (Weiss, *Earliest Christianity*, 1:72-73).

156. Sampley, *Walking Between the Times*, 29.

157. See Cadoux, *Early Church and the World*, 127-28; Cousar, *Introduction to the New Testament*, 158-59; Weiss, *Earliest Christianity*, 1:71-73.

158. Schrage, *Ethics of the New Testament*, 231. Is this not a beautiful way to sustain one's own feelings of righteousness while simultaneously maintaining one's wealth and one's investment in the perpetuation of a status quo which produces things like wealth and poverty in the first place?

and (c) attitudes about work are more likely to refer to those who were slightly better-off who were interested in co-opting and using assemblies of Jesus loyalists for their own advancement. It is useful to repeat these points here because one begins to see their implausibility in light of the material explored above and in prior chapters. But two points should be addressed in greater detail. First, the injunctions against coveting and, second, the voluntary nature of participation in the Collection.

Beginning with the remarks against coveting, one should be careful not to read too much into what is written. Greed and covetousness are clearly condemned, but what does it mean to be greedy and to covet that which belongs to others? According to the argument made in this chapter, greed would be claiming that one should be able to own, use, or dispose of that which does not, in fact, belong to one's own self but, instead, belongs to the community to be shared with whomever has the greatest need. Claiming exclusive property rights over things (or even over people who were treated as things) is an example of greed *par excellence*. Indeed, this would actually be theft—as Ambrose of Milan later writes: "When you give to the poor, you give not of your own, but simply return what is his [sic], for you have usurped that which is common and has been given for the common use of all."[159] Consequently, the injunction against coveting is best understood as a command to reject the dominant legal conceptions of private property. Claiming and defending exclusive rights to private property is a way of coveting that which belongs to people who are poor or in need. This is especially true when we recall that imperial wealth (like all wealth) is entirely premised upon stealing from the poor, colonizing the lands of others, and exploiting the vulnerable. Therefore, by claiming that which they need, not simply in order to survive but to participate in the abundant life that is found in the Anointed (regardless of whom the law says owns those necessities), those who have been impoverished are not coveting the property of those who are wealthy. The opposite is actually occurring when those who are wealthy try to lay claim to and hoard goods they have stolen from others and refuse to return or even share with those others even when this has lethal consequences.

Of course, this is not stated explicitly by Paul and his coworkers in the passages that condemn greed, covetousness, and thievery, but, as many of the spokespeople of the early churches realized, it is an implication that follows naturally from their practices and from the kinds of

---

159. Ambrose of Milan quoted in González, *Faith and Wealth*, 191.

relationships they were fostering within the assemblies of Jesus loyalists. It is not greedy for a sibling to expect to receive what they need from their siblings—that was supposed to be the default and assumed position within a family. It *is* greedy for a sibling to refuse to share what they have to address the needs of their siblings.

Turning to the second point, we should recall that the voluntary nature of the Collection did not mean the Pauline faction thought Jesus loyalists could take a laissez-faire attitude to participation. That participation was not mandated, despite the Collection's obvious centrality to Paulinism, suggests to some that the Pauline faction did not have the authority to demand or enforce participation. The fact is that the Pauline faction did not desire to have the authority to force others to do what they wanted. Given that siblings were to relate to one another horizontally and as equals, and given the ways in which the imposition of any vertical hierarchies was resisted by participants of the early Jesus movement (especially in relation to money and material goods), it would make no sense for Paul and his coworkers to desire or attempt to claim this kind of authority over others within the movement. This has always been the challenge of anti-hierarchical movements—how do they remain true to their values as they continue to grow and as their influence spreads? After all, the more that impoverished and oppressed populations of people within the eastern portion of the Roman Empire were drawn into the Jesus movement because of the abundant life it offered to people within the here-and-now, the more higher-ranking members of society would be attracted to it. As more influential members joined it—at least in part because they saw it as a means of advancing their own status (as we already see with the Super Apostles in Corinth)—the more the values of the movement will be pressured to shift. Sharply delineated hierarchies will begin to appear, as the dominant values of the well-off are brought in with those who benefit from them. Inevitably, rather than recognizing that participation in a transnational sibling-based economics is voluntary because Paul and his coworkers are trying to avoid the creation of hierarchies within the movement, the voluntary nature of the Collection is emphasized in order to permit those who choose not to participate to continue to hoard what they want to claim as their own. And this rapidly became the point of view that dominated the history of Christianity up until today when we arrive at Pauline scholars, who may even consider the New Testament to be authoritative in some way in their own lives, yet who are rooted within places of power, high status, wealth, and privilege.

Other Economic Practices

Having come to these conclusions, it is worth observing the ways in which other material practices of the assemblies of Jesus loyalists associated with the Pauline faction also expressed this sibling-based way of sharing against private property. Here we will look at the hospitality and table fellowship practiced by the early members of the movement. We will then examine how this relates to the call to "care for the poor" that was a central and distinctive feature of the movement.

Hospitality

Hospitality was a highly prized virtue throughout the ancient Near East and the eastern portion of the Roman Empire.[160] This was equally true of Judeans as it was of Greeks, and demonstrating hospitality to strangers was often associated with their religious practices—Abraham was held up as a model of hospitality and synagogues often served as hospices while, at the same time, Greek temples were places of sanctuary and Zeus was called the protector of the rights of hospitality.[161] The widespread nature of this cultural practice would have been essential to those like the Pauline faction, who were itinerant workers.[162] Indeed, it is precisely the demonstration of this kind of hospitality that leads them to praise the Galatians.[163] When Paul came to Galatia he was in a trying "condition" of "physical infirmity" that could have led him to be "scorned" or "despised"—indeed, that may have led him to be ineligible in the eyes of the general public for standard practices of hospitality—but the Galatians "welcomed him as a [messenger] of God, as [the Anointed] Jesus" (Gal 4:13–14). Therefore, just as sibling-based practices of mutuality were adopted as standards within the household of God, so also the early Jesus movement adopted this culturally-rooted practice of showing hospitality to strangers. Thus, Philemon is asked to prepare a room for Paul's arrival (Phlm 20), the Jesus loyalists at Rome are asked to welcome Phoebe and help her with anything she requires (Rom 16:1–2), and Gaius hosts Paul

---

160. See Bird, "Early Christianity," 236–37; Meeks, *Origins of Christian Morality*, 104–5; Dunn, *Beginning from Jerusalem*, 516–17. For longer studies, see Koening, *New Testament Hospitality*; Pohl, *Making Room*.

161. Dunn, *Beginning from Jerusalem*, 516–17.

162. Meeks, *Origins of Christian Morality*, 105.

163. See Longenecker, *Remember the Poor*, 212–13, including 213n5.

in Corinth (Rom 16:23). However, some modifications are made pertaining to the basis for this practice. In particular, for those loyal to Jesus, this hospitality becomes an expression of messianic welcome and of the communal embodiment of God's justice.[164] As Paul and his coworkers state in Rom 15:7: "Welcome one another, therefore, just as [the Anointed] welcomed you, for the glory of God."[165]

This is also a part of what it means for Jesus loyalists to reorient their lives as siblings with one another. As siblings, the hospitality that is offered to those in need extends to offering support to a sibling who resides in a different location than the group that is demonstrating the hospitality. Consequently, not only is the Pauline faction hosted by Jesus loyalists like Gaius, but Jesus loyalists from different cities send financial support so that they will not burden others wherever they reside (see 1 Cor 16:6; 2 Cor 1:16, 11:8–9; Phil 4:10–20). Hospitality is shown not only by caring for those who arrive where one resides but also by caring for the provision of those who reside elsewhere.

Table Fellowship

One of the most important ways in which people showed hospitality, friendship, and solidarity was in the practice of table fellowship. Sharing a meal was a profound expression of fellowship.[166] In the ancient Near East, table fellowship functioned as a social boundary that revealed who was "in" and who was "out," and so eating together demonstrated acceptance.[167] As Joachim Jeremias says: "To invite a man [sic] to a meal was an honor. It was an offer of peace, trust, brotherhood [sic], and forgiveness."[168] Similarly, to refuse table fellowship to a person denied that person's acceptability. Therefore, within the early assemblies of Jesus loyalists, eating with one another—as slave and freed, Judean, Greek, and Gaul, people of all genders, more poor and less poor—was an essential

---

164. See Jennings, *Reading Derrida/Thinking Paul*, 114–15, 117–20.

165. This practice is also encouraged as an expression of the belief that the Jesus loyalists were citizens of heaven (Phil 3:20) and now resided within the empire as aliens and strangers in a strange land. For an excellent meditation on this, see Stringfellow, *Ethic for Christians*.

166. Banks, *Paul's Idea of Community*, 83–85.

167. See Dunn, *Jesus Remembered*, 601–2.

168. Jeremias, *Proclamation of Jesus*, 115.

expression of the conviction that all, having been accepted by God, were now accepted and welcomed together as equals.[169]

By eating together in this way, the early assemblies of Jesus loyalists were continuing the tradition that Jesus initiated regarding eating with the poor, the sinners, tax collectors, prostitutes and sex workers, and others who were excluded and who were denied fellowship within mainstream society. All of this was a part of Jesus's proclamation of liberation and the forgiveness of sins. Indeed, it is the practice of table fellowship that makes Jesus's message of forgiveness comprehensible (but shocking). Jesus was celebrating the eschatological banquet—the celebratory meal of those brought out of exile—but he was doing so with all the wrong people. It was by eating with "the poor" and "the sinners" that Jesus revealed and enacted that they were the ones who had been forgiven and welcomed into new life according to the justice of God. Eating with the excluded revealed that God's hospitality was both more extravagant and more partisan than it had ever been imagined to be; those who knew themselves to be on the outside were the ones invited to the eschatological feast of the kingdom wherein eating was an act of acceptance, forgiveness, and mercy (and those who assumed *they* would always have a place at that table were told that they were mistaken).[170]

Others in Judea related table fellowship to these themes, but they chose to eat with rather different parties of people, thereby embodying different allegiances. Thus, the Pharisees and Essenes understood their practice of table fellowship as a gathering of the part of Israel set apart for YHWH. Jesus's practice of an open table radically confronted these allegiances: "What for many Pharisees and Essenes was a sinful disregard for covenantal ideals was for Jesus an expression of the good news of the kingdom."[171] By eating with the poor and the sinners, Jesus was not simply committing a breach of etiquette; rather, he was defying both purity regulations and the ordinances that were in place for restoring violators of the law to the covenant community. Even more radically, Jesus was turning the tables (quite literally eventually) on who was ultimately considered to have violated the justice upon which the law based its claim to exist and wield force.

---

169. See Dunn, *Beginning from Jerusalem*, 288–89; Weiss, *Earliest Christianity*, 1:66.

170. On this train of thought, see Dunn, *Jesus Remembered*, 526–33; Moltmann, *Church in the Power of the Holy Spirit*, 117.

171. Dunn, *Jesus Remembered*, 605.

Of course, the culminating meal of Jesus's ministry is the "last supper," which was celebrated in connection with and continuation of the exodus tradition.[172] All along, Jesus's meals had been linked to liberation, and the Last Supper, linked to the old exodus meal, symbolized the new exodus. Thus, the Last Supper must be seen as a continuation of Jesus's other meals. It is not something radically different but is the climax of the meals that came before. It was within this context of a shared meal among equals—now all experiencing the liberation and forgiveness of God the Father of Jesus—that the meals were shared in remembrance of the execution of Jesus on behalf of the movement of which he was a part.[173] Indeed, the remembrance of these things required Jesus loyalists to engage in a form of table fellowship that recognized the equal status of all the participants and their respective exoduses from bondage. Paul, his coworkers, and all the members of the early assemblies of Jesus loyalists were to gather together and eat together—as siblings on equal footing with one another—as a way of remembering and enacting the exodus tradition which spanned from Moses, to Jesus, to their own liberation from the oppression and bondage experienced under the rule of Rome and her law.

1 Cor 11:23–34

We see this most clearly in 1 Cor 11:23–34. First, observe how the food and drink consumed in remembrance of Jesus are shared in the context of an assembly that is gathered to participate in an actual meal. This meal was eaten as a part of the Jesus loyalists' daily sustenance.[174] Indeed, given that most participants lived at or near the subsistence level, it is quite possible that this was the most significant or only meal of their day.

Second, we see how tensions have arisen regarding the ways in which meals were being shared in Corinth. This is unsurprising given that sharing meals together and engaging in table fellowship was a common practice among other assemblies and associations at that time. However, other groups practiced table fellowship in a manner that reinforced the socioeconomic and theopolitical stratification of society. Shared meals

---

172. Wright, *Jesus and the Victory of God*, 558–59.

173. Jewett notes how many readings or practices of the Eucharist have neglected the communal element of this practice (Jewett, *Paul*, 74–75).

174. Goguel, *Primitive Church*, 334; Dunn, *Beginning from Jerusalem*, 645.

demonstrated and reinforced where one was ranked within society. Consequently, problems arose in Corinth because some participants tried to import these dominant hierarchical practices into the meals shared among Jesus loyalists.[175] Some of the *relatively* less-poor members were eating more than others and leaving poorer members, who probably worked longer and arrived later, without enough food. This was standard practice within Graeco-Roman society. The more affluent members would eat more courses and would eat the best quality food at a meal, while the poorer members would arrive later, eat fewer courses, and be given the worst quality food.

While this may have been standard practice within the dominant culture, the Pauline faction found it appalling that something like this could be done among Jesus loyalists and among those who are now called to relate to one another as siblings. To import social rank into exodus-based meals rooted in the proclamation of liberation and the remembrance of Jesus's death in solidarity with the exploited and oppressed is to transform that which is life-giving into that which is death-dealing (while presenting that death-dealing practice as though it were life-giving). This goes against everything the table fellowship of Jesus loyalists was intended to represent and actualize.[176] It means that those who eat in this way are actually forgetting Jesus and what he did—while claiming to remember him![177]

---

175. Goguel, *Primitive Church*, 334; Dunn, *Beginning from Jerusalem*, 644, 814–16.

176. See Harink, *Paul Among the Postliberals*, 127–28; Heen, "Role of Symbolic Inversion," 131–33; Cousar, *Letters of Paul*, 69–71; Dunn, *Beginning from Jerusalem*, 814–16; Winter, *After Paul Left Corinth*, 154; Horrell, *Social Ethos*, 150–55. Horrell emphasizes that the Pauline faction is arguing for a behavior that is internal to the assemblies of Jesus loyalists and that they are not pushing a revolutionary social program for society at large. On the one hand this is true. Paul and his coworkers are speaking about the kind of activity that is to define the ways in which Jesus loyalists assemble together. On the other hand, Horrell's emphasis is misplaced because he fails to factor in the consideration that the assemblies of Jesus loyalists and their members were actively working to infiltrate society at large and spread from city to city (creeping up to Rome) and, just as importantly, would have been considered a revolutionary threat by the dominant Powers within that society.

177. See Longenecker, *Remember the Poor*, 154. All of this further emphasizes that Paul and his coworkers were focused upon "the social unity of the church [sic]—not merely its spiritual oneness" (Cousar, *Letters of Paul*, 70)—a point that should be well established by this point. Horrell also emphasizes how the Lord's Supper and baptism were both rites that promoted a new solidarity that abolished prior distinctions (Horrell, *Solidarity and Difference*, 102–10). Sanders makes the interesting argument that the reason why the Lord's Supper moved from being a real meal to being a token

Third, we should reiterate that the presence of this socioeconomic division among the participants at Corinth need not be taken as de facto evidence of the presence of wealthy members within the assembly (or assemblies) that gathered there. This has often been assumed to be the case, once the economic element of the conflict mentioned in 1 Cor 11:23–34 is recognized.[178] However, as argued in volume 1 of this series, this way of thinking demonstrates a lack of awareness of the very real stratifications that can occur within poor communities, where there is a world of difference between the experiences and status of a household that lives just below the subsistence level and a household that lives just above the subsistence level. This assumption also fails to consider the ways in which people who are oppressed and colonized may still replicate the values and ideology of their colonizers and then engage in lateral violence or go on to act in ways that are oppressive to those who are less well-situated than themselves.[179] Hence, it seems that this assumption is rooted in two related errors. First, a binary form of thinking wherein now-dated scholarship assumed that people were either "rich" or "poor." In part, this assumption arose from the proper observation that a middle-class was absent from the eastern portion of the Roman Empire in Paul's day (thereby correcting some of the errors made by earlier scholars). Thankfully, this assumption is being corrected, as we saw when we analyzed the stratification that existed within the vast numbers of poor people. Second, and not unrelated to the first point, is the distance that New Testament scholars tend to have from contemporary communities of people who have been dispossessed. If more scholars were rooted within impoverished communities, then assumptions such as this one would not be so prevalent and would not appear to be so compelling. Indeed, some may see the lives of these scholars as exhibiting the same kind of egregious betrayal of

---

meal was to ensure that all participants received an equal amount (Sanders, *Paul: The Apostle's Life*, 280–81). This seems plausible although, if true, it would be further evidence of the betrayal of the values held by the Pauline faction and the triumph of practices favored by members like the Super Apostles.

178. See, for example, Dunn, *Beginning from Jerusalem*, 653; Goguel, *Primitive Church*, 334; Cousar, *Letters of Paul*, 69; Horrell, *Social Ethos*, 156; Crossan and Borg, *First Paul*, 199.

179. This is also known as "punching down." Much of this has been explored in postcolonial race theory and Indigenous studies. A few particularly good examples, which also posit a way forward for Indigenous peoples on Turtle Island, include Simpson, *Dancing on Our Turtle's Back*; Coulthard, *Red Skins, White Masks*; Simpson, *Mohawk Interruptus*.

Jesus's memory that Paul condemns in 1 Cor 11:23–34. The Corinthians were actually forgetting (and thereby denying) Jesus because of the way they were going about engaging in table fellowship with one another, and many New Testament scholars are actually forgetting (and thereby denying) Paul because of the ways in which they go about studying him. This is how exodus traditions are incorporated into the smooth functioning of an oppressive status quo.

Returning to the passage at hand, however, we can observe the stark poverty of some Jesus loyalists when Paul and his coworkers state that the Corinthian practice of table fellowship has resulted in some people experiencing weakness, illness, and even death (11:30). The Pauline faction's suggestion that this is the result of God's judgment of the community has led to something of a mystical interpretation of this passage. For example, Bruce Longenecker writes that "in Paul's view, if the poor are disadvantaged, the power dimension of the Lord's Supper is short-circuited."[180] Perhaps that is the case, but it makes good sense to understand weakness, illness, and death to be things that result from malnourishment (and not some vaguely defined short-circuit of power, whatever that means). Some Jesus loyalists at Corinth were living below the subsistence level. Others would be at the subsistence level but not above it. Being deprived of a meal, perhaps after a hard day of manual labor when one had just barely been able to eat the day before, would have an impact upon the health of a person. When those who lived slightly above the subsistence level (and who did have some reserves of food at their own homes [see 11:34]) deprived those at or below the subsistence level from partaking in a meal at the end of the day, this could have the fatal consequences the Pauline faction describes. Consequently, it is more plausible to understand the situation they describe as a conflict occurring between members who are at different levels of poverty—not a conflict that is occurring between the wealthy and the poor. What is clear, however, from the Pauline point of view, is that the sibling-based economics pursued in the Collection is also to be the basis for other material interactions between Jesus loyalists.

Gal 2:11–14; Rom 14:1–15:7; 1 Cor 8:1–11:1

Having seen the significance of sharing meals together within the general culture of the eastern portion of the Roman Empire, and having seen

---

180. Longenecker, *Remember the Poor*, 153–54.

how meals were to function as a proclamation of liberation, friendship, and equality within the early assemblies of Jesus loyalists, one begins to understand why they were frequent flashpoints of conflict within the movement. In Gal 2:11-14 (and possibly extending to v. 21), the Pauline faction recounts a conflict with their peers that arose when Cephas, Barnabas, and other Judeans began to eat apart from Jesus loyalists from other regions after a delegation came from James. Here the matter is not so much one of economics—it appears that there was enough food for all involved—but of inscribing pre-existing hierarchies and purity codes into meals that were intended to proclaim one's liberation from those things in the liberated and newly constituted household of God. This is why the Pauline faction refers to the actions of Cephas et al. as "hypocrisy" (v. 13) and charges them with "not acting consistently with the disclosure [*aletheia*] of the gospel" (v. 14). However, all of this does have direct economic implications. As soon as status hierarchies are established within any community, these hierarchies are then employed to justify material and economic imbalances (thus, for example, as we saw in chapter 2, once a firm hierarchy of leadership is established within the Jesus movement, this becomes the justification for redeploying money that had previously been employed to manumit slaves and using it to support the status, rank, and privilege of the "leaders").

Similar arguments are made in Rom 14:1-15:7 and 1 Cor 8:1-11:1. Given the importance of eating meat to these debates, money was a factor in the conflict. Although, as we have seen, meat was more available to poor people than some have argued, it would be the relatively less poor who could indulge in this more than those at or below the subsistence level. Once again, in both passages, the emphasis is upon the need to care for one another in concrete practical ways. In order to do this, Paul and his coworkers confront an elitist haughtiness that tried to lay claim to one's individual "rights" without any regard for one's siblings in the Anointed.[181] In both passages, the Pauline faction subordinates the (in the proper context) legitimate desires of "the strong" to the impact that fulfilling those desires would have upon "the weak" (this is a constant throughout, but see especially Rom 14:13; 15:1-2; 1 Cor 8:9-13; 10:23-31). By making this argument, we see the same kind of countercultural subordination and reversal at work that is a consistent theme

---

181. See Thielman, *Theology of the New Testament*, 448-51; Meeks, *In Search of the Early Christians*, 148-49, 157-58.

Pauline Solidarity

in the Pauline writings.[182] Those living somewhat above the subsistence level, "the strong," are to prioritize those who live at or below the subsistence level and act in ways that first considers the impact of their actions upon "the weak." Hence, shortly after the passage in 1 Cor 8:1–11:1, Paul moves on to the body analogy and speaks of the members of the body who "seem to be weaker" are actually indispensable and those members of the body "we think less honorable" actually merit greater honor (1 Cor 1:22–27).

Living in this way could carry threatening socioeconomic consequences for "the strong." This comes through more clearly in the passage in the discussion of eating meat sacrificed to idols in 1 Cor 8:1–13 and 10:14–29. On the one hand, apart from offending the consciences of some siblings, Paul and his coworkers see no problem with eating meat that was sold in the marketplace after having been used as a part of a religious ceremony—or, for that matter, eating meat prepared by others which may have also been purchased from the same source (10:25–27). However, on the other hand, they make it clear that Jesus loyalists should not partake in ceremonies where meat is sacrificed to another god and then consumed. This is to be avoided for the sake of the consciences of others (8:4–11), but also because one risks becoming an idolater by doing so (10:6, 14–21; that is to say, one risks practicing loyalty to another god and thereby becoming disloyal to the god who is taken to be the Father of Jesus).[183] Those who were "strong" would have difficulty avoiding this—such cultic meals were a standard part of participation in any civic celebration or ceremony and would also be a standard part of table fellowship within any Graeco-Roman association. Therefore, withdrawing from participation in this kind of meal would cause "the strong" to lose their limited and already fragile social and professional contacts.[184] This could quite easily lead to an experience of ostracism that would result in them moving from living slightly above the subsistence level to living at or below that level. For those who dared to do this, the pooling of resources would become all the more indispensable as new networks would need to be established in order to guarantee the survival of one's family and one's own self.

---

182. A point emphasized in Meeks, *In Search of the Early Christians*, 93–95.

183. On the latter point, see Meeks, *In Search of the Early Christians*, 149.

184. See Horrell, *Solidarity and Difference*, 142–50; Schottroff, "'Give to Caesar,'" 248–49.

Conclusion

In all of this, we see a practice of table fellowship that is structured to encourage sibling-based relationships between Jesus loyalists—relationships that are expressed in material ways and carry material consequences. Dominant ways of sharing meals re-inscribed dominant hierarchies of patronage and power, but the Jesus loyalists were encouraged to continue the practices established by Jesus and eat together in ways that concretely disclosed both their liberation from those hierarchies and their mutual respect and care for one another. Thus, as Crossan and Reed write, God's "egalitarian 'share-meal' opposes and replaces the normalcy of Rome's 'hierarchically patronal meal.'"[185] Indeed, this continues to be another element of the rejection of patrons and patronage found within a sibling-based economics. This is the case because common meals tended to be hosted by patrons on behalf of their friends and clients. One's own status and bond with the patron who hosted the meal determined what one ate, how much one ate, and where one sat. Yet, in the accounts of meals found in the letters written by Paul and his coworkers, no mention is made of patronage and, despite it being a ubiquitous practice, one hears nothing of libations being poured out for patrons during the meal.[186] When those in Corinth begin to instate a form of patron-based practice—as we saw in 1 Cor 11:23–34—the Pauline faction is quick to condemn it and see it as a (literally) fatal threat to the movement and its members. Sibling-based economics cannot be paired with hierarchical power structures which masquerade as charitable institutions.[187]

---

185. See Crossan and Reed, *In Search of Paul*, 338–41; Crossan, *God and Empire*, 170.

186. A point highlighted in Dunn, *Beginning from Jerusalem*, 646.

187. Heen has an essay comparing the practice of table fellowship associated with Paul with the Roman festival of Saturnalia (Heen, "Role of Symbolic Inversion," 124–44). He notes the following similarities: (1) the enthronement of a deity; (2) the beginning of a utopian rule; and (3) the reversal of status between the weak and strong in society in an egalitarian ethic (Heen, "Role of Symbolic Inversion," 124). However, by Paul's day, Heen notes that Saturnalia had been thoroughly domesticated and lost its subversive edge (124, 135–37). Therefore, Heen argues that Paul guards against a comparable accommodation within the Jesus movement by emphasizing a "theology of the cross" (124). Hence, Saturnalia offers a "preparatory type" for Paul's Christology, and the practices of the assemblies associated with Paul offer a more genuinely liberating alternative to that of Saturnalia, as it was practiced in Paul's day—because, ultimately, the inversion found in the Jesus movement should lead to the leveling of all social distinctions in an egalitarian community (130–31, 144). I find this comparison fascinating, not so much because I believe that Saturnalia was a festival that Paul was

Pauline Solidarity

Care for "the Poor"

In all of this, we see a consistent focus upon prioritizing the needs of the more vulnerable, isolated, and oppressed members of the assemblies. Essentially, we find the theory and praxis of liberation theology within the movement as imagined by the Pauline faction.[188] Here care for "the poor" is at the core of the identity and activities of the Jesus loyalists—as both the Pauline faction and the Jerusalem-based faction recognized from the beginning (see Gal 2:10). However, as we have seen throughout, this is care for the poor that is engaged in *by the poor*. This is a form of communal self-care that transcends all the boundaries that are used to divide and conquer colonized peoples. As such, it is a very distinct thing from standard approaches to charity or from contemporary practices rooted within the "non-profit industrial complex."[189] This kind of solidarity removes the need for top-down forms of charity, like patronage, which, as we have seen, were actually instrumental in maintaining the gap between the poor and the rich, the colonized and the colonizers.[190] It also liberates the community from other Graeco-Roman practices of charity. What was occurring within the early Jesus movement falls outside of all hierarchical charitable models which existed either then or now.

This is an important point to make because scholars who have emphasized the care for the poor demonstrated within these assemblies have generally done so in order to emphasize the importance of charity and

---

deliberately mimicking or incorporating into his practice, but because it demonstrates one of the other subversive events that occurred in the Roman Empire. It also shows how subversion could be ritualized and incorporated into imperial power dynamics and, as such, it serves as something of a warning and a prototype of what would quickly happen with the Jesus movement.

188. Here I have in mind the stream of liberation theology that gained attention in Latin America in the sixties and then spread around the globe from there (see, for example, Sobrino, *No Salvation Outside the Poor*; Boff and Boff, *Introducing Liberation Theology*; Gutierrez, *Theology of Liberation*).

189. On that terminology, see INCITE!, *Revolution Will Not be Funded*. Some people oppressed by poverty also refer to the parties who make up this complex as "poverty pimps"—i.e., as those who exploit the bodies, stories, and lives of poor people in order to make money. For further excellent studies, see Willse, *Value of Homelessness*; Barry-Shaw and Jay, *Paved with Good Intentions*; Eubanks, *Automating Inequality*.

190. Eduardo Galeano's quote regarding the distinction between charity and solidarity is worth recalling here: "I don't believe in charity. I believe in solidarity. Charity is so vertical. It goes from the top down. Solidarity is horizontal. It respects the other person. I have a lot to learn from other people" (Galeano quoted in Barsamian, *Louder than Bombs*, 146).

have seen the Jesus movement as prototype of the non-profit industrial complex. The influential (and in many ways exciting) writings of Bruce Winter are a good example of this. The title of his most relevant study, *Seek the Welfare of the City: Christians as Benefactors and Citizens*, aptly summarizes his argument.[191] Against those like Meeks, who argued that the early Jesus movement was focused on internal matters and not on external engagement, Winter argues that the Pauline faction wanted the Jesus loyalists to enhance the lives of all people in the cities in which they lived.[192] According to Winter, Paul is urging the Jesus loyalists to adopt the model of charitable concern and civic responsibility that is adopted by well-meaning socially conscious Christians today. He sees Paul as the innovator of this kind of consciousness and practice.

Furthermore, Winter sees this as requiring the "abolition of the patronage system" and as the instantiation of an "unprecedented social revolution of the ancient benefaction tradition."[193] This occurs for two reasons. First, because those who are benefactors should do good simply "because good needed to be done," and they should do so "without expectations of reciprocity or repayment."[194] As such, this good was to be performed for all—including parties traditionally considered too poor or insignificant to be the recipients of patronage and benefaction.[195] In this way, when it comes to benefactors, Paul wishes to "break the strong social convention" of patronage because it limited the ability of Jesus loyalists to do good.[196] Second, patronage and benefaction are challenged from the other side as well. Those who are living as clients are required to move from a "parasitic" existence to active engagement in benefaction.[197] "The secular client must now become a private Christian [sic] benefactor."[198] By urging this, "Paul's purpose was to wean such persons away from the welfare syndrome."[199] Furthermore, when taken together, this twofold reorientation of benefaction "undermined many of the foundations of

---

191. Winter, *Seek the Welfare of the City*.
192. Winter, *Seek the Welfare of the City*, 1–3, 201–2.
193. Winter, *Seek the Welfare of the City*, 60, 209.
194. Winter, *Seek the Welfare of the City*, 60.
195. Winter, *Seek the Welfare of the City*, 45.
196. Winter, *Seek the Welfare of the City*, 48.
197. Winter, *Seek the Welfare of the City*, 42–43, 48–51. Winter quotes 1 Thess 4:10–12; 2 Thess 3:8–11 to support his argument here.
198. Winter, *Seek the Welfare of the City*, 42.
199. Winter, *Seek the Welfare of the City*, 53.

PAULINE SOLIDARITY

Roman culture," so when this change was enacted "it must have been the most distinctive public feature of this newly-emerging religion in the Roman East."[200]

Winter's study was ground-breaking and provided an excellent trajectory for subsequent scholars to follow (especially regarding the relation of patronage to the assemblies associated with Paul and his coworkers), but there are critical flaws that undercut his conclusion.[201] The most obvious problem is what I take to be Winter's dated assumption regarding the socioeconomic status of some of the Jesus loyalists.[202] Specifically, Winter's argument is premised upon the belief that there were "Christians [sic] of very considerable means" and of "significant social status and wealth" within the assemblies associated with Paul and his coworkers.[203] He believes that Erastus is an Aedile in Corinth, and Stephanas and Phoebe are taken as examples of wealthy and influential members of society who engage in the sort of subversion or inversion of patronage he describes.[204] Unfortunately, as we have already seen, this conclusion about the socioeconomic status of the Jesus loyalists is considerably less plausible than the conclusion that the socioeconomic differences we see reflected in the letters written by Paul and his coworkers are differences between relative degrees of poverty. Consequently, it would be well beyond the means of the Jesus loyalists to seek to care for the welfare of the cities in which they lived in anything like the manner that Winter suggests. Much of the focus of the assemblies would be on ensuring the survival of all the members of the assemblies (locally and, as we have seen, transnationally). There simply would not be the resources to engage in the kind of benefaction Winter envisions.

Second, and related to his conclusions regarding the high socioeconomic status of some of the Jesus loyalists, Winter's supposedly "radical"

---

200. Winter, "Roman Law and Society," 99; *Seek the Welfare of the City*, 42, respectively.

201. For some who fit within this anti-patronage trajectory, see deSilva, *Honor, Patronage, Kinship, and Purity*, 152–54 (Paul removes patronage from the realm of competition); Strom, *Reframing Paul*, 142–54 (Paul follows the pattern of benefaction but removes the grounds for boasting).

202. Winter's *Seek the Welfare of the City* was published prior to the studies by Meggitt, Oakes, Friesen, and Longenecker that I explored in volume 1 of this series.

203. Winter, *Seek the Welfare of the City*, 37; see also 39–40.

204. Winter, *Seek the Welfare of the City*, 195–204.

Paul actually ends up being fundamentally conservative.²⁰⁵ Although this Paul does indeed challenge patronage in some significant ways, there is no fundamental break from the system as a whole. Indeed, Winter argues that in partnership with the dominant ideology, Paul "shares a common concern for concord and being law-abiding" and accepting "the existing structures."²⁰⁶ This is likely also why Winter views the poor, and not the rich, as those who live in a "parasitical" manner. Consequently, without affecting "the fabric of the old ranking system," Winter's Paul was trying to transform the system "with a revolution in the use of the resources of the patrons."²⁰⁷ This reformist position is essentially conservative—the law, socioeconomic hierarchies, vertical exchanges, and the system as a whole (which includes the valorization of the rich and the demonization of the poor, given the ability of the rich to hoard both goods and goodness) are left intact. Indeed, given that patrons were already supposed to act as though they gave without thought of return and clients were to never forget their indebtedness (as we saw in volume 2 of this series), there is actually very little mentioned here that distinguishes the imagined practices of Jesus loyalists from dominant practices of patronage. Winter misses how truly radical and thorough-going the Pauline faction was in this regard. The sibling-based economic model that they were seeking to implement within assemblies of poor and colonized populations throughout the Roman Empire was much more radical than Winter suggests (or, perhaps, desires). What we see in the assemblies of Jesus loyalists is the pursuit of solidarity and not the practice of charity. This is not about wealthy members engaging in law-abiding forms of charity that actually end up reinforcing power hierarchies. This is about marginalized people engaging in a form of sharing against private property that threatens the entire social structure.²⁰⁸

In a more recent study, Bruce W. Longenecker offers an updated examination of the centrality of the priority of caring for the poor within

---

205. Winter refers to Paul as a "radical critic of the prevailing culture" (Winter, "Roman Law and Society," 99).

206. Winter, *Seek the Welfare of the City*, 207. I will have more to say in relation to Paul being "law-abiding" in chapter 5.

207. Winter, *Seek the Welfare of the City*, 204.

208. In light of the above, one should recall Kahl's argument that Paul's criticisms targeting "works of the law" are actually criticism of Graeco-Roman euergetism, which Paul counters with faith working through love (Kahl, *Galatians Re-Imagined*, 197–99).

the assemblies associated with Paul and his coworkers.[209] Longenecker's thesis is that "care for the poor" is an integral part of the good news that Paul and his coworkers proclaimed:

> For Paul, economic assistance of the poor was not sufficient in and of itself, nor was it exhaustive of the good news of Jesus; but neither was it supplemental or peripheral to that good news. Instead, falling within the essentials of the good news, care for the poor was thought by Paul to be a necessary hallmark of the corporate life of Jesus-followers who lived in conformity with the good news of the early Jesus-movement.[210]

Just as the Pauline faction sought the realization of "new creation now" in other areas of life, so also this new creation was pursued in the economic domain. The eschatological vision of the Pauline faction does not exclude economics but rather required the reorientation of this realm of life—in order to privilege the poor—just as it reoriented other areas of life in a liberating way.[211] Consequently, Longenecker calls for "a moratorium on the ill-considered view that Paul though it unnecessary to [deal] with socioeconomic problems at any great length."[212]

In order to consider what may or may not have been unique about the model of care for the poor found within the context of the early Jesus movement, and in order to understand the context of Paul and his coworkers, Longenecker surveys how charity was practiced in the Graeco-Roman world as well as in the Judean context. He respects the commonly-held view that Judaism and then Christianity were responsible for the spread of charitable practices and institutions within the Roman Empire. He also observes how Judeans were known for this kind of practice—for example, within the Second Temple Period, when people whose origins were outside of Judea wanted to honor the deity of Israel, they did so by showing generosity to others, especially to the poor—and this was

---

209. See Longenecker, *Remember the Poor*. Longenecker is responding to what he identifies as a general neglect of the economic dimension of the New Testament within dominant scholarship and he criticizes three trajectories—(1) those who think Paul saw economics as inconsequential because he was focused on more important matters; (2) those who only discuss economics in relation to the Collection; and (3) those who make grand economics claims without providing a base for their arguments (Longenecker, *Remember the Poor*, 1–12; in the third category, Longenecker includes such scholars as Elliott, Lopez, and, to some degree, Crossan and Borg).

210. Longenecker, *Remember the Poor*, 1; see also 12, 140.

211. Longenecker, *Remember the Poor*, 137–38, 155.

212. Longenecker, *Remember the Poor*, 156.

seen as one of the distinctive markers of Second Temple Judaism(s).[213] Thus, Longenecker concludes that "concern for the economically insecure is strongly attested as integral to Jewish identity, precisely because it's integral to the concerns of Israel's deity."[214] Not surprisingly, then, care of the materially poor was also integral to the proclamation and activities of Jesus and the early communities of Jesus loyalists.[215] This continues for some time so that, from the second to the fourth century CE, care for the poor became a hallmark of the "proto-orthodox" church.[216]

However, Longenecker also observes that this does not mean that charity was wholly absent within the Graeco-Roman world.[217] In this regard, he notes practices that could be considered generous but would not necessarily always qualify as charitable.[218] For example, he highlights the generosity and benefaction that could occur in Graeco-Roman associations—yet he also notes how this was a way of advancing the status of the association. Furthermore, this was generally a way of sharing within one's peer group (and peers who were already well removed from the lower levels of the economic scale Longenecker constructs), and it would only occur in temporary extenuating circumstances.[219] The same "class" distinctions applied to the practices of hospitality and table fellowship.[220] Similarly, grand acts of euergetism almost always focused upon the benefits these produced for the civic elites.[221] In this regard, Longenecker observes that patronage, which excluded the poor, should not be confused with charity.[222]

---

213. Longenecker, *Remember the Poor*, 109–13. Longenecker notes that this is the case because care for the poor is deeply embedded in Judean Scriptures (113–14). See also Dunn, *Beginning from Jerusalem*, 458–59.

214. Longenecker, *Remember the Poor*, 114.

215. Longenecker, *Remember the Poor*, 115–31.

216. Longenecker, *Remember the Poor*, 135. This fits with the observations made above regarding the approach that the early Jesus movement takes against private property.

217. Longenecker, *Remember the Poor*, 60–67.

218. Longenecker, *Remember the Poor*, 67–74.

219. Longenecker, *Remember the Poor*, 68–69.

220. Longenecker, *Remember the Poor*, 70–71. It should be noted that the grain distributed at Rome was only given to citizens, so all recipients were probably higher than ES6 (88–89).

221. Longenecker, *Remember the Poor*, 72.

222. Longenecker, *Remember the Poor*, 73–74. Here, Longenecker also highlights how the tradition that flows from the Judean Scriptures to Second Temple Judaism

Pauline Solidarity

However, this does not mean some other (still somewhat problematical) forms of charity did not exist within Graeco-Roman society.[223] Almsgiving did occur and even the Stoics, who spoke against pity, did not speak against the act of giving alms (they only spoke against certain motives for giving).[224] But charity was not frequent. This was the case because the elite tended to be protected from the poor by their servants, clients, and lectors, because they did not trust the poor and suspected them of being lazy, immoral loiterers looking for free hand-outs, and because "elite generosity rarely existed without a healthy dose of self-interest mixed in with it."[225] Plus, the wealthy were not fools—they knew their wealth was premised upon the annihilation, dispossession, and enslavement of others. So, they were not inclined towards charity. Yet there were exceptions. A very small number of people did give to the poor out of what could be described as an "humanitarian" concern, and others who gave out of a sense of religious obligation (which was one of the reasons why the poor often congregated around temples).[226] Consequently, Longenecker concludes that charity was not completely absent prior to the spread of the Jesus movement. Indeed, the Jesus movement could have appealed to the exceptional few who were already concerned with the well-being of the poor.[227] That may have been the case, but Longenecker's next conclusion is problematical. Against conservative contemporaries who are critical of the charity model, Longenecker makes the following statement:

> If the elite were not going to change the structures, the sub-elite certainly could not. It was simply not feasible for those at lower economics structures to even contemplate anything more than a charitable posture towards the needy. But this in no way renders charitable acts of the Greco-Roman world as a part of the problem of ancient economic injustice . . . [instead they are] worthy of commendation.[228]

---

to the early Jesus movement completely counters the hegemonic acquisitiveness and control exercised by the elites within Graeco-Roman society (27–35).

223. Longenecker, *Remember the Poor*, 74–87.

224. Longenecker, *Remember the Poor*, 75–77.

225. The final quote is from Longenecker, *Remember the Poor*, 96. On the prior two points, see 80–85.

226. Longenecker, *Remember the Poor*, 86–87, 98–104.

227. Longenecker, *Remember the Poor*, 106.

228. Longenecker, *Remember the Poor*, 107.

Based on what we have already seen in this chapter, it seems that Paul and his coworkers would beg to differ with Longenecker here (as would a good many people I have known or know who have lived or live in abject poverty but do not take kindly to people with PhDs telling them what they can or cannot contemplate).

Disagreeing with Longenecker does not require us to conclude that the members of the early assemblies of Jesus loyalists did not care for the poorer members in concrete material ways. Indeed, given that this topic has often been neglected, forgotten, or avoided, Longenecker does an excellent job of highlighting many of the ways in which this occurs. For example, he highlights how the generosity of the Corinthians requested in 1 Cor 9:13 is not an isolated event but an instantiation of a general practice of caring for all who are in need.[229] Likewise, the exhortation to "do the good" on behalf of others found in Gal 6:9–10 is a call to support one another in material ways as the term "to do the good" (*ergazometha to agathon*) is "technical terminology in the ancient world for bestowing material benefits on others."[230] Similarly, he notes how the call to "help the weak" in 1 Thess 5:12–22 would be a call to help those who are economically vulnerable (as the term "the weak" is applied to the same party in 1 Cor 1:26–29; 8; 9:22, and when Paul talks about his own economic vulnerability).[231] The same applies to the call to care for the "needs" of others found in Rom 12:13—these needs would include material needs for food, clothing, and shelter—and the same expectation is present in the call to "associate with the lowly" in Rom 12:16.[232]

These other references, and this survey of background material and practices, leads Longenecker to reexamine the affirmation of the call to remember the poor found in Gal 2:10. He is emphatic that this passage refers to those who are materially and economically poor. Previously (generally conservative) scholarship has been dominated by a reading of a reference to "the poor" as those who are not really economically poor (rather, the poor is taken as a synonym for "the saints" or the people of God in general, regardless of their socioeconomic status), but, as Longenecker notes, this reading goes against the interpretation of this passage

---

229. Longenecker, *Remember the Poor*, 141.
230. Longenecker, *Remember the Poor*, 142.
231. Longenecker, *Remember the Poor*, 143.
232. Longenecker, *Remember the Poor*, 144–45.

that dominated the first four centuries of Christianity.[233] Hence, a shift in scholarship can be observed in more recent years to support a reading of this passage that understands "the poor" as the economically deprived (although this language does not recognize that poverty is actually produced when some people impoverish others—poverty is dispossession, it is oppression, and not simply a part of "the way things are"). After all, as Thompson notes, this understanding of the poor is consistent with other Pauline uses of that term (see Rom 15:26; 2 Cor 6:10; 8:2, 9; Gal 4:9).[234] James Dunn also concludes that the poor in Gal 2:10 are those who lacked the resources to live at (let alone above) the subsistence level.[235] Consequently, this focus upon care for the poor continues the Judean tradition of asking just foreigners to demonstrate their righteousness by communally caring for the economically poor—within the context of Galatia, care for the poor replaces circumcision as a primary binding marker of the people of God.[236] Brigitte Kahl is exactly right to observe that, within Gal 2, "material solidarity with the poor" becomes the seal of being in the Anointed.[237]

Second, the request to remember the poor should not be taken as a sign that this was something that the Pauline faction was failing to do prior to the meeting in Jerusalem. The verb form that we read as "to remember" can also mean "continue to remember," and the Pauline faction is not expressing an unfulfilled desire when describing Paul's response but rather is stating that Paul already had been focused on this.[238] This is why the Pauline faction can say that the Jerusalem-based ambassadors of (the) Anointed "added nothing" to what they were already doing.[239]

Finally, as Longenecker demonstrates, Gal 2:10 is not peripheral to the remainder of the content of the letter to the Galatians. The "present evil age" that is condemned in Gal 5:19–21 is defined by savage competition and self-interest, whereas the way of life patterned after Jesus "who gave himself" (Gal 1:4; 2:20) and enlivened by the Spirit of Jesus

---

233. Longenecker, *Remember the Poor*, 205–21, 157–82. And it begs the question as to why "the saints" might have been synonymous with "the poor" in the first place.

234. Thompson, "Paul's Collection," 25–27.

235. Dunn, *Beginning from Jerusalem*, 458–59.

236. Dunn, *Beginning from Jerusalem*, 359.

237. Kahl, *Galatians Re-Imagined*, 279.

238. Longenecker, *Remember the Poor*, 190–95.

239. Longenecker, *Remember the Poor*, 196–97.

is characterized by self-giving in solidarity with the crucified.[240] In light of this, the stipulation to remember the poor is not simply admirable moral exhortation; rather, it lies at the heart of the "truth of the gospel" that Paul was defending in Jerusalem because it is wholly in line with the cruciform configuration of living life together.[241] Therefore, as Longenecker observes: "In Paul's view what the apostles were rubber-stamping in Jerusalem was not merely a decision about circumcision. Instead it was a decision about the moral matrix that was to mark out all communities of Jesus-followers, and at the heart of that matrix lies care for the vulnerable."[242] This is what it means to "do good to others" (Gal 6:9–10), and this is what love looks like according to Paul and his peers—"the gritty realities of self-giving for the benefit of others."[243]

Conclusion: The Spread of the Jesus Movement and the Failure of the Pauline Faction

Thus, we return again to the conclusion that the poorest, most oppressed members of the assemblies of Jesus loyalists were situated at the very core of the assemblies—both locally and transnationally.[244] This is a holistic, all-encompassing vision of sibling-based economics practiced over against all the hierarchies that divide people. As such, it is a form of sharing that is against private property, but it is also more than that—it is a form of sharing that goes well beyond charity and, in many ways, is critical of charity. What we see here is not the establishment of hierarchies, wherein those above are called to relate charitably to those below—instead, what we discover is a household of siblings whose relationships with one another are now built upon the foundation of grace and the abundance of God. This grace brings into being (and is) the practice of concrete material solidarity among diverse parties of oppressed, colonized, and marginalized populations who have been scattered and divided throughout

240. Longenecker, *Remember the Poor*, 210.
241. Longenecker, *Remember the Poor*, 211.
242. Longenecker, *Remember the Poor*, 211.
243. Longenecker, *Remember the Poor*, 215, 217–18. One of the implications of this, as Dieter Georgi notes is the way in which money is evaluated—the value of money is determined based on whether or not it is being put to use in the service of the poor (Georgi, *Remembering the Poor*, 161–64).
244. On the Collection understood in this way, see Georgi, *Remembering the Poor*, 184–89.

the Roman Empire but who are now united in the body of the Anointed. It is this economic solidarity that is the true "explosive power" of the early Jesus movement.[245]

This survey also adds depth to earlier remarks suggesting that the material practices of the early Jesus loyalists were the most significant factor responsible for the rapid spread of the Jesus movement throughout the Roman Empire.[246] Practicing this kind of sibling-based economic solidarity would result in very tangible liberating changes to the lives of those who were at the bottom of the socioeconomic and theopolitical strata. Those who were starving, those who would be forced into prostitution, those who became transient day laborers, those who sold their children into slavery—all these people could find new and abundant life in the movement. In these assemblies, goods were to be shared in the ways described above so that there was enough for everybody. No wonder, then, that the Jesus movement exploded into the empire and had assemblies in all the major cities from Jerusalem to Rome within one generation.[247]

As Longenecker mentions, this means that the early Jesus movement would be most attractive to the impoverished members of society who lived at or below the subsistence level, who did not qualify for patronage, who fell outside the security of a household, and who were not welcome to join other associations (according to Longenecker's scale: ES6–7).[248] Conversely, those at the top of the socioeconomic and theopolitical pyramids of power would have little or no interest in participating in these assemblies (ES1–3).[249] In fact, they would be threatened by these

---

245. The quotation is from Schottroff, "Give to Caesar" 249; see also 246–49. Schottroff sees care for the poor within the early Jesus movement as explosive when juxtaposed with the values and norms of Roman society (although she misses the true and perhaps even literal explosiveness of this because she is still caught up in a charity model of care).

246. See Longenecker, "Poor of Galatians 2:10," 205–21; Bird, "Early Christianity," 236–37. In a later work, Longenecker notes Tertullian's assertion that it was concern for the materially poor that attracted the gentile nations to Christianity (Longenecker, *Remember the Poor*, 162–63).

247. No wonder, also, that scholars who consistently ignore, trivialize, or avoid economic or political engagements with the New Testament continue to remain mystified by the spread of the early Jesus movement (see, for example, Hurtado, *Destroyer of the Gods*, 35, 184–85).

248. Longenecker, *Remember the Poor*, 259–61.

249. Longenecker, *Remember the Poor*, 161.

assemblies and do what we have observed time after time—seek to have them branded as terror cells populated by impious atheists and criminals, worthy of punishment and death.

This leaves those Longenecker places at ES4–5. Longenecker notes that a person from ES4 could be attracted to become a benefactor within a Graeco-Roman *collegium* because: (1) it would permit that person to be a "big fish in a (relatively) small pond"; (2) because it would increase that person's social visibility and public honor; and (3) because it allowed that person to start building connections with some more prominent patrons.[250] However, none of these are relevant to the early assemblies of Jesus loyalists: (1) all members were to be considered as equals in status and those who wished to appear as patrons were resisted; (2) association with Jesus loyalists would be unappealing and would actually cause a loss of public honor; and (3) the dubious relationship of the groups to Roman imperialism made it risky to be associated with them.[251] So members of ES4 would not likely be involved. The same observation applies for members of ES5. While the assemblies of Jesus loyalists may have been attractive to them due to the absence of (any mention of) membership fees, they would still end up being burdened with a great deal of financial responsibility and could quickly end up losing the relatively little surplus they had accumulated with the relatively small (but far from insignificant) advance in status that surplus had the potential to bring them.[252] Consequently, Longenecker concludes that the early assemblies of Jesus loyalists were primarily composed of those who lived at or below the subsistence level. He further concludes that the few who lived above the subsistence level were likely from the small portion of Graeco-Roman society who practiced the more genuine (but also much more exceptional and rare) form of charity described above or those devout "Gentiles" who wished to participate in Judean worship by engaging in care for the needy.[253] If these were the people attracted to the early Jesus movement, another level of the conflict between the assemblies of Jesus loyalists and diasporic Judean communities becomes clear. If those who had (relatively) more than those who had just enough to get by (or nothing at all) were the ones leaving one community to go to another, this

---

250. Longenecker, *Remember the Poor*, 263–65.
251. Longenecker, *Remember the Poor*, 264–71, 280–87.
252. Longenecker, *Remember the Poor*, 271.
253. Longenecker, *Remember the Poor*, 272–80. Here, Longenecker cites Gal 4:12–15 and the initial reception Paul received when he arrived in Galatia.

would be considered a threat to the survival of not only the abandoned group but also the individuals who participated therein.

However, after his valuable study, Longenecker makes a troubling conclusion—one that shows how his association with the charity model is problematical, even if his desire to see people act more charitably is admirable. The conclusion that Longenecker draws is that economic differences exist within the early assemblies of Jesus loyalists and that *this is fine*, as long as the *most basic* needs of (the poor) are being met.[254] It is the latter part of this conclusion that is problematical. Granted, there were economic differences between Jesus loyalists (although not nearly so great as Longenecker's scale imagines) but participation within the body of the Anointed was to lead to the leveling of those differences. The point is not to simply say that one is a part of a community where the most basic needs of the poor are being met (after all, if two thousand years of charity have taught us anything, it is that the rich and the poor differ quite considerably on what exactly constitutes "meeting the basic needs" of the poor); the point is to demonstrate the liberating equality that is now experienced in every possible way. The call here is not to be slightly nicer or more sensitive—the call is to be a genuinely new creation, existing in a mutually liberating form of solidarity with the groaning parts of creation, and thereby becoming the embodiment of the righteous justice of God (see 2 Cor 5:17–21; Rom 8:1–39). In other words, not just bread but bread *and roses*, as anarchists have been wont to emphasize.

But, of course, all of this is contested from the very beginning of the spread of the Jesus movement. Given the rapidity of that spread among poor and colonized populations, there was bound to be some creep towards mainstream values. Those with *slightly* higher status than the majority of participants in the movement would see an opportunity to boost their own status if they were able to gain members of the movement as allies or clients, especially if they were able to impose their values upon the group. Thus, as membership trickles up the socioeconomic and theopolitical scale, so also the values of the higher status members can easily trickle down into the group—especially if those higher status members are able to gain some kind of material or economic control over the group and its functioning. It is exactly this drift that the Pauline faction was combating with the Super Apostles at Corinth. From the perspective of Paul and his coworkers, it is not okay for economic differences to

---

254. Longenecker, *Remember the Poor*, 287–90.

continue to exist, no matter how charitable the higher status members claim to be. Consequently, the Pauline faction is adamant that those with relatively higher status (at this point, those slightly above the subsistence level) are not to enjoy any of the benefits that this relatively higher status grants them within the dominant culture and are to engage a way of sharing life together that makes the status of all parties equal.

Therefore, while people experiencing various degrees of impoverishment were initially attracted to the Jesus movement—and while the high numbers of people who rapidly joined the movement could potentially attract those at a slightly higher level—it remained to be seen whether or not it would continue to be acceptable to maintain hierarchical (and ultimately oppressive) charitable ways of structuring life within the community, or whether the sibling-based political economy of grace would prevail and abolish the hierarchies that divided people and sustained inequality.

Unfortunately, the Pauline faction failed to accomplish what it hoped.[255] It is quite possible that the Super Apostles triumphed in Corinth. Similarly, when one reads Acts, it is hard to arrive at anything but the conclusion that the Collection for siblings experiencing poverty in Jerusalem was rejected along with Paulinism. Furthermore, as we see with the Pastoral Epistles, conservative forces very rapidly gained influence in the assemblies that were related to the Pauline faction, and the name of Paul was used to advocate for the deployment of status quo gendered, economic, and status divisions within those assemblies. Thus, it is sloppy history to posit that the betrayal of the Jesus movement occurred with a marked "Constantinian shift" in the fourth century CE.[256] In actuality, things began to be compromised from the very beginning and what we see with Constantine is simply the formalization of what was accomplished long before.[257]

This sort of trajectory and rapid corruption is common among radical or revolutionary movements that grow and spread rapidly but are able to sustain themselves over time instead of being totally annihilated at the outset. What begins as one thing quickly becomes something else. Yet it should not be forgotten that, according to the Pauline faction, this kind of transformation would be seen as a complete betrayal of the gospel of

255. See Friesen, "Paul and Economics," 51.

256. See Clapp, *Peculiar People*, 23.

257. What comes after Constantine—the various permutations of Christian imperialism—is simply faithfully and loyally following in this trajectory.

Anointed Jesus, which was to be assembled in the household of God, wherein siblings engaged in an economy of grace, embraced cruciform shame as honor, and rejected charity, private property, and the hierarchies of power that both sustained and were sustained by the death-dealing rulers of their present evil age.

Excursus

THE AUTHORITY OF PAUL WITHIN THE EARLY ASSEMBLIES OF JESUS LOYALTIES

Introduction

IN THE LAST CHAPTER, I suggested that part of the reason for the voluntary nature of the Collection was that the early assemblies associated with the Pauline faction were attempting to form anti-hierarchical ways of structuring life together wherein all members were to relate to one another as siblings within the newly constituted household of God. As we have seen, each member was said to be filled with the powerful Spirit of Life and the true authorities over the community were Jesus (the already ascendant and Anointed firstborn from the dead and left-for-dead) and God (the Father of Jesus). These authorities are not represented by any one person within the assemblies; rather, the Spirit gives gifts to all and establishes horizontal relationships of mutual care between all members.

Given this, how is one to understand the authority that Paul may or may not have within the assemblies of Jesus loyalists associated with him and his coworkers? In this brief excursus, I will survey a number of positions taken by scholars—spanning a spectrum from those who consider Paul as committed to inscribing a vertical hierarchy within the assemblies of Jesus loyalists (with himself at the top), to those who straddle something of a middle-ground and view Paul as a "charismatic authority" (along the lines of Max Weber's model), to those who see Paul as an anti-authoritarian whose commitment to establishing horizontal relationships between people prevented him from trying to establish himself as *the* authority figure.[258] Upon completing this survey, I will draw some of my own conclusions.[259]

Paul as an Authority Figure: Criticisms of the Apostle

In 1999, Sandra Polaski published *Paul and the Discourse of Power*, a critical contribution to Pauline studies and the nature of the authority Paul did or did not seek to claim for himself in the assemblies of Jesus loyalists. In it, Polaski uses Foucault to question Paul and to examine power dynamics that may be masked by the surface rhetoric of the (uncontested) letters.[260] Like some early scholars who examined the nature of Paul's authority (more on whom, momentarily), Polaski argues that Paul's authority is of a "charismatic nature" of the Weberian sort, wherein Paul is viewed as an exceptional person who is capable of following his own initiative with the expectation that others would follow him.[261] Consequently, although the Spirit is said to be at work tearing down old divisions and barriers, asymmetrical power relationships were still brought to bear upon the assemblies of Jesus loyalists—and Paul himself becomes the power-broker who cannot be superseded no matter how much authority is granted to others.[262] This is because, as an apostle, Paul is "someone to whom God entrusts the gospel, and therefore someone who speaks on the basis of that revelation."[263] Furthermore, Polaski argues, Paul's discourse about grace further reinforced his claim to authority because of the extent of grace that he had received.[264] Not only this, but because others may misconstrue

---

258. Charismatic authority, here, takes place within the context of "social relations of asymmetric power distribution considered legitimate by participating actors" (Holmberg, *Paul and Power*, 3; see also 5–7).

259. Some of this material is anticipated by previous remarks regarding the nature of Paul's apostleship and his socioeconomic status, and some of this material, in turn, anticipates our subsequent discussion of the nature of the *ekklesiai*—the assemblies of Jesus loyalists—so this section will be relatively brief.

260. Polaski, *Paul*, 13–14, 21.

261. Polaski, *Paul*, 28–29. Further, as Polaski argues, given the fundamentally unstable basis of this kind of authority, those who wield it—like Paul—will often try to routinize it in order to perpetuate it over time (30–31).

262. Polaski, *Paul*, 23, 31–33.

263. Polaski, *Paul*, 95–96. This position is seriously problematized by the understanding of "the gospel" proposed in chapter 5.

264. Polaski, *Paul*, 106–11. Even if, Polaski also notes, this grace is given to Paul on behalf of others (114).

or reject grace, even though they may also be recipients of it, Paul must continually function as an overseer within the *ekklesiai*.[265] Consequently, within the hierarchy of charismata that Paul establishes, it is no surprise to discover his own gifts at the top.[266]

Polaski supports these conclusions by examining the letters ascribed to Paul and draws special attention to the letters to Philemon, Galatia, and Corinth. Beginning with Philemon, she notes how Paul, even while praising the letter's primary recipient, establishes himself as the one best fit to judge the situation with Onesimus and Philemon—even though Paul employs the language of mutuality.[267] Furthermore, Paul relies heavily upon the charismatic nature of his authority throughout this letter because he did not have the legal or political power to compel the manumission of Onesimus and so his authority to command Philemon to act a certain way remains beneath or behind the text as an unsubstantiated claim.[268] However, the reader should not be deceived: Paul is urging Philemon to accept new power relationships that would diminish the power currently held by Philemon, and Paul is trying to manipulate Philemon into accepting this—not least by writing a letter that is seeking agreement rather than negotiation that would be publicly read before an entire assembly of Jesus loyalists.[269] Second, in the letter to the Galatians, Paul is writing to counter challenges that have been made against his authority and is trying to reestablish his authority over the Galatians.[270] Hence, he is keen to prove that he has received divine revelations that grant him a special status and which also make him the authorized interpreter of revelations given by God (the Father of Jesus) over against anybody else who wishes to claim this.[271] Finally, in Corinth, Polaski notes that Paul refuses money from the Corinthians because he did not want to be caught in a patron-client relationship with them, where he would be in the position of the client.[272] Consequently, in light of these things, Polaski concludes that Paul's liberating rhetoric consistently masks the imposition of

---

265. Polaski, *Paul*, 114–17.
266. Polaski, *Paul*, 118.
267. Polaski, *Paul*, 60–61.
268. Polaski, *Paul*, 64, 68.
269. Polaski, *Paul*, 69–70.
270. Polaski, *Paul*, 75.
271. Polaski, *Paul*, 79, 81, 101–2.
272. Polaski, *Paul*, 97–98.

hierarchies of power and authority within the newly constituted assemblies of Jesus loyalists.

Graham Shaw comes to similar conclusions to those of Polaski although, perhaps, in a less charitable manner, as he imputes ill intentions to Paul. Shaw claims that Paul clearly had political motives for claiming authority over his readers, making blatant claims to power, praying manipulative prayers, inculcating anxiety by means of eschatology, adopting a persecution complex in response to all criticisms, and using the rhetoric of deliverance and reconciliation to domineer and divide.[273] This leads Shaw to conclude that Paul is "brittle" because he is "delusional."[274]

Elizabeth Castelli proposes a similar argument to those of Polaski and Shaw by exploring the theme of mimesis (imitation) within the letters ascribed to Paul.[275] Since, within mimesis, one is always dealing with a model and an imperfect copy, Castelli argues that Paul uses appeals to imitation as a strategy of power which expresses hierarchical relationships and valorizes sameness over difference.[276] Therefore:

> Paul's discourse of mimesis uses rhetoric to rationalize and shore up a particular set of social relations of power relationships within the early Christian [sic] movement. His use of the notion of mimesis, with all of its nuances, reinforces both Paul's own privileged position and the power relations of the early Christian communities as somehow "natural."[277]

These, then, are three scholarly examples of what has actually become quite a popular view—that Paul was something of an insecure, oppressive, power-monger who led the Jesus movement astray and into the domain of what became hierarchical, death-dealing, institutional Christianity. However, others have offered equally scholarly readings of Paul and his relation to authority and have come to different conclusions.

---

273. Shaw, *Cost of Authority*, 181-83.
274. Shaw, *Cost of Authority*, 182.
275. Castelli, *Imitating Paul*, 14 (and throughout).
276. Castelli, *Imitating Paul*, 14-16. This fits with the standard ways in which the trope of mimesis was employed in antiquity (see 59-87). Further, for those who wish to assert that all of this is ultimately understood as mimesis of the Anointed, Castelli argues that the Anointed Jesus is an afterthought and Paul is the primary person to be imitated (90-91; see, however, 1 Thess 1:6-7; 2:14; Phil 3:17; 1 Cor 4:16; 11:1; Gal 4:12).
277. Castelli, *Imitating Paul*, 116.

Paul as a Non-Domineering Charismatic Authority

Among others who understand Paul as a charismatic authority in the Weberian sense, there exists a broader spectrum of readings. Bengt Holmberg, who helped to launch this area of study among Pauline scholars, lays the foundation for such charismatic readings by noting the ways in which Paul pushes back against the more traditional hierarchies of power (and, in the case of the Jesus movement, the assembly [or assemblies] of Jesus loyalists in Jerusalem), even though Paul still wants recognition from those authorities.[278] Consequently, in his conflicts with both authorities from Jerusalem and local leaders, Paul draws attention to himself as an extraordinary person (called by God, possessing miraculous powers, and engaging in salvific activity) with a radical mission, inspiring others to view him with devotion as a hero and establishing the pattern of behavior for those who come after him.[279] Therefore, for the assemblies Paul is helping establish, Holmberg argues that Paul desires to have a profound and ongoing (i.e., permanent) spiritual, intellectual, ethical, and social influence upon the participants.[280] However, Holmberg also notes that this is an ideal (for Paul) that was limited in actuality by other traveling ambassadors, by direct experiences of the Spirit, and by other patriarchal figures—as demonstrated by Paul's constant efforts to rationalize, explain, and appeal to his readers.[281] Consequently, where Polaski, Shaw, and Castelli are inclined to see Paul as something of a manipulative dictatorial figure, Holmberg argues that while Paul may aspire to that sort of power, he doesn't actually possess it. Thus, while Holmberg paves the way for the three scholars just mentioned, he stops short of drawing the conclusions they draw.

More charitable readings, within the Weberian camp, have been offered by John Schütz, Hans von Campenhausen, and James Dunn. Schütz argues that, over against "leadership"—which is often power taken by force—"authority" is understood as the right to power and, as such, is the interpretation of power.[282] Looking at Paul's own interpretation of his claim to power, Schütz argues that Paul's claim is grounded in his commission to preach the gospel, which permits him to be continually

---

278. Holmberg, *Paul and Power*, 56, 70, 153.
279. Holmberg, *Paul and Power*, 149–60.
280. Holmberg, *Paul and Power*, 70–74.
281. Holmberg, *Paul and Power*, 184–87.
282. Schütz, *Paul*, 3, 9, 14.

responsible for the assemblies of Jesus loyalists, which is a role to which Paul has been called, and which includes the ongoing interpretation of the gospel, primarily embodied in the life of Paul himself, who is always there to correct others if they fail to interpret and embody things correctly.[283] Furthermore, all of this is posed over and against those who wish to identify authority with tradition and history.[284] This then prompts Schütz to ask the following question: "Is Paul's rigorous subordination of everyone and everything to the gospel not really a mask for the subordination of others to himself as an apostle?"[285] Unlike Polaski et al., Schütz responds to this question with a resounding, "No!" Paul, like the others in the assemblies, is bounded by a telos, and the apostle is subject to the power that manifests itself in the gospel, just like all others await the full unveiling of the power of the gospel in the eschaton.[286]

Von Campenhausen's argument is similar, albeit slightly less optimistic. He is more interested in exploring the relationships between charismata and offices of power and the ways in which these things overlap and conflict.[287] Von Campenhausen claims that the early Jesus movement was very charismatic in nature, lacking institutionalized authorities, but that Paul sought to change this by identifying as the apostle to the gentiles and laying claim to the world outside of Judea.[288] As such, Paul claims to have autonomy and freedom from all other authorities, and he claims equal status with any other people who have claimed to be apostles.[289] However, von Campenhausen argues, while Paul does see himself as a father figure and *the* authority, he also argues that Paul does not seek to develop this into a sacral relationship of spiritual control and subordination but rejects this idea to pursue corporate freedom under the Anointed's Lordship.[290] Hence, Paul belongs to the assemblies and not vice versa.[291]

---

283. Schütz, *Paul*, 281–82. Again, this understanding of "the gospel" is seriously problematized in chapter 5.

284. Schütz, *Paul*, 283.

285. Schütz, *Paul*, 285.

286. Schütz, *Paul*, 185–86. And the loss of this eschatological horizon, Schütz argues, gives rise to both orthodox and gnostic power structures.

287. Campenhausen, *Ecclesiastical Authority*, 1.

288. Campenhausen, *Ecclesiastical Authority*, 29–31.

289. Campenhausen, *Ecclesiastical Authority*, 31–33.

290. Campenhausen, *Ecclesiastical Authority*, 44–46.

291. Campenhausen, *Ecclesiastical Authority*, 47.

This is also why Paul gives guidance instead of orders.[292] According to von Campenhausen, the Spirit is the key to understanding the dynamics that exist between authority and freedom since the Spirit is the one who gives gifts to different members, even though there still remains some hierarchy among the gifts.[293] This hierarchy does permit Paul to place himself at the top in a place of permanent authority and also to elevate others he deems appropriate.[294] Over time, the tension with the freedom of the Spirit and the subordination of the apostles to the assemblies gives way before these elevated individuals who end up establishing permanent offices of power.[295]

Dunn also highlights the early absence of offices and titles within the assemblies of Jesus loyalists associated with the Pauline faction. Given that Greek and Roman associations and Judean gatherings within the diaspora often mimicked the structures of municipal life (with titles like magistrates, curators, prefects, secretaries, treasurers, overseers, rulers, and elders), the absence of these things is notable.[296] Consequently, those who did end up functioning as leaders were recognized as such because of their work and service on behalf of the assemblies. Hence, once again, this is taken to be a charismatic authority structure where previously existing social statuses were not relevant factors, although, Dunn argues, those who actually did function as leaders tended to be the wealthier or higher status people who had the time to serve the assemblies in this way.[297] However, even with these charismatic leaders in place, Dunn still asserts that it is ultimately the assembly as a whole which was finally responsible for the order and discipline practiced in the meetings.[298]

---

292. Campenhausen, *Ecclesiastical Authority*, 47.

293. Campenhausen, *Ecclesiastical Authority*, 56–59.

294. Campenhausen, *Ecclesiastical Authority*, 60–63.

295. Campenhausen, *Ecclesiastical Authority*, 46–69.

296. Dunn, *Beginning from Jerusalem*, 637–38.

297. Dunn, *Beginning from Jerusalem*, 640. Dunn's argument about wealth and status at this point should probably be rejected in light of what we have said earlier about the probable social status of the members of the early assemblies of Jesus loyalists. Granted, there would be those with *relatively* higher wealth or status within any given assembly, but it would be a mistake to think that the slightly less poor have *significantly more* free time to devote to serving the assembly than the slightly more poor.

298. Dunn, *Beginning from Jerusalem*, 640.

Subverting Authority and Equal Membership: Paul as Anti-Authority

Finally, on the far end of the spectrum is the position that takes Paul to be anti-authoritarian in a more consistent manner. As has been demonstrated throughout this text, Paul and his coworkers were continually challenging and seeking to subvert or totally replace the hierarchies of power and authority that existed within the Roman Empire. Thus, Neil Elliott asserts, Paul wants to express power relations in a way that is subversive to the imperial power relations that trickled down and dominated all parts of society.[299] Consequently, Elliott goes on to observe, Paul is faced with the challenge of trying to spread this subversive way of sharing life together and confronting rivals who wish to instate other dynamics of power within the assemblies of Jesus loyalists, without, at the same time, engaging in the kind of power play that Paul himself condemns.[300]

Does Paul succeed at doing this? Some scholars would say that Paul does succeed by not actually possessing any formal power—understood as the ability to impose his will by force upon the members of the assemblies. In this regard, Robert Jewett argues that Paul was not an authoritarian but tried to pursue the "radical democratization" of the assemblies of Jesus loyalists.[301] Maurice Goguel makes the same claim, arguing that the assemblies operated on a principle of "majority rule, which is precisely why Paul had to beg, plead, and argue in order to try and make his case—if Paul had any real power, such begging and pleading and arguing, done with so much desperation and vigour, would not be necessary."[302] J. Paul Sampley makes a similar case by examining how the theme of partnership in the Anointed builds upon Roman notions of partnership found within consensual *societas*.[303] The consensual *societas* was a partnership made between parties who were considered to be equals and who were to each contribute something towards a common goal, which united the parties beyond any boundaries of background or social standing.[304] The foundation was voluntary mutual trust and reciprocity in a context free

---

299. Elliott, "Apostle's Self-Presentation," 72.
300. Elliott, "Apostle's Self-Presentation," 72–75.
301. Jewett, *Paul*, 116–19.
302. See Goguel, *Primitive Church*, 232.
303. See Sampley, *Pauline Partnership in Christ*, x.
304. Sampley, *Pauline Partnership in Christ*, 11–14, 62–71.

from coercion.[305] However, although all were equals, some people could act as designated representatives of a *societas*. This did not elevate those representatives above the other members but simply gave them a representative role.[306] According to Sampley, then, this is how Paul understands his own role and the consensual *societas* becomes one of the models Paul employs to help build the network of assemblies of Jesus loyalists throughout the Roman Empire.

Conclusion: An Anarchist Parallel

What, then, are we to make of this spectrum of opinions? Was Paul an authoritarian power-monger or a person who viewed himself as under the authority of the assemblies, just like every other Spirit-empowered individual member, or was he something in between, like a kind-hearted boss or mentor? It is certainly true that, in his impassioned rhetorical appeals, Paul does make certain claims—like that of being the father (or, more frequently, mother) of the members of the assemblies to which he writes—but were such claims accepted as de facto truths? Did the assemblies reject Paul's claim to fatherhood or motherhood or apostleship or anything else? Well, it is quite possible that some of the assemblies, like those at Corinth, did exactly that. Yet is it possible for a person to make such claims and still be committed to what Jewett called the "radical democratization" of the assemblies of Jesus loyalists?[307] I believe that it is. Here, once again, we must remind ourselves that the letters written by Paul and his coworkers are letters of passion more than they are academic theses. Having been personally involved with some anarchist collectives and other groups involved in grassroots community mobilization based upon core beliefs regarding the equal significance, value, and contributive ability of all members, I have certainly witnessed times when the rhetoric of a discussion went outside of the beliefs held by the members speaking—particularly when those speakers felt that some fundamental

---

305. Sampley, *Pauline Partnership in Christ*, 14.

306. Sampley, *Pauline Partnership in Christ*, 15. However, Sampley notes, the consensual *societas* tended to be short-lived because members became greedy and self-centered and began to exploit others instead of treating them with mutuality (16–17). Consequently, when this kind of dissension arose, Paul, because of his commitment to the equality of the members—i.e., precisely because he was not trying to build up his personal power—appealed to other models (113–14).

307. Jewett, *Paul*, 116–19.

component of the community was threatened. Working towards the creation of anti-hierarchical, egalitarian structures within a movement, within the context of a broader world that is marked by hierarchies and power struggles at all levels, is no easy task—and this was just as true in Paul's day as it is in ours. How, exactly, is one to go about advocating for a particular way of life or embodiment of belief within the movement without falling into the trap of using force or coercion to impose that way of life onto others? Often, just when one thinks one has avoided this trap, one falls directly into it, and so one learns, by a process of trial and error, how to advocate (or evangelize, I suppose) while also respecting the autonomy and value of others. I reckon Paul was figuring this out along the way, just like anybody else who has grown up enmeshed within power structures they disliked. Uprooting them is an ongoing process.

Certainly, the obvious desperation in the rhetoric employed by Paul and his coworkers suggests to me that there was no foundation for the authority granted to him apart from the will of those who granted it to him. In this regard, Paul likely was a charismatic authority in the Weberian sense and did not possess any traditional or institutional base for his authority that he could fall back on if the will, interests, desires, or allegiances of the members of the assemblies changed. Again, an appeal to anarchist collectives or grassroots egalitarian communities may be beneficial in understanding this. Within these communities-without-leaders, some members' words carry more clout than the words of some other members. This can occur for a number of reasons that are often combined: perhaps the member has a demonstrated ability to think well about the matter under discussion, perhaps the member was there from the beginning, perhaps the member has shown continual commitment to the radical goals of the collective and has, because of this commitment, suffered personal injury or loss, been targeted by state-based, legally-sanctioned violence, worked tirelessly towards the betterment of the collective or the community, or perhaps the member is particularly well-situated to speak to the matter under discussion (hence, for example, the prioritizing of the voices of women, trans*, non-binary, and genderqueer folks in discussions related to patriarchy, or the prioritizing of voices from black, Indigenous, or other people of color when discussing racism, or prioritizing the voices of Indigenous people when it comes to colonization, and so on). Such people can become "charismatic authorities" even within groups that are deliberately anti-hierarchical and egalitarian. But this is because the other members of the community respect and admire these people and often feel that these people are capable of better expressing what they themselves believe. However, if this ever changes and this respect is lost or charismatic authorities begin to express views that consistently and sharply contradict what the other members believe, then others will begin to function as charismatic authorities and there is nothing, apart from rhetoric, to which the previous people can appeal to maintain their influence—if, that is, they even desire to do so.

I think that this contemporary parallel makes the best sense of the sort of authority we find reflected in the letters written by Paul and his coworkers. The institutionalization of authority that comes after was likely necessary to begin the process of reestablishing hierarchies between men and women, slaves and freedpeople, the relatively less poor and the relatively more poor, and different ethnic groups. To impose hierarchies upon people who were seeking liberation from precisely those hierarchies requires an institutional power base that forces people to accept inequalities. Paul and his coworkers, however, fought desperately against those who wished to take the early assemblies of Jesus loyalists in that direction.

That said, I understand that I am open to the charge of projecting my own experiences back into the reading of the texts, and I understand that I may simply be finding the Paul I want to find there. This is possible. It seems to me, in discussions of Paul's authority, what people find, as in so many other areas of Pauline research, seems to be pretty closely tied to what people go looking for and hoping to find. Those who dislike Paul tend to find an abusive power-monger. Those who like Paul tend to find someone more likable. Given the paucity of reference material we actually possess in this regard, each position does have some plausibility, and that plausibility is often dependent upon the broader context of how one understands the early Jesus movement and reads the Pauline Epistles. However, for the reasons outlined above, and in light of the rest of the argument of this series, I believe that the position I have outlined is the most plausible.

5

THE LAWLESSNESS OF GOOD NEWS IN THE MAKING: JUSTICE, JESUS LOYALTY, AND LOVINGLY ORGANIZING TREASONOUS LIFE

Introduction: What Do We Talk about When We Talk about the Pauline Gospel?

THE STAGE IS NOW set for us to explore the themes that scholarship and tradition have clustered around the motif of "Paul's gospel." These are themes related to Jesus, justice, the law, loyalty (or faith), and love—as they are negotiated and expressed in the formation of the practices of the assemblies of Jesus loyalists who were associated with Paul and his coworkers. In this chapter, I will argue that the good news, according to the Pauline faction, is precisely the formation, spread, and networking of assemblies dedicated to overcoming and annihilating the oppressive hierarchies of power, property, permission, and dispossession under which their members have grievously suffered. The good news is that people are, now, together, related and relating to one another as liberated siblings within the household of God and that, as such, they are pursuing their fuller liberation (along with the liberation of all who have been vanquished, colonized, oppressed, dispossessed, and enslaved by Rome) in economic, material, familial, political, treasonous, creative, communal, and festive ways. As we have already seen, this manifests in a multitude of practical ways in the day-to-day lives of the members of the assemblies—sometimes by ensuring that socioeconomic hierarchies are not replicated when local assemblies gather for a meal, sometimes by pooling money in order to care for those in other locations who risk losing everything due to extreme poverty, sometimes by telling stories about a state-executed terrorist named Jesus who was justly condemned according to the law and crucified at the behest of both international and local authorities, but whom, wonder of wonders, God raised from the dead, and who now haunts a transnational uprising of all of those who have been left for dead.

Thus, over against the great majority of scholars who talk about Paul's gospel as some kind of proposition about salvation by faith or some kind of narrative about Jesus's death, resurrection, and lordship (or some combination of these two options), I will argue that, for Paul and his coworkers, the good news primarily refers to what is happening in their present moment in the assemblies of which they are a part. This is not to say that Jesus, whether as the terrorist who was crucified by Rome, or as the resurrected heavenly Lord, or as the Spirit who empowers the members of the assemblies (both individually and collectively) has nothing to do with the Pauline *euangelion*. Jesus is an essential element. He played (and continues to play) a critical role in making such assemblies possible.

Indeed, as we will see, the contrast and conflict between Jesus and Caesar is the final point of rupture between Paul and the cornerstones of the ideo-theology of Rome. We have already seen how Paul and his coworkers oppose Graeco-Roman hierarchies related to the family unit, gender, and slavery, with the fictive kinship of all of those who are liberated as siblings in the household of God. We have also seen how the Pauline faction opposes Graeco-Roman notions of honor by embracing shame in solidarity with the crucified. And we have seen how the Pauline faction opposes the hoarding of wealth enabled by the oppressive practices of patronage by establishing transnational networks for sharing money in a manner that prioritizes need over thieving possessiveness, where each gives according to one's ability and each receives according to one's need. So, also, we will now discover that over against the ideo-theology of Rome—its concerted campaign to distribute the good news officially sanctioned by the emperor (which was also a collective reshaping of justice, loyalty, love, and how people shaped life together), and focused on the divine Caesars—the Pauline faction posits Jesus as the true Lord and Savior who triumphed over the greatest enemy, Death. As a result, Jesus is now superior to all the spiritual powers (notably Sin and the rule of law) and their earthly representatives (notably the entire authority network implicated in the crucifixion of Jesus) who all operate in the service of Death. This victory reveals Jesus to be the true Son of God, the true first among equals, the one and only Lord, and the truly Anointed. As a result, Jesus is said to be the one who truly brings the merciful gift of peace to all the peoples of the world who, despite Roman claims, actually continue to exist, not in freedom but in bondage until this present time.

This chapter will proceed in six parts. In this first part, I will examine the conversation that has taken place regarding the political (or not) nature of the *euangelion* heralded by Paul and his coworkers. In the second part, I will examine the Pauline faction's understanding of Jesus by more fully exploring the titles ascribed to him and the conclusions drawn about him. This will then lead, in part three, to an examination of the implications these conclusions about Jesus have in relation to justice, the law, love, and faith. In part four, I will turn to the gospel proper and examine how the gospel was assembled within the uprising advanced by Paul and others who had been left for dead. Finally, in part five, I will turn to the vexing question of how to read Rom 13:1–7. Part six will offer a conclusion and reflect upon Paul's probable death in the state-sanctioned extermination of Jesus loyalists that followed the firing of Rome during the reign of Nero in 64 CE.

The Politics of Gospel Language

In order to proceed with this argument regarding the Pauline *euangelion*, I want to first examine the various positions scholars have taken regarding the possible political overtones of the language Paul and his co-authors use in relation to the gospel and Jesus. There are some who argue that there is nothing political about Pauline gospel language and there are those who argue that the language is thoroughly political. However, within that second group there is a spectrum of contradictory opinions. On one extreme are those who argue that the political nature of this language signifies Paul's approval of the imperial political system. On the other extreme are those who argue that this language signifies a thoroughgoing opposition to Roman imperialism. In between these extremes are those who argue that the situation is more complicated than a simple for-or-against binary allows. Some scholars who make this argument lean towards more conservative conclusions about the Pauline faction while other scholars who make this argument favor more politically dangerous conclusions. I will briefly examine each of these positions, moving from most to least conservative. I will then engage in a necessary aside to clarify claims and counterclaims about "hidden" transcripts in the Pauline texts before examining the standard definitions of "the gospel" in order to highlight why I think they are misleading and inadequate.

The first position is held by those who argue that any of the language used in relation to the *euangelion* gospeled by the Pauline faction is entirely spiritual and devoid of political significance. Although once popular among theologians and readers of Pauline texts prior to the rise of historical and other criticisms, and although this reading remains popular in Christian faith communities that favor what they call a "plain reading of Scripture" (i.e., a reading devoid of any thoughtful contextualization or analysis, performed primarily to reinforce previously conceived notions that, not coincidentally, have tended to advance the material, sociopolitical, and economic power of those who formulated and enforce these notions), this is now a minority position among even conservative scholars who find other ways to wrestle with Paulinism due to the overwhelming nature of the evidence. However, there are still a few scholars who seek to defend this position by arguing that there is nothing at all political in gospel language or the names and titles given to Jesus. Seyoon Kim is likely the most prominent example of someone attempting this despite an overwhelming flood of evidence to the contrary. Thus, he asserts that "the Messiah's reign is not political. . . . Paul's conception of Christ's reign and salvation is categorically different from the Roman imperial rule and [salvation]."[1] The basis of Kim's argument, as we will see, is deeply flawed and essentially rests on ignoring the evidence and accusing others of using texts as proof-texts to verify their preconceived notions so that he can use the texts as proof-texts to verify his preconceived notions.[2] Thus, Kim argues that those who see a dangerously political Paul in the epistles are engaging in a "parallelomania" and finding anti-imperialism in texts where this is "no clear anti-imperial intention."[3] In fact, Kim argues, "it is difficult to find any political dimension" in various concepts (specifically, righteousness/justice, peace, and freedom) as they are discussed in the epistle to the Romans because, really, what Paul has in view is "sinners'

1. Kim, *Christ and Caesar*, 18–19 (and throughout).
2. See Kim, *Christ and Caesar*, 32, where he also professes puzzlement as to how "some sophisticated exegetes" could fall into this kind of oh-so-obvious prooftexting.
3. Kim, *Christ and Caesar*, 28.

THE LAWLESSNESS OF GOOD NEWS IN THE MAKING

relationship with God . . . without reflecting on its social corollary."[4] Unfortunately, Kim never demonstrates why he can so firmly conclude that political dimensions are lacking from all of this. In fact, by ignoring the evidence that has accumulated (some of which I have already discussed, some of which will be discussed more later in this chapter), Kim misses how certain words will always have certain connotations or overtones in certain contexts. Thus, for example, if one were today to speak of Jesus as the true president tasked with bringing peace, justice, freedom, and democracy to those who have been colonized by America and its foolish rulers in this present evil age, one could not help but recognize that this language carries political connotations (even if the nature of those connotations is contested). However, Kim discards the notion of Pauline language carrying political overtones because it is based, in his opinion, on a faulty deductive argument that too hastily and incorrectly assumes the following six things: (1) there was an all-pervasive Roman imperial cult in the east that thoroughly integrated religion and politics; (2) Paul was an heir of Judean apocalyptic dualism and saw Rome as one component of a present evil age doomed to destruction; (3) because Jesus was crucified by Roman authorities, the Pauline faction must have an anti-Roman bias; (4) the use of the word *ekklesia* must have political connotations; (5) Paul's refusal of patronage in Corinth had anti-imperial implications; and (6) that the frequent imprisonments and persecutions Paul experienced from local authorities must have been grounded in solid political reasons.[5] Kim hastily dismisses all of these points without wrestling overly much with any of them (this kind of wrestling is unnecessary from his perspective, given all that he already assumes is clear about the texts) but, as I have labored to show (with the exception of [4], which will be examined in detail in section 4 of this chapter), all of them are solid conclusions to draw. Kim, however, simply continues to assume that it is patently obvious that Paul is actually talking about human sinfulness and never Roman injustice, opposing the Mosaic Law and never the Roman law, and confronting the "nationalistic hubris" of "the Jews" and never that of the Romans.[6] Furthermore, Kim draws upon the evidence that has been passed down from the early church fathers and highlights how these records do not interpret Paul in a counter-imperial

---

4. Kim, *Christ and Caesar*, 18.
5. Kim, *Christ and Caesar*, 30–31.
6. Kim, *Christ and Caesar*, 16–18. That this also smells of anti-Semitism is in keeping with the imperialist Christian tradition in which Kim is rooted.

manner.⁷ Despite their proximity to and fluid use of the language deployed in the Pauline Epistles, these early church interpreters actually try to show Christians how they fit within the empire through prayer for the well-being of the emperor, obedience to the law, and the payment of taxes.⁸ However, Kim's reading is tainted by his participation in a theological tradition that presupposes consistency on all key points, not only within the New Testament canon but also between the New Testament and what are taken to be the divinely inspired orthodox creeds and positions adopted by the (singular and carefully selected) orthodox church throughout history. What Kim fails to recognize is that there have ever only been competing, overlapping, and contradictory traditions and trajectories within what became Christianity or, better still, Christianities. In this regard, I think that the prior discussion related to slavery and what to do with monies collected within the early assemblies of Jesus loyalists (specifically, controversies about whether that money be used to redeem members from slavery or pay wages to professional clergy), when paired with the prior analysis of Paul's conflict with (and probably loss to) the Super Apostles in Corinth, leads to the conclusion that several of the positions taken by the church fathers are a betrayal of the Pauline faction's understanding of the gospel and its response to the question of what is to be done.⁹ Kim continues this betrayal, not least of all because he forcefully asserts that, while the Pauline faction and Roman propaganda may have used the same words, in the Pauline Epistles those words are used in a spiritual context that is "politically innocuous."¹⁰

On this final point, Kim is approvingly quoting the work of Christopher Bryan, who argues that when Paul uses the same words for Jesus that are more commonly used for Caesar, Paul is "hardly using them in the same context, or meaning anything like the same thing by them."¹¹ But even Bryan, for all of his desire to maintain the kind of conservative state-, wealth-, and war-loving Christianity that has flourished in the US since it was first created by slavers (who separated from Britain because

---

7. Kim, *Christ and Caesar*, 32–33, 64.

8. Kim, *Christ and Caesar*, 60–64. Pickett also observes this trend in early Christian literature, noting how 1 Clement pushes back against counter-imperial understandings of Christianity by urging submission to imperial rule (Pickett, "Conflicts at Corinth," 135–37).

9. For more on this betrayal, see Howard-Brook, *Empire Baptized*.

10. Kim, *Christ and Caesar*, 29.

11. Bryan, *Render to Caesar*, 91.

they relied entirely upon a slave-based economy, whereas Britain and other European nations had begun the abolition process), argues that much of the language oriented around Jesus and the gospel overlaps with imperial rhetoric in a manner that carries political significance.[12] However, in a bid to outflank his opponents, Bryan argues that this overlap is not intended to encourage anything like resistance to Roman rule but, to the contrary, is only effective (in a manner similar to the Pauline deployment of familial language to refer to the assemblies of Jesus loyalists) because it views the Roman imperial model *as a positive model*.[13] This position, unlike Kim's, seems to at least possess some initial plausibility but, as we will see in what follows, it quickly falls apart. To maintain its plausibility (especially in light of proclaiming Jesus as *the* Lord of all, while imperial propaganda proclaimed Caesar as *the* Lord of all), a hard and fast distinction of spheres must be maintained. But as we have already seen, the spiritual and religious were (more generally) entirely interwoven in Paul's context, and as we will see below, all of this is (more specifically) complicated to the point of making Bryan's claim entirely implausible when one considers the actual statements made about Jesus, a terrorist justly condemned to death according to the rule of law, but to whom the Pauline faction professed their loyalty while also refusing to worship anyone else.

However, Bryan is at least correct to note the overlap in rhetoric. As the prior chapter on the ideo-theology of Rome should have made abundantly clear, talk about things like crucifixion, resurrection, lordship, divine sonship and favor, being a savior who acts mercifully and brings liberation and peace, referencing things like a *parousia*, all in relation to officially sanctioned good news, is very deeply political talk. As we will also see in this chapter, talk of justice, loyalty (*pistis*), and assemblies (*ekklesiai*) only adds to this case. The scholarly consensus acknowledges this now. Right- and Left-wing scholars equally refer to the Pauline discourse about "the gospel" and Jesus as "heavily steeped in imperial language, metaphor, and ideas," as "political," as deploying "imperial themes," or as using "loaded terms."[14]

---

12. Further to this understanding of the origins of the United States of America, see Horne, *Counter-Revolution of 1776*.

13. Bryan, *Render to Caesar*, 82–85.

14. On "heavily steeped," see Maier, *Picturing Paul in Empire*, 6. On "political," see Gorman, *Apostle of the Crucified Lord*, 108–9; Horsley, "Paul's Counter-Imperial Gospel," 141–47; Wright, "Paul and Caesar," 173–76; Wright, *Paul*, 63–65; "Paul's Gospel

The recognition of this has led some conservative scholars to develop some interesting proposals to explain this overlap. Next to Bryan's creative reading stands Bruce Winter's suggestion that this rhetorical overlap is "an unhappy coincidence" because "there would be no advantage whatsoever for their movement if the first Christians [sic] awarded [Caesar's] titles to Jesus because it would be a highly confrontational move, indeed a treasonable one against Rome."[15] It is surprising and disappointing to see Winter grasping for a conclusion that flies in the face of the evidence he himself provides. It is much more plausible to conclude, as I did earlier when examining the Pauline position that did not retreat from suffering or persecution but, in fact, required a form of Jesus loyalty that would exacerbate those things (thereby further requiring the assemblies of Jesus loyalists to engage in material acts of sibling-based mutuality in order to survive), that this rhetorical overlap is not accidental. It is much more likely that Paul and his coworkers were deliberately engaging imperial language, titles, and themes.[16] As John Dominic Crossan and Marcus Borg ask: "How was it even possible—let alone credible—that the exact same terms and titles were taken by Christians [sic] from Caesar the Augustus on the Palatine Hill in Rome and given to Jesus the Christ on the Nazareth ridge in Galilee—or, even worse, to the 'King of the Jews' on a Roman cross in Jerusalem?"[17] As we will see, it is far more credible to conclude that this contrast is both deliberate and counter-imperial, with the Pauline faction offering the true "fulfillment of the Augustan 'gospel.'"[18] Thus, as Adolf Deissmann observed a century ago, when the Pauline faction attempts to reserve for (the) Anointed the "words already in use for worship . . . [of] the deified emperors," the result is a deliberately "polemical parallelism."[19]

While it is easier to shake one's head at Winter's conclusion, it takes more time to root out the conservatism of N. T. Wright's position given that he not only affirms the overlap between Pauline and imperial Roman rhetoric but also affirms that this overlap is deliberate and that Paul

---

and Caesar's Empire," 164–70. See also Crossan and Reed, *In Search of Paul*, 165–67; Horsley, *Paul and Politics*, 90–93.

15. Winter, *Divine Honours for the Caesars*, 92–93.

16. See, for example, Theissen, *Fortress Introduction to the New Testament*, 89–90; Maier, *Picturing Paul in Empire*, 11.

17. Crossan and Borg, *First Paul*, 96.

18. Tellbe, *Paul Between Synagogue and State*, 205; see also 202–3.

19. Deissmann, *Light from the Ancient East*, 342.

and his coworkers engage in this deliberate overlap in order to push a counter-imperial perspective. In fact, Wright has contributed in considerable ways to the broader acceptance of the political nature of the Pauline understanding of the gospel and Jesus. However, the problem with Wright's position become apparent when one observes his repeated emphasis, over many years, that Paul's key conflict was with *paganism*.[20] Thus, Paul announces the truth that "*paganism* parodies" in order to rescue people from "*pagan* empires" in the conflict that exists "between the gospel and *paganism* in general."[21] Consequently, one discovers that, according to Wright, Paul is not opposed to Roman imperialism because he is opposed to imperialism as such; rather, Paul is opposed to Roman imperialism because it is pagan! As he asserts: "The rulers are wicked and will be judged . . . but God wants the world to be ruled, rather than descend into anarchy and chaos, and [God's] people must learn to live under pagan rule even though it means constant vigilance against compromise with *paganism* itself."[22] Now, one can immediately object to this woefully ignorant understanding of anarchism (which does not seem uncommon among rich and well-established white male New Testament scholars, be they members of the British House of Lords or tenured professors at prestigious American institutions—E. P. Sanders, for example, makes the equally silly claim that "almost any legal system is better than anarchy").[23] However, more to the point, one should note that Wright, while affirming the inextricable connection between religion and politics in Paul's context, subtly redeploys the distinction between those spheres when it comes to his description of Pauline counter-imperialism. And he does this to reinforce a fundamentally law-abiding, authority-honoring ethics today (especially given that contemporary imperialisms have often been Christian). Given the comprehensive nature of Pauline counter-imperialism that we have already explored in this text, it is safe to conclude that Wright is missing the point—not, I should add, because he is lacking

20. See Wright, *What Saint Paul Really Said*, 79–83.

21. See, in order, Wright, *What Saint Paul Really Said*, 85–92; *Paul*, 76–77, 179; emphasis added in all cases.

22. Wright, *Paul*, 66; emphasis added. Wright argues that this is a part of a creational monotheism that sees signs of God's rule even in "fallen worldly structures of government" (69). But never, of course, in anarchism!

23. See Sanders, *Paul: The Apostle's Life*, 548. Sanders goes on to conclude that "if it is a matter of being righteoused, the law is excluded. If it is a matter of ethics, it shows the way" (557). While I appreciate his verbal use of righteous, this position is deeply flawed and I will argue against it, especially in section 3 below.

in good intentions but perhaps because he is situated in a place where it is very hard to see the point. That he, like so many others, understands the Pauline gospel to be primarily a narrative (oral or written) proclamation about Jesus rather than understanding the Pauline gospel to be primarily about what is taking place in the *kairos* of Paul's now-time among the assemblies of Jesus loyalists, facilitates this error.[24]

A more carefully nuanced but cautiously conservative position is that held by Harry Maier.[25] Drawing on postcolonial theory and notions of hybridity and entanglement, as well as Michel de Certeau's notion of "making do," Maier argues that both "the uncontested and contested letters of Paul" do indeed invite re-imagination, but they do so in a way that negotiates Roman imperial realities "in complex and subtle, but not always oppositional ways."[26] Maier concludes that "Paul was neither for nor against 'the Roman Empire' but [was] a skillful negotiator of his imperial context.... Paul 'makes do' with Roman imperial realities by adapting them to his purpose. The result is the creation of a form of imperial hybridity."[27] Thus, Maier goes on to argue that:

---

24. Thus, I have concluded that Wright is only considered a radical because those who view him as such are very conservative, whereas Wright sometimes inclines towards *liberal* positions. However, these liberal positions are far from being emancipatory or Pauline. Take, for example, his position about debt relief that sparked some controversy among Evangelicals ten years ago because they considered it to be far too radical (see Wright, "On Dropping the Debt"). Debt relief is a position that posits European or other wealthy nations to be the rightful keepers of debts from the two-thirds world. These European nations are then called to act in a benevolent manner, like Roman patrons or contemporary philanthrocapitalists, and forgive or relieve these debts. This roots justice and virtue on the side of the Europeans. However, what this analysis neglects to mention is that debts were created in the two-thirds world because Europeans plundered those lands and then drove them into debt (frequently by selling arms to dictators they installed to continue facilitating that plundering process). Therefore, a more proper and Pauline position would speak of theft, of the plundering of the two-thirds world by Europe and other wealthy nations, of the need for economic reparations, and of a massive transfer of wealth from plundering countries to plundered countries. The discourse of debt relief or debt forgiveness does not do this. In fact, it continues to facilitate imperial dynamics while easing resistance to those dynamics and permitting key political and economic rulers to posture and present themselves as merciful and gracious (for analyses of a supposedly noble and multicultural liberal nation that engages in this kind of imperialism, see Gordon, *Imperialist Canada*; Gordon and Webber, *Blood of Extraction*; Engler, *Canada in Africa*).

25. See Maier, *Picturing Paul in Empire*.

26. Maier, *Picturing Paul in Empire*, 21; see also 14, 29, 35, 38–39.

27. Maier, *Picturing Paul in Empire*, 31.

> It is as misleading to describe Paul as "relentlessly opposed" to the Roman Empire as it is to describe him as sympathetic to its aims and political goals. Indeed, as a product of the social and cultural context of his urban environment, Paul, the Roman citizen, was as much of a part of the Roman Empire as he could have been opposed to it.[28]

Maier's analysis is useful and draws on important postcolonial observations about how people negotiate their contexts in complex ways that often complicate models structured around black and white oppositional binaries (even though, well before postcolonialism gained the attention of New Testament scholarship, Robert Banks was well ahead of the curve when he observed how Paul was involved in and affected by the tendencies and tensions of his day and, as a result, "in part contradicted, in part reflected and in part extended the various crosscurrents" operative then).[29] However, Maier's conclusions are heavily influenced by his focus on the deutero-Pauline and Pastoral Epistles—all of which he considers to be representatively Pauline. He also follows Acts quite closely, especially regarding Paul's supposed Roman citizenship.

When the focus is narrowed to the uncontested Pauline Epistles, one may maintain this opposition to black and white binaries, taking into account the complexities related to living as colonized subjects longing for liberation, but still arrive at different conclusions. This is what happens in the work of Warren Carter. Rather than using notions like entanglement or making do, Carter talks more about the complex dynamics of mimicry that accompany acts of subversion performed by oppressed and "powerless" groups negotiating power systems "from below."[30] He observes how this tactical negotiation advances by means of both imitation and contestation.[31] Consequently, while this leaves a legacy that is, at least in part, rhetorically and thematically open to being co-opted back into an agenda that better fits the status quo of the empire (as happens very rapidly after the early days of the movement), Carter concludes that Paul's intention is to thoroughly subvert Roman imperialism, not least by positing Jesus as a superior alternative to the emperor.[32]

---

28. Maier, *Picturing Paul in Empire*, 37.

29. Banks, *Paul's Idea of Community*, 160; see also 13–14.

30. See Carter, *Roman Empire*, x, 88–91; *John and Empire*, 72–81; "Vulnerable Power," 474.

31. See Carter, *John and Empire*, 176–203.

32. Carter, *John and Empire*, 177.

Consequently, scholars who situate themselves somewhere to the Left of mainstream (neo)liberalism (frequently those who have been associated with the so-called "radical Left" in academia), tend to assert some variation of Carter's conclusion, even if there is some disagreement about how successful the Pauline faction was in doing this, or how blind they were to some violent elements from their own context that influenced them, or how open their legacy was to being co-opted by their opponents. Thus, for example, Jacob Taubes calls Rom 1:1–7, "The Gospel as a Declaration of War against Rome" and argues that the epistle to the Romans is "a political theology, a *political* declaration of war on the Caesar."[33] Likewise, John Crossan posits that, by presenting the gospel and Jesus in the manner that they do, Paul and his coworkers have either engaged in "a peculiar joke and a very low lampoon" or "what the Romans called *majestas* and we call high treason."[34] Of course, as Larry Welborn has shown, this need not be an either/or.[35] Paul and his coworkers proclaimed the sick joke that a crucified man was *the* true Son of God and Lord, a joke that moves from being a perverse absurdity to being a terrifying and treasonous political prospect once those who benefited from imperial structures of power and wealth distribution realized that Paul and his coworkers were deadly serious.

A Final Note on "Hidden Transcripts"

In order to further clear the air regarding the political nature of Pauline rhetoric about the gospel and Jesus, it is worth returning to and concluding our conversation about the supposed nature of "hidden transcripts" and what that term is taken to signify. This is necessary because conservative scholars have exploited the seemingly paranoid or conspiratorial overtones the term has when taken outside of its precise, technical context and used with an audience unfamiliar with the work of James C. Scott or those who follow in his footsteps. Thus, while postcolonial scholarship has continued to nuance our understanding of how things like "hidden transcripts" might operate and how challenging it is for many colonized people to pursue full liberation from colonization given their rootedness within that context, some conservative scholars have engaged

---

33. Taubes, *Political Theology of Paul*, 13, 16.

34. Crossan, *God and Empire*, 28.

35. See Welborn, *Paul, the Fool of Christ*.

THE LAWLESSNESS OF GOOD NEWS IN THE MAKING

in a deliberate misinformation campaign in order to try and discredit the idea altogether.[36]

Essentially, in the work of James C. Scott as carried over to New Testament studies (most especially due to the influence of Richard Horsley and Neil Elliott and further developed and nuanced by Warren Carter), the term "hidden transcript" is applied to the observation that people who experience colonization, oppression, and violence from the soldiers, police, laws, and socioeconomic structures of the rulers are not inclined to publicly and explicitly voice their opposition to those rulers, soldiers, police, laws, and structures. Speaking in this way would almost certainly guarantee that grievous and potentially fatal violence would be applied to the speaker and, quite probably, the speaker's loved ones. At the same time, those who are at risk of experiencing that violence, those who are enslaved, colonized, or who have been forced off their land or away from their homes to find work, are not likely to be sincere if they are called upon to sing the praises of those who got rich by putting them in their present situation. Thus, the notion of "hidden transcripts" refers to the complex and subtle ways in which the oppressed speak when they are afraid of being overheard by the censors or others who might report them to the authorities, and when they might be inclined to posture as compliant while still trying to maintain their sense of dignity or fight, as much as they can, against the forces that oppress them.[37] In this way, people experiencing oppression subtly negotiate and play with the dominant narratives spread through the public propaganda of the rulers. These narratives are called "public transcripts."[38] These public transcripts

---

36. I have come to the conclusion that this is a deliberate misinformation campaign because I assume that scholars like Seyoon Kim, to whom we will return very shortly, are responsible enough to have read and understood James C. Scott before spending so much time talking about a concept we owe to Scott. Viewing this as a deliberate misinformation campaign is my best effort to be charitable to Kim as a scholar.

37. The central texts here are James C. Scott's *Domination and the Arts of Resistance* and *Weapons of the Weak*. However, Scott's impressive oeuvre is generally useful for thinking about Paulinism, resistance movements, and, not least of all, anarchism given that New Testament scholars consistently demonstrate their own ignorance of that topic despite their polemics against "anarchy."

38. See Horsley, *Hidden Transcripts and the Arts of Resistance*, 3–5. Tacitus's comments on Roman histories are instructive in this regard. On the one hand he writes: "This I regard as history's highest function, to let no worthy action be uncommemorated, and to hold out the reprobation of posterity as a terror to evil words and deeds" (Tacitus, *Annals* 3.655); but on the other hand he observes: "the histories of Tiberius, Caius, Claudius and Nero, while they were in power were falsified through terror, and

are what I have referred to as the ideo-theology of Rome. However, the rich and powerful also have their own "hidden transcripts." Notably, they are inclined to speak in much harsher, dehumanizing, and mocking ways about the vanquished, colonized, and enslaved in letters they exchange among themselves—letters not intended for public consumption.

Horsley, Elliott, and Carter are key figures who have argued that hidden transcripts of the oppressed are present in the uncontested Pauline Epistles.[39] Something like this idea is also operating in Mikael Tellbe's work, when he compares the letter to the Thessalonians with the letter to the Philippians and concludes that, "the further away from Rome Paul comes, the more explicitly he expresses his distance from and criticism of Rome."[40] Dieter Georgi also concludes that Paul is less overtly political, even if he cannot fully suppress himself, when writing to the Philippians because he writes while imprisoned and is concerned about who might read his letter.[41] In a similar vein, writing about the letter to the Galatians, Brigitte Kahl observes that:

> In the discursive space controlled by the conquerors and shaped by conformity with imperial law and order, a letter like the one Paul is sending to Galatia can hardly talk in a straightforward manner about politically sensitive matters like civic nonconformity or disobedience. It required encoded forms of speech and reading "between the lines."[42]

Therefore, talk of hidden transcripts makes a lot of sense when considering letters written by members of persecuted movements developing in the context of oppression and colonization. It encourages a thoughtful and careful engagement with the Pauline texts.

None of this is captured in Seyoon Kim's discussion of the matter. Kim argues that appeals to "the notion of coding" are a "desperate attempt" to force the Pauline texts to be something they are not.[43] In fact, he argues that any "appeal to the device of coding" always and already

---

after their death were written under the irritation of a recent hatred" (Tacitus, *Annals* 1.1).

39. See Horsley, *Hidden Transcripts and the Arts of Resistance*, 1, 3, 8–9, 11–16; Elliott, "Strategies of Resistance," 110–11; "Paul and the Politics of Empire," 27–33; Carter, *Roman Empire*, 12–13.

40. Tellbe, *Paul Between Synagogue and State*, 284.

41. Georgi, *Theocracy*, 72–73.

42. Kahl, *Galatians Re-Imagined*, 252.

43. Kim, *Christ and Caesar*, 32.

"amounts to an inadvertent admission of the failure of [the counter-imperial] interpretive scheme."[44] Thus, he mocks any who resort to some kind of "alleged" code, leaving the reader to think that counter-imperial exegetes are engaging in an hermeneutical exercise comparable to that performed by Michael Drosnin in his much-ridiculed (but still best-selling!) book, *The Bible Code*.[45] Of course, this is all unsubstantiated nonsense. As even the following very brief summary of the subject demonstrates, Kim is preaching to his choir and not engaging in any kind of serious study of the subject that he oh-so-dramatically misrepresents.

However, when it comes to hidden transcripts, Kim is confused about one point that may also be confusing to others and so it is worth examining this in more detail. Specifically, Kim thinks that any discussion of finding a subversive, radical, or revolutionary political intent in any so-called hidden transcript is a self-contradictory endeavor because the exegete both wishes to say that something had been hidden in the text while also claiming to find that thing in the text even though, presumably, it would not be obvious to those who were much more familiar with the language and terms deployed by Paul and his coworkers.[46] However, counter-imperial readers of the Pauline letters are not claiming to do exactly this. Rather, they are arguing that texts produced by persecuted groups in the context of oppression require special attention lest we misread them, in no small part because we may be situated among those who benefit from oppression today (rather than already being familiar with the hidden transcripts of the oppressed that unfold and constantly evolve every day all around us). Take, for example, the Ethiopian proverb explored by Scott: "When the great lord passes, the wise peasant bows deeply and silently farts." What is the wise peasant doing in this situation? Is the peasant acknowledging the rightful supremacy of the ruler or is the peasant bowing falsely and silently mocking an authority that the peasant believes is oppressive but which, nonetheless, wields a sword capable of killing the peasant? Or is the peasant doing both? Indeed, taken as a stand-alone action, it appears that the peasant is doing both. A surface

---

44. Kim, *Christ and Caesar*, 33.

45. On resorting to alleged coding, see Kim, *Christ and Caesar*, 20.

46. Kim, *Christ and Caesar*, 20, 32. As we have seen, Kim asserts that it is folly to think one can "discover" such a code in the Pauline texts when the "church fathers" could not find it. However, as I argued above, it is more probable to believe that the Christian patriarchs were trying to impose, both via rhetoric and physical force, a non-Pauline interpretation onto Pauline texts. In this effort, they largely succeeded.

level self-contradiction, therefore, stands at the heart of how hidden transcripts operate. It is not surprising, then, to discover that Kim gets confused about this seeming self-contradiction. In order to determine the best way to resolve this apparent contradiction, one must know as much as one can about the other activities of the peasant, what the peasant does when the great lord is not around, how the peasant speaks in other contexts, and so on. In other words, we need to do what counter-imperial interpreters of Paul have been urging us to do. Having covered all the material we have in this series, I think we can safely conclude that the broader evidence strongly favors the counter-imperial reading of Paul and reveals Kim's objections to be baseless, insubstantial, and only worth addressing because of Kim's ability to sway those who are unfamiliar with even the most basic elements of the conversation at hand.

The Gospel: From Propositions and Narratives to a Powerful and Ongoing Happening

We are now well situated to see that Pauline talk about the gospel and Jesus is a political discourse.[47] This is just as true for the term *euangelion* itself which, as we have seen, was a prominent term in the ideo-theology of Rome (commonly referring to the cluster of themes related to the purportedly good news of Augustus's birth, triumph over divisive, corrupt, and immoral forces, and subsequent reign as the Lord, Savior, and Son of God who, through a pious commitment to justice, brings peace and prosperity to all).[48] This is not to say that Paul and his coworkers do not also have an awareness of how gospel language is deployed in the LXX translation of Deutero-Isaiah—they obviously are aware of this, quoting Isa 52:7 in Rom 10:15, with Isa 61:1 lingering in the background, not only there but elsewhere in the Pauline corpus. However, reference to the LXX does not negate the political nature of gospel language. This is so for at least two reasons. First, because the Judeans did not have an apolitical understanding of their sacred writings or of the good news as it appears in Deutero-Isaiah. Second, and more conjecturally, it seems probable that Paul and his coworkers make reference to this theme from

---

47. Which, again, is not to say that it is devoid of what we might consider to be theological content. It is, as Michael Gorman emphasizes, a theopolitical gospel (Gorman, *Apostle of the Crucified Lord*, 107–8).

48. See, for example, Deissmann, *Light from the Ancient East*, 366; Georgi, *Theocracy*, 83–85; Bates, *Salvation by Allegiance Alone*, 29.

Deutero-Isaiah precisely because it fits so well with their counter-imperial mission. Thus, as those like Mark Strom have noted, the language about the gospel used by the Pauline faction is rooted in both the LXX *and* the context of Graeco-Roman imperialism.[49]

Here, the cautiousness of James Dunn plays against him because, I think, he decontextualizes the broader context in which Paul and his co-authors use the word gospel and ignores the implications of the words and terms that accompany its use. Dunn acknowledges that it's possible that the gospel of Jesus is presented to counter the gospel of Caesar but suggests we should be careful and not posit a direct conflict, noting the use of the term in the LXX, and arguing that the gospel is about the power of God for salvation, focused on the Anointed and the vindication of God's faithfulness.[50] What Dunn neglects is the way in which these themes—God's power for salvation, focused on the figure of a divinely anointed savior, who brings about a salvation that demonstrates God's fidelity to justice and loyalty to creation—are all central themes related to Roman imperialism. As a result of this error, Dunn roots the term gospel more exclusively in the LXX and distances it from association with the Caesar cult.[51] Dunn's conclusion would be more plausible (even if it ignores the political nature of the Isaianic texts) if the Pauline faction used the term gospel in isolation from other terms like savior, son of god, anointed, justice, peace, or references to evil rulers in this present evil age, let alone discussions that posit the overthrow of the rule of law or the formation of cell groups that gathered illegally and practiced a threatening form of transnational economic mutuality. If these things were absent, then, perhaps Dunn's reading is convincing. But given this context (and one need look no further than the first chapter of Romans to get a good sense of that), the more cautious conclusion to draw is that there is something very political and something very oppositional to the ideo-theology of Rome in Pauline references to the gospel.

What then is "the gospel"? I will quickly examine two common alternatives, one about consenting to certain theological propositions and one about the presentation of a certain narrative about Jesus, before arguing for a third alternative—one that understands the gospel to be about participation in a powerful and ongoing happening.

49. Strom, *Reframing Paul*, 84–85. Not an uncommon view. See also Wright, *What Saint Paul Really Said*, 45–57.

50. Dunn, *Theology of Paul the Apostle*, 550–53; 164–66.

51. See Dunn, *Theology of Paul the Apostle*, 167–69.

Pauline Solidarity

The first understanding of "the gospel" is common to the Occidental Christian tradition that has been able to stay strongly connected to socioeconomic and political centers of wealth and power and which, therefore, has been able to present itself as "true" or "orthodox" or "real" Christianity. This position argues some variation of the thesis that the gospel is the good news that God sent his Son to die for our sins and that, through our confession of faith in Jesus, we may experience the forgiveness of our sins, be saved from damnation, and go to heaven when we die (or, in slightly more updated versions, participate in the new creation of all things when heaven and earth are both remade after the *parousia* of the Anointed). Thus, to pick just one relatively recent example, Eckhard Schnabel declares that the gospel is contained in Paul's oral proclamation of the good news that the crucified and risen Anointed died for the sins of humankind.[52] As a result of this, and still part of the gospel, people can now find "personal, existential liberation from servitude to false gods and come to faith in the one true God the father of Jesus Christ, who alone can forgive sins."[53] Thus, salvation is from "guilt and sin" and results in "a perfect existence after death."[54] Given what we have examined about Paul and his coworkers and the assemblies of Jesus loyalists thus far, one might be quite puzzled by this conclusion. This definition, however, does make a lot of sense within the context of hundreds of years of Christian imperialism which rose to especial prominence in Europe when local centers of wealth and power were trying to break from the Holy Roman Empire in order to be able to amass more wealth and power for themselves. This gospel is good news to the guilty consciences of oppressors who continue to live as oppressors (and who intend or desire to continue living that way). No wonder then, that those who preach this kind of gospel were more than happy to call on princes to slaughter peasants who dared to participate in an uprising (an *anastasis*) because the peasants wanted to be freed from the oppressive structures of power that dominated their lives.[55] It makes sense that Christians today who benefit from those kinds

---

52. Schnabel, *Paul and the Early Church*, 961, 982.
53. Schnabel, *Paul and the Early Church*, 1343.
54. Schnabel, *Paul and the Early Church*, 1356.
55. See Luther, "Against the Robbing and Murdering Hordes of Peasants." Liberation, it seems, is for princes from popes, not for peasants from princes. Or, as we see later in European history, it is for the bourgeoisie from the aristocracy, not for the proletariat from the bourgeoisie, let alone for slaves from slave-owners (in the later situation, redemption is a balm to the conscience of the slave-owner, not the

of power structures would continue to affirm this understanding of the gospel. However, as far as New Testament scholarship is concerned, this position has fallen out of favor and only remains prominent among evangelical scholars who, one suspects, will continue to assert their position over and over again, regardless of the evidence.[56]

The first understanding of the gospel has fallen out of favor because scholars began to notice that it imported foreign (Reformation- or modern-era) notions into the texts and affirmed ideas that would have been exceedingly strange and often unthinkable to a first-century diasporic Judean living in the eastern portion of the Roman Empire. Furthermore, it didn't seem to make sense of what one finds in the texts when Paul and his co-authors write specifically about the gospel. Thus, this led to the creation of a second perspective on what constitutes the gospel. Essentially, this perspective views the gospel as a story that is told about Jesus. N. T. Wright, whom I believe has been particularly responsible for spreading this view among both conservative and liberal scholars, has pushed especially strongly for this view. Thus, in 1997 he summarizes this gospel story as follows: "Jesus, the crucified and risen Messiah, is Lord."[57] In 2008, he fills this out a bit more: "The gospel, in the New Testament, is the good news that God (the world's creator) is at last becoming king and that Jesus, whom this God has raised from the dead, is the world's true lord."[58] The key point of distinction between this position and that taken by those like Schnabel is that the gospel is more a story about Jesus than it is theses about the present reader and, as such, its content must be shaped by the relevant first-century contexts rather than later contexts.

However, the lines frequently blur between theological propositions and narrative summaries. Thus, for example, while Matthew Bates suggests that the gospel is the narrative proclamation that Jesus is King, he argues that this narrative, to be the gospel proper, must contain at least these eight theses about Jesus. Jesus the king: (1) pre-existed with God the Father; (2) took on human flesh fulfilling God's promise to David; (3) died for our sins in accordance with the Scriptures; (4) was buried; (5) was raised on the third day in accordance with the Scriptures; (6) appeared to many; (7) is seated at the right hand of God the Father; and (8)

---

emancipation of the slaves).

56. See the prior discussion of Seyoon Kim's work.
57. Wright, *What Saint Paul Really Said*, 46.
58. Wright, *Surprised by Hope*, 226–27.

will come again to judge the living and the dead.[59] Thus, very frequently, those who focus on propositions and those who focus on narratives have a considerable amount in common, not only in terms of the conclusions they draw but also in how they frame the gospel. Specifically, both positions assume the gospel is primarily something composed of words (concepts or stories expressed orally or in writing). Proclaiming or declaring the gospel is thus, quite literally, *spreading the word*. Unfortunately, this position collapses when one examines how the Pauline faction actually uses gospel language in the letters they write.

To begin with, this position neglects the way in which Paul and his coworkers use the word gospel in a verbal sense. Thus, in Rom 1:15, the Pauline faction express their desire "to gospel" to those at Rome, noting in 1:20 that they are late in coming to Rome because they were "aspiring to gospel" (my translation) in places where the Anointed had not yet been named. In 1 Cor 1:17, the Pauline faction states that the Anointed did not send them "to evangelize" but "to gospel" (my translation), and in 9:16–18, they state that it is not for them to boast about how they gospel and emphasize that they gospel in such a way as to make the gospel free of charge. In 2 Cor 11:7, they reiterate the emphasis that they freely gospeled the gospel to the Corinthians, and in 10:16, express a desire to gospel in the regions beyond Corinth. In Gal 1:16, the Pauline faction speaks about how God apocalypses his son in Paul so that Paul might gospel that son among the nations and notes, shortly thereafter, in 1:23, that others are shocked to learn that the one who persecuted Jesus loyalists is now gospeling the allegiance which he previously ravaged. Later, Paul and his coworkers remind the Galatians that it was through weakness of the flesh that Paul gospeled to them. English translations of these passages are misleading. They almost always substitute "preached the gospel" or "proclaimed the gospel" for the verbal references to the gospel (with "proclamation" seeming to have the same logo-centric overtones as the notion of preaching). However, although gospel is sometimes used as a noun (more on that momentarily), here it is worth emphasizing that Paul and his coworkers clearly understand the gospel to be something that is done—an action of some kind.

This further makes sense of the passages when Paul and his coworkers speak of the gospel as a powerful thing. Thus, in the opening of the letter, Rom 1:16, they famously say that they are not ashamed of the

---

59. Bates, *Salvation by Allegiance Alone*, 93.

gospel because "it is the power of God for salvation for everyone who is loyal" (my translation) and in the closing of the letter, Rom 16:25, they pray that the Romans will be strengthened according to their gospel. In Rom 15:18–20, they talk about how the Anointed, in order to produce the submissive obedience of the nations, used them in word and work, by power of signs and wonders, by power of the spirit, so they can claim that from Jerusalem to Illyricum, they have *completed* the gospel of the Anointed. Here, for the word "completed," English translations tend to substitute "proclaimed" or some variation thereof—but talk of "completing the gospel" problematizes the logocentric understanding thereof. However, the Pauline faction is clear in 1 Cor 1:17, after proclaiming that they were sent to Corinth to gospel, that they did not gospel "by the wisdom of words," so that the cross of the Anointed would not be emptied of its power. Here, the power of the gospel is actually sharply separated from anything done with words. This understanding is already present in the earliest epistle penned by Paul and his coworkers. In 1 Thess 1:5, they observe that they did not come to the Thessalonians "in word only" but came "in power." It is also present in Rom 16:25, in the conclusion of the final epistle, when the Pauline faction speaks of "my gospel and the kerygma of Jesus Anointed" as two distinct things. So, whatever else it is, the gospel is a powerful thing not limited to or by words.

Granted, multiple scholars have noted this. Saying, for example, that for Paul the gospel is not "just words" or "a *logos* empty in-itself" but is also a "power" or something that contains an "*energeia*."[60] Or, as Matthew Bates observes, the gospel is a "power-releasing story."[61] However, these scholars seem to be at a loss as to how precisely this is the case. The assumption seems to be that the gospel is powerful because it produces faith among those who hear it—but it certainly does not produce faith in *all* those who hear it. Paul and his coworkers, having been sorely persecuted, are well aware of this, and so they also speak about the gospel being veiled and refer to some people who have been blinded to the gospel. So how is the gospel both powerful and yet, all things considered, frequently ineffective? Resolving this tension can lead historians to talk about first-century conceptions about magic words or sixteenth-century conceptions of election and predestination, but, in either case, the end result is a verbal or written proclamation of the gospel that does not really

---

60. On just words/power, see Gorman, *Apostle of the Crucified Lord*, 98–99. On *logos/energeia*, see Agamben, *Time That Remains*, 89–91.

61. Bates, *Salvation by Allegiance Alone*, 30.

seem to be as powerful as Paul and his coworkers make it out to be. Perhaps, then, we need a less logocentric understanding of gospeling.

A significant clue for negotiating our way forward is the observation that Paul and his coworkers most frequently talk about the gospel as something in which people participate. This participation takes place because the gospel is a context in which the Jesus loyalists live (a more passive form of participation), and because the gospel is something in which people partake (a more active form of participation). As context, note the several occasions when Paul and his coworkers speak of being "in the gospel." Thus, Rom 1:9 ("For God is my witness, whom I serve with my spirit in the gospel of his son"); 2 Cor 8:18 ("with him, we are sending the brother whose praise in the gospel is throughout all the assemblies"); 2 Cor 10:14b ("even as far as you, we came in the gospel of the Anointed"); and 1 Thess 3:2a ("And we set Timothy our brother and co-worker of God in the gospel of the Anointed") (all translations mine). This context appears to have both spatial and temporal dimensions. Thus, while Paul, his coworkers, and others in the assemblies of Jesus loyalists are said to be in the gospel, the Pauline faction also speaks of "the beginning of the gospel" when Paul set out from Macedonia and no assembly but that of the Philippians yet shared in an accounting of expenditures and receipts with him (Phil 4:15). However, there is also a strong active component to being in the gospel. Thus, the Pauline faction claims to have begotten the Corinthians "through the gospel" (1 Cor 4:15) and claims to have gone to Troas "for the gospel of [the Anointed]" (2 Cor 2:12). Furthermore, as a publically appointed minister of the Anointed Jesus to the nations, Paul now augustly "ministers" the gospel of God (Rom 15:16). Thus, also, his already mentioned claim to have "completed the gospel of the Anointed" (Rom 15:20; my translation).

Others are also expected to actively participate in this gospel. Thus, Paul and his coworkers describe the Corinthians as fellow partakers of the gospel (1 Cor 9:23). Similarly, they praise the Philippians for their partnership (or sharing in common) in (or into) the gospel from the first day up until the present, and they pair this with reference to an ongoing good work that is taking place in their company, as they have lovingly become joint partners in the grace Paul experiences both in his bonds and in the defense and confirmation of the gospel (Phil 1:5–7). They then urge the Philippians to be citizens worthy of the gospel of the Anointed, being especially united in their allegiance in relation to the gospel (Phil 1:27). This combination of both being contextually rooted within the gospel and actively participating in that same gospel is well summarized in Paul's description of Timothy, whom Paul claims, "slaved with me into the gospel" (Phil 2:22; my translation).

In this regard it is also worth noting that there is a submission or obedience that accompanies becoming partners in the gospel. Thus, while Paul notes that not all submissively obey the gospel (Rom 10:16), he praises the Corinthians for confessing their submissive obedience to the gospel of the Anointed by their (presumed) participation in the Collection on behalf of the poor in Jerusalem (2 Cor 9:13—referred to here as a civic service [*diakonia*] that glorifies God).

We can conclude that, for the Pauline faction, the gospel was primarily an event that possessed a demonstrably large amount of power, in which the Jesus loyalists were located, and in which they obediently and actively participated. Surely, then, the answer as to what constitutes the Pauline gospel is now clear—it is nothing more and nothing less than the unique way of sharing life together that was being developed in the assemblies of Jesus loyalists associated with Paul and his coworkers. It is a powerful and ongoing happening in which Paul, his coworkers, and other Jesus loyalists participate.[62] This, then, immediately makes sense of the Pauline statement, "if our gospel is veiled, it is veiled to those who are perishing, in whose case the god of this age has blinded the minds of the disloyal ones (i.e., those who have different allegiances), to prevent the shining forth of the light of the gospel of the glory of the Anointed who is the image [*eikon*] of God" (2 Cor 4:3-4; my translation). Here, the Pauline gospel is juxtaposed with the gospel of Caesar, the most august god of the age, who was commonly understood to be the very image of a god (but here is a darkening and blinding force who causes people to perish). Of course, as the Pauline faction already made clear in 2 Cor 9:13, the glory of the Anointed Jesus is found in the economic mutuality practiced among those loyal to Jesus, but this gospel is veiled to those who have bought into the imperial Roman propaganda in part because the way of

---

62. This is where those who incline to an apocalyptic interpretation of Paul are on the right track when they deploy Badiou's notion of the Event to talk about the gospel. Unfortunately, as far as I can tell, what they tend to overlook is the ongoing participatory nature of this Event—the Event is more than a chance occurrence or a retelling, and focusing all one's energy on appropriating the Event with the logos (as they get side-tracked by arguments about historical continuity, the relevance or possibility of a *novum*, arguments with Barthians or those like Cullmann who push for something like "salvation history," and so on), not only misses the point but might actually be a betrayal of the Event itself.

Jesus is so contrary to the way of Caesar and, in part, because veiling the gospel (i.e., keeping one's way of life a secret from those who are allied with Rome) is a wise strategy. Presumably, this is also why Paul chose to have private discussions about the gospel when he met prominent members of the assemblies of Jesus loyalists in Jerusalem. The meeting was held secretly out of a desire to avoid "false" siblings who "crept in to spy on our freedom, which we have in [the Anointed] Jesus, so that they might enslave us" (Gal 2:4). Given what we have seen about the early Jesus movement, the Pauline faction is not being metaphorical here—members were experiencing radical forms of freedom and, if exposed, were at risk of being enslaved in new or harsher ways.

We then see that the enemies of the gospel, according to the Pauline faction, are those who wish to import a different way of sharing life together into the assemblies of Jesus loyalists. The Super Apostles in Corinth are said to herald another Jesus, and, according to Paul and his coworkers, want the Corinthians to receive a different spirit and a different gospel (2 Cor 11:4). This is the case because, as we have seen, the Super Apostles want to establish abusive hierarchies of power within the assemblies at Corinth. Similarly, this sheds light on how we understand the Pauline struggle with the Galatians. Paul and his coworkers are worried the Galatians are being turned to "a different gospel, which is not another" but, rather, a perversion of the gospel of the Anointed (Gal 1:6–7). In other words, some have shown up in Galatia who are saying similar things about Jesus but encouraging a different lifestyle, and it is this shift in lifestyle that is taken to be a perversion of the gospel as such. Thus, Paul and his coworkers go on to say, "If we or a herald from heaven should gospel to you besides that which we gospeled to you, let that one be accursed. As we previously said, and now again I say, if anyone gospels to you differently than what you have received, let that one be accursed" (Gal 1:8–9; my translation). What does gospeling a different gospel look like? Well, apparently it looks like Cephas withdrawing from eating with people of other nationalities and trying to compel them to live according to Judean customs. By doing this, the Pauline faction accuses Cephas of "not walking correctly with respect to the disclosure of the gospel" (Gal 2:14; my translation). The word "disclosure" (*aletheia*) is important here. Although English translations tend to translate *aletheia* as "truth" (thereby favoring a logo-centric understanding of the gospel), it is more accurately translated as "disclosure," or "the state of being evident" or "unconcealedness" or even "the opening of presence"—all concepts not immediately apparent in common English understandings of "truth."[63] Perhaps Cephas does betray the truth of the gospel, but the truth (*aletheia*) of the gospel has more to do with how people share life together than it has to do with post-Enlightenment language games. Thus, those who violate that truth of the gospel as a way of sharing life together are also the enemies identified in Rom 11:28. What matters here, as in Galatia, is neither circumcision nor uncircumcision but rather loyalty working through love (Gal 5:6). Alter that, and you are no longer gospeling the gospel.

Now, this does not mean that within the Pauline faction the gospel has no propositional content, no relation to Jesus, or no narrative associated with it. Certainly, stories and statements would have been part of what Paul shared in his task of heralding the gospel (see Rom 10:15; 1 Cor 9:14; 2 Cor 11:4; 1 Thess 2:9; Phil 1:12–18). Furthermore, when describing the gospel Paul gospeled with the Corinthians (and *in* which the Corinthians have stood), Paul mentions "the word I gospeled to you" when he handed on "some of the first things [Paul] also received," which are presumably summarized in the subsequent verses relating to Jesus and his ambassadors (1 Cor 15:1–11; my translation). And there is no doubt that the Pauline faction associates the gospel with something that they spoke in Thessalonika (see 1 Thess 2:2–9). Presumably, this kind of oral presentation also took place when Paul, according to an apocalypse, went to Jerusalem and laid the gospel that he heralds among the nations before those who "seemed to be a big deal" (Gal 2:2; my translation). Finally, there is no doubt that the Pauline faction speaks about a verbal defense (*apologia*) of the gospel in Phil 1:7 and 1:18. However, this verbal defense is not the gospel *qua* gospel, and it is telling that the word *apologia* is only used in connection to the gospel when Paul is in prison and preparing to verbally defend himself before the courts. When it comes to the Pauline faction, the emphasis is far more on the themes developed above and less on that relating to the word (a blindspot in scholarship that is perhaps in part explained by the observation that gospel scholars tend to be logocentric rather than active participants in the act of gospeling as per the Pauline faction, although, I reckon, they tend to confuse the two).

At this point, an analogy might help. Imagine the gospel as a modern-day surgical operation. Note, immediately, the many ways in which

---

63. See Heidegger, *Being and Time*, 196–211.

one can speak of this operation. It is a noun ("the operation was a success"), it is a verb ("we are operating on the patient's heart"), and it is a context ("we go into the operation at noon"). However, when operating, one should possess the knowledge required to participate in that operation (let us call this learning the relevant propositions), and one should be aware of relevant case studies (let us call this learning the relevant narratives). However, neither the knowledge gained nor the case studies are the surgical operation itself. A surgical operation is only a surgical operation when it is being completed by the necessary team of people, all of whom play their part as they strive towards their commonly agreed-upon goal. So also with the Pauline gospel. The Pauline gospel is neither background information nor descriptive story-telling. The Pauline gospel is ever only something that is completed by the necessary team of people, all of whom play their part as they strive towards their commonly agreed-upon goal. However, background information and story are still important to the gospel (imagine someone operating while lacking those things and you will come close to feeling the horror Paul felt when he learned what the Super Apostles were gospeling at Corinth), so it is to those things that we can now turn.

The Foundation of the Gospel: Jesus and Why He Matters

What the Pauline faction believes, proclaims, and experiences of Jesus is a critical component of this foundational material that is simultaneously background information, a present experience, and a future hope. The Pauline faction posits Jesus as the true Lord and Savior who triumphed over the greatest enemy, Death, and as a result, is also now superior to all the spiritual Powers (notably Sin and the rule of law) and their earthly representatives (notably the entire authority network implicated in the crucifixion of Jesus) who operate in the service of Death. Apart from apocalypsing Jesus as the Lord and Savior, this victory also reveals Jesus to be the true Son of God, the true first among equals, the one and only Lord and the truly Anointed One. Thus, as a result, Jesus is said to be the one who truly brings the merciful gift of peace to the world. This shift in power dynamics dramatically alters what is possible within the present evil age as justice begins to spread through the assemblies of Jesus loyalists who both acknowledge and experience the *aletheia* of this and transfer their loyalty (*pistis*) to Jesus, while communally and individually, through the power of the Spirit of Life (the Spirit of the Anointed Jesus, the Spirit of God), they experience themselves as emancipated subjects defined not by the hierarchies of power that were previously inscribed on their bodies and in their subjectivities but by the love and solidarity that they continually demonstrate in material ways with one another. We will explore justice, faith, and love in more detail in section 3 below. In this section, we will look at the claims made about Jesus in relation to Jesus being: (1) the Lord; (2) and Savior; (3) who emancipates people from slavery (*apolytrosis*); (4) to the elements, powers, principalities, and rulers; (5) and whose victory is apparent through his resurrection and his current reign; (6) wherein he practices mercy and the giving of good gifts to those whom he rules; (7) notably, the gift of a peace that transcends prior divisions and overcomes previous animosities; (8) thereby revealing him to be the true Son of God; (9) the true first among equals (*princeps*); (10) and the truly Anointed One.[64] While we will look at each of these things in isolation, it is important to emphasize that Paul and his co-workers continually relate these things to one another and frequently the mention of one element is accompanied by or interwoven with mention of other elements. Remembering this influences how we understand the ways in which the Pauline faction uses words that have multiple possible overtones in the Pauline context. The Pauline usage of the title "Lord" in relation to Jesus is a particularly instructive example of this.

Jesus Is the Lord

The two titles most frequently applied to Jesus in the Pauline Epistles are "Anointed" and "Lord." Often, they appear together, so it is somewhat artificial to separate them, but I will begin this discussion of Jesus with the title "Lord" and conclude with the discussion of the title "Anointed" because I believe they are appropriate bookends and because this will, then, facilitate our transition, in what follows, to the discussion of what it means to live life "in the Anointed."

What is at stake when the Pauline faction refers to Jesus as Lord, as the Lord, as our Lord, as the one Lord, as the Lord of all, and so on? The plurality of ways in which lordship language was used in the first-century

---

64. In what follows, I am revising and considerably expanding material that I presented in a lecture at Regent College on July 20, 2010. That lecture content is available in Oudshoorn, "Reading Paul in the Context of Empire."

Mediterranean world has resulted in an equal plurality of scholarly opinions. I. Howard Marshall notes at least five ways in which lordship language was used: (1) as a general term of respect; (2) especially for seniors and people of higher status; (3) or for masters and owners; (4) or political rulers and the emperor; (5) or gods.[65] Those invested in a divine Christology have emphasized the ways in which lordship language is used to refer to gods or to the presence of the divine.[66] Thus, some argue that Paul uses this language to parallel Jesus with gods and figures worshiped in "pagan religions" and "mystery religions" who were also called "lord."[67] Some, however, note that these pagan religions would also include imperial cults, while also noting that lordship language was a common way of referring to (often also divine) kings and emperors—thus, religious and political domains are, yet again, not so easily separated.[68] Others draw more attention to lordship language in relation to slave-owners, with slavery mostly understood in an apolitical manner.[69] Others deploy a de-politicized understanding of eschatology to see Jesus's lordship as primarily eschatological in nature, even if eschatology is not entirely removed from ethics per se.[70] This then results in some, notably James Dunn, cautiously trying to find some kind of baseline that everyone can agree upon. For Dunn, lordship languages denotes, at the very least, "an asserted or acknowledged dominance and right of disposal of superior over inferior. . . . To confess someone as one's 'lord' expressed an attitude of subserviency and a sense of belonging or devotion to the one so named."[71]

This plurality of uses, especially when recognized by those who remove the Pauline usage of lordship language from a discussion of the

---

65. Marshall, "Jesus as Lord," 130–31.

66. See, for example, Tenney, *New Testament Times*, 113; Davies, *Jewish and Pauline Studies*, 206; Meeks, *Origins of Christian Morality*, 166; Tilling, *Paul's Divine Christology*; Moule, *Origin of Christology*, 35–44; Hurtado, *Lord Jesus Christ*, 108–18.

67. Ziesler, *Pauline Christianity*, 34.

68. See Deissmann, *Light from the Ancient East*, 349–51; Barclay, *Obeying the Truth*, 189; Meeks, *Origins of Christian Morality*, 166.

69. See Weiss, *Earliest Christianity*, 2:458–60; Kümmel, *Theology of the New Testament*, 158–59; Davies, *Jewish and Pauline Studies*, 206.

70. See Furnish, *Theology and Ethics in Paul*, 162–71.

71. Dunn, *Theology of Paul the Apostle*, 247. Meanwhile, Sanders manages to altogether avoid discussing the implications of Pauline lordship language, even though he argues that the lordship of Jesus, paired with the cross and resurrection, are at the heart of Paul's gospel (Sanders, *Paul*, 21–22).

terms and themes consistently paired with it, leads some to conclude that there is no conflict between the lordship of Jesus and the lordship of Caesar. Dunn, again, is cautious almost to the point of equivocation when he argues that there is no "sharp antithesis," in Paul's time, between the statements that "Jesus is Lord" and "Caesar is Lord," even though the proclamation of Jesus's lordship "was likely to send a shiver up and down many a spine, since it could so easily be represented as a direct antithesis to the loyalty owed to the emperor."[72] Dunn does not see lordship language as "necessarily subversive" (especially given that other cults also used the term in a manner that was not threatening to Rome), and so he understands the use as "more fanciful than subversive."[73] Here, Dunn is rather vague about what constitutes a "sharp" versus a less sharp antithesis. He also does not explore why oppressed people may choose to avoid sharp antitheses in their rhetoric. And, by arguing against the conclusion that lordship language is not *necessarily* subversive (and who said that it was?), he brackets out other more nuanced perspectives. However, Dunn is not alone in his conclusions. Marshall uses his survey of possible uses of the word "Lord" to conclude that the early Jesus loyalists did not think of Jesus as a political Lord but, instead, saw Jesus as a religious Lord and, as such, imported language from their political context to talk about Jesus that way.[74] Schreiner concurs, arguing that lordship language is about religious confession.[75] Two things are worth observing here. First, this position rests upon a now discredited and implausible understanding of the separation of religion and politics in Paul's context. In this regard, Marshall's move is especially interesting—first, religion is depoliticized and then political language is brought into that depoliticized religious context and used in a depoliticized way! Given what we've already seen, this seems highly implausible. Second, Jesus seems to be a rather weak kind of Lord. Thus, again according to Marshall, Jesus is Lord in a fairly passive way as Caesar and his representatives are left in charge of most things that matter here and now.[76] This contradicts what we have already seen about the ethics of the early assemblies of Jesus loyalists, and it also

72. Dunn, *Theology of Paul the Apostle*, 247, 430.
73. Dunn, *Theology of Paul the Apostle*, 553.
74. Marshall, "Jesus as Lord," 132–33.
75. See Schreiner, *Paul*, 162–63. See also Meeks, *Origins of Christian Morality*, 168.
76. See Marshall, "Jesus as Lord," 144–45.

contradicts what we examined above, regarding the gospel being a powerful and ongoing happening in which Jesus loyalists participate.

A closer examination of some passages wherein the Pauline faction uses lordship language makes a different interpretation more plausible. Specifically, the position that makes the best sense of the evidence is that Paul and his co-authors deploy lordship language in a manner that is intended to present Jesus as a superior alternative to Caesar. Thus, Rom 10:9–12 states the following:

> If you confess with your lips that Jesus is Lord and believe in your heart that God raised him from the dead, you will be saved ... there is no distinction between [Judean] and Greek; the same Lord is Lord of all and is generous to all who call on him. For "Everyone who calls on the name of the Lord shall be saved."

Here, Jesus is not presented as one Lord among many, or the Lord over one specific domain. He is presented as the Lord of all. Rom 15:9–11 also clearly presents Jesus as Lord over the nations. Thus:

> "I will praise you among the nations [*ethne*], and sing praises to your name";
>
> and again he says,
>
> "Rejoice, O nations [*ethne*], with his people";
>
> and again,
>
> "Praise the Lord, all you nations [*ethne*], and let all the peoples praise him."

Jesus, then, is presented as Lord of all people and of all nationalities, everywhere. This belief dethrones all other lords, as 1 Cor 8:5–6 states:

> Indeed, even though there may be so-called gods in heaven or on earth—as, in fact, there are many gods and many lords—yet for us there is one God, the father, from whom are all things and for whom we exist, and one Lord, Jesus [Anointed], through whom are all things and through whom we exist.

Finally, it is worth repeating the lordship language already examined in Phil 2:9–11:

> Therefore God also highly exalted [Jesus] and gave him the name that is above every name, so that at the name of Jesus every knee should bend, in heaven and on earth and under the earth, and every tongue should confess that Jesus [Anointed] is Lord, to the glory of God the father.

In these passages, one finds little room for the acknowledgment of any other lords. Several of these passages contain ideas or themes that are political in nature (from the *apotheosis* of Jesus to the refusal of any other gods or lords, including the Caesars, on earth or in heaven), so one may much more plausibly conclude that the Pauline usage of lordship language is, indeed, political and politically problematical from the Roman perspective.[77]

Deissmann's analysis is instructive here as he shows the mimicry and contestation involved in the subversive rhetoric related to Pauline discussions of "the Lord's treasury" (1 Cor 11:10), "the Lord's service" (Rom 12:11), and "the Lord's day" when the Collection is to take place (1 Cor 16:1–2). Within Roman constitutional law, the language of *kuriakos* ("belonging to the Lord") is translated as "imperial"—thus, for example, the "imperial treasury," "imperial service," and the "imperial day" of Sebaste (the Greek version of the name Augustus) when financial payments often became due.[78] By speaking the way they do, Deissmann argues that the Pauline faction is subverting these imperial-related motifs. Similarly, when mention is made of *apeleutheros kyriou* (freedpeople of the Lord) in 1 Cor 7:22, the Pauline faction is deploying a term that was commonly used for people freed by the emperor.[79] Yet, according to Paul and his coworkers, it is not the emperor who rules over and liberates all the people who reside in the empire; rather, it is Jesus who is the true Lord over all people and who liberates them from the reign of the emperor.

This discourse is not simply potentially subversive—from the perspective of the Roman authorities, it is treasonous. This is not only true of the passages quoted above. It also applies to the Pauline manner of speaking about Jesus as *the* Lord.[80] Lords require loyalty, and they require that this loyalty be expressed in the behaviors, values, and ways of living day-to-day life of those who are loyal to them.[81] While Caesar was will-

---

77. As concluded by Deissmann, *Light from the Ancient East*, 338, 353–55; Gorman, *Reading Paul*, 102–3; Horsley and Silberman, *Message and the Kingdom*, 156; Wright, *Paul*, 5; Cadoux, *Early Church and the World*, 102; Tellbe, *Paul Between Synagogue and State*, 250–51; Oakes, "God's Sovereignty over Roman Authorities," 126, 133–39.

78. Deissmann, *Light from the Ancient East*, 357–61.

79. Deissmann, *Light from the Ancient East*, 377.

80. Something Weiss already highlights (*Earliest Christianity*, 2:457–58), although he misses the implications of this, which are drawn out by Crossan and Borg (*First Paul*, 109).

81. See Cullmann, *Christ and Time*, 144, 211–12; Oakes, *Philippians*, 204–6;

ing to acknowledge other lesser lords and permit people to demonstrate loyalty to those lesser lords as long as that loyalty took place within the context of an overall loyalty to Caesar, Caesar would neither permit any other lords to claim the right to the universal loyalty of all people nor permit others to claim to be the one and only Lord of all. Claims like these violated the unanimous consensus Caesar required to rule and to justify his reign.[82] Those who made such claims and who refused to comply with the acknowledged universal rule of Caesar—the one Lord of all, the Lord who should be praised by the nations, and all people regardless of their nationalities—would be the subjects of violent campaigns that targeted them for assimilation or extermination. Such religious-political parties were considered treasonous, and treason itself was considered an impious religious offense as much as it was a political offense (which is why during the reign of Augustus, for example, the Greeks began to translate the Roman charge of *maiestas* with the word *Theiotes*, describing "treason as impiety").[83] Thus, numerous "foreign cults," from the druids in Gaul and Britain, to some Egyptian cults, to the influence of apocalypticism, magic, and astrology, to the early Jesus movement, were all targeted for political suppression or total extermination.[84] Here, religion, theology, and the politics of treason are inextricably connected.

However, before moving on to explore the disclosure of Jesus as Savior, it should be noted that, by deploying imperial themes, even if only to subvert them, the Pauline faction leaves a legacy open to being co-opted and worked back into the abusive hierarchies found in an imperial status quo (much as their use of patriarchal language for "God the Father of Jesus" leaves their legacy open to re-appropriation by oppressive gendered relationships). Here, one thinks immediately of Elizabeth Schüssler-Fiorenza's criticism of the kyriocentrism present in the Pauline discourse.[85] From the Super Apostles, to the pastoral epistles, to the early

---

Meeks, *Origins of Christian Morality*, 168; Gorman, *Reading Paul*, 101–3.

82. See Ando, *Imperial Ideology*, 30.

83. Ando, *Imperial Ideology*, 30–31, 395.

84. Drawing here on material already discussed above as well as Garnsey and Saller, *Roman Empire*, 169, 173. Hurtado also suggests that Paul himself used violence against the Jesus loyalists earlier in his life because he saw Jesus as a "messiah-claimant, and as such a king, which would have amounted to a challenge to Rome's rule" (Hurtado, *Destroyer of the Gods*, 19).

85. See Schüssler-Fiorenza, *In Memory of Her*, xxi (and throughout). Also, Horsley, "Introduction," 23.

church fathers, and through the entire history of orthodox and imperial Christianity, up to and including the words of scholars like Seyoon Kim, one cannot help but acknowledge the force of Schüssler-Fiorenza's conclusions. The Pauline legacy is one that is open to being co-opted for counter purposes and used by precisely the people whom Paul and his coworkers tried to resist.[86]

And Savior

The Pauline faction also regularly talks about Jesus as the Savior, as the bringer or cause of salvation, and as one who is actively engaged in saving those who loyally acknowledge him as Lord. Thus, Rom 10:34 states: "Everyone who calls on the Lord's name will be saved" (see also Rom 1:16; 5:10; 10:9–10; 1 Cor 1:18, 21; 15:2; 2 Cor 2:15; 6:2; Phil 1:28; 3:20; 1 Thess 5:8–9). Again, given that the world of the Roman Empire had already been saved by a Savior who brought salvation to all, and given that this was taken to be true not only of Augustus but was also repeated by other Caesars (like Nero at his ascension), this Pauline perspective would be greatly troubling to those situated in positions of power.[87] And for good reason. Within the Judean Scriptures, salvation was and is consistently a concrete, historical, communal-political event.[88] For the Judeans, salvation was always caught up with socioeconomic and political

---

86. On this point, by thoroughly rejecting the title of "Messiah," I believe Jesus was actually doing something more radical than even the Pauline faction. Jesus as he wanted to be perceived, as far as I can tell, was not so much the Anointed as the anti-Anointed, not so much the Christ as the anti-Christ (given the ways he not only rejects but mocks messianic pretensions—for my own exploration of some of that, see Oudshoorn, "Going to Die"). That said, I do think the Pauline faction is sensitive to some of these issues, which is why the talk of "the kingdom of God" that dominates the Synoptic Gospels is absent in Paulinism and, instead, one finds regular mention of the justice of God (*dikaiosyne theou*). Given that Paul and his coworkers wrote before the Synoptics, it's interesting to consider which term (kingdom or justice) is more loyal to Jesus and those who first gathered with him.

87. See Deissmann, *Light from the Ancient East*, 363–64; Carter, "Vulnerable Power," 473–74.

88. See Georgi, *Theocracy*, 29; Carter, *John and Empire*, 188–89; Miranda, *Marx and the Bible*, 168–73; Tellbe, *Paul Between Synagogue and State*, 252–53; Bates, *Salvation by Allegiance Alone*, 131. Bates, however, as we will see when discussing faith as allegiance, tends to warp his conclusions about salvation and faith because he is still hung up on the question of what kind of salvation might take place after death or after the return of Jesus—whichever comes first.

ways of structuring life together—which is also why the Judeans had a stubborn habit of revolting against oppressive empires. Consequently, when the Pauline faction talks about salvation, they do so in a manner that competes with and contradicts the ideo-theology of Rome. They make different claims: (a) about the identity of the Savior of the world; (b) about the kind of peace accomplished by the Savior; (c) about who or what people have been saved from; and (d) about the means by which the peace that results from salvation was accomplished. As we have seen, according to the dominant propaganda, Augustus (and then his heirs, up to and including Nero) was the Savior of the world, he had brought a peace that benefited Romans and their elite allies, and he had accomplished that peace by conquering, killing, or subduing not only his Roman rivals, who plunged the world into civil war, but also by saving foreign nationals from themselves and their own rulers, thereby incorporating them into the Roman Empire. All of this is contradicted by the Pauline faction. According to them, Jesus was the Savior of the world, he brought about a peace for all who had suffered under both Roman conquest and occupation and the rapacious rule of their magistrates or allies, and he accomplished this peace by dying on a cross as a terrorist publically executed by Rome. As Michael Gorman has observed, these are "mutually exclusive" narratives about salvation.[89] While the emperor claimed the title of savior because he killed people like Jesus in order to "secure the peace," the Pauline faction gives Jesus the title of Savior because Jesus gave his life in such a way that he was able to overcome the power of Rome.[90]

Who Emancipates People from Slavery (*Apolytrosis*)

Picking up on the Pauline language of "redemption" or "emancipation" (*apolytrosis*) helps us to understand something more of the political nature of salvation as understood by Paul and his coworkers. Rom 3:24 relates this emancipation to both what took place with Anointed Jesus and the possibility of now being able to freely live as just people (i.e., people who can enact and experience justice because of the ways in which they structure their corporate life together). Likewise, in 1 Cor 1:30, the emancipation of the Jesus loyalists and their ability to truly live

---

89. Gorman, *Reading Paul*, 102–3. See Crossan and Reed, *In Search of Paul*, 141, 149.

90. See Wengst, *Pax Romana*, ix, 2–4.

life is again related to who Anointed Jesus is and what he accomplished. And *emancipation from slavery* is precisely what Paul and his co-authors are talking about when they discuss *apolytrosis*. As multiple scholars have noted, *apolytrosis* is a technical term related to slavery laws and, more specifically, to liberating captives and prisoners of war from slavery either by a victory over their former masters or by ransoming them from their masters.[91] Those who, like Johannes Weiss, believe that Paul's language of "redemption" is strictly about liberation from "sin" (understood in an apolitical sense) are entirely missing the point.[92] They are also forgetting that the great majority of those addressed by Paul and his coworkers— and many of those doing the addressing—were literally either enslaved because of Roman conquest or were the immediate descendants of those who had been enslaved. One does not need to grasp for metaphorical meanings here—people who are literally enslaved are being addressed and they are being addressed by people who, it seems, had a habit of pooling resources to literally emancipate people from slavery. This, then, helps us to answer the question regarding from whom or from what those in the Anointed are being saved. But to answer this, we need to pick up the question of the Pauline understanding of what the Pauline faction

---

91. See Sampley, *Pauline Partnership in Christ*, 2; Jewett, "Corruption and Redemption," 45. James Dunn argues that a more probable source for the Pauline usage of this language is the account of Israel being ransomed from Egypt, but I'm not sure that this makes as much of a difference as Dunn seems to think it makes (Dunn, *Theology of Paul the Apostle*, 227–28). As has proven to be the case multiple times over the last two millennia, the exodus event can inspire struggles against contemporary manifestations of slavery so, again, it seems like that Paul and his coworkers can hold both historical Judean and contemporary notions about *apolytrosis* in hand without abandoning either.

92. Weiss actually thinks that Paul strips redemption language of its political significance but it seems more probable, at least to me, that Weiss is the one doing that (see Weiss, *Earliest Christianity*, 2:514–15). Of course, many of the more theologically inclined readers of Paul interpret redemption in this way. In 2003, for example, Theissen talks about Christ's triumph creating "freedom towards the criteria of the world" (Theissen, *Fortress Introduction to the New Testament*, 78), which is too bad, because in 1992 he seemed closer to what the Pauline faction was on about when he argued that within Pauline soteriology the themes of liberation, redemption, pardon, and reconciliation are related to "a restricting of relations of domination through the saving event," and he went on to ask, "is there not an implicit longing here—the longing that, for once, not only should the rulers be changed but that rule itself should lose its subjugating character?" (Theissen, *Social Reality*, 164–65). Indeed there is that longing here and, more than a longing, there are those who experience themselves as emancipated in the process of bringing such a transformation about.

variously refers to as the elements, the principalities, the powers, and the rulers.

To the Elements, Powers, Principalities, and Rulers

Saviors are designated as such because they save people from beings, things, experiences, actions, or circumstances that threaten or harm those who are saved or who are in the process of being saved. Similarly, slaves are redeemed from those who previously enslaved them. Paul and his coworkers find various ways to name those from whom Jesus loyalists have been saved. This includes the "god of this age" mentioned in 2 Cor 4:4—a god who is likely counted among the many so-called gods who exist in heaven and on earth (1 Cor 8:5) and the dull and blind rulers of this age (1 Cor 2:6–8). As we have seen, there is no more ideal candidate for the title "god of this age" than Caesar. Furthermore, given that Caesar is a plurality—spanning from Augustus to Nero and including several members of the extended imperial family—it is no surprise to see that the god of this age may also be made of many gods, some of whom, like Augustus, are in heaven, others of whom, like Nero, are on earth.

However, the Pauline faction is not always so explicit, and other names are frequently ascribed to those from whom the Jesus loyalists are being saved. Thus, in Rom 8:38, the Jesus loyalists are assured of the impotence of the "powers"; in 1 Cor 15:24, the ultimate annihilation of all "dominion, authority, and power" is foretold; in Gal 4, the Jesus loyalists are said to be liberated from "elements" that used to enslave them; and the nations are also said to be under the rule of both "idols" (1 Cor 12:2) and "demons" (1 Cor 10:20). What, then, are we to make of these things? If saving people from those things that used to enslave them is at the core of the Pauline understanding of Jesus's significance—and I agree with Paula Fredriksen that it is—then what are all these things?[93]

Various proposals have been made. First, are those who wish to emphasize the spiritual identity of the powers, who also often emphasize this in order to argue that one should not understand the powers in any kind of sociopolitical way.[94] Thus, Jesus is said to liberate people from

---

93. See Fredriksen, *From Jesus to Christ*, 56–58; Elliott, *Liberating Paul*, 123–24; Harink, *Paul Among the Postliberals*, 32.

94. See, for example, Kümmel, *Theology of the New Testament*, 186–89; Schreiner, *Paul*, 127–50, 233–34. I should note that, going forward in this section, I sometimes use the term "the powers" to refer to the cluster of things—powers, principalities,

the worship of false gods, from the thrall of demons, and from sin and death—all of which are understood in a strictly spiritual and theological manner. James Dunn, for example, describes the powers as "heavenly beings, subordinate to God and his Christ, with the potential to intervene between God and his creation, and hostile to his purposes and people" and goes on to say that they are more existential than ontological "supraindividual, suprasocial forces, spiritual realities, which influence events and conduct."[95] For conservative scholars who hold this position, any political identification of "the powers" is denied. The underlying idea is that state structures (at least the structures of the states in which they reside) are not things from which people need to be liberated but are, rather, things one should continue to obey. Some liberal scholars come to similar conclusions whether via a demythologizing existential hermeneutic that understands liberation as more to do with experiences internal to individuals rather than any change in external circumstances or via a reading that sees the powers as including socioeconomic or political structures but which then views these powers as morally neutral so that they can be redeemed and put into the service of the good.[96]

---

rulers, elements, idols, demons, gods—from whom Jesus is said to emancipate anyone willing to transfer their allegiance to him. It is regrettable that Walter Wink's analysis has heavily dominated the use of this term, especially given Wink's reliance on deutero-Pauline epistles (for more on that, see Elliott, *Liberating Paul*, 118–19) and some of his problematical conclusions (explored below), but I could not think of a better umbrella term. Martyn's discussion of the identity of the elements in Gal 4 is helpful for tying these things closely together as he concludes that the worship of basic elements (earth, water, air, fire) has been reworked, in the Graeco-Roman context, to the worship of their traditional gods, who from the Judean perspective, were viewed as idols or demons (Martyn, "Christ," 16–22, 30–31, 126). Ramsay MacMullen also helpfully notes that the notion of *daimones*, in Greek culture, was not necessarily a bad thing and *daimones* were simply beings who existed in an "intermediate though still superhuman and supernatural realm" as "powers that fill the heavens, fill the air" (MacMullen, *Changes*, 132). Weiss anticipates much of Martyn's work on this point, although he is emphatic that this all has to do with mysticism and spirituality devoid of material or political points of reference (see Weiss, *Earliest Christianity*, 2:239, 248, 248n46, 249, 251, 494–95, 599–603.)

95. Dunn, *Theology of Paul the Apostle*, 106, 109–10.

96. Bultmann, of course, is the classic existentialist example (see Bultmann, *Theology of the New Testament*, 1:230, 256–59; *Primitive Christianity*, 190). He also mostly sees the powers as morally neutral and composing an environment where one must continually choose Jesus as one's personal Lord. Conzelmann also adheres closely to this position (Conzelmann, *Outline of the Theology*, 193–94). In terms of liberal scholars who view the powers in more political terms but who also view them as morally neutral and redeemable, Wink is the classic example (see Wink, *Naming the Powers*;

Thus, some of the scholars who incline towards liberalism hold that the Pauline discussion of the powers is a way of referring to socioeconomic, cultural, and political structures and authorities. When looking for modern-day examples, these scholars mention things like racism, militarism, or nationalism (as per Gorman), Mammon and Aphrodite (Wright), or may emphasize that more abstract spiritual powers are always working through specific human instruments (Elliott).[97] Some in this camp do this to undercut what they perceive to be a misplaced emphasis on the spiritual or, at the very least, on the spiritual to the exclusion of all else.

Indeed, while exploring the topic of "the powers," it is important to take both spiritual and political components seriously and refuse to separate the two from each other. The language of the powers likely refers to cosmic angelic-demonic spiritual forces.[98] However, individual nations were also understood to have their own guardian angel (or *daimon*). These angels/demons were intimately connected to the identity, rule, and power of those nations.[99] And they were especially intimately connected with the people who ruled those nations. Thus, the powers both transcend and include socioeconomic and political structures and actors.[100] As Herman Ridderbos observes, they encompass "the totality

---

Unmasking the Powers; Engaging the Powers; see also Cullmann, *Christ and Time,* 196–203; *State in the New Testament,* 60–64; Harink, *Paul Among the Postliberals,* 116–19; Cadoux, *Early Church and the World,* 109–10). Rom 13:1–7 (explored below) is pretty much *the* passage in the Pauline Epistles used to support this position and the other relevant passages already mentioned are mostly ignored. It is Cullmann who cautions about comparing any other governments—including that of Nero—to that of Hitler's Germany in order to argue for disobedience to the state as a divinely appointed power. Thus, he observes (in a statement that hopefully at this point strikes the readers as implausible due to what we have learned about Roman imperialism): "Only the Roman State's surpassing of its limits in the imperial cult and the therewith connected aggression against the Christians, but not its general exercise of its functions as a State, can be compared with the State demonism that we have experienced." This is in keeping with the law-loving and law-abiding Paulinism of N. T. Wright and E. P. Sanders mentioned above. It's not likely in keeping with what the Pauline faction believed.

97. See Gorman, *Apostle of the Crucified Lord,* 587–88; Wright, *What Saint Paul Really Said,* 155–57, 160–61; Elliott, *Liberating Paul,* 122.

98. See Schnackenburg, *Moral Teaching,* 284–85; Schweitzer, *Mysticism of Paul the Apostle,* 55, 63–65; Sugai, "Paul's Eschatology," 114–15; Vos, *Pauline Eschatology,* 92, 279–81; Ridderbos, *Paul,* 89.

99. See Ziesler, *Pauline Christianity,* 16; Cullmann, *State in the New Testament,* 68, 100–14; Davies, *Jewish and Pauline Studies,* 192–93.

100. See Roetzel, *World That Shaped,* 99, 127; Georgi, *Theocracy,* 52, 56–57;

of unredeemed [i.e., unemancipated, i.e., enslaved] life" dominated by Sin and Death, and for this reason, according to Ridderbos, it is not inappropriate to understand the political persecutions experienced by Paul and his coworkers as "demonic threats."[101]

The mention of Sin and Death is not inconsequential here.[102] From the Pauline perspective, Death is the arch-power, ruling over *all* the other powers.[103] Thus, in 1 Cor 15:20–28, the Pauline faction observes that the ultimate enemy is Death, to whom all things were previously placed in subjection, but from whose rule, through the triumph of Jesus, all things can now be liberated. Death, as they go on to celebrate, has been swallowed up in victory (1 Cor 15:54) and so, quoting the prophet Hosea they mockingly ask, "Where, O Death, is your victory?" and "Where, O Death, is your sting?" (1 Cor 15:55). Yet, they go on to immediately observe that the sting of Death is *Sin* and the power of Sin is *law* but, even in these domains, Jesus loyalists experience victory (1 Cor 15:56–57). Thus, for the Pauline faction, Death is the ultimate power governing all the other powers, Sin is that which brings death about, and the rule of law—which, according to its own standards, justly crucified Jesus—is deeply implicated in all of this. This should cause us to be cautious about positions that are quick to exonerate the powers and see them as neutral or potentially good. One does not find such statements in the uncontested Pauline letters. Instead, as 1 Cor 15:24 makes clear and other passages imply, Paul and his coworkers eagerly anticipate the *destruction* of the powers.[104]

Davies, *Jewish and Pauline Studies*, 199–200; Sampley, *Walking between the Times*, 26–27; Harink, *Paul Among the Postliberals*, 32–37; Cullmann, *Christ and Time*, 104–5, 192–93.

101. Ridderbos, *Paul*, 91–92.

102. See Beker, *Paul the Apostle*, 189, 214–15. Beker's way of connecting Death to Sin heavily influences what follows. On this point, it's also worth observing that Crossan and Reed are over-reaching (perhaps influenced by a scientific perspective that views death as a natural part of life and also influenced by the pacifism they regard as the best alternative to American militarism?) when they argue that Paul doesn't take issue with death so much as he takes issue with violence and violent death in particular (see Crossan and Reed, *In Search of Paul*, 389).

103. Making an anarchist, from the Pauline perspective, ultimately nothing more than someone who opposes any ordering of the world under the rule of Death. For, as anarchists from Proudhon onwards have repeated, "Anarchy means order" (hence the most famous anarchist symbol, an "A" inside of an "O"). It is just that anarchists want the order of things to serve Life rather than Death (see Proudhon, *Selected Writings*).

104. As observed by Roetzel, *World That Shaped*, 99, 127; Elliott, *Liberating Paul*, 122–24; Georgi, *Theocracy*, 56–57.

Pauline Solidarity

Death is not the kind of thing that is redeemed—it is the kind of thing that is defeated, overthrown, and ultimately annulled in the resurrection (*anastasis*) of the dead. And all the powers that operate in the service of Death, the many heads of Sin sitting on the hydra of the rule of law, are to meet the same fate as their lord. This defeat is signaled in the uprising (*anastasis*) of the left-for-dead that is taking place in the illicit assemblies of Jesus loyalists who now practice what Ted Jennings aptly calls "outlaw justice."[105] Thus, the defeat, overthrow, and annulment of Death signals the defeat, overthrow, and annulment of Roman imperialism, which, like the contemporary Occidental forms of government applauded by almost all New Testament scholars (conservative or liberal), was utterly dependent upon theft, murder, colonization, dispossession, hoarding, and assigning large numbers of people to dislocation, slavery, and death. Speaking of redeeming imperialism is as nonsensical as speaking of redeeming rape (and, of course, the two are not mutually exclusive). Or, perhaps more technically accurate, speaking of redeeming imperialism is like speaking of emancipating slavery. How can slavery be liberated from slavery? It cannot be. It can only be abolished. And according to Paul and his coworkers, Jesus Anointed has accomplished the liberation of all peoples from all these things.[106]

And Whose Victory Is Apparent through His Resurrection and His Current Reign

Three closely interwoven things associated with participation in the powerful and ongoing happening of the gospel provide Paul and his coworkers with a basis for their claim that Jesus has won this victory and triumphed over the powers. The first is Jesus's resurrection, the second is Jesus's current reign as Lord (alongside of his Father in heaven), and the third is the ongoing and powerful activity of Jesus's spirit in the assemblies of Jesus loyalists.[107]

---

105. See Jennings, *Outlaw Justice*. More on this in section 3.

106. Thus, Rom 7:25, which leads into Rom 8.

107. Different scholars want to focus more exclusively on each of these individual elements, arguing that a single element is the decisive moment of victory. Thus, for example, Crossan and Borg emphasize the resurrection (Crossan and Borg, *First Paul*, 151–52; see also Theissen, *Fortress Introduction to the New Testament*, 7). Calvin Roetzel emphasizes Paul's meeting with the risen Jesus (Roetzel, *Letters of Paul*, 49). I think it better to hold these things together instead of prioritizing one element over

In terms of the first point, it is clear that everything that the Pauline faction believes is taking place, everything in which they have invested themselves, is entirely dependent on the *anastasis* of Jesus—as they say in 1 Cor 15:14–17, if the Anointed has not been raised from the dead, then their kerygma and the Corinthians' loyalty are both in vain and everyone is still in bondage to the power of Sin. As we have already seen and as Paul and his coworkers go on to say, Sin is but the "sting of Death" which is granted power through the law, but as the firstfruit of the resurrection of the dead, Jesus not only triumphs over all these things but also gives that same victory to those who participate in the gospel with him (1 Cor 15:57). Therefore, asserting that Jesus rose-up from the dead was not simply a way of comforting those who were mourning the deaths of loved ones (deaths that were quite possibly violent deaths brought about by local persecutions).[108] Granted, there would be a comforting element present in this, but the emphasis here is on motivating those left-for-dead who, through the triumph of Jesus and with the aid of the Spirit of Life, partake in their own uprising.[109] This relates to the observation that Jesus is not only said to have risen from the dead but also said to be seated at the right hand of God the father in heaven (as per Rom 8:34 and Phil 2:9). It would be impossible for first-century inhabitants of the empire to understand this outside of Roman imperial propaganda about the *apotheoses* of various emperors.[110] By ascending in this way, Jesus triumphs over those who are said to have ascended into heaven and who were welcomed into the company of the gods because they pacified the world by crucifying people like Jesus.

---

another. Ditto for those who wish to claim that the true victory of Jesus will not take place until his *parousia* (see, for example, Carter, "Vulnerable Power," 473). This ties into the discussion of an "inaugurated but not yet consummated" eschatology already discussed in volume 1 of this series.

108. *Pace*, for example, Malherbe, *Paul and the Popular Philosophers*, 8, 74; *Social Aspects of Early Christianity*, 64–65.

109. Thus, the observations already mentioned in prior volumes, that the very idea of resurrection was intimately linked to revolutionary movements while being resisted by centrally established authorities. Wright often uses this language (see Wright, *Surprised by Hope*, 214), but he, like many so-called radical New Testament scholars, tends to bleach the word "revolutionary" of any substantial meaning which is partly why I tend to avoid using it altogether (as far as I can tell, the words "revolutionary" and "radical" in scholarship often have more to do with branding than they have to do with ethics).

110. See Horsley and Silberman, *Message and the Kingdom*, 154; Horsley, *Religion and Empire*, 90; *Jesus and Empire*, 134; Carter, *John and Empire*, 315–34.

Second, as the firstborn of the dead, Jesus, according to Paul and his coworkers, currently reigns as the Lord. Paul believes he has directly encountered Jesus in this capacity (see Gal 1:16; 1 Cor 15:8; 9:1), and it is this encounter that seems to have brought about his transfer of allegiance to Jesus.[111] Thus, in 1 Cor 4:9 and again in more detail in 2 Cor 2:14–16, the Pauline faction uses the language of an imperial triumph to describe the manner in which Jesus vanquished Paul.[112] Now Jesus currently reigns as Lord alongside of God. Hence, as we have seen, the many references to Jesus as Lord. He is also described as reigning in this way in both Phil 2:9–11 and 1 Thess 4:15–17.[113]

Third, Jesus does not reign at a distance. He is intimately involved in the assemblies of Jesus loyalists. In fact, because Jesus is present both in individual members and in the assemblies as a whole, it is possible to see the assemblies and their component parts as the body of Jesus himself continuing to gospel in the here-and-now. This will be explored in more detail below, when speaking of what it means to be "in the Anointed" as members of the "body of the Anointed" (over against being "in the flesh," which is a way of speaking of participating in the imperial body politic). Here, I wish to emphasize that the same spirit that raised Jesus from the dead is said to be present in a powerful and active way in the individual and communal lives of the Jesus loyalists (see Rom 8:9–11; 15:16, 19; 1 Cor 6:11; 2 Cor 3:3; 13:14; Gal 5; Phil 1:19, 27; 2:1). This Spirit—sometimes closely related to God, sometimes closely related

---

111. The accounts in Acts (Acts 9:3–9; 22:6–21) are somewhat questionable and not entirely consistent but, the general point that Paul had some kind of dramatic, personal encounter with one whom he believed to be the risen Anointed Lord Jesus seems to be very much in keeping with how Paul speaks about his own trajectory from one who persecuted the Jesus loyalists to one who became an ambassador of Jesus to the nations.

112. See, for example, Maier, *Picturing Paul in Empire*, 41–45.

113. Here I wish to object to those who impose kingship language onto Jesus or, via Jesus, onto God, which is done by both right-leaning and left-leaning scholars (see Wright, *How God Became King*; Meggitt, *Madness of King Jesus*; Jipp, *Christ is King*; Bates, *Salvation by Allegiance Alone*). The Pauline faction does not use kingship language. They do use lordship language, and I understand that lords and kings often blur together, but it is not insignificant that the language of kingship does not appear in the Pauline texts (especially given the later focus on the Kingdom of God in the Synoptic Gospels), and I do not think we should rush to use that terminology. This also ties into concerns I have about the legacy of the kyriocentric language of the Pauline texts and how that coheres (or does not cohere) with the anarchism of the Pauline position related to the rule of law, the powers, and rulers of this present evil age. Again, it is not the kingdom of God but the justice of God that has pride of place in Paulinism.

to Jesus, sometimes closely related to Life, often spoken of as an entity distinct from those things—is the powerful force uniting the assemblies and also enabling them to act in new ways.[114] Thus, in all three of these ways—through his resurrection and ascension, through his current reign as Lord, and through his active work in the assemblies of Jesus loyalists—the victory of Jesus over the powers that previously enslaved the Jesus loyalists is disclosed.

However, because all of this is only just beginning, because the germ of resurrection life has only just begun to spread among the vanquished and the left-for-dead, and because the foolish and blind rulers have not realized their defeat but persist in thinking they can take, enslave, rape, kill, and crucify as they see fit, there is still a war that is being waged. Thus, military images and metaphors related to imperial games frequently appear in the Pauline Epistles.[115] The Thessalonians are urged to put on armor (1 Thess 5:8). The Philippians are urged to strain forward for the goal and the prize (Phil 3:12–14) and Epaphroditus is described to the Philippians as a "fellow soldier" (Phil 2:25). The Galatians are also urged to run well (Gal 5:7). So, too, are the Corinthians, whom Paul and his co-authors encourage like runners and boxers (1 Cor 9:24–27), and to whom they state that Paul fought with wild animals at Ephesus (1 Cor 15:32). It is also to the Corinthians that Paul's role as an ambassador is compared to military service (1 Cor 9:7), even as he later encourages them to stand firm like strong men (1 Cor 16:13). Thus, in 2 Cor 6:7 the Pauline faction describes the Corinthians working in the power of God with "the weapons of justice" in their right and left hands. Shortly thereafter, in 2 Cor 10:3–6, warfare language is again explicitly deployed and the Pauline faction is clear that the weapons they use are not "fleshy" but are "powerful" and capable of overthrowing strongholds, taking even thoughts captive and making them submissive to the Anointed, while also being ready to avenge any disobedience (2 Cor 10:3–6). Similarly, the Romans are urged to not be vanquished by evil but to be victorious over evil with good (Rom 12:21). To do this, they too must dress in armor, even if this is "the armour of light" (Rom 13:12—more on that below).

---

114. See Fee, *Paul, the Spirit, and the People of God*, 63–73, 870–876; Hays, *Moral Vision*, 43–45; Judge, "Did the Churches Compete," 52; Blanton, *Materialism for the Masses*, 155–56.

115. See Krentz, "Paul, Games, and the Military," 354. Note that militarism and games were deeply interwoven in the Graeco-Roman world (345–47).

Thus, it seems that the gospeling of Jesus loyalists not only contradicts the gospeling of Rome—these gospels are, in fact, at war with each other.

Many Christian interpreters, be they bourgeois academics or Christian peace activists, are quick to interpret this language as strictly metaphorical, existential, or spiritual—they want to be clear that this talk about taking up arms and armor and fighting or boxing (or racing), does not refer to literal weapons or literal physical acts of violence.[116] However, Edgar Krentz is more cautious about imposing a strict pacifist reading on these texts. He notes that Pauline discourse tends to use military language in an acritical manner in order to motivate others to engage in a serious work that involves deep commitment and personal suffering.[117] While Krentz takes this as evidence that the Pauline faction lacked any serious criticism of Roman militarism (a suggestion that seems implausible given the case built so far in this text), it seems to me that one can still heed Krentz's observations while avoiding his conclusion *and* remaining cautious about agreeing with pacifist conclusions regarding the way the Pauline faction modifies their talk about weapons and armor. Paul and his coworkers are writing as members of an oppressed and persecuted group. When speaking of war and weapons, it is probably a good safety measure to use modifiers that create plausible deniability if questioned by the authorities. Thus, for example, the NRSV translates 2 Cor 10:4 as saying "the weapons of our warfare are not merely human," and this captures the possible ambiguity of the passage quite well. Possessing weapons that are not *merely* human does not preclude one from arming oneself with weapons that are also human, even if those weapons are taken to be something more besides. This is worth keeping in mind for subsequent discussions of peace and of Rom 13:1–7. However, at this point, it is clear that Jesus has triumphed and that Jesus's triumph continues to work itself out in a militant way that, from the Pauline perspective, can be called a war with and against the gospeling of the empire.

---

116. See, for example, Georgi, *Theocracy*, 27–28; Cadoux, *Early Church and the World*, 118–19.

117. Krentz, "Paul, Games, and the Military," 344–47, 355–63; see also Oakes, *Philippians*, 201–4. Krentz also observes how this language would resonate in cities and colonies with a high population of veterans or which were famous for the games they hosted (351, 355). This point is also made in Tellbe, *Paul Between Synagogue and State*, 246–48.

THE LAWLESSNESS OF GOOD NEWS IN THE MAKING

Wherein He Practices Mercy and the Giving of Good Gifts to Those Whom He Rules

The outcome of Jesus's victory, which is continually enacted in the current assemblies of Jesus loyalists, results in practices of mercy and the giving of good gifts to those who recognize Jesus as Lord. This is the context in which much of the conversation about the Pauline conception of grace should be situated, but having already discussed grace in the context of Graeco-Roman patronage and the alternative economics of the networked assemblies of Jesus loyalists, it is worth emphasizing that the outpouring of God's grace, resulting in a theology of abundance and the practices of economic mutuality, is intimately connected with what Jesus is said to have accomplished. Thus, in Rom 3:24, Paul and his coworkers argue that justice is brought into the lives of the Jesus loyalists through a free gift of grace brought about by (and exhibited within) the emancipation of the slaves accomplished by and in Anointed Jesus (see also Rom 5:15–17, 21; 1 Cor 1:4). Here, justice, loyalty (*pistis*), and grace, which is freely experienced as a gift from the victor to the people emancipated by that victory and under the ongoing reign of that victor, are intimately connected and equally opposed to the rule of law—hence, people are said to be made just—that is to say, to be in just relationships with one another—by a loyalty that is demonstrated, not by performing the deeds required by the law, but by following "the law of loyalty" (Rom 3:27–28; my translation).

Thus, like the Caesars, Jesus shows mercy to the vanquished. Indeed, as Neil Elliott has shown, this contrast is at play in the discussions of divine mercy contained in Rom 9–11.[118] However, as Rom 5:6–11 demonstrates, the mercy of Jesus also exceeds and reverses standard expectations related to mercy as victors practiced it toward the vanquished.[119] The Caesars showed mercy to people with considerable wealth and status in order to consolidate their hold on a local population by co-opting the most powerful and greedy members. The mercy of Jesus extends not only to vanquished enemies but also to those who are weak, ungodly, and unjust—and, as Paul details in 1 Cor 4:10–13, it even extends to the nobodies and the nothings who are like a disease-ridden scum infecting various cities. In fact, it was precisely in order to liberate these people that Jesus fought and won his triumph. Thus, the victory of Jesus brings a free,

---

118. Elliott, *Arrogance of Nations*, 100–111.
119. Something Maier observes in his *Picturing Paul in Empire*, 55–57.

merciful, and gracious gift to these people who are now liberated in the assemblies of Jesus loyalists. However, at the same time, this act is simply the realization of justice because the weakness, sinfulness, bondage, and godlessness of "the wretched of the earth" was only brought about in the first place because of the injustice of the rulers, gods, and powers of this age.[120]

One of the primary ways of speaking about this gift is by saying that those who are united in Jesus's uprising have been given the gift of life, or age-long, unending, or eternal life, or of the life of the new age (see esp. Rom 6:1–23; but also Rom 2:7; 5:21; 8:6, 11; 1 Cor 15:45; 2 Cor 2:16; 3:6; 4:10–12; Gal 6:8; Phil 2:16). This makes sense given that the first thing taken from those left-for-dead is life itself. In an empire ruled by Death, it is precisely life that Death wishes to steal and hoard so that Death can continue to reign. But if resurrection life comes, even after Death has done its worst (and there was nothing worse than death on a cross), then all those living in the shadows of their own crosses have grounds for believing that the reign of death is broken and that life, true life, real life, abundant life, is possible to them now.

However, salvation, justice, and life are not the only gifts Jesus distributes as a merciful victor. These things become possible within the assemblies of Jesus loyalists because the Spirit of Life now distributes a multitude of more specific and personalized gifts to all the members (see Rom 12:6–8; 1 Cor 7:7; 12:4–31; 14:1–40). Thus, according to the Pauline faction, Jesus both liberates people from the powers that enslaved them and also gives them the gifts they need in order to stay free as they pursue new life together within and against the death-dealing socioeconomic and theopolitical practices of the empire in which they are embedded.

Notably, the Gift of a Peace that Transcends Prior Divisions and Overcomes Previous Animosities

The grace of Jesus (and of the God taken to be his Father) is constantly paired with peace. Hence, their well-remarked upon pairing at the opening of the uncontested epistles (see Rom 1:7; 1 Cor 1:3; 2 Cor 1:2; Gal 1:3; Phil 1:2; 1 Thess 1:1; Phlm 3). The Pauline faction also maintains a

---

120. Jennings does a lot to explore the connection between justice and mercy and also their relation to the law (Jennings, *Outlaw Justice*). On "the wretched of the earth," see Fanon, *Wretched of the Earth*.

unique emphasis upon God as "the God of peace" (see Rom 15:33; 16:20; 1 Cor 14:33; 2 Cor 13:11; Phil 4:9; 1 Thess 5:23—a term that only appears in one other place in the New Testament, Heb 13:20). There is no doubt that, just as the triumph of Augustus and the rule of subsequent Caesars is said to accomplish and maintain peace, so also the victory of Jesus accomplishes a peace that overcomes previous divisions. Thus, people (who were previously unable to live justly) experience peace with God (Rom 5:1), peace with one another (Rom 14:19; 1 Cor 14:33; 2 Cor 13:11; 1 Thess 5:13), and, insofar as it is possible to them, peace with all (Rom 12:18; 1 Cor 7:15). Thus, peace is also one of the great gifts graciously and freely given by Jesus in coordination with God the Father and the Spirit of Life (Rom 8:6; 14:17; 15:13; Gal 5:22; Phil 4:7).

Given that this peace comes about through the exultation of a person who was crucified in order to maintain the *pax Romana*—i.e., that peace is accomplished by the triumph of a person who was condemned as a terrorist and a threat to world peace—this peace is necessarily different than the peace promoted by the Caesars.[121] Others have tried to express this in various ways. For example, Ted Jennings states that "ultimately, peace is the goal of Paul's messianic politics—not . . . the peace of pacification but the peace of diversity rejoicing in harmony."[122] Similarly, Harry Maier argues that Paul and his coworkers, along with God, Jesus, and the Spirit, establish "an order of peace and concord achieved by other than Roman diplomatic and military means."[123] In the same vein, Crossan and Reed, and then Crossan and Borg, argue that the Pauline faction presents an alternative vision of "peace through justice" or "peace through distributive justice" (which is contrasted with the unjust and punitive system of Roman justice).[124] For Crossan and Borg, as for many others, this peace

---

121. Klaus Wengst astutely points out that the crucifixion of Jesus was performed in order to secure the peace (Wengst, *Pax Romana*, 2–4). Georgi also develops this point well when talking about how Paul modifies the political ideology of reconciliation and peace—a task Plutarch assigned to Alexander the Great and which was taken over by the Caesars—and notes how dramatically this is reworked by saying that the death of the Savior is an entirely new emphasis (leaders sacrificed subordinates, never themselves), leading to a view of humanity "controlled by the mutual solidarity of life born out of a common death" (Georgi, *Theocracy*, 65–71).

122. Jennings, *Outlaw Justice*, 222.

123. Maier, *Picturing Paul in Empire*, 120.

124. Crossan and Reed, *In Search of Paul*, 74, 403; Crossan and Borg, *First Paul*, 116, 121; Crossan, *God and Empire*, 149.

produces a picture of multicultural diversity paired with concord and mutual acceptance.[125]

However, this picture of liberal multiculturalism somewhat (but not altogether) misses the point. As we already saw with the warfare imagery deployed above and the consistent opposition to the rulers, gods, and powers of the age (and the institutions and structures that all, ultimately, serve Death), the Pauline faction is not at peace with all people, all parties, all systems, and all arrangements. They are, in fact, at war with the peace imposed by conquest, military occupations, and elite betrayals, which both maintains and is maintained by the Roman Empire. Thus, in 1 Thess 5:1–11, they openly mock Roman claims regarding "peace and security," because, they claim, those who rely on Rome for such things are in for a devastating surprise (because Roman peace is not real and Roman security is false).[126] Thus, the peace experienced among the assemblies of Jesus loyalists is not a truly universal peace that incorporates everyone regardless of property, status, loyalties, and so on. Rather, it is the kind of peace that is necessary to create solidarity networks among colonized, enslaved, and oppressed peoples so that they can collectively work to produce life-affirming and life-giving ways of structuring life together with and against the agents and structures of the death-dealing empire. This is the work of reconciliation now being accomplished by the ambassadors of the Anointed, who bring new creation and justice wherever they go (2 Cor 5:17–21).

That said, even in the context of this struggle, there is no doubt that humility, a willingness to suffer personal loss, bodily harm, and political persecutions as well as a novel embrace of non-retaliation are all things valued by the Pauline faction. However, Pauline scholars, especially those responding to the militarism and eternal warmongering of nations like

125. See Crossan and Borg, *First Paul*, 158–84; for another study that emphasizes this, see Horrell, *Solidarity and Difference*; these themes are generally strong in liberal Pauline scholarship.

126. See, especially, Tellbe, *Paul Between Synagogue and State*, 123–26; Smith, "'Unmasking the Powers'" 47–66. See also Carter, "Vulnerable Power," 473; Georgi, *Theocracy*, 28. Alternatively, Ernst Bammel argues that, in 1 Thess 4:15–5:11, Paul is using a state-based ideology to engage in the sort of self-criticism encouraged by the state itself (and so, according to Bammel, Paul criticizes one part but never questions the whole; see Bammel, "Romans 13," 375–80). I think this series, as a whole, highlights the implausibility of this assertion. As a third alternative, Seyoon Kim repeats some of his arguments about how language cannot be nuanced or have multiple layers of meaning and then says the whole passage is really just about what happens to believers who have died (Kim, *Christ and Caesar*, 8–9).

Britain or the United States (either to condemn or affirm these states), tend to overstate this. Thus, to pick two examples, Michael Gorman asserts that the turn to nonviolence is at the very heart of Paul's gospel and Ben Witherington argues that Paul stresses pacifism as "a social program, not just a survival tactic."[127] Here, a great deal is made of Paul's prior involvement in violently persecuting the early Jesus movement, wherein Paul likely understood himself as standing in the tradition of Israel's "hero of zeal" who were willing to use violence against other Judeans because of their blasphemy and their disregard of the law (which compromised the holiness of Israel and threatened Israel's set-apartness for God).[128] Paul's encounter with the Jesus, whom he previously persecuted, is said to have converted Paul to a strict pacifism. Considerable attention is then given to Rom 12:9–21, wherein Jesus loyalists are called to bless their persecutors, to not repay evil for evil, to love enemies in tangible and meaningful material ways (thereby overcoming evil with good), and, as much as they can, live at peace with all people.

The injunction to not repay evil for evil also already appears in 1 Thess 5:15, but there is a question as to the extent of this and to whom this applies or does not apply. Paul and his coworkers, for example, are not afraid to say that those who gospel different gospels should be accursed (Gal 1:8–9). They also are not averse to calling those who gospel other gospels "dogs" and wishing that terrible physical harm (like castration) would befall them (Phil 3:2; Gal 5:12). Similarly, they are not averse to wishing vengeance upon their enemies—this vengeance is simply postponed to the *parousia* (see, for example, Rom 2:5–11; 2 Cor 5:10; Gal 1:8–9; Phil 3:18–19; 1 Thess 1:9–10; 2:16). Now, one could argue that Paul and his coworkers are operating with imaginations limited (and still colonized) by their context and so they fail to see the full implications of their own teachings . . . or, alternatively, one could argue that Paul has no desire to be as thorough-going a pacifist as (in my experience, mostly bourgeois and White) liberal Christians make him out to be.[129]

127. Gorman, *Reading Paul*, 17–18, 120; Witherington, *Paul Quest*, 184; see also 181–84. See Cadoux, *Early Church and the World*, 103–4; Wengst, *Pax Romana*, 86–88. I've also made this mistake myself in the past; see Oudshoorn, "New Testament and Violence."

128. See especially Dunn, *Beginning from Jerusalem*, 339–45; Wrede, *Paul*, 5–6; Witherington, *Paul Quest*, 174. Note Paul's mention of zeal in Gal 1:13–14 and Phil 3:6.

129. The same bourgeois, mostly White liberals tend to engage in similar acts of bleaching the historical record in relation to other movements that were willing to take

Furthermore, despite what happened when he encountered Jesus, Paul praises the Jesus loyalists for their *zeal* and exhorts them to further zeal (see 1 Cor 14:12; 2 Cor 7:7, 11; 9:2; Rom 12:11). Given that the zeal referred to in a number of these passages seems to refer to nonviolent actions, one should be cautious about reading too much into Paul's reference to his prior zeal. Was it so strictly related to a willingness to use violence? If it was, does Paul's ongoing approval of zeal mean that he still sometimes values violence as a tactic? Or has zeal now been redefined? Or was zeal never as heavily focused on violence as we have made it out to be? Caution should be exercised here, and drawing a rather large conclusion that Paul and his coworkers were utterly devoted to pacifism at all times in all ways seems unwarranted. Other solutions are equally or more plausible. Thus, for example, one could argue that Paul and his coworkers urged non-retaliation for two inter-related reasons. First, because they wished to avoid lateral violence and, second, because they had not found meaningful ways to strike back at the rulers and still survive as life-giving and life-affirming assemblies. In terms of lateral violence, Paul and his coworkers may have be concerned about colonized, enslaved, and oppressed peoples lashing out at others who were also colonized, enslaved, and oppressed (who, in the day-to-day lives of the members of the Jesus loyalists were likely to be the most immediate proximate cause of oppression—like neighbors ratting out other neighbors for hosting an illegal gathering or like reaffirming dehumanizing stereotypes about "Others" that the empire used to divide and rule the vanquished), rather than fostering the kind of unity necessary to overcome the context of colonization, slavery, and oppression. This would be a misplaced form of violence that actually furthered the agenda of the colonizers (after all, Rome maintained peace by fostering disagreements between the colonized and then playing the role of mediator). Indeed, the wish to avoid lateral violence fits well with the recognition that most of the Pauline references to peace speak of the kind of peace that is to exist, not in the world generally, but in the assemblies of Jesus loyalists. However, given their minority status and vulnerability, exercising extreme caution about retaliating is (*pace* Witherington) less of a universal social program and more of a necessary survival strategy for right now. Situational analyses, like understandings of when and how God's vengeance might take place, are context-driven

---

up arms—like the Black civil rights movement in the United States of America (for criticisms of this, see, for example, Cobb, *This Nonviolent Stuff'll Get You Killed*; Umoja, *We Will Shoot Back*; Hill, *Deacons of Defense*; Gelderloos, *Failure of Nonviolence*).

and continually open to shifts and changes and developments. Such a change may have taken place in Rome in 64 CE. We shall see.

Thereby Revealing Himself to Be the True Son of God

As the Lord and Savior who triumphed and emancipated those loyal to him from Death and all the powers operating in the service of Death, as the one who shows mercy and grace, bringing about a peace that transcends prior divisions—as a person who, in other words, matches and surpasses Caesar on all the key foundational points of the imperial gospel of Rome—and as a person who has risen from the dead and also ascended to the right hand of God in heaven, it is also no surprise to see Jesus referred to as the Son of God. Thus, as we have already seen, God is primarily understood as the Father of Jesus and references to Jesus as God's Son abound in the Pauline Epistles.[130] There is no way to square this claim of divine sonship with the claims to divine sonship made by the Caesars—especially since the claims made about both argue that they are *the greatest* son of *the greatest* god. This cannot be the case of both the crucifier and the crucified. To give this title to Jesus is to simultaneously deny it to Caesar, which amounts to nothing less than an act of calculated treason.[131]

Indeed, it seems to me that this parallel with the dominant ideo-theology of Rome best explains how first-century Judeans came to view Jesus as divine. It seems to me that an early high Christology is the result of the hybridity and mimicry that arose from the early Jesus loyalists attempting to dethrone Caesar—both in theory and in practice. Therefore, the lack of engagement with motifs related to the imperial ideology that dominated the eastern part of the empire at the time of Paul among New Testament scholars arguing for an early high Christology is rather striking in this regard.[132] With so many parallels existing between how Paul and his coworkers speak about Jesus and how the imperial propaganda spoke about Caesar, concluding that Jesus, like Caesar, must also be a divine son of God ends up feeling inevitable. Unfortunately, for many

---

130. See Rom 1:3–4, 9; 5:10; 8:3, 29, 32; 1 Cor 1:9; 15:28; 2 Cor 1:19; Gal 1:16; 2:20; 4:6; 1 Thess 1:10.

131. See Crossan and Reed, *In Search of Paul*, 11.

132. I discuss this in relation to Larry Hurtado's work in Oudshoorn, "Response to Larry Hurtado," but similar criticisms can be made of Dunn and Tilling. Hurtado offered a response of sorts to my criticisms in Oudshoorn, "Hurtado Responds."

engaged in the early high Christology conversation, this thesis appears to be rejected a priori because they are not only interested in Jesus as one among many other historical figures who were treated as divine—they also want to understand Jesus as divine now. Seeing the divinity of Jesus as implicated in a (as we have already seen) not always positive process of co-opting and subverting imperial propaganda might have more troubling implications for what we are to make of questions related to Jesus's divinity today.

The True First Among Equals (*Princeps*)

That said, precisely in his role as the Son of God, Jesus also becomes the firstborn of many siblings who are also adopted into the household of God (see especially Rom 8:14–32, along with the discussion that follows in Rom 9–11; Gal 3:26–4:31). I have already described this in detail above when I discussed the fictive kinship that now exists among Jesus loyalists who are now grafted into the family of God. However, by describing Jesus as the firstborn, Jesus is positioned as a first among equals. This is the proper meaning of the title "*princeps*," which, as has already been noted, was one of the titles most valued by Caesar Augustus. However, as the trajectory of Phil 2:5–11 makes clear, the equals here are not only all children adopted by God but also were all of those in the company of the crucified and left-for-dead.[133] Recalling that it was the Caesars who claimed to be adopted sons of God, and recalling that the proof of that claim was found in how they pacified the empire (through conquest, crosses, and the rule of law), it is hard to overstate how offensive and threatening it would be to claim that the left-for-dead are the ones who are the truly adopted children of god and that a person crucified to maintain Caesar's peace is the true first among equals.

And The Truly Anointed One

Finally, we can conclude by looking at the title most frequently applied to Jesus: (the) Anointed.[134] The political nature of Judean messianism has

---

133. See Georgi, *Theocracy*, 73–74; Tellbe, *Paul Between Synagogue and State*, 200–202, who follows in the steps of Georgi.

134. A title used 383 times in the Pauline letters (Schnabel, *Paul and the Early Church*, 1405).

THE LAWLESSNESS OF GOOD NEWS IN THE MAKING

already been well established and I do not believe it necessary to repeat all that I have already said on this topic. Suffice to say, the Anointed was always understood to be one who would be specially favored by God to liberate God's people from unjust, oppressive, and colonizing rulers, laws, and hierarchies of power. Not all are convinced, of course. Schnabel, for example, recognizes that the title "Christ" or "Messiah" was "potentially dangerous" because it could be understood as a political title, but asserts that there is "no evidence that Paul proclaimed, with a deliberately provocative focus, the political implications of Jesus the Messiah."[135] In fact, when it comes to this matter, Schnabel concludes that seeing Pauline messianism as politically subversive is "both unrealistic and anachronistic, formulated at conference tables in the secure ivory towers of modern scholars whose lives are not in danger."[136]

At the risk of sounding foolish (see 2 Cor 11), I can only say that I cannot comment on such conferences because I have neither the time nor money needed to attend them. I have been too busy trying to gospel in the company of the left for dead, where I have sometimes found myself intervening into knife fights, where I have been assaulted multiple times by police officers and riot cops, where I have been thrown into cells, where we have shared life together in ways not bound by the rule of law or the rule of Death, and where many of my loved ones are not only in danger of dying but have already died. I think, for example, of my friend Mike Smith (not his real name), who, unbeknownst to me, saw me on the bus with my son, and who always praised me for how well I loved my son because he knew, just from looking at us, how deep our love was for each other. I think about how my friend Mike Smith died from an infection related to injection drug use, because people who have to find alternate ways to deal with their pain, loneliness, and trauma are often turned into criminals, so he used in unsafe places with unsafe gear. I think about saying goodbye to my friend Mike Smith when he was in a coma on a hospital bed and his artificial leg had been removed and there were tubes in his arms and down his throat and also in his jugular (or was it his carotid?), and his wrists were tied to the sides of his bed (for his own safety, I was told), and I said goodbye to him, and I stroked his arm and told him I loved him, and told him it was okay to let go and leave this world where he was ever only crucified—and, for the life of me, all I could see

---

135. Schnabel, *Paul and the Early Church*, 1483.
136. Schnabel, *Paul and the Early Church*, 1406.

was the battered body of the Anointed One after it had been through the gauntlet of Roman torture and taken down from the cross where it was nailed and where it finally completely shattered—and I know that Mike Smith is only one of a great cloud of witnesses whom I have known . . . and I think about the words of Schnabel, and I think he has no idea what the fuck he is talking about.

However, part of what is striking about the Pauline usage of this title is how it frequently seems to function as a name.[137] Hence, the common English translations of "Jesus Christ" (rather than Jesus the Christ) and "Christ Jesus" (rather than the Christ, Jesus). I find these translations problematic, in part because "Christ" is simply a way of referring to "Messiah," and both Messiah and Christ mean "Anointed," the term I prefer to use. I think rendering the word more literally, as "Anointed" or "the Anointed," helps to better capture the parallel that the Pauline faction is drawing upon—because the contrast here is between Jesus Anointed and Caesar Augustus. Caesar, it should be remembered, was a surname of the Julian gens and the name Augustus was an honorific title given to Octavian saying that he was August—i.e., that he was duly recognized as consecrated and inspiring reverence. Hence, he can also be the August Caesar in the same way that Paul and his coworkers refer to the Anointed Jesus. In both cases, proper names and titles are paired, names become titles, and titles become names. Furthermore, this highlights the clash between the Anointed and the August. The latter receives all the proper honors from all the proper people and has utilized all the proper channels to get there. The former has the Spirit of Life. And so there is a clash between institutional and charismatic powers, between those who would hoard life for themselves, who make their living dependent upon the deaths of others, and those who still, in the overflowing of life, live and refuse to accept dying as their lot. Because, as we have already begun to see and will see more of shortly, the Anointed is never only One—the Anointed is multitudinous. It is the August who announce there can and must be only one—one Lord, one God, one creed, one baptism, one people, one *imperium*, one market, one peace, one way, one life. But the company of the left-for-dead, the company of the living, know otherwise. There are countless roads to freedom and countless people on the way in the *anastasis* of the dead who experience a second life and who only look like a zombie apocalypse to those who piled them into mass graves in

---

137. On the use of "Christ" as a name, see Fredriksen, *From Jesus to Christ*, 56.

the first place. Slaves who dream of freedom are a nightmare only to the slave-owners, slave-sellers, and those who share in the slave market. They are a nightmare to the August. But, for the slaves themselves, it is the world of the August that is the nightmare, and it is to this world that one proclaims that the Anointed is risen, that the anointing is spreading, that people walk with tongues of fire above their heads, and they are already inside the house.

Implications Concerning Justice, the Law, Love, and Loyalty

This, then, is the background information about Jesus that Paul and his coworkers felt was necessary for gospeling the gospel in the Roman Empire. This information has significant implications for how the gospel is gospeled. This is especially true in relation to three themes that were of major importance, not only to Paul and his coworkers, but to Roman imperialism as well. These themes are justice (and the law), love, and loyalty (also known as "allegiance," "fidelity," or "faith"). We will examine each of these in order to fill out what gospeling the gospel requires according to the Pauline faction.

Justice and the (Rule of) Law

As we saw in volume 2 of this series, the rule of law was fundamental to the spread of Roman imperialism and the justification of the emperors along with all those who ruled under them.[138] The law justified, valorized, enforced, maintained, and strengthened the massively unequal distributions of wealth, freedom, power, and property that were foundational to the status quo of the empire. The rule of law ensured that vanquished nations remained vanquished, subservient, and incorporated into the empire.[139] Hence, Rudolf von Jhering's assertion that Rome conquered the world three times: first with armies, then with religion, then with laws.[140] Compared to simply using lethal force (as in a military conquest),

---

138. As explored above. See also Garnsey and Saller, *Roman Empire*, 20; Koester, *History, Culture, and Religion*, 309–12; Ando, *Imperial Ideology*, 340.

139. See Garnsey and Saller, *Roman Empire*, 109–10; Jeffers, *Greco-Roman World*, 154–57.

140. Jhering cited in Graeber, *Debt*, 198.

ruling through law is not without its challenges. As Florus observes in his history of Rome (from its founding until Augustus closed the Temple of Janus in 25 BCE): "It is more difficult to govern a province than to acquire one: for they are conquered by force, but they must be retained by law."[141] Therefore, in order to try and make the imposition of the Roman rule of law more palatable (or at least harder to fight), the Romans were adamant that not only were they granted rule because of their commitments to piety and justice (as we have already seen) but also because Roman law transcended any merely human creation—their law was a natural law that reflected the proper order of all things. Thus, during Augustus's reign, Dionysius of Halicarnassus asserts that Roman rule "is established according to reason, for it is a law of nature, one common to all men, which the passage of time will not destroy, that the strong shall always rule over the weak."[142] Slightly earlier, and in a more circumspect manner, Cicero explains:

> Just as the laws preside over the magistrates, so the magistrates preside over the people, and truly it is possible to say that a magistrate is a speaking law, while the law is a silent magistrate. For nothing is so completely suited to justice and the rightful ordering of nature—when I say that, I wish to be understood as saying the Law—than the legitimate exercise of power [*imperium*]. Without it neither a home, nor a city, nor a nation, nor a human race, nor nature itself, nor even the world can long endure.[143]

This relationship between the magistrate and the law was also critical to the rise of the emperors who, beginning with Augustus, tried to distance themselves from Rome's opposition to dictators and kings, by asserting that even they were subject to the law.[144] Of course, one should not simply take emperors at their word when they speak like this—in many ways, the law was simply what the emperors declared it to be.[145] Indeed, even Cicero is well aware of how his comment on the naturalness of the rule of Roman law stretches credulity. Thus, while exploring the notion that "no departure should be made from the precedents and principles of our ancestors," he also remarks: "I shall not point out here that

---

141. Lucius Annaeus Florus, *Epitome of Roman History* 2.30.29.
142. *Ant. rom.* 1.3.5; 5.2, quoted in Ando, *Imperial Ideology*, 55.
143. Cicero, *Leg.* 3.2-3, quoted in Ando, *Imperial Ideology*, 408.
144. Ando, *Imperial Ideology*, 409.
145. See Ando, *Imperial Ideology*, 109, 378.

THE LAWLESSNESS OF GOOD NEWS IN THE MAKING

our ancestors invariably followed custom in time of peace, but expediency in war, and that they invariably responded to emergencies with new ways of doing things."[146] The rule of law is never as natural or as eternal as it makes itself out to be. It is dependent upon the will of a sovereign who, as Carl Schmitt famously observed, demonstrates sovereignty by being able to determine the state of exception that, as Giorgio Agamben shows, is necessary to form the networks of power and wealth distribution that make imperialism possible, powerful, and persistent.[147] Thus, within the Roman Empire, the law and the word of Caesar (i.e., the word of god) become one and the same. Even as Caesar declares his submission to the law, obedience to the law remained obedience to Caesar. And obedience to the law, especially among conquered peoples, considered to be barbaric, uncivilized, and inferior, was absolutely fundamental to the spread and maintenance of Roman imperialism and the massive transfer of wealth from the provinces to Rome (while local subordinates helped themselves along the way).[148]

This is the context in which we should read Pauline remarks about the law, its power, and its connection to Sin and Death as well as Pauline remarks about justice—how it is simultaneously greater than the law, against the law, and fulfills the law by bringing Life. This is a justice that is deeply connected to love and loyalty (*pistis*), as the conquest achieved and maintained by Roman law is annihilated in the victory won by Jesus and maintained in the assemblies of Jesus loyalists. Thus, Paul and his coworkers are not focused so much on Judean laws (which only merit sustained attention, as we have seen, when they are used to try and shelter the Jesus loyalists from persecution but which are an unacceptable tactic because of how this gospels the gospel wrongly) as they are focused on the imperial Roman law—the same law which, according to its own standard of justice, justifies the actions of those who crucified Jesus and conquered, colonized, and enslaved those to whom Paul and his coworkers are sent as ambassadors (although, of course, Rome presented this violent process

---

146. Cicero, *De imperio Cn. Pompei* 60. See also Agamben's discussion of the *senatus consultum ultimatum* (the final decree of the senate) which led to an *iustitium* (standstill or suspension of law) in times of crisis, which is foundational to the rise of Roman imperialism even if it is distinguished from dictatorial rule (Agamben, *Time That Remains*, 41–51).

147. Schmitt, *Political Theology*; Agamben, *State of Exception*.

148. Brigitte Kahl's discussion of the spread of Roman law to lawless barbarians in Galatia is very useful here (Kahl, *Galatians Re-Imagined*, 42–74, 96 [and throughout]).

as justified and performed as a merciful act of grace given to those who respond with faith).[149] The issue, in other words, is not so much Torah as it is the universal rule of law enforced (at this time) by Rome.[150] Which is why, as we have already seen, the so-called "works of the Law" that are opposed by Paul and his coworkers are the actions and communal events in which members of vanquished and Roman populations would participate in order to demonstrate loyalty to Rome.[151] These are the works of the law-abiding, the law-affirming, and the law-rewarding. They are not works that interest the Pauline faction—in fact, they are viewed as a return to slavery in Gal 4–5. Thus, José Miranda correctly asserts that Pauline faction "wants a world without law. Exegesis which avoids this fact makes an understanding of the Pauline message impossible. Neither Kropotkin nor Bakunin nor Marx nor Engels made assertions against the law more powerful and subversive than those Paul makes."[152] This, of course, is precisely how the Romans feared that barbarians like the Gauls (i.e., Galatians as the Greek "*Galatai*" is translated into Latin as "*Galli*" which is "Gauls" in English) and rebellious Judeans might respond to their rule of law.[153] Such people were not known for their acceptance of either Roman justifications of the rule of law or those justified by the Roman rule of law (thus, despite scholars like Sanders who emphasize that diasporic Judeans generally accepted the "pagan" world without protest, one should recall Juvenal's comment that "[the Judeans] look down on Roman law, preferring instead to learn and honor and fear the [Judean] commandments").[154] Vanquished peoples debating the merits of the law, arguing that people have been set free from the law, and asserting that justice is something that exceeds and violates the law (even as it fulfills

---

149. See Jennings, *Outlaw Justice*, 7; Taubes, *Political Theology of Paul*, 23–24; Kahl, *Galatians Re-Imagined*, 3, 7, 75; Wengst, *Pax Romana*, 37–40.

150. See Crossan and Borg, *First Paul*, 169–72. Georgi, *Theocracy*, 51, 101; also 33–45; Jennings, *Outlaw Justice*, 43; Miranda, *Marx and the Bible*, 182–84; Elliott, *Liberating Paul*, 214–15; Carter, "Vulnerable Power," 474. Of course, as a legal system, Torah is also problematical from the Pauline perspective but the Torah is less of a concern for Paul and his coworkers among the nations vanquished by Rome, wherein people were suffering under the imperial legal system.

151. See above as well as Elliott, *Arrogance of Nations*, 140–41; Kahl, *Galatians Re-Imagined*, 75; Hardin, *Galatians and the Imperial Cult*, 116–47.

152. Miranda, *Marx and the Bible*, 187.

153. On this etymology and point of comparison, see Kahl, *Galatians Re-Imagined*, 1–2.

154. Sanders, *Paul: The Apostle's Life*, 333; Juvenal, *Satires* 14.100–101.

THE LAWLESSNESS OF GOOD NEWS IN THE MAKING

it), is all very deeply troubling from the Roman perspective. No wonder, then, that Kahl asserts: "It is not even plausible historically to imagine Jews and Galatians in Paul's time freely discussing and disagreeing about law and lawlessness in a secluded religious space."[155] This kind of conversation cannot be cordoned off from the socioeconomic and political dimensions of life. Such a conversation is only possible in an illegal political gathering that is the stuff of nightmares for emperors.

The Pauline faction is quite clear about their opposition to the law. This is so primarily because the law is ultimately in the service of Death. As Ted Jennings explains, "Law and death are inextricably bound together. Death is the "or else" of law, without which law does not have the force of law."[156] Hence, the law is described in Rom 8:2 as the "Law of Sin and of Death" (and see 1 Cor 15:55–56). The law requires Death, the threat of Death, or various lesser deaths (imprisonment, impoverishment, enslavement) in order to operate. Because it is fundamentally dependent upon Death (and thereby operates in the service of Death), the law contributes to the spread of Sin. Sin, of course, as the "sting of Death," is best understood as that which is death-dealing and which operates in opposition to the abundant Life that God (the Father of Jesus) wishes all people to experience in the economy of abundance and grace that God wishes to institute and affirm in and through Jesus and the Spirit. Thus, everything from conquest, to colonization, to dispossession, to enslavement, to rape (of slaves, for example), to hoarding wealth while others starve—all become enshrined and justified in and by the law. Consequently, as Rom 7:11 states, Sin takes a hold of the law in order to kill people like Paul (i.e., people who are poor, conquered, and of no status) either by simply enforcing the dynamics that belong to the law-abiding status quo (as Anatole France once wrote: "The law in its majestic equality, forbids the rich as well as the poor to sleep under bridges, to beg in the streets, and to steal food"), or by punishing people like Paul when they try to find extra-legal (or illegal) ways to pursue a more life-giving and life-affirming way of structuring Life together. Under this rule of law, Paul experiences himself as "sold into bondage to Sin" and, by living according to this rule of law (thereby expressing his agreement with it and

---

155. Kahl, *Galatians Re-Imagined*, 7.

156. Jennings, *Outlaw Justice*, 19, 118. For some contemporary examples that explore the death-dealing forces that uphold the rule of law, see Williams, *Our Enemies in Blue*; Maynard, *Policing Black Lives*; Taylor, *From #BlackLivesMatter to Black Liberation*; Alexander, *New Jim Crow*.

confessing it to be good), he finds himself doing "the very things I do not want to do" (Rom 7:14–16). Indeed, by living under this rule of law, Paul finds himself unable to do the good he wants to do but, instead, he is trapped enacting the evil he does not want thanks to the power of Sin that colonizes him through the law of the colonizers (Rom 7:18–21). Consequently, although he longs for a more just way of living, he finds himself, while subjected to the rule of law, as being trapped within a body ruled by Death (Rom 7:24).

Therefore, although the law claims to be founded upon justice, the rule of law has fundamentally failed to produce anything like justice. Tragically, the law simply cannot produce justice.[157] And this is true of all legal systems, which is why Rom 3:9–20 asserts that there is no justice for anyone—neither Judean nor Greek—because all are still in bondage to Sin, the death-dealing outworking of the rule of law. For as long as people are under the rule of law, they are under the dominion of Sin and condemned to Death (Rom 6:13–14). The colonized, enslaved, uprooted, dispossessed, and violated peoples to whom Paul and his coworkers addressed this speech would have little trouble understanding this.

Furthermore, according to the Pauline faction, the inability of the law to produce justice becomes evident when one examines the law-makers, law-enforcers, and those most prominently justified by the law. Here, I think it makes good sense to read Rom 1:18–32 as a criticism of what Paul takes to be the ruthless corruption, thieving immorality, and murderous violence of the imperial rulers, especially the emperor and those close to him.[158] This makes especially good sense of Rom 1:32 which states that although those whom the Pauline faction criticizes know that they (the criticized) are engaging in acts that would justly merit a death sentence, they have the ability to both persist in acting this way and the ability to applaud others who act in this way. Only the very powerful can get away with doing this. Therefore, as Dieter Georgi says, "The orderly and upstanding citizens turn out to be rebels, perverting themselves and humanity. Instead of saving the world, they plunge it into

---

157. See Jennings, *Outlaw Justice*, 50, 59, 64, 117; Miranda, *Marx and the Bible*, 160–63.

158. See Elliott, *Arrogance of Nations*, 11, 14, 62, 70–83; Fitzpatrick, *Paul*, 69–70. Here, I think, I can agree with this line of criticism even though I disagree with what Paul and his coworkers assume to be natural or unnatural when it comes to sex (except, that is, when it comes to their opposition to the ways in which the powerful sexually exploit and abuse those under their power).

ruin."[159] In the same way, as Bruce Winter observes, the ethical injunctions against drunkenness, promiscuity, and the deeds of darkness found in Rom 13:8–14 read like a criticism of the sexual violence (approved by the license of the age, the *saeculi licentia*) of rich young men at Rome who regularly celebrated their coming of age by raping slaves and freedpeople who lived in poverty.[160] This fits well with what the Pauline faction writes elsewhere. Thus, for example, after exposing the folly and blindness of the rulers of this age—who exhibit their folly and blindness in their sinfulness (i.e., by acting in a death-dealing way) by bringing the full force of the law (i.e., Death) to bear upon the person of Jesus (see 1 Cor 2:6–8), it is no surprise that Paul and his coworkers then urge the Corinthians to avoid Roman-sanctioned law courts altogether—in part, because those who preside over those courts are unjust, wicked, immoral, robbers, and thieves (see 1 Cor 6:1–10).[161] All of these passages seriously undercut the Roman claims that their rulers were granted the right to rule precisely because of their piety and their commitment to justice.[162] Yet, if such unjust people are justified by the law (and they are), then the law itself is fundamentally incapable of producing justice.

159. Georgi, *Theocracy*, 88; see also 12–16, 61–63, 90.

160. See Winter, "Roman Law and Society," 85–89. Of course, rich, young (and old) White men in much of the Occident still engage in acts like these with total impunity, as the recent examples of Brett Kavanaugh, Brock Turner, and Donald Trump so vividly illustrate.

161. See Sampley, *Pauline Partnership in Christ*, 3; Winter, *Seek the Welfare of the City*, 109–13. Various scholars have tried to tone down this passage by arguing that the issue here is spiritual and not political and pertains to the argument that "pagans" should not be permitted to judge "Christians" (see Lietzmann, *Beginnings of the Christian Church*, 138–40;), or that the real issue is avoiding Christians fighting other Christians in a public manner (see Pilgrim, *Uneasy Neighbors*, 33–34. Similarly, see Winter, *Seek the Welfare of the City*, 70, 113–15, who stresses that this way of managing an inter-familial conflict would be "unheard of"), or that the motive to avoid the courts is really due to a commitment to nonviolence (see Cadoux, *Early Church and the World*, 104–5), or that the "rulers" are evil *spiritual* forces, and the criticism has less to do with how the courts enact justice and more to do with "pretentious elitism" or "humanistic wisdom" which, really, is applicable to all people everywhere (see Kim, *Christ and Caesar*, 21–25). Given all that has already been argued in this series, I don't think one needs to engage these arguments point by point to see that they are (more and less creatively) simply seeking to avoid the central thrust of the passage—i.e., that the courts, and those who preside over them, are corrupt and unjust. And, furthermore, the Jesus loyalists are to work out a justice system superior to that of the courts, not least of all, because they will one day sit in judgment over those courts (see Sampley, *Pauline Partnership in Christ*, 3–6; Cullmann, *State in the New Testament*, 65).

162. As well observed by Knust, "Politics of Virtue and Vice," 155–64.

This is not to say that the Pauline faction believes that justice, particularly God's justice, is something that it is impossible to experience here and now as a fundamental component of how people go about structuring life together. In fact, as Rom 1:17 makes clear, God's justice has now been apocalypsed in the loyalty of Jesus to the people who now demonstrate a comparable loyalty to the God of Life (see also Rom 3:26). This justice (which is the more accurate translation of the dikai-language that English translations interpret as "righteousness") is understood to be against the law, greater than the law, and, simultaneously, the fulfillment of the law.[163] It is against the law, most immediately and obviously, because it is illegal to proclaim that a terrorist is the true and proper Lord, Savior, Son of God, First Among Equals, and Anointed. Jesus was justly crucified according to the law and as a part of the justification of all things accomplished by Rome, and so transferring one's allegiance to Jesus would automatically place one in opposition to the law.[164] No wonder, then, that after noting the inability of the law to produce justice, Paul and his coworkers go on to argue that the justice of God has been manifested apart from the law through the emancipation accomplished in the Anointed Jesus (Rom 3:21–24). The Anointed is the end of the law so that justice may flourish among all those who are loyal to him (Rom 10:4; see also Phil 3:9). Indeed, if justice comes through the law, then the death of the Anointed is meaningless when it comes to the matter of justice (Gal 2:21). Thus, justice exists outside of the bounds of the law, beyond the law,

---

163. On translation of *dikai-* words as "justice," see Jennings, *Reading Derrida/Thinking Paul*, 1–2, 5; Elliott, *Arrogance of Nations*, 5–6, 75–76; Wright, "Paul's Gospel and Caesar's Empire," 170–73; Damholt, "Rightwiseness and Justice," 413–432. As Damholt especially notes, part of the problem with the English translation is that, in older English "rightwiseness" (or righteousness) still carried more explicit overtones of justice but these overtones have been systematically eroded over time (in no small part due to the theological work of the *adikon*, although Damholt doesn't say this). And, granted, it is true that Graeco-Roman notions of justice also incorporated a sense of what we consider "righteousness" more colloquially today, but one severely truncates justice if one strictly limits it to that sense.

164. See Kahl, *Galatians Re-Imagined*, 10, 80; Miranda, *Marx and the Bible*, 188–91; Jennings, *Outlaw Justice*, 63. Here, some of the apocalyptic scholars inspired by Badiou are less than helpful and tend to obfuscate the issue when talking about the resurrection event (which induces a subject and leads to the production of a truth) as being "against the law" because it overcomes the autonomy of desire (also called "the problem of the unconscious") unleashed by the law and the subsequent gap this produces between thinking and doing (see Holsclaw, "Subjects between Death," 160). I am pretty sure we don't have to worry about anything illegal, let alone revolutionary, coming from this camp.

as something that is both other than the law and superior to the law.[165] Ted Jennings's term, "outlaw justice," is well chosen—this justice is both against the law and outside of the law.[166] However, this justice can also be said to fulfill or confirm the law (as per Rom 3:31) because the law always claims justice as its basis. Proper justice fulfills the mandate and purpose of the law *qua* law, even if this takes place in extra-legal spaces or through the performance of illegal actions.[167] This is why Paul and his coworkers speak of two different laws. On the one hand, there is "the Law of God" (Rom 7:22, 25; 1 Cor 9:21), or "the Law of [the Anointed]" (1 Cor 9:21; Gal 6:2), or "the Law of the Spirit of Life, " and these are contrasted, on the other hand, with the rule of "the law" more generally, which is defined more accurately as the "Law of Sin and of Death" (Rom 8:2). In this way, the Pauline faction affirms the commitment to justice, which is taken as the foundation and telos of any legal system, while also deconstructing all legal systems in order to encourage people to structure their lives together in a liberating manner that both exceeds and violates categories of legality. These references to "the law of God" or "the law of the Anointed" are essentially references to loving in a manner unrestricted by what the law says is or is not permissible—such as, for example, engaging in an illegal transnational financial Collection on behalf of poverty-stricken Jesus loyalists in Jerusalem. Hence, tangibly and meaningfully "bearing one another's burdens" is how one fulfills "the Law of [the Anointed]" (Gal 6:2).[168] I will say more about this below. Here, we need to emphasize that Paul and his coworkers can make these claims about God's justice violating, exceeding, and fulfilling the law because, while the law serves Death and is defined by the many death-dealing structures of Sin that operate within it, the outworking of God's justice results not only in life but in new life that arises among those who have passed through death. While Death exercises dominion over those under the law (and even before the law, Death exercises dominion because Sin came and brought Death, so the law merely exacerbates or exponentially amplifies the death-dealing potential of Sin and the domain of Death), now justice in the domain of Jesus's lordship is revealed through the abundant Life available to all who transfer their allegiance to Jesus (see Rom 5:12–21). Jesus loyalists

---

165. See Jennings, *Outlaw Justice*, 3, 8, 10, 32–43.

166. Jennings, *Outlaw Justice*, 101 (and throughout).

167. See Agamben, *Time That Remains*, 98, 107; Jennings, *Outlaw Justice*, 19, 44–47, 91; Engberg-Pedersen, *Paul and the Stoics*, 161.

168. See Horrell, *Solidarity and Difference*, 223–31.

then enter into this Life by passing through Death with Jesus in the rite of baptism (Rom 6:3–4). And this is Life experienced as an *anastasis* (a resurrection, an uprising), wherein one is liberated from slavery to all that is death-dealing—i.e., Sin (Rom 6:5–12). Thus, while the wages of Sin—implemented by the force of law—is Death, the free gift (*charisma*) of God is Life in "Anointed Jesus our Lord" (Rom 6:23). This is more than rhetoric for the Pauline faction. They have solid proof to back up their statements. They can point to the violence and death that accompanies the rule of Roman law into the world (and into the lives of the Jesus loyalists while they were still enslaved to the powers that dominated them before they transferred their allegiance to Jesus). Behold, the Death the law brings as it spread Sin into the world. But, simultaneously, they can point to what is happening in the assemblies they have helped to plant in various cities in the eastern portion of the empire; they can point to how people are experiencing tangible and meaningful liberation from power hierarchies and dynamics that formerly oppressed them as they find new, concrete ways to care for one another. Behold, the in-breaking of God's justice which gives life where the law took it away. This is the gospel in which the Jesus loyalists stand and through which they are in the process of experiencing salvation (1 Cor 15:1–2). No wonder, then, that it all collapses for the Pauline faction if Jesus has not been raised from the dead (1 Cor 15:12–19). Jesus is the *princeps* of this uprising, the one whose *anastasis* enables the *anastasis* of those loyal to him, until Death itself is (not redeemed but) utterly destroyed (1 Cor 15:20–26). Ultimately, then, the justice of God is revealed in the victory of Jesus and the practices of those loyal to him (Rom 1:17). Life arises out of Death, justice triumphs over Sin, emancipation from the rule of law is accomplished, and the crucified overthrow the crucifixion-system. This, then, helps us to understand the emphasis upon "faith" in the Pauline letters, but before exploring that, I wish to say more about love.

Love Justifies the Breaking of the Law

Love, it has been widely noted, is at the core of Pauline ethics.[169] The *anastasis* of Jesus, the lowly, slavish one executed on a cross, is a shocking

---

169. See, for example, Bultmann, *Existence and Faith*, 171; Wright, *What Saint Paul Really Said*, 135–50; Cadoux, *Early Church and the World*, 90; Cullmann, *Christ and Time*, 229; *Salvation in History*, 338; Furnish, *Theology and Ethics*, 235; Meeks, *Writings of St. Paul*, 443–44; Ladd, *Theology of the New Testament*, 567–68; Schnackenburg,

revelation of the love of God. It is shocking because, according to the Pauline faction, it reveals that God loves not those whose wealth, power, morality, and high status has been justified by the law, but those who have been condemned by the law, those who have been vanquished by Rome, those who have been dispossessed, raped, and enslaved by the wealthy. These nobodies, these nothings, these scum, these problems, these disposables, these threats to the peace and security of the empire are revealed as the beloved of God. Thus, the love of God has now been poured out into the hearts of the Jesus loyalists (Rom 5:5), whom God loved even while they were enslaved within death-dealing structures, and while they, too, may have contributed to that which is death-dealing (Rom 5:8), and whom, because of this great love, God has now liberated from slavery—now nothing can separate them from this love (Rom 8:35-39). Consequently, the love of God prompts those who are in the gospel to also be defined by love.[170] The injunction to love is repeated throughout the epistles, often as an umbrella statement summarizing the entire Pauline ethics (see Rom 12:9-10; 13:8-10; 14:15; 1 Cor 8:1; 14:1; 16:14; 2 Cor 6:6; 8:7-8, 24; Gal 5:6, 13-14, 22; Phil 1:9; 2:2; 1 Thess 1:3; 3:12; 4:9; 5:8). In fact, when writing to a dramatically divided assembly (or cluster of assemblies) the Pauline faction gives us one of the most enduring odes to love ever written (1 Cor 13:1-13).[171] While passion is evident here (and Pauline passion frequently drifts into hyperbole), Paul and his coworkers are adamant that love is primarily something that is performed or enacted or demonstrated by how one goes about being in

---

Moral Teaching, 275-77; Schweitzer, *Mysticism of Paul the Apostle*, 304-9; Theissen, *Fortress Introduction to the New Testament*, 73; Ridderbos, *Paul*, 282-95; Weiss, *Earliest Christianity*, 1:569-73; Horrell, *Solidarity and Difference*, 252.

170. Meeks and Schnackenburg both do a good job of highlighting the responsive nature of love within Pauline ethics (Meeks, *Writings of St. Paul*, 443-44; Schnackenburg, *Moral Teaching*, 275-77).

171. Here, Richard Hays does a disservice to Paulinism when he discards love as a core motif of New Testament ethics. He does so because of what he sees as a paucity of references outside of Paul and John, because he feels that the motif of the cross better communicates what the New Testament means when it talks about love, and because he (and I suspect this is the core issue) believes that love has become debased in contemporary popular discourse (Hays, *Moral Vision*, 200-203). On a related note, Hays also does another equal disservice to Paulinism when he discards "liberation" as a core motif because he prioritizes the deutero-Pauline epistles over the uncontested letters and because, in Hays's opinion, the word liberation is overly imminent or political and not spiritual enough (203-4).

relationships with others.[172] This is signified in talk about sibling-based devotion being manifested in a love that is "without hypocrisy" (Rom 12:9–10) or in the injunction that love is to be "genuine" or "sincere" (2 Cor 6:6; 8:8). It is also why participation in the Collection is considered a "proof" of love (2 Cor 8:24). It is also why loyalty is said to "work through love" (Gal 5:6) or is paired with talk of the "labour of love" (1 Thess 1:3; see also 5:13).

What, then, does this love look like? Essentially, it looks like the establishment of networks of mutual care wherein comprehensively liberating all members from need or, at a bare minimum, meeting the needs of the most vulnerable and oppressed is the top priority.[173] Thus, as Gerd Theissen aptly notes, love is rooted in an ethics of solidarity.[174] This love-as-solidarity, expressed in meaningful actions and the development of communal structures within a particular trajectory, is heavily focused upon the assemblies of Jesus loyalists but also extends beyond those assemblies to all those who are suffering and oppressed by Rome, the rule of law, Sin, and all the other powers who operate in the service of Death.[175] This outwards expansion is, after all, precisely what Paul and

---

172. See Clarke, "Jew and Greek," 107; Ridderbos, *Paul*, 297.

173. Various scholars come close to expressing this in different ways, with the general consensus being that Pauline love is essentially a self-sacrificing love that focuses on serving others or meeting their needs, making them (rather than oneself) the priority. Thus, for example, Gorman, *Cruciformity*, 156–61, 176 (and, in relation to faith and hope, Gorman, *Apostle of the Crucified Lord*, 583–86; *Reading Paul*, 146–66); Schrage, *Ethics of the New Testament*, 211–13, 217; Käsemann, *Perspectives on Paul*, 30; Fowl, *Story of Christ*, 88–92; Winter, *Seek the Welfare of the City*, 174–75; Welborn, *Paul's Summons to Messianic Life*, 71; Ziesler, *Pauline Christianity*, 115–17.

174. Theissen, *Fortress Introduction to the New Testament*, 62.

175. On this point, I think that Weiss and Cadoux overstate their case by trying to make love strictly limited to something that takes place within Pauline communities (see Cadoux, *Early Church and the World*, 90–91; Weiss, *Earliest Christianity*, 2:569–73). Theissen comes close to balancing this well (Theissen, *Religion of the Earliest Churches*, 69). Further, while I appreciate the emphases of Welborn and Käsemann, who argue that it is important not to neglect the outward movement of this love beyond the assemblies themselves (see Welborn, *Paul's Summons to Messianic Life*, 2, 7–8, 58–59; Käsemann, *Perspectives on Paul*, 30), I do think they are a bit too universalizing in their pushback because I think the Pauline emphasis still targets specific groups (i.e., the oppressed and left-for-dead) rather than simply focusing on anyone or everyone equally. Kee's focus is actually slightly better when he says this love extends to all "humans who were in need," although this "need" needs to be understood as material need rather than simply people who are in need of "the gospel" understood in some kind of immaterial manner (Kee, *Beginnings of Christianity*, 410).

his coworkers were trying to engage in as they moved into the nations as ambassadors of the Anointed. If love was strictly limited to Jesus loyalists, there would be no motive for the Pauline mission. But because the love of God for the nobodies, the enslaved, and the vanquished has now been revealed, the kerygma of this love is heralded to all those enslaved by the rule of imperial law as the gospel spreads like a virus across the empire.

Furthermore, it is precisely this love that is said to fulfill the law (see Rom 13:8–10; Gal 5:14). It does so in a manner similar to the way in which justice is said to fulfill the law (i.e., accomplishing what the rule of law theoretically claims it exists in order to accomplish, but what the actually existing rule of law fails to accomplish), which means that love also fulfills the law by exceeding it and transgressing it when necessary.[176] As Hans Conzelmann suggests, the question of obedience to any specific law is resolved by looking at what love requires (especially the love of and among the oppressed).[177] Or, as Jennings says, the driving ethical question is how to avoid violating the neighbor rather than the question of how to avoid violating the law.[178] Love, in other words, is not something that is opposed to justice or outside of the domain of justice—it is, in fact, what happens when people treat one another justly, regardless of what the law prioritizes or requires.[179] As such, it is love that justifies both the breaking of the law and those who break the law in the manner encouraged by the Pauline faction. This is what justification is all about—love making justice real, first and foremost, for the victims of injustice (and doing so within horizontal or rhizomatic solidarity networks that refuse and annul practices of patronage or charity, which posture as models of

---

176. Thus, Barrett is right to see that "trimming" the law to love is not a "liberalization" but a "radicalization" (Barrett, *Paul*, 135). Bornkamm misses all of this when he argues that love "does not place itself beyond the limits and ordinances of custom" (Bornkamm, *Early Christian Experience*, 182).

177. Conzelmann, *Outline of the Theology*, 279.

178. Jennings, *Outlaw Justice*, 195. As Brigitte Kahl puts it: "Love means continual mindfulness in discerning, disobeying and unfreezing the antithetical *nomos* of self versus other" (Kahl, *Galatians Re-Imagined*, 269). I like this but I think it depoliticizes the parties involved too much. Perhaps better stated we could say, "Love means continual mindfulness in discerning, disobeying, and unfreezing the antithetical nomos of the rich versus the impoverished" or "the colonizers versus the colonized" or "the one percent versus life as we know it," and so on.

179. Crossan gets at some of this although I find his language somewhat questionable since he talks about love being like "the soul of justice" or "the spirit of justice," which, to my mind, counters the very embodied Pauline conception of love as a thing *that is done* (see Crossan, *God and Empire*, 190; Crossan and Borg, *First Paul*, 304–5).

care but which, in fact, perpetuate inequalities).[180] Indeed, if we do not start there, what hope do we have of ever arriving at a life-giving way of structuring life together? Justice is not the kind of thing that trickles down. It begins in the unmarked graves of the crucified. It begins with the unjustly executed and left-for-dead. And, from there, carried on a swell of love, it rises up.

Loyalty to Jesus and to One Another

Therefore, we are now well-positioned to understand the role of faith (*pistis*) in the assemblies of Jesus loyalists associated with Paul and his coworkers. *Pistis*, as has been widely noted, can have a range of meanings such as "reliability, confidence, assurance, fidelity, faithfulness, commitment, and pledged loyalty."[181] It can also include the notion of "trust" which incorporates the idea of mental assent or belief.[182] This idea of faith as trust demonstrated in mental assent or belief has been the primary way in which Protestant theologians have interpreted the Pauline notion of "faith," especially as they have desired to juxtapose "faith" and "works." However, it has become increasingly obvious that this understanding of "faith" neither does justice to what the Pauline faction are talking about when they use *pistis* language nor makes sense of how *pistis* language is used more generally in the Pauline context.[183] "Faith" is better rendered as "faithfulness," "loyalty," or "allegiance," and this faith is not primarily something that is related to mental assent or logocentric confessions—it is primarily something that is lived out in one's own life and in one's relationships with others.[184] Of course, mental assent and trust accom-

---

180. See Kahl, *Galatians Re-Imagined*, 163.
181. See Bates, *Salvation by Allegiance Alone*, 3.
182. See Bates, *Salvation by Allegiance Alone*, 90.
183. Richard Hays broke significant ground here, and his work has inspired a great deal of debate (see Hays, *Faith of Jesus Christ*; and, subsequently, Westerholm, *Perspectives*; Easter, "*Pistis Christou* Debate," 33–47). At this point, I take it as well established that the notion of faith that dominated Protestantism does not have its roots in Paulinism but, rather, in forms of Christianity that are premised upon accommodating themselves to the status quo and working to justify the hierarchies of power and wealth distribution established therein.
184. On faith understood in this way, see especially Bates, *Salvation by Allegiance Alone*, 5, 8–9, 77; as well as Elliott, *Liberating Paul*, 214; Strom, *Reframing Paul*, 16–17; Meeks, *Origins of Christian Morality*, 31; Furnish, *Theology and Ethics of Paul*, 185, 192, 199–205; Jennings, *Outlaw Justice*, 21; Agamben, *Time That Remains*, 116. I also

pany this, but they are neither the primary focus nor the *sine qua non* of faith.[185] Paul and other ambassadors of the Anointed are not going around gathering the intellectual assent of the nations—they have been set apart to bring about the "obedience of faith" (*hypakoen pisteos*) of the nations (Rom 1:5; also 16:26).[186] This "obedience of faith," or "obedience of loyalty" or "obedience that arises from allegiance" is a way of being that is revealed in how one acts in relation to others. It is a loyalty that is revealed in tangible acts of love that prioritize the oppressed and thereby results in a justice that simultaneously fulfills the intentions of the law while violating the rule of law as it is experienced at this present time.

---

like how Sanders emphasizes this by, appropriately, translating faith as a verb (to faith) (Sanders, *Paul: The Apostle's Life*, 507). Bates does a good job of showing how this translation of *pistis* fits with how the word is used in various related texts from Josephus to 1 Maccabees, to 3 Maccabees to the Addition to Esther to the Graeco-Roman political environment (see Bates, *Salvation by Allegiance Alone*, 4–5, 79–80, 87–89).

185. Matthew Bates, despite the good work he does translating *pistis*, unfortunately focuses almost exclusively on allegiance as intellectual agreement and verbally professed fealty (Bates, *Salvation by Allegiance Alone*, 92–100). He does mention that enacted loyalty is also an element of allegiance but he devotes most of his attention to logocentric elements. Thus, *pistis* is defined as allegiance but then allegiance is defined as faith in the traditional Protestant sense! Thus, Bates's concern is attaining eternal salvation by mentally agreeing with the eight theses he argues define "the Gospel" ("the bare minimum of facts to which me [Freudian *sic*?] must cognitively agree before we are saved"). This agreement is then affirmed through some kind of public verbal profession of allegiance. But what this looks like in terms of enacted or embodied allegiance, Bates hardly says. Vague moral admonitions like "fight the good fight" and "pursue the virtues" (98) are paired with injunctions to stay away from sensuality and lots of stuff to do with sex or getting drunk, plus, you know, avoiding idols and sorcery (125). Just don't sin, be righteous, don't be worldly and love other Christians (126). A vaguely defined bourgeois Christian moralism, in other words. Hence, not surprisingly, one also finds affirmations of middle-class acts of piety or paternalistic acts of charity when Bates tries to get more concrete (208–9). But Bates is open to some negotiation here. What is not open to negotiation, according to Bates, is the assertion that one really needs to believe the key points about the gospel in order to not be doomed (200). This is paired with an "overarching *desire* to actualize that confession through lived obedience" (123; emphasis added; note how desire replaces any kind of concrete content in terms of action). And, in this way, Bates thinks his allegiance is enough to allow him to participate in heaven when it finally comes to earth. That's nice for Bates but probably has little to do with the empire-shaking threat of the movement we have been examining.

186. Bates does touch on this (Bates, *Salvation by Allegiance Alone*, 85–86) and originally what he says sounds quite hopeful until he gets into talking about what this actually means.

Pauline Solidarity

For the Pauline faction, loyalty is similar to love because it, too, arises as a response to God's initiative. Through Jesus, God has apocalypsed God's loyal allegiance, not to the wealthy and powerful, not to the rulers and conquerors, not to the slave masters and profiteers, but to the crucified, the criminals, the enslaved, the cast-out, and the left-for-dead (see Rom 1:17; 3:21–25; 5:6–11; Gal 2:15–21; 3:26; Phil 3:8–11; 1 Cor 1:21). God has allied Godself with these people and, as the work of the gospel now makes clear, this allegiance is one that is powerful, emancipatory, and ongoing.[187] Thus the faithfulness—i.e., the loyalty, fidelity, and active allegiance—of God becomes the model for the faithfulness—i.e., the loyalty, fidelity, and active allegiance—of the Jesus loyalists.[188] Injunctions to "stand firm in your faith" (as per 1 Cor 16:13; 2 Cor 1:24) are not commands to "keep on intellectually assenting to theses that others may find hard to believe and which may cause you to have doubts" but are commands to continue to demonstrate loyalty to Jesus and the household of God despite pressures (often life-threatening pressures) to transfer one's allegiance back to the empire and its local rulers.

Furthermore, it is of critical importance to emphasize that the loyalty encouraged by the Pauline faction is not only loyalty to Jesus or to God the Father of Jesus but also loyalty to other members of the assemblies, including members in different locations.[189] Thus, those who are faithfully (i.e., loyally) gospeling the gospel are to stand firm in one spirit and strive side by side with one mind (Phil 1:27). Faith, in other words, is also loyalty to the movement. Here, again, Jesus loyalists are urged to model their behavior after what has been apocalypsed in Jesus. Loyalty to God requires loyalty to those to whom God is loyal.[190] And this breaches the boundaries created and enforced by rulers, past and present. Hence,

---

187. Hence, 1 Cor 15:14 states the obvious: If the Anointed has not been raised, your loyalty is in vain. Or, again, in 1 Cor 15:17: If the Anointed has not been raised, your loyalty is futile.

188. On this, see Meeks, *Origins of Christian Morality*, 160–61.

189. Here, I like how Ward Blanton emphasizes that faith is something partisan, employed by "those who side with the "nothings" (Blanton, *Materialism of the Masses*, 85; emphasis removed). However, I struggle with his talk about faith as a performative speech-act (73) because I worry that this still prioritizes the logos too much.

190. This, of course, is one of the central assertions of liberation theology—an assertion, I can not help but note, that is rarely tested but nonetheless almost unanimously rejected by middle-class theologians and biblical scholars (see Boff and Boff, *Introducing Liberation Theology*; Sobrino, *No Salvation Outside the Poor*; Gutierrez, *Theology of Liberation*).

neither circumcision nor uncircumcision count for anything, but the only thing that counts is loyalty working through love (Gal 5:6). This is a loyalty that works together for the good of all the oppressed and, most especially, those who now count themselves as members of the "family of the loyal" (Gal 6:10) who, already, in their relationships with one another, experience the fruit of the Spirit of Life.

Assembling the Gospel: The Uprising of the Dead

Community Orientation

Therefore, all of these things—justice, lawlessness, love, loyalty, the lordship of Jesus, and the gospel—are inextricably related to what is going on in the communities of people associated with Paul and his coworkers. These things are not abstract principles or theses whose strengths rest upon their logic or coherence within a particular narrative but are, instead, powerful precisely because they describe the politics put into practice by the Pauline faction. The righteousness of God is revealed because Paul and his coworkers can point to the lives of the Jesus loyalists with whom they are associated—they can point to the emancipation of slaves, the honors granted to the oppressed, the elevation of the vanquished or those considered to be of little value, and they can point to concrete actions of economic mutuality rooted in a sibling-based solidarity that prove the abundant grace of God and say, look, there it is. Hence, as has been widely noted, Pauline ethics are remarkably social and, more than other first-century voices, they are rooted in an indispensible community-orientation.[191] It is impossible, from the Pauline perspective, to be in the Anointed, to be in the gospel, or to be loyal to Jesus outside of this community context. Talk of justification, of "justice-ification," or of justice being embodied in the establishment of proper relationships between people (which then requires the redistribution of

---

191. See Engberg-Pedersen, *Paul and the Stoics*, 36–37; Beker, *Paul the Apostle*, 304–5; Banks, *Paul's Idea of Community*, 10–11; Cousar, *Letters of Paul*, 133–34; Scroggs, *Paul for a New Day*, 39–41; Wrede, *Paul*, 30–38, 56, 60; Hays, *Moral Vision*, 41–43; Horsley, "1 Corinthians," 144–45; Elliott, *Arrogance of Nations*, 157–58. Curiously, Cadoux posits that the gospel, prior to Paul, was heavily focused on the individual and that Paul is the one who develops this in a communal way (see Cadoux, *Early Church and the World*, 79–80). It seems far more likely to me that Paul and his coworkers were actually continuing the kind of politics and grassroots community mobilization already begun by those who gathered with Jesus prior to Paul's transformation.

wealth and the flattening of hierarchies of power) makes no sense if talking about a person in isolation from others. The same goes for talk of love or loyalty or Jesus's lordship. As Dunn accurately observes, "the individual as individual, therefore, could hardly hope to live out Paul's ethical principles solely on his or her own."[192] Wayne Meeks is especially useful on this point: "We cannot begin to understand [the Pauline] process of moral formation until we see that it is inextricable from the process by which distinctive communities were taking shape. Making morals means making community."[193] Meeks then describes that process in this way: "becoming a Christian [sic] meant something like the experience of an immigrant who leaves his or her native land and then assimilates to the culture of a new, adopted homeland. Such a transfer of allegiances and transformation of mores requires a resocialization."[194] Meeks goes on to say that understanding this personal transformation through the transfer of allegiances to a new lord as expressed in a resocialization to a new community is not adequately captured in contemporary conversations about "theology and ethics."[195] Similarly, asserting that Paul and his coworkers are focused on "the Church," especially when that "Church" is exclusively or even primarily understood as a religious institution (defined over against other religious institutions and in contradistinction to political institutions), fails to adequately describe what was going on with the assemblies of Jesus loyalists.[196] Not only this but, while those who use the more innocuous term "community" help us escape theological categories for a better historical and sociological analysis of the early assemblies of Jesus loyalists, they still fail to capture what Paul and his coworkers were

---

192. Dunn, *Theology of Paul the Apostle*, 672. Hence, also, Welborn's observation that it is not an individual but a collective, the *ekklesia*, that is the subject of the awakening the Pauline faction describes (Welborn, *Paul's Summons to Messianic Life*, 60–61).

193. Meeks, *Origins of Christian Morality*, 5–6.

194. Meeks, *Origins of Christian Morality*, 12. See also Scroggs, *Paul for a New Day*, 41.

195. Meeks, *Origins of Christian Morality*, 150–51.

196. For examples of those who stress this, see Cousar, *Letters of Paul*, 133–34; Goguel, *Primitive Church*, 26, 33, 52; Bockmuehl, *Jewish Law in Gentile Churches*, 178–79. However, a lot of New Testament scholars and English translations of the New Testament contribute to this by using the word "church" (a term that does not really begin to rise to prominence until about 200 years after Paul) as a substitute for the word "assembly" (*ekklesia*) that is used by the Pauline faction.

on about.¹⁹⁷ Their work and focus was much more properly understood as an all-encompassing experimental politics or political economy that proposed a unique vision for how society is to be structured, how goods are to be distributed, how value and status are to be distributed, how power is to be acknowledged (or leveled), how justice is to be practiced, and how care is to be shown (and what priorities that care is to have) within the pursuit of peace and the common good. In other words, it is a process of imagining, affirming, and then creating (or embodying or manifesting) "a better world" or a "concrete alternative social utopia."¹⁹⁸ This is politics through and through.

Titles

This political understanding of the community-oriented gospeling of Paul and his coworkers makes the best sense of the titles most frequently applied to individuals and groups within the assemblies of Jesus loyalists. As we have already seen, the title *apostolos* was applied to a delegate, envoy, ambassador, messenger, authorized emissary, herald, or diplomat.¹⁹⁹ For first-century Greek-speakers, this language is unmistakably political. Yet it is, of course, the title the Pauline faction use most frequently in relation to Paul—often in passages loaded with language that is equally political (see Rom 1:1, 5; 11:13; 1 Cor 1:1; 4:9; 9:1–5; 15:9; 2 Cor 1:1; 12:12; Gal 1:1; the use of *presbeuomen* in 2 Cor 5:20 also fits with this). Others in the faction are also described in this way (1 Cor 12:28–29; 1 Thess 2:7; Phil 2:25), notably Andronicus and Junia, whose prominent apostleship is paired with a reference to their political imprisonment (Rom 16:7). Even those with sometimes questionable or fully oppositional relationships to the Pauline faction are granted the title, notably James and Peter

---

197. See, for example, Banks, *Paul's Idea of Community*; Hays, *Moral Vision*.

198. See, respectively, Yeo, *Chairman Mao*, 15–17; Georgi, *Theocracy*, 51; *Remembering the Poor*, 153. Also, Judge, "Did the Churches," 521; Horsley and Silberman, *Message and the Kingdom*, 149–51; Carter, "Vulnerable Power," 475–76; and, in a somewhat subdued manner, Boyarin, *Radical Jew*, 16–17, 32, 40, 52–56.

199. See Deissmann, *Light from the Ancient East*, 374; Elliott, "Apostle Paul and Empire," 98; Kahl, *Galatians Re-Imagined*, 248; Dunn, *Beginning from Jerusalem*, 351, 531–32 (although Dunn downplays the political elements of this by positing an eschatological emphasis that is depoliticized; see 536–39). Malina and Pilch also somewhat lose the political significance of this when they talk of an apostle as being a "change agent" who is authorized to innovate based upon the desires of the "change agency" (i.e., Israel's God). See Malina and Pilch, *Social-Science Commentary*, 20–21, 335–36.

and those associated with them at Jerusalem (1 Cor 15:7; Gal 1:15, 17; 2:8) and the so-called Super Apostles in Corinth (2 Cor 11:5, 13; 12:11). This is understandable from a political point of view. These various ambassadors represent different factions and, in some cases, at least from the Pauline perspective, serve different lords. This is a political conflict pertaining to how assemblies go about organizing their collective life together. There is conflict regarding how the gospel is gospeled.

The title *diakonos* (variously translated as "deacon," "minister," or "servant") is also frequently employed by the Pauline faction to speak of some Jesus loyalists (see Rom 12:7; 16:1; 1 Cor 3:5; 2 Cor 3:6; 6:4; 11:15, 23; Phil 1:1). It, too, is a political title, applied to state-appointed ministers, who are also heralds, envoys, and personal representatives of the Lords who appoint them.[200] The same connotations exist with the title *leitourgon* applied to Paul (and others?) in Rom 15:16 and to Epaphroditus in Phil 2:25. A *leitourgon* was an officially elected civic minister who (at their own expense) was appointed to attend to the public good in tangible, material, financial, and spiritual ways. Hence, the origins of the notion of a "liturgist" or of the English word "liturgy" are found, in the Pauline context, in political officials who personally funded works for the common good.[201] The same connotations apply to the language of being "subordinate officers" or "attendants" (*huperetes*) in 1 Cor 4:1, where that term is paired with the language of being "household (and also sometimes civic) managers" or "stewards" (*oikonomous*). Here, the household language is intertwined with political organization (as it is throughout the Pauline discourse) but this also fits with the political power held by those who were *oikonomous* in the households of Caesar and his subordinates throughout the empire. Further language that blurs these categories include times when the Pauline faction refer to those who are "slaves of the Anointed" or "freedpeople of the Lord," titles which parallel those who are taken as slaves of other lords, especially Caesar, but also, more prominently, those who are freedpeople of the emperor (a significant parallel given that emperor-cults were spreading especially strongly among freedpeople who saw themselves as having been emancipated by

---

200. See Deissmann, *Light from the Ancient East*, 376; Georgi, *Opponents of Paul*, 27–32.

201. Although, of course, given what we have seen of Graeco-Roman patronage, these works for the common good often did not benefit the poor, the enslaved, or those considered outsiders, as "the common good" was the domain of freeborn (mostly male) citizens.

THE LAWLESSNESS OF GOOD NEWS IN THE MAKING

Caesar, whom they then considered the head of their corporate body).[202] Caution is appropriate here, but given that the freedom and slavery of those in the Anointed is paired with an understanding of how Jesus has liberated those who are loyal to him from the bondage that Rome imposed, I believe it is fair to suggest titles like slave and freedperson have political resonance.

I think it is also fair to suggest that the usage of titles like "holy" (1 Cor 1:2; 2 Cor 1:1; Phil 1:1; Rom 1:7) and "elect" (1 Thess 1:4; Rom 8:33; 1 Cor 1:27; Rom 16:13) and emphasizing things like being "called" (1 Cor 1:9; 7:15, 17–24; Gal 1:6, 15; 5:8, 13; 1 Thess 2:13; 4:7; 5:24) and "beloved" (Rom 1:7; 1 Thess 1:4; also Rom 5:5, 8; 8:35–39; 15:30; 2 Cor 5:14; 13:11, 13) and "known" (1 Cor 8:3; Gal 2:9) by God also carry both political and anti-imperial connotations.[203] As we have already seen, it was Rome, and especially Rome as represented in the person of the emperor, that saw herself as holy, elect, called, beloved and known by god. This was a fundamental component of the justification of Roman rule. Not only this, but Rome made this an exclusive claim about herself and, as such, viewed the vanquished, colonized, dispossessed, and enslaved as profane, godforsaken, barbaric, strangers to god and justice and virtue, whom god had given over to the Romans to kill or possess or transform as they saw fit. To challenge this claim, to assert that honors Rome had hoarded for herself belong to those whom Rome has enslaved, and to do this in the context of the other claims being made, surely makes this politically problematical.

This is only heightened when we turn to the Pauline claim that those who are in the Anointed possess a new, alternative citizenship. Writing to those oppressed and impoverished within the Roman colony of Philippi, wherein many of the citizens of the city were also granted Roman citizenship (in fact, many of them were former Roman soldiers), the Pauline faction first belittles those who are "enemies of the cross of the Anointed," whose current glory will be lasting shame, who are known by their greed, and who are doomed for destruction (Phil 3:17–19), and then go on to assert that the Jesus loyalists have a citizenship in the heavens, where the Lord Jesus Anointed currently resides and from whence he will come to transform their current shame into lasting glory when Jesus subjects all to his rule (Phil 3:20–21). Thus, Jesus loyalists are citizens of a domain

---

202. See Deissmann, *Light from the Ancient East*, 376–77.

203. Meeks explores this cluster of titles, although not in a political way (see Meeks, *First Urban Christians*, 85–86).

PAULINE SOLIDARITY

where Caesar's lordship is not recognized and, indeed, where it is asserted that Caesar's subjection of all things to his rule will be overthrown. Hence, just as Philippi is a colony "defended from a distance by the ruler of the city [in this case, Rome] to which [the Philippians] ultimately belong," so now the Jesus loyalists colonize Philippi while remaining defended from a distance by the ruler of the heavens (and earth) to whom the Jesus loyalists ultimately belong.[204] Therefore, the Philippians are asked to citizen in a manner that adequately gospels the rule of the Anointed. Citizening in this way, as Tellbe notes, sustains and escalates a conflict with those who citizen as Romans.[205]

Consequently, it is not surprising that the Pauline faction also uses the image of "the body of the Anointed" to describe the ways in which individual members of the assemblies relate to the whole (1 Cor 10:17; 12:12-27; Rom 12:4-5). As has been widely noted, the use of body imagery was commonly deployed in Graeco-Roman political discourse to urge for unity even in the midst of entrenched stratifications and hierarchies of power.[206] Over against this Graeco-Roman ideal, the "body of the Anointed" reverses this hierarchy, giving greater honor to the lesser members. Hence, we again discover a subversive politics at work. However, what has been much less widely noted is how this political metaphor may relate to times when Paul and his coworkers refer to "the body of sin" and "the body of death." What body is this? Well, if death to the (rule of) law comes through membership in the (political) body of the Anointed (Rom 7:4), and if this brings about the destruction of the body of sin (Rom 6:6), a very literal destruction given that members are torn from that body and grafted into the body of the Anointed (Rom 11:17-24),

---

204. I'm slightly reworking Oakes's astute observation in "God's Sovereignty," 138. On this more broadly, see Theissen, *Social Reality*, 273; Bockmuehl, *Jewish Law*, 139; Tellbe, *Paul Between Synagogue and State*, 268-75; Taubes, *Occidental Eschatology*, 64; Barclay, *Obeying the Truth*, 235; and even Wright's appropriation of the language of "frontline outposts" (Wright, *Surprised by Hope*, 249).

205. See Tellbe, *Paul Between Synagogue and State*, 239-43. N. T. Wright waters all of this down into something rather bland and non-Pauline when he argues that the talk of citizenship in Philippians urges Jesus loyalists to "sit light on their civic status and be prepared to hail Jesus, not Caesar, as Lord" (Wright, *Paul*, 72; see also 71-72). First of all, the Jesus loyalists at Philippi had no civic status worth mentioning and, secondly, they are already hailing Jesus as Lord and doing so in a way that denies central claims related to Caesar's lordship—or, indeed, the rule of any other lord or house of lords.

206. See Maier, *Picturing Paul in Empire*, 57-59; Horrell, *Solidarity and Difference*, 82, 124-25; Grant, *Early Christianity and Society*, 36-37.

THE LAWLESSNESS OF GOOD NEWS IN THE MAKING

even as it rescues those very members from the body of death (as per Rom 7:24), then surely it makes sense to understand the body of sin and death to be the body politic of Roman imperialism. *Life in the flesh, in other words, is life lived as members of the body of which Caesar is the head,* wherein one is subjected to the death-dealing machinations of the law and the rule of Death (Rom 7:25). In the flesh, people are sold into slavery and dominated by Sin (Rom 7:14). In this flesh, there is nothing good (Rom 7:18). Thus, those who are citizens of the heavens now no longer live in the flesh but begin to rise up as a "spiritual body" (1 Cor 15:44). They do not set their minds on the things of the flesh—the virtues and honors and laws of Rome—because, as they well know, those things lead to death but, instead, set their minds on the things of the Spirit—the *anastasis* Spirit—because this results in life and peace (Rom 8:4-6). No wonder, then, that life in the flesh is described as hostile to God and unable to submit to the law of God (Rom 8:7) or fulfill the law of the Anointed (Gal 6:2). The fleshy (imperial) body is already ruled by another Law and another Lord, so life lived in the flesh cannot please God (Rom 8:8). But those inhabited by the Spirit now live in the Spirit (Rom 8:9; also Gal 6:8). Thus, the Jesus loyalists are no longer debtors according to their place within the imperial body politic—indeed, if they continued to live there, they would not be long in dying in slavery or poverty or on a cross—but, instead, put to death the deeds of that body—deeds like slavery, dispossession, rape, and dehumanization—in the body politic of the Anointed (Rom 8:12-13; see also Gal 5:16-6:2).[207] Consequently, when the Super Apostles attempt to infuse some of the death-dealing and legally-validated hierarchies of power into the assemblies of Jesus loyalists at Corinth, and when the arguments of these people are found to be compelling, what do Paul and his coworkers say? By bringing dynamics of the imperial body politic into the assemblies, you are acting like people of the flesh (see 1 Cor 3:1-3; 5:5). Similarly, the Galatians, when tempted to adopt similar dynamics, are warned against starting with the Spirit and ending with the flesh (Gal 3:3). Being in the body of the Anointed means no longer living in the ways that made sense in the Augustan or Neronian body.

---

207. Hence, why Paul also refers to Judeans as his kindred according to the flesh (Rom 9:3-8) because they, too, represent another body politic (see also Rom 4:1 and the discussion of circumcision in Gal 6:12-13). This is not to say that body and flesh are always on every occasion used in this way by the Pauline faction.

No wonder, then, that the Jesus loyalists were expected to organize themselves in such a way as to be able to perform functions that were, externally, performed by civic bodies or individuals. Thus, the injunction to avoid the unjust courts of the corrupt rulers in 1 Cor 6 is premised upon the expectation that the Jesus loyalists would find their own ways, internal to their assemblies, to resolve tensions and produce just outcomes to conflicts.[208] In this regard, Bruce Malina highlights how the Pauline faction rejects the rule of law in favor of "custom."[209] By this, Malina means that behaviors that are considered appropriate, right, or just are internally sanctioned (by customs that are developed within the assemblies) rather than being externally sanctioned (by the societal law). Thus, influenced by the agent of God's power (the Spirit of Life), the authority of dominant political institutions is rejected and new norms are created that, in turn, give rise to new institutions or new ways of ordering the assemblies of Jesus loyalists. How precisely people order themselves is constantly being improvised and worked out in the contexts of the various assemblies and in negotiation with various factions. This leads to some confusion (and, as I have argued, ultimately results in an institutionalization process that, although seemingly inevitable on a large scale once revolutionary movements hit a certain tipping point, betrays the values and expectations of the Pauline faction), but the central point is that members of the assemblies of Jesus loyalists are to take over responsibility for handling themselves in ways that were previously viewed as the jurisdiction of the governing authorities.

Ekklesiai

All of this is further confirmed when one examines the word *ekklesia*, which is the word most frequently deployed when Paul and his coworkers speak of the assemblies of Jesus loyalists.[210] What is an *ekklesia*?

---

208. See Grant, *Early Christianity and Society*, 39–40; Sampley, *Pauline Partnership in Christ*, 5; Cullmann, *State in the New Testament*, 65; Meeks, *First Urban Christians*, 104; Malina and Pilch, *Social Science Commentary*, 9.

209. See Malina, "Social Levels, Morals, and Daily Life," 155–56.

210. On *ekklesia* being the most frequently deployed term, see Sanders, *Paul: The Apostle's Life*, 9. Kee's observation that, during the republic, the state replaced the family as the center of social identity is also interesting here (Kee, *Christian Origins*, 82). What actually happened with the Caesars was the welding of a family to the state and its structures. The same thing appears to be taking place in the assemblies populated

Quite literally, it is a political "assembly" by which is meant "a gathering of citizens called out from their homes into a public space."[211] Within the Graeco-Roman context, this *ekklesia* made the decisions that were necessary in order to govern a city and guide it towards a mutually-agreed-upon telos. However, a considerable number of Christian scholars are keen to quickly assert that Paul and his coworkers do not intend to use the word *ekklesia* in the way that it is overwhelmingly used in their context. Instead, these scholars emphasize that the *ekklesia* (usually taken to be "the church," although that is a mistranslation and one that deploys a term that didn't come into favor until more than two hundred and fifty years after Paul) is a term that refers to those whom God has gathered for worship—and "worship," too, is understood as an activity that falls entirely outside of the domain of politics, so this gathering is focused on the "heavenly" and that which is "supranational" and "supratemporal."[212] These scholars are adamant that there is nothing political or provocative going on with the *ekklesiai* associated with the Pauline faction or with the language that faction uses to describe those assemblies.[213] Thus, instead of contrasting, comparing, or competing with political civic assemblies, the points of contrast are generally taken to be Judean synagogues and Hellenistic cults.[214] The way in which the LXX uses the word *ekklesia* to

---

by the household of God.

211. See Hurtado, *Destroyer of the Gods*, 97; Meeks, *Moral World*, 20–27; Horsley, "Building An Alternative Society," 206–9; Deissmann, *Light from the Ancient East*, 112; Georgi, *Theocracy*, 57–59; Malina and Pilch, *Social Science Commentary*, 356–57; Howard-Brook and Gwyther, *Unveiling Empire*, xxii; Pickett, "Conflicts at Corinth," 122; Carter, "Vulnerable Power," 476; Gorman, *Cruciformity*, 356–60.

212. See Banks, *Paul's Idea of Community*, 37; Cerfaux, *Church in the Theology*, 191, 205; Goguel, *Primitive Church*, 24, 27; Weiss, *Earliest Christianity*, 2:615–18; Witherington, *Paul Quest*, 79–82.

213. See especially the assertions made by Weiss, *Earliest Christianity*, 2:618; Judge, "Did the Churches," 514. Judge's comment is especially interesting because it relates to how the assemblies would be viewed by outsiders (as unprovocative and as nothing to be feared) even though he also says that the Pauline assemblies were engaging in an act of community building motivated by an intellectual challenge to the reigning culture and manifested in far more social activism than other groups (Judge, "Did the Churches," 514). Hence, Judge even goes on to suggest that "Parliament" or "Congress" may be a better interpretation of the word "*ekklesia*" and argues that the assemblies are "all community and no cult" (502). How Judge holds to this, while arguing that the peers of the Jesus loyalists would not find them a scary, threatening, or provocative presence in the civic community, mystifies me.

214. See Banks, *Paul's Idea of Community*, 35; Goguel, *Primitive Church*, 24–25; Weiss, *Earliest Christianity*, 2:618; Witherington, *Paul Quest*, 79, 81.

refer to the "assembly of YHWH" is used to justify this reading.[215] Of those who press this point, I believe Dunn wrestles with the evidence most honestly and, consequently, ends up in a somewhat conflicted position. Dunn recognizes that the term *ekklesia* is used most frequently in the Pauline context to refer to the official assembly of a city, but he thinks that Paul is drawing more on the LXX usage of the term in a manner that is theological-not-political and not subversive . . . but, at the same time, he also argues that the overtones of being an assembled body of citizens, perhaps of a heavenly city, make communal life "deeply, but not openly, subversive."[216]

However, the supposed contrast here between civic assemblies and the assembly of YHWH falls apart quite rapidly when one recalls that the assembly of YHWH, like other *ekklesiai*, was simultaneously deeply political and deeply religious. Its laws were equally religious, economic, political, and social, and its liturgies were as much about concretely developing the common good as they were about engaging in rituals oriented around praising a deity (which, of course, also contributes to the common good). The assembly of YHWH is, in other words, a political (but not-less-than-religious) body which, in all likelihood, is why the translators who composed the LXX chose the term *ekklesia* for the Greek translation. Consequently, rather than positing an either/or between how one understands the Pauline usage of the word *ekklesia*, one can see that Paul and his coworkers are drawing both on the LXX and on the usage of the term *ekklesia* throughout the empire because, in fact, the term is being used in the same way in both situations.[217]

Furthermore, it is absurd to argue that the assemblies of Jesus loyalists associated with Paul and his coworkers were apolitical because their very existence, and the regularity with which they met, was against the law. Augustus, as we have seen, had initiated legislation that made it illegal for any association to meet more than once per month, and

---

215. See Cerfaux, *Church in the Theology*, 95–117; Goguel, *Primitive Church*, 24–25; Weiss, *Earliest Christianity*, 2:616–17.

216. See Dunn, *Beginning from Jerusalem*, 549–55, 599–60 (this pushes his earlier remarks in a more spiritual direction [see Dunn, "Diversity in Paul," 121–22]). Dunn seems to *want* the *ekklesiai* to be religious bodies but, at the same time, the evidence is heavily favored in terms of a political understanding and, instead of simply ignoring the evidence like others in his camp, he acknowledges it and wrestles with it and, consequently, ends up with a rather tortured conclusion.

217. Michael Gorman holds this together pretty well. See Gorman, *Reading Paul*, 132–34; Pate, *End of the Age Has Come*, 165–66.

THE LAWLESSNESS OF GOOD NEWS IN THE MAKING

the Judeans were unique in having received permission to meet once a week.[218] Thus, contemporary scholars can try to assert that the assemblies were spiritual-but-not-political, but this ignores the fact that they broke the law in order to meet every week and, as an illicit regular gathering, would be perceived by the authorities as a treasonous threat to the public good. Hence, also, the persecutions that followed the Pauline faction everywhere they gospeled. There is no question that the assemblies associated with Paul and his coworkers would be considered political by their contemporaries.

It is also the strikingly political nature of this organizing—from the titles used, to the economic practices of the Jesus loyalists, to the views they held about crucifixion (among other things), to everything else already explored above—that distinguishes the assemblies from other collegia, professional associations, burial association, religious cults, or philosophical groups.[219] Various scholars have proposed various degrees of similarity to one or more of these associations.[220] However, while conservative scholars have tended to push back against this in order to present some version of Christian exceptionalism, what has been less frequently noted (but not altogether neglected) is that all of these various associations and groups tended to operate in a fundamentally conservative manner, replicating and mirroring the hierarchies of power, status, and inequality present in mainstream society.[221] It is this conservatism, this mirroring and replicating, that are absent within the assemblies of Jesus loyalists associated with Paul and his coworkers. In place of that

---

218. See Winter, *Divine Honours for the Caesars*, 194; Winter, "Roman Law and Society," 72–73; and this ties in with Jeffers, *Greco-Roman World*, 99. As we saw in volume 1 of this series, the desire to shelter under the Judean exemption goes a long way towards explaining why people might be drawn to circumcision. Tellbe argues that meeting in small groups in households was another tactic used to try and avoid persecution (Tellbe, *Paul Between Synagogue and State*, 199).

219. For various descriptions of these groups, see Garnsey and Saller, *Roman Empire*, 156–57; Bird, "Early Christianity," 240; Crossan and Reed, *In Search of Paul*, 46–47; Jeffers, *Greco-Roman World*, 74–77; Dunn, *Beginning from Jerusalem*, 613–15; Deissmann, *Paul*, 116, 123–25; Georgi, *Opponents of Paul*, 152–53, 158, 160; Horsley, *Religion and Empire*, 27–28.

220. See, for example, Maier, *Picturing Paul in Empire*, 37; Schüssler-Fiorenza, *In Memory of Her*, 183–84; Dunn, *Beginning from Jerusalem*, 620–21; Banks, *Paul's Idea of Community*, 15–22.

221. See Garnsey and Saller, *Roman Empire*, 157; Crossan and Reed, *In Search of Paul*, 304–5; Jeffers, *Greco-Roman World*, 77. Groups that did not operate in this manner were, of course, marked for extermination.

conservatism, we find a comprehensive, treasonous, utopian politics.²²² Here, Badiou's description of the early Jesus loyalists as "a small group of militants" wherein the language of siblings ("brothers") is used in a manner comparable to the use of the word "comrades" in nineteenth- and early-twentieth-century revolutionary organizing is helpful.²²³ So, too, is the way Jennings reads Paul through the lens of Friedrich Engels: "Paul is like the early leaders of the social democrats who launch cells of workers among the proletarian masses of the cities and towns of Europe and leave the rest to them—and to history's inevitable triumph."²²⁴ It is no wonder that scholars who have little experience engaging in grassroots community mobilization within or as members of oppressed populations (i.e., scholars with little or no experience of gospeling) struggle to classify the model that best describes the early assemblies of Jesus loyalists. Models and parallels are endlessly presented, disposed of, and argued over, but for those who are familiar with what it is to live and move and have their being within communities of solidarity, resistance, and liberation, the resemblances are as striking as the conclusions are inescapable.

Being and Gospeling in the Anointed

This, then, describes what it means to be "in the Anointed," a term that the Pauline faction frequently favors when speaking of the way of life

---

222. Meeks paves the way for this reading, noting how the Pauline assemblies draw from both the household and Greek notions of the polis, while not being modeled after voluntary associations, synagogues, philosophy schools, or other cults and collegia (Meeks, *Moral World*, 75–84; *First Urban Christians*, 108–9, 113–20, 183–84; *In Search of the Early Christians*, 167–71, 179). Meeks observes that the Pauline assemblies are neither the sum of these other groups nor their mere synthesis and, I believe, understanding the political nature of the Pauline assemblies explains why this is the case. Jeffers also highlights key differences between the Pauline assemblies and voluntary associations and concludes that Paul and his compatriots may have used the voluntary association model as a legal cover but did not model themselves on those associations in any meaningful way (see Jeffers, *Greco-Roman World*, 72, 79–80). Others who pick up on the political conflict between the Pauline *ekklesiai* and conventional collegia include Winter, "Roman Law and Society," 75, 79; Horrell, *Social Ethos*, 126–42; Horsley, "Rhetoric and Empire," 84, 91 (Horsley's comments on how Paul requires people to violate the *sensus communis* and form alternative allegiances are interesting to read, especially in light of Ando's comments—already explored above—about the importance of consensus to Roman imperialism).

223. See Badiou, *Saint Paul*, 20–21.

224. Jennings, *Outlaw Justice*, 217–18.

that is to define Jesus loyalists as both individuals and collectivities.[225] As we have seen, to be in the Anointed is to be torn from the fleshy body of Roman imperialism and grafted into the spiritual body of those who are rising-up from the dead (2 Cor 12:27; Rom 12:5). It also means being members of the household of God (see Gal 3:26). But to be in the Anointed is ultimately to be in the domain of Jesus's lordship, wherein those who are loyal to Jesus are also the recipients of Jesus's loyalty and the gracious gifts his rule provides—notably emancipation (*apolytrosis*), justice, and life (e.g., Rom 3:22, 24; 5:15-21; 6:23; 8:1; 1 Cor 1:4, 9, 30; 7:22; 15:18-31; 16:24; 2 Cor 1:21; 3:14; 5:17-19; 12:2; Gal 1:22; 2:4, 16-20; 3:14; 5:6; Phil 3:3, 9; 4:7, 19, 21; 1 Thess 2:14; 4:16; Phlm 23). To be in the Anointed, as Ziesler argues, is to be "in [the Anointed's] sphere of power," which also means that life in the Anointed is "the opposite of life under the old dominations and powers."[226] Now, there is undoubtedly a "mystical" or, perhaps better stated, deeply personal experiential component to all of this.[227] There is a profound intimacy that is experienced by those who are simultaneously in the Anointed and have the Anointed in them. However, this is also a communal experience, and being in the Anointed is most often a name given to the way of life shared and developed by the assemblies of Jesus loyalists. Thus, being in the Anointed is a way of talking about the communal pursuit of love and justice expressed in actions

---

225. On the frequency and prominence of "in Christ" language, see Schweitzer, *Mysticism of Paul the Apostle*. See also Deissmann, *Religion of Jesus*, 158–80; Longenecker, *Ministry and Message of Paul*, 89.

226. Ziesler, *Pauline Christianity*, 61. See also Deissmann's remarks about "belonging to Christ" paralleling those who "belong to Caesar" which he then uses to juxtapose "Christians" with "Caesareans" (Deissmann, *Light from the Ancient East*, 377). Similarly claims are made more implicitly by others like Ridderbos, *Paul*, 205, 211, 223–24, 237, 258–59; Wright, "Paul and Caesar," 188.

227. See, of course, Schweitzer, *Mysticism of Paul the Apostle*, viii, 1–3, 23 (and throughout); Deissmann, *Paul*, 139–40, 149; *Religion of Jesus*, 195–200. As one would expect, Schweitzer emphasizes the eschatological nature of all of this, although I believe volume 1 of this series demonstrates why his understanding of eschatology is problematical. Deissmann tends to emphasize that this is "in Christ" *mysticism*, an experience of intimacy that is responsive and premised upon God's act of drawing near. Other scholars, particularly with a more conservative slant, tend to attempt to remove some of the more "mystical" elements of this (wherein one experiences a deeply personal intimacy with the Anointed). Thus, for example, Kümmel argues that the notion of being in Christ "denotes the Christian's relation to the eschatological saving event and the Christian community that is founded thereby" (Kümmel, *Theology of the New Testament*, 219).

and attitudes reflecting meaningful solidarity and unity.[228] This is what a transfer of allegiance and location to the domain of the Anointed makes possible. And all of these things are experienced in an equally personal and profoundly intimate way. The poverty-stricken family in Jerusalem that receives money from families in Corinth and Macedonia and, as a result, does not have to sell children into slavery or uproot themselves from their community to pursue work elsewhere, will both experience a "mystical" intimacy with the Anointed (whose love and rule makes this kind of wealth redistribution possible) and a life-saving change in their material circumstances.[229] Mysticism and materialism need not be opposed to one another here. Similarly, while liberal and conservative scholars have gone back and forth arguing about whether "in Christ mysticism" or "justification" is at the "core" of "Paul's theology," this exposition demonstrates that one needn't choose between the two. *Being in the Anointed is the domain wherein the process of making things just takes place.* Thus, Paul and his coworkers frequently refer to being in the Anointed not only as a context but as something that is done, as a work, as a labor, or as something active (e.g., Rom 16:3, 7, 9–10; 1 Cor 4:10, 15, 17; 2 Cor 2:12–17; 12:19; 13:3–5; Phil 1:1, 26; 2:1; 3:14; 1 Thess 1:3; Phlm 20). The body of the Anointed is apocalypsed through the ways in which its members practice a lawless justice which brings Life where Death used to reign. Thus, justice is actualized "in the way of life of the messianic cells" as people collectively and quite literally become the justice of God.[230]

---

228. On the relation of being in the Anointed to a community-oriented ethics that prioritizes these things, see Deissmann, *Religion of Jesus*, 245–57; *Paul*, 208–9; Crossan and Borg, *First Paul*, 111–12, 185–86; Kahl, *Galatians Re-Imagined*, 269.

229. In this regard, I was struck by Ramsay MacMullen's remark that, in the Pauline context, the "chief business of religion . . . was to make the sick well," such that titles of "Healer" and "Savior" often go hand-in-hand (MacMullen, *Paganism in the Roman Empire*, 49). Thus, MacMullen argues that it was the "supernatural efficacy" of Christianity that produced so many converts (95–96). Indeed, it is precisely the work I have described above—emancipating slaves, practicing a sibling-based economic mutuality, and so on—that shows how the early Jesus movement so effectively made the sick well.

230. Jennings, *Outlaw Justice*, 177–78; Miranda, *Marx and the Bible*, 163. See also, Gorman, *Reading Paul*, 116–20; Scroggs, *Paul for a New Day*, 17–19; Harink, *Paul Among the Postliberals*, 59–60. Crossan and his co-authors are better than the conservatives when it comes to this theme but are still too caught up in a push to counter an American notion of punitive or retributive justice with the idea of distributive or restorative justice, and so they miss the point a bit (although I certainly do not mean

THE LAWLESSNESS OF GOOD NEWS IN THE MAKING

Of course, there are still boundaries to all of this. After all, members of the Anointed's body have been torn from the fleshy body of Roman imperialism and, in fact, this has caused them to die but, having been grafted onto the body of the Anointed, they have been raised to new life beyond Sin, Death, and the law. Hence, the rite of baptism which both symbolized and enacted this transition.[231] Boundaries between people do not entirely vanish—as if one could be a devout member of Caesar's body and a member of the crucified yet resurrected body of the Anointed simultaneously—but these boundaries are significantly redrawn.[232] Specifically, boundaries used to divide, dominate, oppress, dispossess, enslave, violate, and kill people are abolished, and the new boundaries that are established are put in place to prevent people from contributing to death-dealing practices.

With this in mind, we can now do away with three common arguments that have been made in relation to Pauline ethics and their motivations. First, there are those, mostly conservatives, who argue that Pauline ethics—and the boundaries related to the formation of the community of those who are in the Anointed—are driven by a desire to maintain a good reputation with others and, in fact, exhibit an elitism, wherein the Jesus loyalists present themselves as an attractive alternative to mainstream society by outdoing others in (what were commonly recognized as) virtuous behaviors.[233] As we have seen, the appeal of the Jesus movement (an appeal that was limited to those living on the margins of society, those in the place of no place, who were regularly subjected to the normalized violence of the oppressive rule of law) was precisely that people were given the opportunity to break from this notion of virtue, the picture it painted of the world and their place in it, and transfer their allegiance, along with their individual and collective existence, to another domain.

---

that to be a criticism of distributive or restorative notions of justice!). See Crossan and Reed, *In Search of Paul*, 355, 382–84; Crossan and Borg, *First Paul*, 164–66.

231. See Rom 6:3–4; 1 Cor 1:13; 6:11; Gal 3:27–28. See, for example, deSilva, *Honor, Patronage, Kinship, and Purity*, 304–6. This is further remembered in the common meals shared by the assemblies (see 1 Cor 10:16).

232. See Meeks, *First Urban Christians*, 84–95; deSilva, *Honor, Patronage, Kinship, and Purity*, 280–99; Malina, "Social Levels, Morals, and Daily Life," 191–95; Neyrey, *Paul*, 219.

233. See, for example, Cadoux, *Early Church and the World*, 95; Thielman, *Theology of the New Testament*, 442–44; Winter, "Roman Law and Society," 81–85; Theissen, *Social Reality and the Early Christians*, 285; Ziesler, *Pauline Christianity*, 121; Malina, "Social Levels, Morals, and Daily Life," 194.

Second, there are those (mostly liberal scholars) who see the Pauline faction as engaging in a more philosophical project that adopts but spiritualizes Stoic values related to morality and community.[234] However, this enlightened liberalism does not do justice to the conflict that the Pauline faction still presupposes and exacerbates between the wealthy and the impoverished, the supposedly powerful and the supposedly powerless, and between those accustomed to living abundantly and those left for dead. Third, among some of those slightly to the Left of the liberals (who frequently lay claim to the title "radical"), the argument is often made that Paul and his coworkers are calling for secession or apocalyptic withdrawal from the empire and its death-dealing ways in order to try and create a more life-giving alternative (which is generally as far removed from the empire as possible—hence, for example, in this stream we see everything from Mennonites and the new monasticism to Walsh and Keesmaat's organic solar-powered farm).[235] What this position misses, however, is the way in which the Pauline faction went out looking for a fight, as it were, with Caesar, looking to emancipate slaves from right under his nose. Paul and his coworkers are not *fleeing* Caesar so much as *fleecing* him and leaving a series of timed explosives in their wake.[236] Thus, conservative, liberal, and radical positions all miss what is taking place with Paul and his coworkers and what motivates their ethics. They are neither conservative elitists trying to impress their neighbors with how virtuous they are, nor are they enlightened liberals preaching peace regardless of the violence upon which that peace is premised, nor are they seeking to radically remove themselves from the empire altogether—they

---

234. See Engberg-Pedersen, *Paul and the Stoics*, 78 (and throughout); Tellbe, *Paul Between Synagogue and State*, 248–49; Dodd, *Meaning of Paul for Today*, 9–10, 46–48, 146.

235. See, for example, Cousar, *Introduction to the New Testament*, 8–9; Walsh and Keesmaat, *Colossians Remixed*, 159, 172–73; Georgi, *Theocracy*, 102–3; Harink, *Paul Among the Postliberals*, 144–46; Gorman, *Cruciformity*, 359–60. It's probably worth noting that engaging in this kind of lifestyle tends to be expensive . . . in other words, it's a lot easier to develop an organic solar-powered farm when you're earning what professors earn at the University of Toronto than, say, working three part-time jobs as a single parent trying to house, feed, and clothe your children. In other words, apocalyptic retreat, in our context, all too often ends up being one of the ways in which the rich hoard both goods and goodness, and should not be considered a viable option for Jesus loyalists unless it prioritizes creating lines of flight for those whom our society has left for dead.

236. My rhetoric is quite different, but I think Scroggs holds withdrawal and engagement together pretty well in his work (see Scroggs, *Paul for a New Day*, 40, 51–55).

are the dead come back to life and they are spreading like a virus, seizing life back from those who tried to steal it from them, as they demolish fortresses and tear down strongholds until Death itself is finally defeated in the new creation of all things.

It is the communal and material working out of this all-encompassing political (but no less religious) program—oriented around contributing to and affirming that which is life-giving and resisting or destroying that which is death-dealing—that is the gospel according to Paul and his coworkers.[237] Thus, descriptions of "the Church" as God's redemptive instrument in history (between the cross and the *parousia* of the Anointed) or about "the Church" as the agent of God's new creation here and now are inadequate on at least two counts.[238] First, this rhetoric, although perhaps inspiring, is altogether too vague and open to all kinds of abuses or disappointing limitations (as exhibited most obviously in the ethics modeled and encouraged by the bulk of scholars who talk in this way). Second, it misses the point that the assemblies are not simply agents of this or that transformation—the assemblies are, themselves, the gospel and, consequently, according to the Pauline faction, there is no gospel apart from their existence, development, and spread. The gospel, in other words, is something that is always being assembled anew whenever and wherever people begin to refuse the oppressive and death-dealing dynamics of the hierarchies of power that are brought to bear upon them and, consequently, begin to pursue more life-giving and life-affirming ways of mutually sharing in the abundance of life together (and if people gospel another gospel, let them be anathema!). Where and when this happens one can affirm that, yes, the crucified are rising from the dead and yes, justice is materializing and, yes, the Spirit of Life is moving so

237. Schnabel misunderstands things when he says that "next to gospel proclamation, founding local communities was a central element of Paul's 'mission'" (Schnabel, *Paul and the Early Church*, 1371), because founding local communities of the sort I have described is, in fact, the gospel proclamation. Hays does a better job of showing the centrality of this to Paul's gospel (see Hays, *Moral Vision*, 32–41) as do Crossan and Reed (Crossan and Reed, *In Search of Paul*, 141, 409) but I especially like how Banks argues that building community cannot be removed from the proclamation of the gospel because embracing the gospel means entering into a specific community (Banks, *Paul's Idea of Community*, 33).

238. For some examples that emphasize the redemptive agent side, see Cullmann, *Christ and Time*, 145–55; *Salvation in History*, 256–57; Wright, "Paul's Gospel and Caesar's Empire," 182–83; *New Testament and the People of God*, 146; *Simply Christian*, 200–204. For some examples emphasizing new creation see Hays, *Moral Vision*, 198; Kee, *Renewal of Hope*, 135; Harink, *Paul Among the Postliberals*, 71–72, 125–26.

powerfully that even the law and all of its death-dealing components cannot hold it back, and woe, indeed, to you rulers, managers, defenders of private property, enforcers of the rule of law, and profiteers of crucifixion because your time is coming to an end.[239]

And, Finally, Romans 13:1–7

But I have left the most perplexing or potentially troubling passage for last. Rom 13:1–7 is a passage that has long haunted Paulinism. I believe that it was best left until now because a significant amount of context was needed before we examined it. Long the bastion of the law-abiding who place Paul in the service of Death, this passage—arbitrarily raised above others and taken at face value in a way that many other passages are not—has been used as a trump card over the rest of the Pauline corpus and has become the gatekeeper or lens through which everything else is understood. Conducive to enforcing death-dealing socioeconomic and theopolitical structures, it has been used to justify everything from genocidal imperial conquest to the annihilation of any kind of movement wherein the left-for-dead have sought to claim the Life that was stolen from them. However, when read in light of all that we have explored in this series, it strikes the reader as an extremely odd passage. It reads as follows:

> (1) Let every soul be subject to superior designated authorities. For there is no designated authority if not from God and the existing ones have been appointed (commissioned) by God. (2) Therefore, those wholeheartedly (with militant overtones) resisting the designated authorities have resisted those instituted by God and those who resist will receive judgment (with overtones of legal condemnation) on themselves. [Or: those who oppose the order of things are opposing God's ordering of things and, when they act out that opposition, they can expect to be judged and condemned for their actions.] (3) For the

---

239. Therefore, returning to Bates's argument that salvation is premised primarily upon intellectual assent to eight theses that summarize the story of God in Jesus—an assent that is then verified in some kind of verbal proclamation of loyalty to King Jesus—one realizes that it is this assembling practice (brought about by the Spirit of Life), *regardless of the ideologies, faiths, words, or beliefs* of its participants, that is truly the pathway to salvation as salvation is understood by the Pauline faction (i.e., as the creation of just ways of organizing life-giving and life-affirming relationships between diverse parties).

> rulers are not a terror to the good work but to evil. Moreover, do you want to not be terrified by the designated authority? Do the good and you will be appropriately praised by him. (4) For, he is an appointed minister (*diakonos*) of God to you for the good. But if you do evil, be terrified, for he does not bear the sword (the "slaughter-knife") in vain. An appointed minister (*diakonos* again!) of God, he is an avenger, exercising wrath on the one actively performing evil. (5) Therefore, it is necessary to be subjected, not only because of wrath, but also because of conscience. (6) Indeed, also because of this, pay taxes for they are God's appointed ministers (*leitourgoi*—as defined above) totally committed to continually attending to the public good by this means. (7) Render to all their dues (*opheilas*)—taxes to whom taxes are due, tolls to whom tolls are due, terror to whom terror is due, honor to whom honor is due (my translation).

Thus, a specific injunction—pay taxes to the authorities who collect taxes—is paired with a much broader and seemingly more universal statement about rulers, their purpose, their grounds for ruling, and how Jesus loyalists are expected to respond to them. A few things immediately strike the reader as puzzling. First, Paul and his coworkers use the same terms for the political authorities (God's divinely appointed *diakonos* and *leitourgoi*) that they use for themselves. Yet, here, these titles are being given to those whom Paul and his coworkers have explicitly disparaged, seen as wicked, unjust, blind, foolish, opposed to God, and doomed to condemnation. Second, rather than questioning the ability of these authorities to judge well (which they have done previously), the judgments of the authorities (their praise or condemnation) is valued here. Third, Paul and his coworkers affirm the ways in which the designated authorities order things to be a part of God's ordering of things, even though they previously described this order of things as symptomatic of life in "this present evil age" wherein, among other things, the courts were not taken to be places where one could expect to find justice. Fourth, Paul and his coworkers urge submission when, in much of their other writings, they urge the violation and breaking of the law. Fifth, they also affirm structures—like the honor system—that they have explicitly, continually, and adamantly rejected elsewhere as they have embraced shame in the company of the crucified. It is no wonder, then, that Neil Elliott says that what is written here seems like a "monumental contradiction" of Paulinism.[240]

As such, it is tempting to see this passage as a later interpolation. Several scholars have made this argument, drawing especial attention to how the argument of the letter flows seamlessly if you remove the passage and move from Rom 12:21 to 13:8.[241] Others, however, are less convinced of this, noting how the themes found in Rom 13:1–7 both fit with their immediate context and contain strong linguistic and textual links to the rest of the letter.[242] Now, granted, this could simply be proof that the party (or parties) who inserted the passage into the letter did a good job of choosing where to place it and worked to incorporate it with the letter and, yes, nothing seems to be lost in the flow of the letter if this passage is removed, so this argument need not be as weighty as it is made out to be. However, using the "this is too inconsistent with everything else Paul says" argument as the basis for positing an interpolation will, for good reasons, make anyone familiar with the history of the uses and abuses of the New Testament feel very nervous (although there are times when this argument seems persuasive to me). Therefore, while I am sympathetic to the interpolation thesis and do not altogether discount it (it seems quite plausible to me), I do think there is a way of reading the passage that explains how Paul and his coworkers could have included it given everything that I have already written about them.

Generally, scholars from all sides have accepted the authenticity of this passage, although there is a great deal of diversity found in how people have made sense of it. Roughly speaking, scholars are divided into two main camps—those who support a "plain reading" (i.e., a decontextualized, acritical reading) in order to enforce an ethics of submission to governing authorities, and those who—to widely varying degrees—problematize a strict one-to-one enforcement of the text based upon various contextual considerations. Therefore, this section will proceed in three

---

240. Elliott, "Romans 13:1–7," 186. I like the way in which Elliott continually draws the reader's attention to the what-the-fuck-ness of this passage (see also Elliott, *Liberating Paul*, 218; *Arrogance of Nations*, 152–56). He is not alone in doing this. See, for example, Horrell, *Solidarity and Difference*, 254–55; Carter, *Roman Empire*, 133–34.

241. See Kallas, "Romans 13:1–7," 365–74; Walker, *Interpolations*; Welborn, *Paul's Summons*, xvi, 70, esp. 123–24n115, for sources and further discussion. Bammel, even though he accepts the passage, also accepts this disconnect (Bammel, "Romans 13," 367).

242. See, for example, Horrell, *Solidarity and Difference*, 252–57; Tellbe, *Paul Between Synagogue and State*, 173; Furnish, *Moral Teaching of Paul*, 120–22.

parts. Because I began by highlighting the oddity of this passage, I will continue by examining a number of positions that try to contextualize it in order to make sense of it and its implications. I will then examine the arguments made in favor of Pauline obedience to the state and what limits are posited in relation to that obedience. Finally, I will propose my own understanding of the text and argue that Paul and his coworkers are not being entirely honest here—something supported both in the immediate context of this passage and by our broader examination of Paulinism—and that they have good reasons for being dishonest.

Situational Explanations

Given the oddity of the force of the statement made about the designated authorities in Rom 13:1–7, there are some who focus on the specific injunction to pay taxes and contextualize this in such a way as to argue that this context invalidates arguments related to submitting universally to all authorities (at all times). However, others argue that the act of contextualization does not take away from the force of the injunction to submit. Generally, when trying to understand the context that may have prompted the Pauline faction to write in this way, one or more of the following factors is considered relevant: (a) given that the well-being of the assemblies of Jesus loyalists was at stake and that they constantly faced the risk of persecution, the payment of taxes is a survival strategy;[243] (b) given that the Judeans were especially vulnerable to being subjected to pogroms during riots—as had just occurred at Alexandria in 38 CE—and given that tax riots had recently taken place in the vicinity of Rome close to Puteoli, and given that Judeans had only recently returned to Rome after being expelled due to events involving riots, and given that Judeans were already suspected of not paying taxes (because of the exemption they had received to pay the temple tax), Paul and his coworkers urge submission in order to protect the Judeans from both riotous mobs and the subsequent and inevitably violent response from the authorities;[244] (c) furthermore, given the poverty of the Jesus loyalists and given that

---

243. See, for example, Judge, *Social Distinctives of the Christians*, 53; Tellbe, *Paul Between Synagogue and State*, 198–99; Elliott, "Strategies of Resistance," 121; Dunn, *Beginning from Jerusalem*, 921–22; Grant, *Early Christianity and Society*, 44, 48.

244. Tellbe, *Paul Between Synagogue and State*, 178–81; Sanders, *Paul: The Apostle's Life*, 694–96; Elliott, *Liberating Paul*, 222–24; "Romans 13:1–7," 188–96; "Strategies of Resistance," 121; "Disciplining the Hope," 189.

Caesar had crucified their Lord, Paul and his coworkers are concerned that some Jesus loyalists will participate in rebellious activities or riots related to taxation and so they deliberately seek to quell this revolutionary fervor;[245] (d) or, as many argue, there is a good chance that this submission is only advised because Paul and his coworkers were expecting the imminent end of the world;[246] (e) or maybe Paul and his coworkers had gotten caught up in the optimism that circulated among the Roman elite at the beginning of Nero's reign, given Nero's potential to restore peace, salvation, and prosperity to the empire (well before the extent of his depravity was revealed and well before he began to personally persecute the Jesus loyalists);[247] (f) or maybe Paul was simply too naïve and unaware of how violence was structured into the dynamics of imperialism and conquest to be critical of designated authorities in general.[248] Various scholars combine these factors in various ways (and, digging through the literature, it appears that basically every possible combination of these factors has been argued at some point). Thus, for example, E. P. Sanders believes that protecting Judeans after Claudius expelled them from Rome, when paired with what Sanders takes to be Paul's social conservatism and expectation of an imminent end, provide us with the explanation of this

---

245. See Bryan, *Render to Caesar*, 80–81; Ridderbos, *Paul*, 325; Weiss, *Paul and Jesus*, 63–64; Cadoux, *Early Church and the World*, 97–99. Here, again, the law-abiding and law-loving nature of a lot of scholars comes through. Thus, Ziesler argues that the government must be upheld when the only alternative is (gasp) anarchy (Ziesler, *Pauline Christianity*, 119–20). Even Schweitzer falls into this (see Schweitzer, *Mysticism of Paul the Apostle*, 316). Wright, though, is the worst. Hence, he ostentatiously pooh-poohs any kind of "civil disobedience and revolution that merely reshuffles the political cards into a different order" (as if all civil disobedience and revolutionary activity does this), and argues that Paul is clarifying what his "subversive message" does and does not imply (i.e., nothing meaningfully or materially subversive), in order to avoid an "anarchy [that] simply replaces the tyranny of the officially powerful with the tyranny of the unofficially powerful" (Wright, *Paul*, 78; "Paul and Caesar," 190–91).

246. See Furnish, *Moral Teaching of Paul*, 115–16, 124, 127; Hengel, *Property and Riches*, 211–13; Bornkamm, *Paul*, 211–12; Dunn, *Beginning from Jerusalem*, 923; Cullmann, *State in the New Testament*, 56–57; Schottroff, "'Give to Caesar,'" 240–41; Schweitzer, *Mysticism of Paul the Apostle*, 313–17. Horsley and Silberman put a bit of a unique twist on this by arguing that Paul wants the Jesus loyalists at Rome to be submissive so that he can make it to Spain and, thereby, complete the eschatological mission required to bring the world to an end (Horsley and Silberman, *Message and the Kingdom*, 188–91; see also Dewey, "EIS THN SPANIAN," 321–49).

247. See Bryan, *Render to Caesar*, 79; Cadoux, *Early Church and the World*, 112–13; Roetzel, *World That Shaped*, 22–23; Furnish, *Moral Teaching of Paul*, 136.

248. See Fitzpatrick, *Paul*, 78–79.

THE LAWLESSNESS OF GOOD NEWS IN THE MAKING

passage.[249] Mikael Tellbe argues that, essentially, all of this is rooted in the stress to pay taxes to the state because Judeans at Rome would be vulnerable to charges of tax evasion and because Paul was concerned about them being targeted in a pogrom—thus, this passage is highly specific to this situation as a survival strategy that reveals a "tension" in Paul's approach to the state (which, according to Tellbe, contains both elements of political quietism and challenging the state's claims in central and critical ways).[250] Neil Elliott, who understands Paul and his coworkers as political radicals and not as social conservatives, also sees this injunction as rooted in a concern to protect vulnerable Judeans, and he believes that Paul feels it is appropriate to speak this way because the return of Jesus and the fall of Rome is imminent, so Paul can propose this grudgingly as an ad hoc survival strategy.[251]

Frequently, but not always, this act of contextualization is then taken to severely limit the seemingly timeless nature of the command to submit to the designated authorities. Thus, for example, if Paul and his coworkers were wrong about the imminent end of the world, then it is wrong to believe that people everywhere and at all times should always submit to the authorities. Or, it is postulated, that if the Pauline faction had written the letter to the Romans after the Neronian persecution had begun, then they would not have written the same things. Or, again, if one is no longer worried about survival or vulnerable Judeans, then maybe different conclusions—both about the basis of the authority of the rulers and about how one might respond to them—can be drawn. Or, as in the case of Warren Carter, we can note several of these possibilities while observing how little Rom 13:1–7 coheres with what Paul has written elsewhere and conclude that, while we cannot be exactly sure which factor or factors motivated the Pauline faction to write in this way, we can still be fairly certain that this was not intended to be the foundation of an eternally valid ethics of submission.[252]

In response to these proposals, I wish to begin with two points. First, I do not find all of these proposed factors to be equally compelling. For example, given the understanding of apocalyptic Pauline eschatology I outlined in volume 2 of this series, I do not think that a belief in the

249. See Sanders, *Paul: The Apostle's Life*, 694–96.

250. Tellbe, *Paul Between Synagogue and State*, 171–206.

251. Elliott, "Strategies of Resistance," 119–21; *Arrogance of Nations*, 56; *Liberating Paul*, 222–24; "Romans 13:1–7," 186–96; "Disciplining the Hope," 189.

252. See Carter, *Roman Empire*, 135–36.

imminent end of the world or the empire is a factor here (and, it should be noted, that factor weighs heavily in most of these accounts). I also do not find it plausible to think that Paul and his coworkers were caught up in any kind of optimism regarding the early years of Nero's reign. While some elite members of society had high hopes for what Nero might accomplish on their behalf, it is highly unlikely that people living at the subsistence level, people living in slavery, and people from vanquished, colonized, and migrant populations had any higher hopes for Nero than they did for those who came before or after him (suggesting this as a factor is kind of like suggesting that the Iraqis would have had higher hopes for George W. Bush than they had for George H. W. Bush). Paul was intimately familiar with state-based violence and bore the brandmarks of it on his own body. Thus, I also don't think it's plausible to suggest that he was too naïve about the workings of the empire to be able to imagine a more serious criticism of it. That said, I do think that those who connect this passage to concerns related to tax revolts, Judean vulnerability, and group survival raise very plausible points of concern. However, and this is my second point, even if this is the context in which Paul and his coworkers urge the Jesus loyalists at Rome to pay their taxes, this injunction remains paired with a shocking statement about the source of power of the designated authorities, the validity of their judgments, and the submission that is owed to them. Granted, we have already seen that Paul and his coworkers can be rather hyperbolic and get carried away in the heat of an argument, and perhaps that is what is going on here, too, but it leaves the reader wondering if something else prompts the Pauline faction to write in this way. Why not simply say something like: "Given the current state of affairs and the vulnerability of some of those in your assemblies, it is important that you all pay your taxes"? Why the need to frame such a highly situational injunction in such a universal way—especially given the way in which this flies in the face of so much that Paul and his coworkers have argued elsewhere? One is left wondering: if one decides to treat this passage as Pauline, is there another way of understanding this passage that makes better sense of it?

The Grounds and Limits of Obedience

One way of resolving the conflict between the contextual and universal components of this passage is to argue, for one reason or another, that

Paul and his coworkers actually intend this view of the designated authorities to be (for the most part) a timeless view. Again, a number of factors are proposed to defend this and, among those who make these proposals, a diverse array of positions is taken, especially when it comes to understanding the limits (or lack thereof) of submission. I will briefly mention four examples of those who try to limit submission to the state in various ways before looking at the position taken by those who urge a much more unqualified obedience and the reasons that they offer to support this position.

The most obvious way in which submission to designated authorities is limited based upon appeals to Rom 13:1–7 arises from the observation that the authorities themselves are said to be under God's authority. Consequently, submission to the designated authorities should not be acritical but is, in turn, subordinated to submission to Jesus's lordship and the authority of God.[253] Furthermore, as those subordinated to God's authority, the designated authorities are also tasked with rewarding good and punishing evil, and so, some argue, submission to the designated authorities does not require submission when those authorities fail in that mandate and, for example, punish good and reward evil.[254] Of course, this is inferred from the text—Paul and his coworkers do say that the designated authorities only receive authority because God gives it to them, and they do say that this authority has a specific purpose, but they never, in this passage, actually say something like, "If the authorities violate their mandate or if they require you to violate your allegiance to Jesus, you are not to submit to them."[255] This is just taken for granted as an "obvious" conclusion to draw based on how these scholars understand the rest of

---

253. See, for example, Wright, *Paul*, 78; "Paul and Caesar," 190; *Simply Christian*, 78–79; Bryan, *Render to Caesar*, 1–2; Lohse, *Theological Ethics*, 131–33; Schrage, *Ethics of the New Testament*, 238–39; Witherington, *Paul Quest*, 174, 177–81; Cousar, *Letters of Paul*, 156–57.

254. See for example, Jennings, *Reading Derrida/Thinking Paul*, 75; Ziesler, *Pauline Christianity*, 119; Lohse, *Theological Ethics*, 134–36; Wengst, *Pax Romana*, 79–85; even Schrage, *Ethics of the New Testament*, 237–38; Winter, *Seek the Welfare of the City*, 119 (wherein Winter argues that Paul's criticisms of authorities in 1 Cor 6 speak to the failure of local magistrate, while, in Rom 13, Paul upholds the empire-wide rule of criminal Law). Bryan, too, for all of his compliance with oppressive systems still argues that there is room for a "prophetic challenge" at times when the state over-extends itself or betrays its purpose (Bryan, *Render to Caesar*, 78–80).

255. Hence, Schottroff observes that the point here is less open to ever inferring disobedience because the argument is that even unjust authorities are still put in place by God (Schottroff, "'Give to Caesar'"). More on the implications of this in a moment.

PAULINE SOLIDARITY

the Pauline corpus (an understanding rejected by those who urge a more unqualified obedience and who essentially argue that the authorities are *always* working according to God's plan and should, therefore, *always* be obeyed). However, given how these scholars tend to understand the Pauline corpus and how justice and authority are understood in their contemporary contexts, they mostly do not see any clash between Jesus loyalists and the designated authorities. They view disobedience as a very rare or "one-off" event, at least in liberal democracies or when it comes to the states in which they are citizens. They may see it as more appropriate in states opposed by their governments, although even then it sometimes takes something like Hitler understood fifty years after the fact (but probably not Hitler as understood in his historical moment) to get some of these scholars thinking that maybe something more is required than politely and fawningly pointing out something may be off. Be that as it may, some scholars under this umbrella also try to impose further limits to this injunction within an overall framework of de facto submission. Here, I will highlight the positions of Gerd Theissen, Oscar Cullmann, and Ernst Käsemann.

Theissen argues that, after Claudius's edict of 41 CE, which expelled the Judeans from Rome (likely, Theissen thinks, over a conflict related to the early Jesus movement), the Pauline faction is trying to allay fears related to the political risks posed by the presence of the Jesus loyalists there.[256] Hence, Paul "emphasizes his absolute political loyalty" in order to show that he cannot "represent a political threat."[257] However, Theissen believes that the Pauline faction's understanding of the designated authorities in this passage is focused upon "constitutional representatives" and deliberately suppresses any discussion of the emperor. Hence, he argues that Rom 13:1–7 is "an expression of a legitimistic attitude which recognizes only constitutional rule, and not the arbitrary rule of an individual."[258] I believe there are several problems with this reading. First, as I will argue below, I do not think the emperor is absent from

---

256. Theissen, *Fortress Introduction to the New Testament*, 49.

257. Theissen, *Fortress Introduction to the New Testament*, 84.

258. Theissen, *Fortress Introduction to the New Testament*, 84. Hence, while Theissen also argues that the early Jesus movement produced dissidence in political, public, and familial spheres (through, from Theissen's perspective, refusing to participate in official cults, through refusing political offices, and through urging domestic fidelity, heteronormativity, and opposing abortion), the early Jesus loyalists still gave the state "an unreserved ethical legitimation" (Theissen, *Social Reality*, 283; see 281–83).

this passage. People from persecuted groups may have very pragmatic reasons about even mentioning the title of the emperor when they talk among themselves, but I think it is implausible to say that the emperor's presence is thereby suppressed or that the emperor's authority is subtly undercut because he is not named. Second, even those who have been nominated to more limited terms in other superior positions of authority in Rome (i.e., "constitutional authorities," like the *leitourgoi* mentioned in v. 6) would have only been appointed or commissioned to these positions at the behest of Nero or his ministers. Third, given all we have seen of the interweaving of the word of the emperor and the letter of the law, it is not so easy to separate "constitutional authority" from "the arbitrary rule of an individual." Thus, while Theissen's reading fits with the politics of his own state (and opposes the politics espoused by states opposed by his state), it may be wishful thinking to imagine that this is a Pauline understanding of things.

Cullmann suggests that an "eschatological attitude" which sees "the Church" as the *politeuma* of the coming age while recognizing the provisional nature of the state for as long as the old age persists explains the Pauline approach in Rom 13:1–7. This "leads neither to renunciation nor uncritical acceptance."[259] Thus, for as long as it remains, the state is willed by God and the Jesus loyalists are required to aid it, unless it becomes totalitarian, in which case it is to be resisted.[260] As with most reformists, it takes a lot (in fact, the bar always seems to be moving just out of reach) for certain states to be considered "totalitarian." In fact, from Cullmann's perspective, the execution of Jesus was just one big misunderstanding as Jesus was "in no sense an enemy of the State on principle, but rather a loyal citizen who offered no threat to the State's existence."[261] This read-

---

259. See Cullmann, *Salvation in History*, 3–4; 337; *State in the New Testament*, 4–5. Pate, among others, follows Cullmann on this point and argues that this is basically Luther's doctrine of the two kingdoms wherein both the Kingdom of God and the kingdoms of this world interact but neither rules the other until the return of Jesus (Pate, *End of the Age has Come*, 189–90—again, anarchy is mentioned as something associated with evil and the repression of which justifies the existence of the state. Luther, too, is well known for his counter-revolutionary attitude and his urging of the princes to slaughter the peasants when they rose up and sought to create a more life-giving situation for themselves).

260. Cullman, *State in the New Testament*, 50–51, 69–70.

261. Cullmann, *State in the New Testament*, 53–54. Sampley comes to the same conclusions as Cullmann: "Believers are to deal with governing authorities eschatologically, that is, knowing that the final power resides with God, but seeing the present as the arena in which life must be lived" (Sampley, *Walking Between the Times*, 26)—even

ing, then, comes very close to those who posit an unqualified obedience to the state because it makes all material, political, economic, or social matters somewhat inconsequential (because the root problem is "Satan" or "Sin" understood in a strictly spiritual sense).[262] By arguing this, Cullmann is engaging in a form of theological overcoding that, instead of clarifying the matter at hand, obfuscates the issue. Because Cullmann is bringing a lot into this passage that is not immediately obvious there, if you accept his general eschatological outlook, this makes sense. However, having already outlined an alternative (more plausible) apocalyptic eschatology related to Paul and his coworkers, wherein eschatology and politics are not opposed to each other but are shown to be very deeply interwoven, Cullmann's solution is much more deeply indebted to the magisterial reformers (whose nascent imperialism should not be denied) and their doctrine of the two kingdoms than it is to Paulinism.

Over against Cullmann, Ernst Käsemann argues that Paul is not engaging in any kind of eschatologically-oriented theological ethics in this passage.[263] Käsemann also wishes to distance any understanding of this passage from the Lutheran doctrine of two kingdoms and argues Rom 13:1–7 is oriented not around the metaphysics or nature of the state but around its function.[264] Therefore, Käsemann argues that submission is related to worshiping God in a way that encompasses all areas of life.[265] Christians can worship God by faithfully serving the state. However, according to Käsemann, "Christian obedience comes to an end at the point where further service becomes impossible—and only there."[266] And where precisely is that? Well, according to Käsemann, it is "when the suggestion is made to the Christian that he [sic] should deny his existence as a Christian and abandon his particular Christian task."[267] In fact, when

---

though he disagrees with Cullmann's argument about the execution of Jesus being a misunderstanding and, instead, notes how Paul's regular experiences of punishments, persecutions, and the failure of the law to protect him, led him to view jurists as contemptible, courts as hopeless, and rulers as doomed to perish, not least because they also killed Jesus (25).

262. See, for example, Schottroff, "'Give to Caesar,'" 241–43; Bornkamm, *Paul*, 214–15.

263. See Käsemann, *New Testament Questions of Today*, 199.

264. See Käsemann, *New Testament Questions of Today*, 200–205.

265. Käsemann, *New Testament Questions of Today*, 199–200.

266. Käsemann, *New Testament Questions of Today*, 214.

267. Käsemann, *New Testament Questions of Today*, 214.

this takes place, there may also come a time when it is appropriate for "Christians" to participate in a revolution—specifically, according to Käsemann, when the designated authorities begin to radically destroy the ties that hold a community together in a bond of mutual service and "when all acts of service become a part of common self-destruction, then Christians should revolt."[268] I think Käsemann speaks in a sensible, albeit somewhat vague and over-simplified way. I believe his position collapses once a more thoroughgoing socioeconomic or political analysis of the state takes place. For example, can one worship God by contributing to the well-being of a settler colonial state whose existence is premised upon the ongoing annihilation of Indigenous peoples as Indigenous peoples, even if those who are accepted as citizens within that state are valued and treated charitably and granted human rights? I also believe that his position is not one that encourages action but can easily and endlessly defer subversive or rebellious activity. When, for example, can one know that *all* acts of service to the state are now fundamentally contaminated? Finally, it should also be noted that the limits that Käsemann places on obedience are not found in the passage at hand and are inferred from elsewhere in the Pauline corpus.

However, when Rom 13:1–7 is read in isolation from that corpus (or from other possible contextual provisos), or when Rom 13:1–7 is made the definitive text that interprets how the rest of the Pauline corpus is read and interpreted, it appears to be making a strong case for an atemporal, unquestioning obedience to the designated authorities—a position often taken by conservative Christian scholars. Thus, for example, Herman Ridderbos argues that Christians show submission to God by submitting to authorities and, for Paul, this is a "deeply rooted conviction" that cannot be overturned simply because one observes "the misdeeds of a specific government."[269] Christian service to Jesus takes place "within the boundaries set for it by the civil authorities."[270] Consequently, Ethelbert Stauffer concludes that Paul's "theologia imperii" (imperial theology) is

---

268. Käsemann, *New Testament Questions of Today*, 215–16.

269. Ridderbos, *Paul*, 321–22. Indeed, Weiss concludes that Paul's view of the state in this regard is only possible because he both "shuts his eyes to many disagreeable facts" and "finds some divine element for reverence within the State" (Weiss, *Paul and Jesus*, 63; see also Weiss, *Earliest Christianity*, 2:592). Schreiner, like Schottroff (already mentioned above) simply thinks Paul urges obedience to good and evil rulers because God ordains both (Schreiner, *Romans*, 450; similarly, see Furnish, *Moral Teaching of Paul*, 133–34).

270. Ridderbos, *Paul*, 324.

manifested in the belief that, after "the Fall," civil authorities, like Caesar, are needed to restrain the forces of chaos.[271] Hence, "the Pauline Church" constantly intercedes for the state, obeys it, and prays for its well-being, praising God for blessing Caesar and thanking God for the *pax Augusti*.[272] This *pax Augusti* and the law and order that went with it are often taken to be something Paul valued because it permitted him to travel and spread "the Gospel" in an "unhindered" manner.[273] Indeed, Victor Paul Furnish concludes that, as a world traveler, Paul would be able to better appreciate the "social, economic, and political stability that Roman rule had made possible even in the farthest reaches of the Empire."[274] Therefore, Troeltsch concludes that Paul not only recognized the validity of the state but "prized it" because of its commitment to justice and order and morality.[275] More generally, then, a lot of blanket statements are made about the duty of Jesus loyalists to obey the government and serve the current order of things (and it is emphasized that paying taxes is only one small part of this).[276] The end result of this is an "unqualified acceptance" of the government and an equally unqualified submission to it, regardless of specific contextual factors related to this-or-that government or eschatological expectations regarding the imminence (or lack thereof) of Jesus's return.[277]

In order to make this case, the designated authorities are often taken to be distinct from "the powers," whom even conservatives agree that Paul is critical of elsewhere. Although Käsemann also rejects linking the authorities to the powers (because he focuses more on the function than the metaphysics of authority), generally the logic here is cyclical. Thus, Thomas Schreiner argues that there is no link between the state and the powers because Paul would never counsel submission to the powers, so

---

271. Stauffer, *New Testament Theology*, 81–85.

272. Stauffer, *New Testament Theology*, 193–97. Meeks argues that this follows diasporic Judean views of Rome as a friend who protected Judeans from the violence that would befall their communities in a breakdown of power hierarchies (Meeks, *First Urban Christians*, 106).

273. See for example, Kee, *Christian Origins*, 120; Kim, *Christ and Caesar*, 42–43.

274. Furnish, *Moral Teaching of Paul*, 129.

275. Troeltsch, *Social Teachings*, 1:80–81.

276. See, for example, Roetzel, *World That Shaped*, 22; Bultmann, *Theology of the New Testament*, 1:218; Pilgrim, *Uneasy Neighbors*, 7–11; Schreiner, *Romans*, 448–50.

277. See Pilgrim, *Uneasy Neighbors*, 27–30.

they cannot be in mind here since Paul is counseling submission.[278] This seems like a difficult thesis to maintain, given that Paul and his coworkers use the same terminology when condemning the powers elsewhere and given the interweaving we have already observed between the religious and political (the powers and the rulers) in Paul's day.[279]

However, this position is also more frequently justified by appealing to the call to suffer patiently, love enemies, and refuse to engage in violence towards enemies, which immediately precedes this passage (Rom 12:9–21). This can play out in two ways. First, Jesus loyalists can refuse to enact vengeance because they accept the state's role in enacting vengeance.[280] Second, it means that even when the designated authorities behave as enemies of Jesus loyalists, the Jesus loyalists are to continue to submit to them as a manifestation of this nonviolent love of enemies.[281] Now, granted, the history of Christianity is full of stories about victims of violence being told to passively continue to submit to those who enact that violence (from patriarchs to soldiers to kings to cops to capitalists). But, as we have already seen, Paul and his coworkers did have a clearly articulated belief in the need to fight back against unjust and oppressive structures. The Pauline call for peace and concord is more about facilitating alliances among peoples who had been previously divided so that they could be united against their common enemy—the structures of Roman imperialism. Therefore, I think those who try to connect Rom 13:1–7 to Rom 12:9–21 in this way are doing a disservice to Paulinism.

Ultimately, this isolated reading of Rom 13:1–7 is untenable because it flies in the face of everything else we have learned about Paulinism. There is a fundamental conflict of loyalties here. Elsewhere, Paul and his

---

278. See Schreiner, *Romans*, 448.

279. Hence, Schreiner's argument that the paying of taxes is an "earthly" and not "spiritual" activity also collapses (see Schreiner, *Romans*, 448).

280. Cullmann, *State in the New Testament*, 57; a position immediately problematized by our prior reflection on 1 Cor 6.

281. See, in various permutations, Wright, *Paul*, 78; "Paul and Caesar," 190; Jennings, *Outlaw Justice*, 188–89; Schottroff, "'Give to Caesar,'" 224–27, 234–37; Cousar, *Letters of Paul*, 156–57; Schrage, *Ethics of the New Testament*, 236. Jewett relates this love of enemies and submission to the state to Judean uprisings and suggests it communicates the following message: "Your obligation to Israel does not mean participating in their war on Rome" (Jewett, *Christian Tolerance*, 114–16). Crossan and Borg also think that Paul, motivated by a self-sacrificing love of enemies, engages in a bit of "rhetorical panic" because he is afraid that Christians might get caught up in some revolution fervor and, consequently, kill instead of being killed (Crossan and Borg, *First Paul*, 118–20).

coworkers have made it clear that those who are loyal to the crucified Anointed Jesus cannot also be loyal to the crucifying August Caesar. Because of this conflict of loyalties, Paul himself, along with many (all?) of his coworkers, suffered a great deal of persecutions and punishments. In light of this, it seems absurd to suggest that the Pauline faction appreciated the *pax Romana*. If anything, their travels in and among various vanquished, oppressed, colonized, enslaved, and impoverished populations gave them far greater insight into the violent and death-dealing nature of Roman authority. How, then, are we to make sense of this passage?

A Time to Lie

I believe the explanation that best makes sense of Rom 13:1-7 is one that posits that Paul and his coworkers are deliberately lying in order to mislead any spies, censors, or unreliable parties who might get their hands on the letter or hear it being read.[282] This, then, explains why the Pauline faction can refer to the foolish, wicked, and blind authorities who have persecuted them at every step, as *leitourgoi* or as a *diakonos* of God (terms they have applied to themselves elsewhere). It also makes sense of their sudden reversal regarding the value of the judgments made by the authorities and their ability to reward good and punish evil. It explains why a person who has boasted of all the times he has been subjected to the terror of state-based punishment, who has urged communal practices that put people at risk of experiencing the same, can now warn people to live in a way where they submit to the governing authorities and avoid being terrorized by the state. This is also why a call to submission is paired with a call to honor those to whom honor is due, even though the Pauline faction has spent considerable time and effort dismantling and devaluing Graeco-Roman notions of honor in order to embrace shame in the company of the crucified.

When viewed as an act of deception, it is important to ask about the identity of the "God" mentioned in Rom 13:1-7. Surely, from the perspective of any Roman censors or spies, this God would be understood as the divine Caesar (whom, it should be recalled, the Pauline faction has already referred to as "the god of this age" in 2 Cor 4:4 and whose

---

282. For those who make suggestions along these lines, although generally not fully following through on them, see Sanders, *Paul: The Apostle's Life*, 693-95; Jennings, *Outlaw Justice*, 191-92; Carter, *Roman Empire*, 133-34; and especially Herzog, "Dissembling," 339-60.

THE LAWLESSNESS OF GOOD NEWS IN THE MAKING

extended family is also included in the reference to the many so-called gods in heaven and on earth in 1 Cor 8:5), who appoints and commissions the superior designated authorities. Thus, the governing authorities are *leitourgoi* and a *diakonos* of Caesar, whereas Paul and his coworkers are *diakonoi* and *leitourgoi* of Jesus. To illustrate this, it is fruitful to reread the passage, substituting the word "Caesar" for the word "God":

> (1) Let every soul be subject to superior designated authorities. For there is no designated authority if not from [Caesar] and the existing ones have been appointed (commissioned) by [Caesar]. (2) Therefore, those wholeheartedly (with militant overtones) resisting the designated authorities have resisted those instituted by [Caesar] and those who resist will receive judgment (with overtones of legal condemnation) on themselves. [Or: those who oppose the order of things are opposing [Caesar's] ordering of things and, when they act out that opposition, they can expect to be judged and condemned for their actions.] (3) For the rulers are not a terror to the good work but to evil. Moreover, do you want to not be terrified by the designated authority? Do the good and you will be appropriately praised by him. (4) For, he is an appointed minister (*diakonos*) of [Caesar] to you for the good. But if you do evil, be terrified, for he does not bear the sword (the "slaughter-knife") in vain. An appointed minister (*diakonos* again!) of [Caesar], he is an avenger, exercising wrath on the one actively performing evil. (5) Therefore, it is necessary to be subjected, not only because of wrath, but also because of conscience. (6) Indeed, also because of this, pay taxes for they are [Caesar's] appointed ministers (*leitourgoi*—as defined above) totally committed to continually attending to the public good by this means. (7) Render to all their dues (*opheilas*)—taxes to whom taxes are due, tolls to whom tolls are due, terror to whom terror is due, honor to whom honor is due (my translation).

The passage makes perfect sense when read in this way. Thus, over against the various provisos or explanations offered by scholars from all camps, I believe Rom 13:1–7 actually urges completely unqualified obedience to Caesar. The value of the passage to the Pauline faction is that it (hopefully) deceives any censors or "false siblings" (like those mentioned in Gal 2:4) who would be troubled or confused by what they had read or heard thus far and who might respond to the letter by reporting the assembly (or assemblies) at Rome to the designated authorities.[283]

283. Interestingly, Schottroff argues that appeals to this passage would be deemed

Part of what reveals this to be an act of deception is the recollection that the Pauline faction affirms that there is ultimately only one God, the father of Jesus, who has adopted all Jesus loyalists into his family, and one Lord, Jesus (see, most obviously, 1 Cor 8:6), and so those who are aware of the work of the Pauline faction cannot take the injunction in Rom 13:1–7 seriously. But I also believe that Paul and his coworkers signal that they are lying while also trying to maintain the deception in the verses that immediately follow this passage. Thus, in Rom 13:8, immediately after talking about rendering everyone their dues (*opheilas*—whether those dues be taxes, tolls, terror, or honor), Paul and his coworkers immediately write that Jesus loyalists are to owe (*opheilete*) no one anything but are, instead, to love one another in the law-fulfilling (which, as we have already seen, is also a law-violating) manner already mentioned. Now, this may make the ears of the censors tingle, and so the Pauline faction is quick to placate them again and argue that loving in this law-fulfilling way means avoiding things like adultery, murder, theft, and coveting (Rom 13:9).[284] But then, Paul and his coworkers quickly return to saying that loving others in a way that causes them no harm (i.e., in a way that prioritizes the well-being of one's neighbor over the rule of law) is the fulfillment of the law (Rom 13:10). This then leads in Rom 13:11 to a fuller expression of an anti-imperial sentiment which posits that the Jesus loyalists are now nearer to salvation than when they first believed (i.e., they are nearer to salvation as members of the body of Jesus than when they were members of the body of Caesar and participants in the salvation he offered), and so, given that they still exist in a time of conflict and night when the works of darkness continue to be practiced, they are to put on armor of light (Rom 13:12). Here, again, the censors may become concerned, so Paul and his coworkers placate them once again by describing the works of darkness in terms of orgies, drunkenness, and sexual immorality (Rom 13:13). However, in Rom 13:14, the Pauline faction conclude by urging the Jesus loyalists at Rome to put on the Lord Jesus Anointed and make no provisions for the flesh (which, as we have seen, refers to the body of Caesar) and its lusts.

---

insufficient by any concerned authorities who would find statements made in the rest of the letter too troubling to be placated by what is written in Rom 13:1–7 (Schottroff, "'Give to Caesar,'" 227–29).

284. Even though, as mentioned above, there is likely a veiled criticism of elite Roman males in this passage.

Consequently, it seems more plausible to read Rom 13:1–7 as an example of one of the ways in which members of oppressed but resistant populations lie in order to serve Life and resist Death.[285] They play a game of cat and mouse and try to pull a fast one over on the bosses, even as they wink and nudge and signal what they are on about to those more deeply involved in the movement. If there was any confusion, Phoebe would be well-equipped to work this out in person once she determined who was safe and who was not among the Jesus loyalists at Rome. Indeed, it is likely that the only reason this truly unique passage exists in the letter to the Romans (if we decide to treat it as though it is not an interpolation) is because Paul and his co-workers are writing to an assembly (or assemblies) they have never visited, situated at the central hub of the empire. They may know several people involved there, but they may be much less certain about those on the periphery of the movement, how closely it is being watched (given the recent return of Judeans to Rome after Claudius expelled them), or how safe it is to speak openly. What is clear based on this reading, however, is that Jesus loyalists are no more to submit to the authorities than they are to view Caesar as god, or owe anything to anyone except to love them in ways that exceed, violate, and fulfill the law.

Conclusion: The Fire This Time

This, then, brings our study of Paulinism to an end. I have tried to leave no stone unturned and present as comprehensive an image as possible. At the end of the day, when it comes to the socioeconomics and politics of Paul and his coworkers, I believe that this reading is the most plausible one. Furthermore, I believe that one of the strengths of understanding Paulinism in this way is that it intimately links the so-called "Pauline mission" to what Jesus was doing in Judea prior to Paul. The Pauline faction essentially took an Indigenous resistance movement and extended it into a resistance movement that transcended divisions (between Judeans and other nationalities, between people of diverse genders, between slaves

---

285. And I, too, in my journey to become a safe and useful friend and accomplice to people experiencing oppression have found that lying to death-dealing authorities is often a useful tactic to deploy when operating in the service of Life and pursuing the kind of law-fulfilling but law-breaking love that does no harm to one's neighbor. As for oppressed people themselves, lying is simply a part of surviving at times. I personally learned this lesson well when I was a child growing up in a home with an unstable, violent (but devoutly Christian) father.

and freedpeople) used by Rome to divide, conquer, and perpetually rule those whom they vanquished and left for dead. However, further developing that thesis regarding the relation of the Pauline faction to Jesus's work in Judea would potentially take another volume the size of this one. I would simply like to conclude with a hypothesis about the burning of Rome in 64 CE and the death of Paul.

Given the ways in which Paul intimately identified with Jesus and tried to follow his trajectory, I sometimes wonder if Paul went to Rome for the same reason that Jesus went to Jerusalem. That is to say, I wonder if he went to Rome to engage in an act of property destruction at the very heart of the empire he sought to resist, knowing that doing so would almost certainly result in his own death at the hands of imperial administrators of justice. Setting fire to Rome, to Nero's very palace and the central neighborhoods of the city at the center of the world, would be just such a powerful and symbolic act. After all, just like Jesus's action in the Jerusalem temple during Passover signified much more than simply flipping a few tables, so also arson, in the Roman political discourse, was associated with the assassination of rulers, a Saturnalian reversal of values, and the destruction of the state.[286] Engaging in this kind of action will also fit with the image we have of Pauline zeal (a zeal the Pauline faction continues to speak positively of throughout their letters), the warfare imagery they deploy, and the limits they place around love. This would also make good sense of the interpretation of Rom 13:1–7 that I have offered—if you are going to Caesar's house to burn it down, you probably do not want to proclaim this in advance but, instead, would want to present yourself as coming in a non-threatening, friendly manner. Consequently, when a fire sweeps through Rome in 64 CE—almost completely destroying ten of fourteen districts and partially destroying Nero's palace—and when Paul is killed in the subsequent persecution of Jesus loyalists (as he likely was), one must ask the question: who started the fire?[287]

---

286. See, for example, Cicero, *Cat.* 1.6; 2.10; 3.21.

287. On the details of what the fire destroyed, where it was started, and how Nero responded, see Tacitus, *Annals* 15:38–44. Of course, as Neil Elliott points out, the observation that Paul himself was executed by Rome bears implications for how we understand him. As Elliott says, "Perhaps the greatest irony of Paul's legacy in our day is just this: that we cannot hear the blow of the executioner's sword let alone the sharp-edged proclamation that brought that blow down upon the apostle's neck, above the chorus of imperial acolytes around us who hymn [Rom 13:1–7] as a magic charm to protect the policies and profits of the already rich" (Elliott, *Liberating Paul*, 226).

Nero blamed the Jesus loyalists, but later historians, especially those with either an anti-Nero or pro-Christian bias, tend to blame Nero.[288] Even anti-imperial Pauline scholars incline to this interpretation. Thus, for example, Brigitte Kahl argues that in "Nero's fire," the Jesus loyalists are an ideal substitute that can be blamed and then executed because of their "transgression of civil order, their transnational character, their 'conquest' of Rome and blasphemous neglect of its god(s), and their origin from a man whom Rome had publicly exihibited [sic] as a Dying Jew and disposed of as a Dead Jew."[289] The early Jesus loyalists are, indeed, an ideal scapegoat—so ideal that it may actually make better sense to view them as the actual culprits. After all, some historians present a different image of Nero's response to the fire. Tacitus argues that Nero not only tried to extinguish the blaze and assist others once he learned that Rome was burning, but he also suffered considerable losses during the fire, and Tacitus highlights that, although some argued that Nero was simply trying to clear ground to build a new palace, the fire started well away from where that palace ended up being built (and the new palace incorporated elements that Nero salvaged from the palace that was damaged during the fire and replicated other parts of it that had been lost). Was Nero trying to pull a fast one over on the Romans and things got more out of control than he had intended—or did someone else start the fire? Personally, I find it quite plausible to imagine that Jesus loyalists associated with the Pauline faction started the fire.[290] Nero may have used the fire to his own ends, but this does not mean that he started it. After all, even if Nero did start the fire, who actually cast the torches? Did Nero become aware of the Jesus loyalists' plot to burn Rome and pave the way for it to succeed— for example, by pulling the guards away from certain districts at certain times—so that he could use it to his own ends? This is certainly a strategy that imperial powers have used many times over the course of history. Be that as it may, participation in such a plot seems like a fitting final act for Paul, the international ambassador of the crucified and risen Anointed Jesus who resisted the death-dealing powers of his day by participating in the gospeling of a treasonous uprising of Life. Indeed, as the fire raged, it is hard not to imagine Paul exultantly saying, "burn motherfucker, burn!"

288. Suetonius, *Twelve Caesars*, 38; Cassius Dio, *Historiae Romanae* 62.

289. Kahl, *Galatians Re-Imagined*, 297.

290. It was a footnote in Cadoux's work that first planted the possibility of this in my mind, even though Cadoux distances those who may have started the fire from Paul himself (see Cadoux, *Early Church and the World*, 100–101n3).

even though he may well have been aware that he would not survive what followed. When he was subsequently fed to animals or slaughtered in games, crucified on the Appian way, or set ablaze as a human torch at a rich man's garden party (or simply struck down where he sat or stood when the guards rushed in on a newly discovered terror cell), as his dying eyes looked out on the smoke still rising from the devastated Palatine and Caelian hills, one must imagine Paul happy.[291]

---

291. I am, of course, riffing on the concluding line of Albert Camus's *The Myth of Sisyphus* (111), an appropriate point of comparison, in my opinion, because it seems to me that history teaches us that the Pauline task is a particularly Sisyphusean endeavor.

POSTSCRIPT BY DAVE DIEWERT

Dan,

You have taken on a massive project here; a Herculean attempt to slay the dragon of empire-affirming readings of Paul that have been built up for centuries into a virtually unassailable fortress defending the material and ideological structures of imperial power. You have carefully worked your way around that fortress, examining the bricks that comprise its walls, finding those that are loose, decaying, or weak, breaking them apart, until significant portions of the wall begin to crumble and those who have been trapped inside, enduring the death-dealing conditions of the imperial order, find their way out.

I must admit that reading through your work has been a challenging task. Your careful consideration of the vast array of scholarly research and arguments, and your thoughtful engagement with the various theories and interpretations of the Pauline material is impressive, and I'm sure under-appreciated by those (like me) unfamiliar with this particular academic field. At the same time, you walk through the thicket of previous Pauline studies at a pace that makes it possible to follow where you're going, and for that I'm grateful.

What is quite remarkable is that you have plunged into the fray of Pauline scholarship and debate from a standpoint outside of the academy. Although you are clearly versed in the numerous issues and arguments surrounding the interpretation of Paul and his coworkers, you approach it with both feet clearly planted in the life and death struggle of people and communities "left for dead." In addition, you have nothing to gain from your work on this project in terms of career advancement or social status. I think this gives you a vantage point that is particularly significant; you see the fallout of empire-affirming readings of Paul on the bodies and in the lives of those around you. Eschewing any notion of objectivity, you enter this work knowing where you stand and with whom, and you're not afraid to name it. This doesn't mean you short-circuit careful analysis or rigorous thought; but you know what's at stake for the masses of oppressed and exploited people forced into conditions of premature death by the ruling class and the structures of power they violently erect and maintain.

Your work has severely weakened the dominant imperial reading of Paul and opened up new possibilities for collective, embodied praxis in the struggle for liberation and life. I want to reflect on some of those openings here in connection with the work on the ground that has occupied my thinking and energy for the past few years. Although I'm not going to make specific links to the many themes you have examined in this work (i.e., mutual aid, transnational associations of oppressed communities, the hegemonic function of law, the death-dealing ways of imperial power, ideologies that solidify domination, etc.), I think they will be evident.

Homeless Communities as Those "Left for Dead"

For the past two decades, homelessness has been on the rise in Vancouver and its surrounding municipalities as I'm sure it has been in your own region. Beginning in 2002, there have been official point-in-time homeless counts across the Metro Vancouver region every three years;[1] and the City of Vancouver has implemented its own homeless count on an annual basis since 2010.[2] Although these stats are always acknowledged to be undercounts and have significant limitations, they provide a baseline for tracking the phenomenon of homelessness. Every year the number has gone up, despite mayoral promises to end homelessness or provincial efforts to increase shelter spaces or limited projects of supportive "welfare rate" housing. The most recent regional count registered an increase of 30

---

1. In 2002 the number of homeless people counted was 1,121 and in the latest count (2017) the number was 3,605. These counts occur over a 24-hour period and include sheltered and unsheltered homeless. They are always an undercount because they are limited in scope and don't include those who are the "hidden" homeless.

2. In 2010, the number of homeless people counted in the City of Vancouver was 1,715; in the most recent count (2019), it was 2,223—a 30-percent increase despite numerous efforts by various levels of government to acquire and build low-income housing throughout the city.

percent and in March 2019, Vancouver recorded its highest count ever. In the City of Surrey, the second largest municipality in the province, the most recent numbers (2017) showed a 50-percent increase in homelessness, and in July 2019, bylaw officials reported to city council that they had identified 95 homeless encampments throughout the city.

The common liberal explanation for the increasing number of people living in our cities without secure shelter focuses on individual misfortune or personal failure. People are homeless because they live with mental illness, are drug-addicted, have suffered injury or personal tragedy, or are just lazy and refuse to work. Depending on where a person lands on this spectrum of explanations, they are deserving of help or deserving of containment and punishment.

One of the striking demographics of the homeless population in my region is the disproportionate number of Indigenous people. Although they make up roughly 4–5 percent of the population, they account for 35–40 percent of homeless people, a discrepancy that clearly cannot be ascribed to individual failure. It's not hard to trace this back to the ongoing impacts of settler colonialism, with its endless quest for Indigenous land, dispossession of Indigenous people from their traditional territories, nations, and cultures, and implementation of various strategies of elimination. Forcibly removed from their land, pushed onto reserves, targeted for genocide, and thrust into deep poverty, many move to the cities and survive as best they can on the streets or in cheap housing where they are displaced repeatedly by the forces of gentrification.

When those who experience homelessness are asked why they survive in shelters or on the streets, they identify reasons beyond their individual control: rents are too high, income is too low, and vacancy rates are shrinking fast. These point in the direction of societal failure, a refusal to distribute collective wealth in a way that would meet the basic needs of everyone. And this failure is not due to some bureaucratic miscalculation or technical flaw in the system. Massive inequality is inevitable in a colonial and capitalist social order that is based on the theft of Indigenous land and resources, the dispossession and elimination of Indigenous people, the prioritizing of profit over people and individual competition over collective solidarity, and a neoliberal politics of austerity. When housing is a commodity that is bought and sold in the market to the highest bidder, when private property is a site of speculation for the sake of capital accumulation, when welfare levels are kept well below the poverty line and wages are suppressed, and when the state refuses to build adequate social housing, the social conditions for ever-expanding homelessness are produced and reproduced.

So I think it's fair to say that people who experience the structural violence of poverty and homelessness are those who fit within your category of the "left for dead." And this is not just a rhetorical phrase or figure of speech: recent reports indicate that homeless people have roughly half the life expectancy as those with housing,[3] and over the course of one year (2015–2016), homeless deaths in BC rose 140 percent.[4] Having to endure the conditions of inclement weather, constant hunger, social stigma, criminalization, and various mechanisms of social control undermines physical, mental, and spiritual health, and thrusts people into a place of premature death.

Imperial Power and Its Collaborators

Although the settler colonial state and the capitalist economy it serves and protects are responsible for the production of homelessness, the ruling class deals with it as a social management crisis, not a structural problem woven into the entire system. With the emergence of capitalism, those who refused to work in the industrial factories were criminalized through vagrancy laws and forced into workhouses or prisons.[5] When vagrancy legislation was struck down, municipal bylaws came into effect that targeted the non-capitalist survival strategies of unemployed workers. Police, bylaw officers, and private security hired by business associations spend much of their time and resources preventing loitering, panhandling, squeegeeing, and dumpster diving, pursuing low-level drug dealing and petty theft, and dismantling homeless encampments. Those who are unemployed and out in the public pose a threat to the interests of private property and business owners, so the carceral apparatus

---

3. See the 2014 report by *Megaphone Magazine* (Condon and McDermid, *Dying on the Streets*). Across the country, "In 2017, there were 22 cities that reported the number of people experience homelessness who lost their lives without a place to call home. Out of those cities that reported, 2,525 homeless community members passed away. Consulting reports about deaths of people experiencing homelessness in 2016, we estimate that at least 13,000 people pass away each year while without housing" (National Coalition for the Homeless, "Remembering Those Lost to Homelessness").

4. Between 2015 and 2016 there were 175 deaths among homeless people in BC, an increase of 140 percent (BC Coroners Service, "Reportable Deaths of Homeless Individuals").

5. See Neocleous, *Fabrication of Social Order.*

of the state is deployed to surveil, remove, and discipline them, and restore "public order."

Criminalization and the use of "hard power" (cops, courts, and prisons) is one of the main responses of the state to the social tensions that emerge with increasing homelessness, and it is usually cloaked in the discourse of "public safety." Of course the "public" whose safety and well-being are of most concern to the ruling class are business and property owners, even though homeless people face greater violence of various forms daily. More recently, we have seen tent cities dismantled through court injunctions based on fire safety issues, another component of the "public safety" argument that is weaponized for the sake of displacement and discipline.

The state also relies on the "soft power" of social institutions like healthcare and social services to manage the presence of unhoused people. Social workers are tasked with moving them into (often unsafe) temporary shelters where they "disappear" from public view and can be regulated by staff who are in regular contact with police. Mental health regimes can be imposed on people such that non-compliance will result in the loss of potential housing, search warrants and arrest, or forced hospitalization. While social and mental health services are important, workers have a great deal of power to regulate and punish those who don't fully comply with policies or procedures, and standing behind or alongside them are "outreach workers" with guns.[6]

Over the past decade, municipal and provincial governments have focused on the construction of (temporary or permanent) "supportive housing" for people who are living in shelters or on the streets, operated by non-profit housing providers. In supportive housing, residents are under constant surveillance, provided minimal food, forced to comply with program agreements with requisite mental health or addiction components, and have restricted visitor policies. It's a form of "soft" incarceration that is marketed as the best solution to the crisis of homelessness

---

6. When a significant homeless encampment emerged along a two-block strip in Surrey, the city implemented a "Surrey Outreach Team" comprised of twelve police and four bylaw officers to surveil, contain, harass, and discipline those surviving on the sidewalks. After eighteen months, the encampment was forcibly removed and people were scattered into temporary trailer units, shelters, the streets, or the bushes. This police-led management and removal strategy paved the way for a massive gentrification plan for the area. Recently RCMP members of this team have been deployed to form a new Police Mental Health Outreach Team, sewing enforcement into mental health interventions.

to the "public" who are vehemently opposed to having social housing projects located in their neighborhood. The emphasis is on management and social control rather than on housing that is dignified, adequate, and secure.

In addition to these state-orchestrated and funded responses to homelessness, there are various community reactions to the presence of unhoused people on the streets or in small encampments. On the one hand, community groups (especially churches or religious organizations) engage in acts of charity, handing out socks at Christmas, opening up soup kitchens, or providing emergency weather shelters. But these acts of charity (as you clearly articulate), while they may relieve immediate survival needs, not only reinforce the system that produces massive inequality, they mask it behind voluntary gestures of benevolence. The violence of poverty is never exposed and opposed; charity paves the way for its entrenchment behind circumscribed acts of compassion.

The other kind of community response, especially in smaller cities, is hostile and aggressive public opposition and vigilante attacks that try to drive homeless people out of the neighborhood in order to restore "public order." Local residents, acting alone or as a group, use various means of intimidation and violence to accomplish their aim of coerced removal. They justify their hostility by claiming that homeless people are criminals and should be jailed, or drug addicts and should be forced into treatment; and that the state is not doing enough to fulfill its policing function and ensure public safety. Vigilante aggression and hate directed against the homeless (and their supporters) in places like Maple Ridge and Nanaimo have taken various forms: verbal insults, threats of bodily harm, thrown objects, slashing or setting fire to tents, and large organized protests and confrontations outside tent cities led by the Soldiers of Odin. Of course more subtle but still harmful and dehumanizing expressions of antagonism can be heard on mainstream media or in public hearings as middle-class homeowners and representatives from business improvement associations rail against the presence of homeless drug users in their neighborhoods.

These state and community responses all target desperately poor unsheltered people for surveillance, containment, punishment, and removal. For them it's a waste management problem; unemployed and unemployable workers who don't contribute to the economy, don't submit to the daily disciplines of waged labor, are outside of civil society, and impede the accumulation of profit by their presence on the streets and their strategies of survival, are deemed disruptive and redundant. Construed as individual failures and threats to the colonial and capitalists social order, they are forced to endure conditions of premature death.

So-called "solutions" (i.e., more shelters, meager and inadequate housing, increased policing and social workers, private security, surveillance cameras, etc.) prove to be completely ineffective because they don't address the root causes (colonial dispossession and capitalist accumulation) but operate within the logic and mechanisms of the market and the carceral state. So as housing costs soar and incomes stagnate or drop, people are continually tossed into the streets to fend for themselves and to be accosted by cops, bylaw, or vigilantes. It's not a question of individual moral failure or tragic circumstances; the real issue is the dominant social order and the structures of ruling class power that violently maintain their material and ideological ascendancy.

People Experiencing Homelessness—a Global Perspective

We talk about "homeless people" as though they are a distinct social group: people without housing presumably due to issues of addiction, mental health, past experiences of trauma, or moral flaws. There's a clear divide between "us" (hardworking tenants or homeowners) and "them." But people move in and out of homelessness for various periods of time and for various reasons, often because they have lost their jobs or can't work, or they have had to leave their Indigenous communities and find ways to survive in urban centers. So it makes more sense to think of homeless people as part of the working class who are currently unemployed and exist in a state of deep poverty; and for Indigenous people, as belonging to diverse Indigenous communities who have been dispossessed from their lands, nations, and cultural practices by the settler colonial Canadian state. Perhaps we should think of homelessness, then, as a condition produced by capitalist and colonial forces that is held out as a threat over the heads of all working class and Indigenous people: abandon your non-capitalist land relations and practices, sell your bodies in the labor market, endure wage exploitation and contribute to the profits of bosses and landlords, or suffer severe material deprivation, exclusion from society, and carceral state violence.

Working class and urban Indigenous people who are forced into the condition of homelessness can and do organize themselves in encampments and work together for their survival. Tent cities create spaces where mutual aid and support are practiced, political consciousness is developed, and collective self-determination is implemented. Residents in tent cities look out for one another in multiple ways, sharing food and clothing, responding to immediate health needs such as practicing harm reduction and responding to overdoses, and protecting each other against aggressive external threats of police, bylaw officers and vigilantes. In addition, they practice non-capitalist, decolonized land relations since their presence on (usually) public land is based on a relation of use not ownership and exchange. The land where they pitch their tents and build their makeshift structures is the basis of survival and collective empowerment, not profit.

In these spaces, unhoused working class and urban Indigenous people build their political power—formulating political demands for dignified housing, pushing back on police and bylaw repression, and organizing their life together outside of the regime of private property. People in these communities belong to a global class struggle and a revolutionary project that aims to overthrow capitalist and colonial power, the true sources of their exclusion and deprivation. They are agents of their own emancipation, not simply recipients of meager social services or voluntary charity. And, like workers who organize themselves to fight back against the exploitation and repression of their capitalist owners, or Indigenous communities defending their territories against colonial theft, people experiencing homelessness build their political power and enlarge their capacity as participants and leaders in the fight for deep social transformation.

Homeless people are not only part of the working class, they are also part of a global movement of displaced people.[7] Imperialist competition for access and control over resources has created a growing flood of migrants and refugees, displaced from their homes, villages and cities, and moving within and across borders in search of survival and safety. After they risk their lives crossing land and sea, they end up in places often hostile to their presence, in makeshift camps, under the surveillance of state police and the management of institutions and NGOs. Here they develop their own structures of mutual aid and support, economic distribution, and political organization. These camps of externally and internally displaced people usually end up being demolished by the state

---

7. See Chen and Drury, "Dead End of Homeless Nationalism."

because poor people who organize are always seen as a threat to those in power; but inevitably the camps are rebuilt as acts of self-determination, defiance and resistance that push beyond survival to life and liberation.

The same forces that create the conditions of global mass displacement and migration are at work in the cities of my region, driving people out of their homes and neighborhoods into shelters, tent city encampments and the streets. Rather than see these precarious communities of homeless people as a unique social group, we should view them as part of the growing swell of globally displaced people. People thrust into these spaces for survival, seeing themselves as sharing the same fate and facing the same enemies of imperialism, colonialism, and capitalism, can build communal links and dual power that can resist and overcome the death-dealing imperial powers that crush us all, and struggle for a world that can contain and nourish multiple worlds of human solidarity and flourishing.

Perhaps it's in the multitudinous encampments of those left for dead—homeless tent cities, Indigenous communities, refugee camps—that we will witness a global movement of rebellion against the dominant powers, and a revolutionary uprising in pursuit of freedom and life. And if you are right, my friend, that's where the spirit of Jesus and Paul can be found as well—not in the middle-class churches sanctioned by imperial powers, but in the communities of subaltern humanity forging a new world of intercommunal solidarity, material sufficiency, and mutual care.

BIBLIOGRAPHY

Agamben, Giorgio. *Homo Sacer: Sovereign Power and Bare Life*. Edited by Werner Hamacher and David E. Wellbery. Translated by Daniel Heller-Roazen. Meridian: Crossing Aesthetics Series. Stanford: Stanford University Press, 1998.
———. *State of Exception*. Translated by Kevin Attell. Chicago: University of Chicago Press, 2005.
———. *The Time That Remains: A Commentary on the Letter to the Romans*. Edited by Werner Hamacher and David E. Wellbery. Translated by by Patricia Dailey. Meridian: Crossing Aesthetics Series. Stanford: Stanford University Press, 2005.
Agosto, Efrain. "Patronage and Commendation, Imperial and Anti-Imperial." In *Paul and the Roman Imperial Order*, edited by Richard A. Horsley, 103–23. Harrisburg, PA: Trinity, 2004.
Alexander, Michelle. *The New Jim Crow: Mass Incarceration in the Age of Colorblindness* Foreword by Cornel West. New York: New Press, 2015.
Ando, Clifford. *Imperial Ideology and the Provincial Loyalty in the Roman Empire*. Berkeley: University of California Press, 2000.
Badiou, Alain. *St. Paul: The Foundations of Universalism*. Translated by Ray Brassier. Cultural Memory in the Present. Stanford: Stanford University Press, 2003.
Bakunin, Michael. *Bakunin on Anarchy: Selected Works by the Activist-Founder of World Anarchism*. Edited and translated by Sam Dolgoff. Preface by Paul Avrich. New York: Alfred A. Knopf, 1972.
Bammel, Ernst. "Romans 13." *Jesus and the Politics of His Day*, edited by Ernst Bammel and C. F. D. Moule, 363–85. Cambridge: Cambridge University Press, 1984.
Bammel, Ernst, and C. F. D. Moule, eds. *Jesus and the Politics of His Day*. Cambridge: Cambridge University Press, 1984.
Banks, Robert. *Paul's Idea of Community: The Early House Churches in Their Historical Setting*. Grand Rapids: Eerdmans, 1988.
Barclay, John M. G. "The Family as the Bearer of Religion in Judaism and Early Christianity." In *Constructing Early Christian Families: Family as Social Reality and Metaphor*, edited by Halvor Moxnes, 66–80. London: Routledge, 1997.
———. *Obeying the Truth: A Study of Paul's Ethics in Galatians*. Studies in the New Testament and Its World. Edinburgh: T & T Clark, 1988.
Barrett, C. K. *Paul: An Introduction to His Thought*. Louisville: Westminster John Knox, 1994.
Barry-Shaw, Nikolas, and Dru Oja Jay. *Paved with Good Intentions: Canada's Development NGOs from Idealism to Imperialism*. Winnipeg: Fernwood, 2012.

Barsamian, David. *Louder than Bombs: Interviews from the Progressive Magazine*. New York: South End, 2004.

Bartholomew, Craig, et al., eds. *A Royal Priesthood? The Use of the Bible Ethically and Politically: A Dialogue with Oliver O'Donovan*. Scripture and Hermeneutics Series 3. Grand Rapids: Zondervan, 2002.

Barton, Stephen C. "Money Matters: Economic Relations and the Transformation of Value in Early Christianity." In *Engaging Economics: New Testament Scenarios and Early Christian Reception*, edited by Bruce W. Longenecker and Kelly D. Liebengood, 37–59. Grand Rapids: Eerdmans, 2009.

Bates, Matthew W. *Salvation by Allegiance Alone: Rethinking Faith, Works, and the Gospel of Jesus the King*. Foreword by Scot McKnight. Grand Rapids: Baker Academic, 2017.

Beker, J. Christiaan. *Paul the Apostle: The Triumph of God in Life and Thought*. Philadelphia: Fortress, 1984.

Bird, Frederick. "Early Christianity as an Unorganized Ecumenical Movement." In *Handbook of Early Christianity: Social-Scientific Approaches*, edited by Anthony J. Blasi et al., 225–46. New York: Altamira, 2002.

Blanton, Ward. *A Materialism for the Masses: Saint Paul and the Philosophy of Undying Life*. Insurrections: Critical Studies in Religion, Politics, and Culture. New York: Columbia University Press, 2014.

Blasi, Anthony J., et al., eds. *Handbook of Early Christianity: Social-Scientific Approaches*. New York: Altamira, 2002.

Bockmuehl, Markus. *Jewish Law in Gentile Churches: Halakhah and the Beginning of Christian Public Ethics*. Grand Rapids: Baker Academic, 2000.

Boff, Leonardo, and Clodovis Boff. *Introducing Liberation Theology*. Translated by Paul Burns. Maryknoll, NY: Orbis, 1992.

Bormann, Lukas, et al., eds. *Religious Propaganda and Missionary Competition in the New Testament World: Essay Honoring Dieter Georgi*. Leiden: Brill, 1994.

Bornkamm, Gunther. *Early Christian Experience*. Translated by Paul L. Hammer. The New Testament Library Series. London: SCM, 1969.

———. *Paul: Paulus*. Translated by D. M. G. Stalker. New York: Harper & Row, 1971.

Bourgois, Philippe, and Jeffrey Schonberg. *Righteous Dopefiend*. Berkeley: University of California Press, 2009.

Boyarin, Daniel. "Paul and the Genealogy of Gender." In *A Feminist Companion to Paul*, edited by Amy-Jill Levine with Marrianne Blickenstaff, 13–41. Cleveland: Pilgrim, 2004.

———. *A Radical Jew: Paul and the Politics of Identity*. Berkeley: University of California Press, 1994.

British Columbia Coroners Service. "Reportable Deaths of Homeless Individuals, 2007–2016." March 21, 2019. Online. https://www2.gov.bc.ca/assets/gov/birth-adoption-death-marriage-and-divorce/deaths/coroners-service/statistical/homeless.pdf.

Bryan, Christopher. *Render to Caesar: Jesus, the Early Church, and the Roman Superpower*. Oxford: Oxford University Press, 2005.

Bultmann, Rudolph. *Existence and Faith: Shorter Writings of Rudolph Bultmann*. Edited and Translated by Schubert M. Ogden. London: Collins Clear-Type, 1964.

———. *Primitive Christianity: In Its Contemporary Setting*. Translated by R. H. Fuller. London: Thomas and Hudson, 1956.

———. *Theology of the New Testament*. Vol. 1. Translated by Kendrick Grobel. London: SCM, 1952.
Cadoux, Cecil John. *The Early Church and the World: A History of the Christian Attitude to Pagan Society and the State Down to the Time of Constantinus*. Edinburgh: T & T Clark, 1955.
Callahan, Allen Dwight. "Paul, Ekklesia, and Emancipation in Corinth: A Coda on Liberation Theology." In *Paul and Politics: Ekklesia, Israel, Imperium, Interpretation. Essays in Honor of Krister Stendahl*, edited by Richard A. Horsley, 216–23. Harrisburg, PA: Trinity, 2000.
Campenhausen, Hans von. *Ecclesiastical Authority and Spiritual Power in the Church of the First Three Centuries*. Translated by J. A. Baker. Stanford: Stanford University Press, 1969.
Camus, Albert. *The Myth of Sisyphus*. Translated by Justin O'Brien. Introduction by James Wood. London: Penguin, 2000.
Carter, Warren. *John and Empire: Initial Explorations*. New York: T & T Clark, 2008.
———. *The Roman Empire and the New Testament: An Essential Guide*. Nashville: Abingdon, 2006.
———. "Vulnerable Power: The Roman Empire Challenged by the Early Christians." In *Handbook of Early Christianity: Social-Science Approaches*, edited by Lukas Bormann et al., 453–88. New York: Altamira, 2002.
Castelli, Elizabeth A. *Imitating Paul: A Discourse of Power*. Literary Currents in Biblical Interpretation. Louisville: Westminster John Knox, 1991.
Cavanaugh, William T. *The Myth of Religious Violence: Secular Ideology and the Roots of Modern Conflict*. Oxford: Oxford University Press, 2009.
Cerfaux, Lucien. *The Church in the Theology of St. Paul*. Translated by Geoffrey Webb and Adrian Walker. London: Herder and Herder, 1959.
Chen, Listen, and Ivan Drury. "The Dead End of Homeless Nationalism: From Refugee Camps to Tent Cities, Displaced Peoples Unite!" *The Volcano* (blog), September 9, 2019. Online. http://thevolcano.org/2019/09/09/the-dead-end-of-homeless-nationalism-from-refugee-camps-to-tent-cities-displaced-peoples-unite.
Chow, John K. "Patronage in Roman Corinth." In *Paul and Empire: Religion, Power, and the Life of the Spirit*, edited by Richard A. Horsley, 104–25. Harrisburg, PA: Trinity, 1997.
Clapp, Rodney. *A Peculiar People: The Church as Culture in a Post-Christian Society*. Downers Grove, IL: InterVarsity, 1996.
Clarke, Andrew D. "Jew and Greek, Slave and Free, Male and Female: Paul's Theology of Ethnic, Social and Gender Inclusiveness in Romans 16." In *Rome in the Bible and the Early Church*, edited by Peter Oakes, 103–25. Carlisle: Paternoster, 2002.
Cobb, Charles E., Jr. *This Nonviolent Stuff'll Get You Killed: How Guns Made the Civil Rights Movement Possible*. New York: Basic, 2014.
Coggan, Donald. *Paul: Portrait of a Revolutionary*. London: Hodder & Stoughton, 1984.
Cohn-Sherbok, Dan, and John M. Court, eds. *Religious Diversity in the Graeco-Roman World: A Survey of Recent Scholarship*. Sheffield: Sheffield Academic, 2001.
Condon, Sean, and Jenn McDermid. *Dying on the Streets: Homeless Deaths in British Columbia*. Vancouver, BC: Street Corner Media Foundation, 2014.
Conzelmann, Hans. *History of Primitive Christianity*. Translated by John E. Steely. New York: Abingdon, 1973.

———. *An Outline of the Theology of the New Testament*. Translated by John Bowden. New Testament Library Series. London: SCM, 1969.
Coulthard, Glen Sean. *Red Skins, White Masks: Rejecting the Colonial Politics of Recognition*. Minneapolis: University of Minnesota Press, 2014.
Countryman, Louis William. *The Rich Christians in the Church of the Early Empire: Contradictions and Accommodations*. New York: Edwin Mellen, 1980.
Cousar, Charles B. *An Introduction to the New Testament: Witnesses to God's New Work*. Louisville: Westminster John Knox, 2006.
———. *The Letters of Paul*. Interpreting Biblical Texts. Nashville: Abingdon, 1996.
Crossan, John Dominic. *God and Empire: Jesus Against Rome, Then and Now*. San Francisco: HarperSanFrancisco, 2007.
Crossan, John Dominic, and Jonathan L. Reed. *In Search of Paul: How Jesus's Apostle Opposed Rome's Empire with God's Kingdom. A New Vision of Paul's Words and World*. San Francisco: HarperSanFrancisco, 2004.
Crossan, John Dominic, and Marcus J. Borg. *The First Paul: Reclaiming the Radical Vision Behind the Church's Conservative Icon*. New York: HarperOne, 2009.
Crow, Scott. *Black Flags and Windmills: Hope, Anarchy, and the Common Ground Colective*. Foreword by Kathleen Cleaver and John P. Clark. San Francisco: PM, 2014.
Cullmann, Oscar. *Christ and Time: The Primitive Christian Conception of Time and History*. Translated by Floyd V. Filson. Philadelphia: Westminster, 1964.
———. *Salvation in History*. New Testament Library. Translated by Sidney G. Sowers. London: SCM, 1967.
———. *The State in the New Testament*. New York: Scribner's Sons, 1956.
Dahl, Nils Alstrup. "Euodia and Syntyche and Paul's Letter to the Philippians." In *The Social World of the First Christians: Essays in Honor of Wayne A. Meeks*, edited by L. Michael White and O. Larry Yarbrough, 3–15. Minneapolis: Fortress, 1995.
Dahl, Nils Alstrup, with Paul Donahue. *Studies in Paul: Theology for the Early Christian Mission*. Minneapolis: Augsburg, 1977.
Damholt, Ronald. "Rightwiseness and Justice: A Tale of Translation." *Anglican Theological Review* 97 (2015) 413–32.
Davies, William David. *Jewish and Pauline Studies*. Philadelphia: Fortress, 1984.
———. *Paul and Rabbinic Judaism: Some Rabbinic Elements in Pauline Theology*. Philadelphia: Fortress, 1980.
Deissmann, Adolf. *Light from the Ancient East: The New Testament Illustrated by Recently Discovered Texts of the Graeco-Roman World*. Translated by Lionel R. M. Strachan. Grand Rapids: Baker, 1978.
———. *Paul: A Study in Social and Religious History*. Translated by William E. Wilson. New York: George H. Doran, 1926.
———. *The Religion of Jesus and the Faith of Paul: The Selly Oak Lectures, 1923, On the Communion of Jesus with God and the Communion of Paul with Christ*. Translated by William E. Wilson. London: Hodder & Stoughton, 1923.
deSilva, David A. *Honor, Patronage, Kinship, and Purity: Unlocking New Testament Culture*. Downers Grove, IL: InterVarsity, 2000.
Dewey, Arthur J. "EIS THN SPANIAN: The Future and Paul." In *Religious Propaganda and Missionary Competition in the New Testament World: Essay Honoring Dieter Georgi*, edited by Lukas Bormann et al., 321–49. Leiden: Brill, 1994.

Dio Cocceianus, Cassius. "Historiae Romanae." In *Dio's Roman History*, edited by Earnest Cary et al. New York: Harvard University Press, 1914. Online. http://www.perseus.tufts.edu/hopper/text?doc=Perseus%3Atext%3A2008.01.0593.

Dodd, C. H. *The Meaning of Paul for Today*. New York: Meridian, 1957.

Donfried, Karl P., ed. *The Romans Debate*. Edinburgh: T & T Clark, 1991.

Downs, David. "Is God Paul's Patron? The Economy of Patronage in Pauline Theology." In *Engaging Economics: New Testament Scenarios and Early Christian Reception*, edited by Bruce W. Longenecker and Kelly D. Liebengood, 129–56. Grand Rapids: Eerdmans, 2009.

Dumbrell, William J. *The Search for Order: Biblical Eschatology in Focus*. Grand Rapids: Baker, 1994.

Dunn, James D. G. *Beginning from Jerusalem*. Christianity in the Making 2. Grand Rapids: Eerdmans, 2009.

———. "Diversity in Paul." In *Religious Diversity in the Graeco-Roman World: A Survey of Recent Scholarship*, edited by Dan Cohn-Sherbok and John M. Court, 107–23. Sheffield: Sheffield Academic, 2001.

———. *Jesus Remembered*. Christianity in the Making 1. Grand Rapids: Eerdmans, 2003.

———. *The Theology of Paul the Apostle*. Grand Rapids: Eerdmans, 1998.

Easter, Matthew C. "The *Pistis Christou* Debate: Main Arguments and Responses in Summary." *Currents in Biblical Research* 9 (2010) 33–47.

Eisenstein, Hester. *Feminism Seduced: How Global Elites Used Women's Labor and Ideas to Exploit the World*. Routledge: New York, 2009.

Elias, Jacob W. *Remember the Future: The Pastoral Theology of Paul the Apostle*. Waterloo: Herald, 2006.

Elliott, Neil. "The Apostle Paul and Empire." In *In the Shadow of Empire: Reclaiming the Bible as a History of Faithful Resistance*, edited by Richard A. Horsley, 97–116. Louisville: Westminster John Knox, 2008.

———. "The Apostle Paul's Self-Presentation as Anti-Imperial Performance." In *Paul and the Roman Imperial Order*, edited by Richard A. Horsley, 67–88. Harrisburg, PA: Trinity, 2004.

———. *The Arrogance of Nations: Reading Romans in the Shadow of Empire*. Paul in Critical Contexts. Minneapolis: Fortress, 2008.

———. "Disciplining the Hope of the Poor in Ancient Rome." In *Christian Origins: A People's History of Christianity*, edited by Richard A. Horsley, 177–97. Minneapolis: Fortress, 2005.

———. *Liberating Paul: The Justice of God and the Politics of the Apostle*. Maryknoll, NY: Orbis, 1994.

———. "Paul and the Politics of Empire: Problems and Prospects." In *Paul and Politics: Ekklesia, Israel, Imperium, Interpretation. Essays in Honor of Krister Stendahl*, edited by Richard A. Horsley, 17–39. Harrisburg, PA: Trinity, 2000.

———. "Romans 13:1–7 in the Context of Imperial Propaganda." In *Paul and Empire: Religion and Power in Roman Imperial Society*, edited by Richard A. Horsley, 184–204. Harrisburg, PA: Trinity, 1997.

———. "Strategies of Resistance and Hidden Transcripts in the Pauline Communities." In *Hidden Transcripts and the Arts of Resistance: Applying the Works of James C. Scott to Jesus and Paul*, edited by Richard A. Horsley, 97–122. Semeia Studies 48. Atlanta: SBL, 2004.

BIBLIOGRAPHY

Engberg-Pedersen, Troels. *Paul and the Stoics*. Edinburgh: T & T Clark, 2000.
Engler, Yves. *Canada in Africa: 300 Years of Aid and Exploitation*. Winnipeg: Fernwood, 2015.
Epp, E. J. *Junia: The First Woman Apostle*. Minneapolis: Fortress, 2005.
Esler, Philip F. *Conflict and Identity in Romans: The Social Setting of Paul's Letter*. Minneapolis: Fortress, 2003.
———. "The Mediterranean Context of Early Christianity." In *The Early Christian World*, edited by Philip F. Esler, 3–25. London: Routledge, 2000.
———. *New Testament Theology: Communion and Community*. Minneapolis: Fortress, 2005.
Esler, Philip F., ed. *The Early Christian World*. Vol. 1. London: Routledge, 2000.
Eubanks, Virginia. *Automating Inequality: How High-Tech Tools Profile, Police, and Punish the Poor*. New York: St. Martin's, 2017.
Fanon, Frantz. *The Wretched of the Earth*. Preface by Jean-Paul Sartre. Translated by Constance Farrington. New York: Grove, 1963.
Federici, Silvia. *Caliban and the Witch: Women, the Body, and Primitive Accumulation*. Brooklyn: Autonomedia, 2004.
Fee, Gordon D. *Paul, the Spirit, and the People of God*. Peabody: Hendrickson, 1996.
Fitzgerald, John T., et al., eds. *Early Christianity and Classical Culture: Comparative Studies in Honor of Abraham J. Malherbe*. Supplements to Novum Testamentum Volume 60. Leiden: Brill, 2003.
Fitzpatrick, Joseph P. *Paul: Saint of the Inner City*. New York: Paulist, 1990.
Florus, Lucius Annaeus. *Epitome of Roman History*. Translated by Edward Seymour Forster. London: William Heinemann, 1929. Online. http://www.perseus.tufts.edu/hopper/text?doc=Perseus%3Atext%3A2008.01.0496.
Foucault, Michel. *Abnormal: Lectures at the Collège de France 1974–1975*. Translated by Graham Burchell. Edited by Vario Marchetti and Antonella Salomoni. New York: Picador, 1999.
———. *The Archaeology of Knowledge and the Discourse on Language*. Translated by A. M. Sheridan Smith. New York: Pantheon, 1972.
Fowl, Stephen E. *The Story of Christ in the Ethics of Paul: An Analysis of the Function of the Hymnic Material in the Pauline Corpus*. Journal for the Study of the New Testament Supplement Series 36. Sheffield: JSOT, 1990.
Fredriksen, Paula. *From Jesus to Christ: The Origins of the New Testament Images of Jesus*. New Haven, CT: Yale University Press, 2000.
Friesen, Steven J. "Paul and Economics: The Jerusalem Collection as an Alternative to Patronage." In *Paul Unbound: Other Perspectives on the Apostle*, edited by Mark D. Given, 27–54. Peabody: Hendrickson, 2010.
Furnish, Victor Paul. *The Moral Teaching of Paul: Selected Issues*. Nashville: Abingdon, 1979.
———. *Theology and Ethics in Paul*. Nashville: Abingdon, 1968.
Galinsky, Karl, ed. *The Cambridge Companion to the Age of Augustus*. Cambridge: Cambridge University Press, 2005.
Garnsey, Peter, and Richard Saller. *The Roman Empire: Economy, Society, and Culture*. Berkeley: University of California Press, 1987.
Gaventa, Beverly Roberts. *New Testament Theology: Communion and Community*. Minneapolis: Fortress, 2005.
———. *Our Mother Saint Paul*. Louisville: Westminster John Knox, 2007.

———. "Our Mother St Paul: Toward the Recovery of a Neglected Theme." In *A Feminist Companion to Paul*, edited by Amy-Jill Levine with Marianne Blickenstaff, 85–97. Cleveland: Pilgrim, 2004.

Gelderloos, Peter. *The Failure of Nonviolence: From the Arab Spring to Occupy*. Seattle: Left Bank, 2013.

Georgi, Dieter. *The Opponents of Paul in Second Corinthians*. Translation supervised by the author. Philadelphia: Fortress, 1986.

———. *Remembering the Poor: The History of Paul's Collection for Jerusalem*. Abingdon: Nashville, 1965.

———. *Theocracy: In Paul's Praxis and Theology*. Translated by David E. Green. Minneapolis: Fortress, 1991.

Given, Mark D., ed. *Paul Unbound: Other Perspectives on the Apostle*. Peabody, MA: Hendrickson, 2010.

Gloer, W. Hulitt, ed. *Eschatology and the New Testament: Essays in Honor of George Raymond Beasley-Murray*. Peabody, MA: Hendrickson, 1988.

Goguel, Maurice. *The Primitive Church*. Translated by H. C. Snape. London: George Allen & Unwin, 1964.

González, Justo L. *Faith and Wealth: A History of Christian Ideas on the Origin, Significance, and Use of Money*. San Francisco: HarperSanFrancisco, 1990.

Gordon, Todd. *Imperialist Canada*. Winnipeg: Arbeiter Ring, 2010.

Gordon, Todd, and Jeffrey R. Webber. *Blood of Extraction: Canadian Imperialism in Latin America*. Winnipeg: Fernwood, 2016.

Gorman, Michael J. *Apostle of the Crucified Lord: A Theological Introduction to Paul and His Letters*. Grand Rapids: Eerdmans, 2004.

———. *Cruciformity: Paul's Narrative Spirituality of the Cross*. Grand Rapids: Eerdmans, 2001.

———. *Reading Paul*. Cascade Companions. Eugene, OR: Cascade, 2008.

Graeber, David. *Debt: The First 5,000 Years*. New York: Melville, 2011.

Gramsci, Antonio. *Selections from the Prison Notebooks*. Edited and Translated by Quintin Hoare and Geoffrey Nowell Smith. New York: International, 1971.

Grant, Robert M. *Early Christianity and Society: Seven Studies*. San Francisco: Harper & Row, 1977.

Guérin, Daniel, ed. *No Gods No Masters: An Anthology of Anarchism*. Vol. 2. Translated by Paul Sharkey. San Francisco: AK, 1998.

Gutierrez, Gustavo. *A Theology of Liberation: History, Politics, and Salvation*. Translated and edited by Sister Caridad Inda and John Eagleson. Maryknoll, NY: Orbis, 1973.

Hardin, Justin K. *Galatians and the Imperial Cult: A Critical Analysis of the First-Century Social Context of Paul's Letter*. Wissenschaftliche Untersuchungen zum Neuen Testament 2. Reihe 237. Tubingen: Mohr Siebeck, 2008.

Harink, Douglas. *Paul Among the Postliberals: Pauline Theology Beyond Christendom and Modernity*. Grand Rapids: Brazos, 2003.

———, ed. *Paul, Philosophy, and the Theopolitical Vision: Critical Engagements with Agamben, Badiou, Žižek, and Others*. Theopolitical Visions Series. Eugene, OR: Cascade, 2010.

Harland, Philip A. "Connections with Elites in the World of the Early Christians." In *Handbook of Early Christianity: Social-Science Approaches*, edited by Anthony J. Blasi et al., 385–408. New York: Altamira, 2002.

BIBLIOGRAPHY

Harrill, J. Albert. *The Manumission of Slaves in Earliest Christianity*. Wissenschaftliche Untersuchungen zum Neuen Testament 32. Tubingen: Mohr Siebeck, 1995.

———. "Paul and Slavery." In *Paul in the Greco-Roman World: A Handbook*, edited by J. Paul Sampley, 575–607. New York: Trinity, 2003.

———. *Slaves in the New Testament: Literary, Social, and Moral Dimensions*. Minneapolis: Fortress, 2006.

Hays, Richard B. *The Faith of Jesus Christ: The Narrative Substructure of Galatians 3:1–4:11*. Foreword by Luke Timothy Johnson. Grand Rapids: Eerdmans, 2002.

———. *The Moral Vision of the New Testament: A Contemporary Introduction to New Testament Ethics*. San Francisco: HarperSanFrancisco, 1996.

Heen, Erik M. "The Role of Symbolic Inversion in Utopian Discourse: Apocalyptic Reversal in Paul and the Festival of the Saturnalia/Kronia." In *Hidden Transcripts and the Arts of Resistance: Applying the Works of James C. Scott to Jesus and Paul*, edited by Richard A. Horsley, 123–44. Semeia Studies 48. Atlanta: SBL, 2004.

Heidegger, Martin. *Being and Time*. Translated by Joan Stambaugh. SUNY Series in Contemporary Continental Philosophy. New York: State University of New York Press, 1996.

Hengel, Martin. *Crucifixion: In the Ancient World and the Folly of the Message of the Cross*. Translated by John Bowden. Philadelphia: Fortress, 1977.

———. *Property and Riches in the Early Church: Aspects of a Social History of Early Christianity*. Translated by John Bowden. Philadelphia: Fortress, 1974.

Herzog, William R., II. "Dissembling, a Weapon of the Weak: The Case of Christ and Caesar in Mark 12:13–17 and Romans 13:1–7." *Perspectives in Religious Studies* 21 (1994) 339–60.

Hill, Lance E. *The Deacons of Defence: Armed Resistance and the Civil Rights Movement*. Greensboro, NC: University of North Carolina Press, 2004.

Holmberg, Bengt. *Paul and Power: The Structure of Authority in the Primitive Church as Reflected in the Pauline Epistles*. Philadelphia: Fortress, 1980.

———. *Sociology and the New Testament: An Appraisal*. Minneapolis: Fortress, 1990.

Holsclaw, Geoffrey. "Subjects between Death and Resurrection: Badiou, Žižek, and St. Paul." In *Paul, Philosophy, and the Theopolitical Vision: Critical Engagements with Agamben, Badiou, Žižek, and Others*, edited by Douglas Harink, 155–75. Theopolitical Visions Series. Eugene, OR: Cascade, 2010.

Horne, Gerald. *The Counter-Revolution of 1776: Slave Resistance and the Origins of the United Sates of America*. New York: New York University Press, 2014.

Horrell, David G. *The Social Ethos of the Corinthian Correspondence: Interests and Ideology from 1 Corinthians to 1 Clement*. Studies of the New Testament and Its World. Edinburgh: T & T Clark, 1996.

———. *Solidarity and Difference: A Contemporary Reading of Paul's Ethics*. London: T & T Clark International, 2005.

Horsley, Richard A. "1 Corinthians: A Case Study of Paul's Assembly as an Alternative Society." In *Paul and Empire: Religion, Power, and the Life of the Spirit*, edited by Richard A. Horsley, 242–52. Harrisburg, PA: Trinity, 1997.

———. "Building An Alternative Society: Introduction." In *Paul and Empire: Religion, Power, and the Life of the Spirit*, edited by Richard A. Horsley, 206–14. Harrisburg, PA: Trinity, 1997.

———, ed. *Christian Origins*. A People's History of Christianity 1. Minneapolis: Fortress, 2005.

———. "General Introduction." In *Paul and Empire: Religion, Power, and the Life of the Spirit*, edited by Richard A. Horsley, 1–8. Harrisburg, PA: Trinity, 1997.

———, ed. *Hidden Transcripts and the Arts of Resistance: Applying the Works of James C. Scott to Jesus and Paul*. Semeia Studies 48. Atlanta: Society of Biblical Literature, 2004.

———, ed. *In the Shadow of Empire: Reclaiming the Bible as a History of Faithful Resistance*. Louisville: Westminster John Knox, 2008.

———. "Introduction." In *Paul and the Roman Imperial Order*, edited by Richard A. Horsley, 1–23. Harrisburg, PA: Trinity, 2004.

———. *Jesus and Empire: The Kingdom of God and the New World Disorder*. Minneapolis: Fortress, 2003.

———, ed. *Paul and Empire: Religion, Power, and the Life of the Spirit*. Harrisburg, PA: Trinity, 1997.

———, ed. *Paul and Politics: Ekklesia, Israel, Imperium, Interpretation. Essays in Honor of Krister Stendahl*. Harrisburg, PA: Trinity, 2000.

———, ed. *Paul and the Roman Imperial Order*. Harrisburg, PA: Trinity, 2004.

———. "Paul's Counter-Imperial Gospel: Introduction." In *Paul and Empire: Religion, Power, and the Life of the Spirit*, edited by Richard A. Horsley, 140–47. Harrisburg, PA: Trinity, 1997.

———. *Religion and Empire: People, Power, and the Life of the Spirit*. Facets Series. Minneapolis: Fortress, 2003.

———. "Rhetoric and Empire—and 1 Corinthians." In *Paul and Politics: Ekklesia, Israel, Imperium, Interpretation. Essays in Honor of Krister Stendahl*, edited by Richard A. Horsley, 72–102. Harrisburg, PA: Trinity, 2000.

Horsley, Richard A., and Neil Asher Silberman. *The Message and the Kingdom: How Jesus and Paul Ignited a Revolution and Transformed the Ancient World*. Minneapolis: Fortress, 1997.

Howard-Brook, Wes. *Empire Baptized: How the Church Embraced What Jesus Rejected Second to Fifth Centuries*. Maryknoll, NY: Orbis, 2016.

Howard-Brook, Wes, and Anthony Gwyther. *Unveiling Empire: Reading Revelation Then and Now*. Foreword by Elizabeth McAlister. The Bible and Liberation Series. Maryknoll, NY: Orbis, 1999.

Hurtado, Larry. *Destroyer of the Gods: Early Christian Distinctiveness in the Roman World*. Waco, TX: Baylor University Press, 2016.

———. *Lord Jesus Christ: Devotion to Jesus in Earliest Christianity*. Grand Rapids: Eerdmans, 2003.

INCITE! Women of Color Against Violence, eds. *The Revolution Will Not Be Funded: Beyond the Non-Profit Industrial Complex*. New York: South End, 2009.

Jeffers, James S. *The Greco-Roman World of the New Testament Era: Exploring the Background of Early Christianity*. Downers Grove, IL: InterVarsity, 1999.

Jennings, Theodore W., Jr. *Outlaw Justice: The Messianic Politics of Paul*. Stanford: Stanford University Press, 2013.

———. *Reading Derrida/Thinking Paul: On Justice*. Cultural Memory in the Present. Stanford: Stanford University Press, 2006.

Jeremias, Joachim. *The Proclamation of Jesus*. Vol. 1 of *New Testament Theology*. London: SCM, 1971.

Jewett, Robert. *Christian Tolerance: Paul's Message to the Modern Church*. Biblical Perspectives on Current Issues. Philadelphia: Westminster, 1982.

———. "The Corruption and Redemption of Creation: Reading Rom 8:18–23 within the Imperial Context." In *Paul and the Roman Imperial Order*, edited by Richard A. Horsley, 25–46. Harrisburg, PA: Trinity, 2004.

———. *Paul: The Apostle to America. Cultural Trends in Pauline Scholarship*. Louisville: Westminster John Knox, 1994.

———. "Paul, Shame, and Honor." In *Paul in the Greco-Roman World: A Handbook*, edited by J. Paul Sampley, 551–74. New York: Trinity, 2003.

———. *Romans: A Commentary*. Hermeneia Series. Minneapolis: Fortress, 2007.

Jipp, Joshua W. *Christ is King: Paul's Royal Ideology*. Minneapolis: Fortress, 2015.

Judge, Edwin A. "Did the Churches Compete with Cult Groups?" In *Early Christianity and Classical Culture: Comparative Studies in Honor of Abraham J. Malherbe*, edited by John T. Fitzgerald et al., 501–24. Supplements to Novum Testamentum 60. Leiden: Brill, 2003.

———. *Social Distinctives of the Christians in the First Century: Pivotal Essays by E. A. Judge*. Edited by David M. Sholer. Peabody, MA: Hendrickson, 2008.

Juvenal. "Satires." In *Juvenal: The Sixteen Satires*, edited by Peter Green, 65–297. Translated by Peter Green. Penguin Classics. London: Penguin, 1967.

Kahl, Brigitte. *Galatians Re-Imagined: Reading with the Eyes of the Vanquished*. Paul in Critical Contexts Series. Minneapolis: Fortress, 2010.

Kallas, James. "Romans 13:1–7: An Interpolation." *New Testament Studies* 11 (1965) 365–74.

Käsemann, Ernst. *New Testament Questions of Today*. Translated by W. J. Montague. Philadelphia: Fortress, 1969.

———. *Perspectives on Paul*. Translated by Margaret Kohl. London: SCM, 1971.

Kautsky, Karl. *Foundations of Christianity*. Translated by Henry F. Mins. New York: S. A. Russell, 1953.

Kee, Howard Clark. *The Beginnings of Christianity: An Introduction to the New Testament*. London: T & T Clark, 2005.

———. *Christian Origins in Sociological Perspective: Methods and Resources*. Philadelphia: Westminster, 1980.

———. *The Renewal of Hope*. New York: Association, 1959.

Kim, Seyoon. *Christ and Caesar: The Gospel and the Roman Empire in the Writings of Paul and Luke*. Grand Rapids: Eerdmans, 2008.

Kim, Yung Suk. *Christ's Body in Corinth: The Politics of a Metaphor*. Paul in Critical Contexts. Minneapolis: Fortress, 2008.

Klein, Naomi. *The Shock Doctrine: The Rise of Disaster Capitalism*. Toronto: Vintage Canada, 2008.

Knust, Jennifer Wright. "Paul and the Politics of Virtue and Vice." In *Paul and the Roman Imperial Order*, edited by Richard A. Horsley, 155–73. Harrisburg, PA: Trinity, 2004.

Koening, John. *New Testament Hospitality: Partnership with Strangers as Promise and Mission*. Eugene, OR: Wipf & Stock, 2001.

Koester, Helmut. *History, Culture, and Religion of the Hellenistic Age*. Vol. 1 of *Introduction to the New Testament*. Berlin: De Gruyter, 1995.

Krentz, Edgar. "Paul, Games, and the Military." In *Paul in the Greco-Roman World: A Handbook*, edited by J. Paul Sampley, 344–83. New York: Trinity, 2003.

Kropotkin, Peter. *Fugitive Writings*. Collected Works of Peter Kropotkin 10. Montréal: Black Rose, 1993.

———. *Mutual Aid: A Factor of Evolution*. 1906. Online. https://theanarchistlibrary.org/library/petr-kropotkin-mutual-aid-a-factor-of-evolution.
Kümmel, Werner Georg. *The Theology of the New Testament According to Its Major Witnesses: Jesus—Paul—John*. Nashville: Abingdon, 1973.
Ladd, George Eldon. *A Theology of the New Testament*. Edited by Donald A Hagner. Grand Rapids: Eerdmans, 1993.
Lampe, Peter. "Paul, Patrons, and Clients." In *Paul in the Greco-Roman World: A Handbook*, edited by J. Paul Sampley, 488–523. New York: Trinity, 2003.
———. "The Roman Christians of Romans 16." In *The Romans Debate*, edited by Karl P. Donfried, 44–52. Edinburgh: T & T Clark, 1991.
Lassen, Eva Marie. "The Roman Family: Ideal and Metaphor." In *Constructing Early Christian Families: Family as Social Reality and Metaphor*, edited by Halvor Moxnes, 103–20. London: Routledge, 1997.
Levine, Amy-Jill, with Marrianne Blickenstaff. *A Feminist Companion to Paul*. Cleveland: Pilgrim, 2004.
Lietzmann, Hans. *The Beginnings of the Christian Church*. Translated by Bertram Lee Woolf. London: Lutterworth, 1953.
Livy, Titius. *The History of Rome*. Translated by Rev. Canon Roberts. New York: E. P. Dutton, 1912. Online. http://www.perseus.tufts.edu/hopper/text?doc=Perseus%3Atext%3A1999.02.0026
Lohse, Eduard. *Theological Ethics of the New Testament*. Translated by M. Eugene Boring. Minneapolis: Fortress, 1991.
Longenecker, Bruce W. "The Poor of Galatians 2:10: The Interpretative Paradigm of the First Four Centuries." In *Engaging Economics: New Testament Scenarios and Early Christian Reception*, edited by Bruce W. Longenecker and Kelly D. Liebengood, 205–21. Grand Rapids: Eerdmans.
———. *Remember the Poor: Paul, Poverty, and the Greco-Roman World*. Grand Rapids: Eerdmans, 2010.
Longenecker, Bruce W., and Kelly D. Liebengood, eds. *Engaging Economics: New Testament Scenarios and Early Christian Reception*. Grand Rapids: Eerdmans, 2005.
Longenecker, Richard N. *The Ministry and Message of Paul*. Grand Rapids: Zondervan, 1971.
———. *New Testament Social Ethics for Today*. Grand Rapids: Eerdmans, 1984.
———. *Paul, Apostle of Liberty: The Origin and Nature of Paul's Christianity*. Grand Rapids: Baker, 1976.
Lopez, Davina C. *Apostle to the Conquered: Reimagining Paul's Mission*. Paul in Critical Contexts. Minneapolis: Fortress, 2008.
Luther, Martin. "Against the Robbing and Murdering Hordes of Peasants (1525)." In *Martin Luther*, edited by E. G. Rupp and Benjamin Drewery, 121–26. Documents of Modern History. London: Edward Arnold, 1970. Online. http://zimmer.csufresno.edu/~mariterel/against_the_robbing_and_murderin.htm.
MacMullen, Ramsay. *Changes in the Roman Empire: Essays in the Ordinary*. Princeton: Princeton University Press, 1990.
———. *Paganism in the Roman Empire*. New Haven, CT: Yale University Press, 1981.
Maier, Harry O. *Picturing Paul in Empire: Imperial Image, Text, and Persuasion in Colossians, Ephesians, and the Pastoral Epistles*. London: Bloomsbury T & T Clark, 2013.

BIBLIOGRAPHY

Malherbe, Abraham J. "God's New Family in Thessalonica." In *The Social World of the First Christians: Essays in Honor of Wayne A. Meeks*, edited by L. Michael White and O. Larry Yarbrough, 116–25. Minneapolis: Fortress, 1995.

———. *Paul and the Popular Philosophers*. Minneapolis: Fortress, 1989.

———. *Social Aspects of Early Christianity*. Philadelphia: Fortress, 1983.

Malina, Bruce J. "Social Levels, Morals, and Daily Life." In *The Early Christian World*, edited by Philip F. Esler, 369–400. London: Routledge, 2000.

Malina, Bruce J., and Jerome H. Neyrey. *Portraits of Paul: An Archaeology of Ancient Personality*. Louisville: Westminster John Knox, 1996.

Malina, Bruce J., and John J. Pilch. *Social-Science Commentary on the Letters of Paul*. Minneapolis: Fortress, 2006.

Marshall, I. Howard. *A Concise New Testament Theology*. Downers Grove, IL: InterVarsity, 2008.

———. "Jesus as Lord: The Development of the Concept." In *Eschatology and the New Testament: Essays in Honor of George Raymond Beasley-Murray*, edited by W. Hulitt Gloer, 129–45. Peabody, MA: Hendrickson, 1988.

Martin, Ralph. "The Spirit in 2 Corinthians in Light of the "Fellowship of the Spirit" in 2 Corinthians 13:14." In *Eschatology and the New Testament: Essays in Honor of George Raymond Beasley-Murray*, edited by W. Hulitt Gloer, 113–28. Peabody, MA: Hendrickson, 1988.

Martyn, J. Louis. "Christ, the Elements of the Cosmos, and the Law in Galatians." In *The Social World of the First Christians: Essays in Honor of Wayne A. Meeks*, edited by L. Michael White and O. Larry Yarbrough, 16–39. Minneapolis: Fortress, 1995.

———. *Theological Issues in the Letters of Paul*. Nashville: Abingdon, 1997.

Matera, Frank J. *New Testament Ethics: The Legacies of Jesus and Paul*. Louisville: Westminster John Knox, 1996.

Maynard, Robyn. *Policing Black Lives: State Violence in Canada from Slavery to the Present*. Winnipeg: Fernwood, 2017.

Meeks, Wayne A. *The First Urban Christians: The Social World of the Apostle Paul*. New Haven, CT: Yale University Press, 1983.

———. "The Image of the Androgyne." In *In Search of the Early Christians: Selected Essays*, edited by Allen R. Hilston and H. Gregory Snyder, 11–27. New Haven, CT: Yale University Press, 2002.

———. *In Search of the Early Christians: Selected Essays*. Edited by Allen R. Hilston and H. Gregory Snyder. New Haven, CT: Yale University Press, 2002.

———. *The Moral World of the First Christians*. Library of Early Christianity. Philadelphia: Westminster, 1986.

———. *The Origins of Christian Morality: The First Two Centuries*. New Haven, CT: Yale University Press, 1993.

———. *The Writings of St. Paul*. New York: Norton, 1972.

Meggitt, Justin J. *The Madness of King Jesus: The Real Reason for His Execution*. Forthcoming.

———. *Paul, Poverty and Survival*. Studies of the New Testament and Its World. Edinburgh: T & T Clark, 1998.

Miranda, José Porfirio. *Marx and the Bible: A Critique of the Philosophy of Oppression*. Translated by John Eagleson. Maryknoll, NY: Orbis, 1974.

Moltmann, Jürgen. *The Church in the Power of the Spirit: A Contribution to Messianic Ecclesiology*. Translated by Margaret Kohl. Minneapolis: Fortress, 1993.

BIBLIOGRAPHY

Moule, C. F. D. *The Origin of Christology*. Cambridge: Cambridge University Press, 1977.

Moxnes, Halvor, ed. *Constructing Early Christian Families: Family as Social Reality and Metaphor*. London: Routledge, 1997.

National Coalition for the Homeless. "Remembering Those Lost to Homelessness." *National Coalition for the Homeless* (blog), December 21, 2018. Online. https://nationalhomeless.org/remembering-those-lost-to-homelessness.

Neocleous, M. *The Fabrication of Social Order: A Critical Theory of Police Power*. London: Pluto, 2000.

Neumann, Rachel. "We Make the Road by Walking: Lessons from the Zapatista Caravan." *Monthly Review* 53.2 (2001). Online. https://monthlyreview.org/2001/06/01/we-make-the-road-by-walking.

Neyrey, Jerome. *Paul, In Other Words: A Cultural Reading of His Letters*. Louisville: Westminster John Knox, 1990.

Nickle, Keith F. *The Collection: A Study of Paul's Strategy*. Studies in Biblical Theology 48. London: SCM, 1966.

Oakes, Peter. "God's Sovereignty over Roman Authorities: A Theme in Philippians." In *Rome in the Bible and the Early Church*, edited by Peter Oakes, 126–41. Carlisle: Paternoster, 2002.

———. *Philippians: From People to Letter*. Society for New Testament Studies Monograph Series 110. Cambridge: Cambridge University Press, 2001.

———. *Reading Romans in Pompeii: Paul's Letter at Ground Level*. Minneapolis: Fortress, 2009.

———, ed. *Rome in the Bible and the Early Church*. Carlisle: Paternoster, 2002.

Osiek, Carolyn. "Family Matters." In *Christian Origins*, edited by Richard A. Horsley, 201–20. Minneapolis: Fortress, 2005.

Oudshoorn, Daniel. "Going to Die: On Staging Losing Conflicts with the Powers (A Sermon)." Sermon deliverd at "The Story" in Sarnia, Ontario, April 1, 2012. *On Journeying with Those in Exile* (blog), April 1, 2012. https://poserorprophet.wordpress.com/2012/04/01/going-to-die-on-staging-losing-conflicts-with-the-powers-a-sermon.

———. "Hurtado Responds." *On Journeying with Those in Exile* (blog), November 3, 2016. Online. https://poserorprophet.wordpress.com/2016/11/03/hurtado-responds.

———. "The New Testament and Violence. Part Two: The Nonviolence of Paul." *On Journeying with Those in Exile* (blog), November 30, 2010. Online. https://poserorprophet.wordpress.com/2010/11/30/the-new-testament-and-violence-part-two-the-nonviolence-of-paul.

———. "Reading Paul in the Context of Empire." Lecture delivered at Regent College, July 20, 2010. *On Journeying with Those in Exile* (blog), July 21, 2010. Online. https://poserorprophet.wordpress.com/2010/07/21/reading-paul-in-the-context-of-empire-lecture-delivered-10july20.

———. "Response to Larry Hurtado's *Destroyer of the gods: Early Christian Distinctiveness in the Roman World*." *On Journeying with Those in Exile* (blog), October 27, 2016. Online. https://poserorprophet.wordpress.com/2016/10/27/response-to-larry-hurtados-destroyer-of-the-gods.

Pate, C. Marvin. *The End of the Age has Come: The Theology of Paul*. Grand Rapids: Zondervan, 1995.

Peppard, Michael. *The Son of God in the Roman World: Divine Sonship in its Social and Political Context.* Oxford: Oxford University Press, 2011.

Pickett, Ray. "Conflicts at Corinth." In *Christian Origins*, edited by Richard A. Horsley, 113–37. Minneapolis: Fortress, 2005.

Pilgrim, Walter. *Uneasy Neighbors: Church and State in the New Testament.* Overtures to Biblical Theology. Minneapolis: Fortress, 1999.

Pohl, Christine D. *Making Room: Recovering Hospitality as a Christian Tradition.* Grand Rapids: Eerdmans, 1999.

Polaski, Sandra Hack. *Paul and the Discourse of Power.* Gender, Culture, Theory 8. The Biblical Seminar 62. Sheffield: Sheffield Academic, 1999.

Porter, Stanley E., and Cynthia Long Westfall, eds. *Empire in the New Testament.* Eugene, OR: Pickwick, 2011.

Proudhon, Pierre-Joseph. *Selected Writings of Pierre-Joseph Proudhon.* Edited by Stewart Edwards. Garden City: Anchor, 1969.

Remus, Harold. "Persecution." In *Handbook of Early Christianity: Social-Science Approaches*, edited by Anthony J. Blasi et al. eds., 431–52. New York: Altamira, 2002.

Richardson, Peter. *Paul's Ethic of Freedom.* Philadelphia: Westminster, 1979.

Ridderbos, Herman. *Paul: An Outline of His Theology.* Translated by John Richard De Witt. Grand Rapids: Eerdmans, 1975.

Roetzel, Calvin J. *The Letters of Paul: Conversations in Context.* Louisville: Westminster John Knox, 1998.

———. *Paul—A Jew on the Margins.* Louisville: Westminster John Knox, 2003.

———. *The World That Shaped the New Testament.* Atlanta: John Knox, 1985.

Rossing, Barbara R. "Prophets, Prophetic Movements, and the Voices of Women." In *Christian Origins*, edited by Richard A. Horsley, 261–86. Minneapolis: Fortress, 2005.

Sampley, J. Paul, ed. *Paul in the Greco-Roman World: A Handbook.* New York: Trinity, 2003.

———. *Pauline Partnership in Christ: Christian Community and Commitment in Light of Roman Law.* Philadelphia: Fortress, 1980.

———. *Walking Between the Times: Paul's Moral Reasoning.* Minneapolis: Fortress, 1991.

Sanders, E. P. *Paul.* Past Masters Series. Oxford: Oxford University Press, 1991.

———. *Paul: The Apostle's Life, Letters, and Thoughts.* Minneapolis: Fortress, 2015.

Sandnes, Karl Olav. "Equality Within Patriarchal Structures: Some New Testament Perspectives on the Christian Fellowship as a Brother- or Sisterhood and a Family." In *Constructing Early Christian Families: Family as Social Reality and Metaphor*, edited by Halvor Moxnes, 150–65. London: Routledge, 1997.

Scheid, John. "Augustus and Roman Religion: Continuity, Conservatism, and Innovation." In *The Cambridge Companion to the Age of Augustus*, edited by Karl Galinsky, 175–94. Cambridge: Cambridge University Press, 2005.

Schmitt, Carl. *Political Theology: Four Chapters on the Concept of Sovereignty.* Edited and translated by George Schwab. Foreword by Tracy B. Strong. Chicago: University of Chicago Press, 2005.

Schnabel, Eckhard J. *Paul and the Early Church.* Vol. 2 of *Early Christian Mission.* Leicester: Apollos, 2004.

Schnackenburg, Rudolf. *The Moral Teaching of the New Testament*. Translated by J. Holland-Smith and W. J. O'Hara. London: Burns & Oates, 1967.

Schottroff, Luise. "'Give to Caesar what Belongs to Caesar and to God What Belongs to God': A Theological Response of the Early Christian Church to Its Social and Political Environment." In *The Love of Enemy and Nonretaliation in the New Testament*, edited by Willard M. Swartley, 223–57. Louisville: Westminster John Knox, 1992.

Schrage, Wolfgang. *The Ethics of the New Testament*. Translated by David E. Green. Philadelphia: Fortress, 1988.

Schreiner, Thomas R. *Paul: Apostle of God's Glory in Christ*. Downers Grove, IL: InterVarsity, 2001.

———. *Romans*. Baker Exegetical Commentary on the New Testament. Grand Rapids: Baker, 1998.

Schüssler-Fiorenza, Elisabeth. *In Memory of Her: A Feminist Theological Reconstruction of Christian Origins*. New York: Crossroad, 1994.

———. *Rhetoric and Ethic: The Politics of Biblical Study*. Minneapolis: Fortress, 1999.

Schütz, John Howard. *Paul and the Anatomy of Apostolic Authority*. Society for New Testament Studies Monograph Series 26. Cambridge: Cambridge University Press, 1975.

Schweitzer, Albert. *The Mysticism of Paul the Apostle*. Translated by William Montgomery. London: Black, 1931.

Scott, James C. *The Art of Not Being Governed: An Anarchist History of Upland Southeast Asia*. New Haven, CT: Yale University Press, 2010.

———. *Domination and the Arts of Resistance: Hidden Transcripts*. Yale: Yale University Press, 1992.

———. *Weapons of the Weak: Everyday Forms of Peasant Resistance*. Yale: Yale University Press, 1987.

Scroggs, Robin. *Paul for a New Day*. Philadelphia: Fortress, 1977.

———. *The Text and the Times: New Testament Essays for Today*. Minneapolis: Fortress, 1993.

Seneca, Lucius Annaeus. *Seneca: Dialogues and Essays*. Translated by John Davie. Oxford World's Classics. Oxford: Oxford University Press, 2007.

Shaw, Graham. *The Cost of Authority: Manipulation and Freedom in the New Testament*. Philadelphia: Fortress, 1982.

Simpson, Audra. *Mohawk Interruptus: Political Life Across the Borders of Settler States*. Durham: Duke University Press, 2014.

Simpson, Leanne Betasamosake. *Dancing on Our Turtle's Back: Stories of Nishnaabeg Re-Creation, Resurgence and a New Emergence*. Winnipeg: Arbiter Ring, 2011.

Smith, Abraham. "'Unmasking the Powers': Toward a Postcolonial Analysis of 1 Thessalonians." In *Paul and the Roman Imperial Order*, edited by Richard A. Horsley, 47–66. Harrisburg, PA: Trinity, 2004.

Sobrino, Jon. *No Salvation Outside the Poor: Prophetic-Utopian Essays*. Maryknoll, NY: Orbis, 2008.

Stauffer, Ethelbert. *New Testament Theology*. Translated by John Marsh. London: SCM, 1955.

Stringfellow, William. *An Ethic for Christians and Other Aliens in a Strange Land*. Eugene, OR: Wipf & Stock, 2004.

BIBLIOGRAPHY

Strom, Mark. *Reframing Paul: Conversations in Grace and Community*. Downers Grove, IL: InterVarsity, 2000.

Suetonius Trannquillus, C. *The Twelve Caesars*. Translated by Robert Graves. London: Folio Society, 2005.

Sugai, Yasko. "Paul's Eschatology and his Ethical Thought in Relation to It." MCS thesis, Regent College, Canada, 1982.

Swartley, Willard M., ed. *The Love of Enemy and Nonretaliation in the New Testament*. Louisville: Westminster John Knox, 1992.

Tacitus, Publius Cornelius. *The Complete Works of Tacitus*. Translated by Alfred John Church and William Jackson Brodribb. Edited by Moses Hadas. The Modern Library. New York: Random, 1942.

Taubes, Jacob. *Occidental Eschatology*. Translated by David Ratmoko. Cultural Memory in the Present. Stanford: Stanford University Press, 2009.

———. *The Political Theology of Paul*. Cultural Memory in the Present. Edited by Aleida Assmann et al. Translated by Dana Hollander. Stanford: Stanford University Press, 2004.

Taylor, Keeanga-Yamahtta. *From #BlackLivesMatter to Black Liberation*. Chicago: Haymarket, 2017.

Tellbe, Mikael. *Paul between Synagogue and State: Christians, Jews, and Civic Authorities in 1 Thessalonians, Romans, and Philippians*. Coniectanea Biblica New Testament Series 34. Stockholm: Almqvist & Wiksell International, 2001.

Tenney, Merrill C. *New Testament Times*. London: Lowe & Brydone, 1965.

Thatcher, Tom. "'I Have Conquered the World': The Death of Jesus and the End of Empire in the Gospel of John." In *Empire in the New Testament*, edited by Stanley E. Porter and Cynthia Long Westfall, 140–63. Eugene, OR: Pickwick, 2011.

Theissen, Gerd. *Fortress Introduction to The New Testament*. Translated by John Bowden. Minneapolis: Fortress, 2003.

———. *The Religion of the Earliest Churches: Creating a Symbolic World*. Translated by John Bowden. Minneapolis: Fortress, 1999.

———. *Social Reality and the Early Christians: Theology, Ethics, and the World of the New Testament*. Translated by Margaret Kohl. Minneapolis: Fortress, 1992.

———. *The Social Setting of Pauline Christianity: Essays on Corinth*. Edited and translated by John H. Schütz. Philadelphia: Fortress, 1982.

Thielman, Frank. *Theology of the New Testament: a Canonical and Synthetic Approach*. Grand Rapids: Zondervan, 2005.

Thompson, Richard. "Paul's Collection for the Jerusalem Church and the Inclusion of the Gentiles." ThM Thesis, Regent College, Canada, 2000.

Tilling, Chris. *Paul's Divine Christology*. Wissenschaftliche Untersuchungen zum Neuen Testament 2. Reihe 323. Tübingen: Mohr Siebeck, 2012.

Troeltsch, Ernst. *The Social Teachings of The Christian Churches*. Vol. 1. Translated by Olive Wyon. Introduction by H. Richard Niebuhr. New York: Harper & Row, 1960.

Umoja, Akinyele Omowale. *We Will Shoot Back: Armed Resistance in the Mississippi Freedom Movement*. New York: New York University Press, 2014.

Vergilius Maro, Publius. *The Aeneid*. Translated by Robert Fitzgerald. Vintage Classics. New York: Vintage, 1990.

Vos, Geerhardus. *The Pauline Eschatology*. Grand Rapids: Eerdmans, 1972.

Walker, William O., Jr. *Interpolations in the Pauline Letters*. New York: Sheffield Academic Press, 2001.

Walsh, Brian J., and Sylvia C. Keesmaat. *Colossians Remixed: Subverting the Empire.* Downers Grove, IL: InterVarsity, 2004.

Wan, Sze-kar. "Collection for the Saints as Anticolonial Act: Implications of Paul's Ethnic Reconstruction." In *Paul and Politics: Ekklesia, Israel, Imperium, Interpretation. Essays in Honor of Krister Stendahl,* edited by Richard A. Horsley, 191-215. Harrisburg, PA: Trinity, 2000.

Weber, Max. *The Protestant Ethic and the Spirit of Capitalism.* Translated by Talcott Parsons. Introduction by Anthony Giddens. New York: Routledge, 2006.

Weiss, Johannes. *Earliest Christianity.* Translated by Frederick C. Grant et al. 2 vols. Gloucester, MA: Peter Smith, 1970.

———. *Paul and Jesus.* Translated by H. J. Chaytor. London: Harper & Brothers, 1909.

Welborn, L. L. *Paul, the Fool of Christ: A Study of 1 Corinthians 1-4 in the Comic-Philosophic Tradition.* Early Christianity in Context Series. Journal for the Study of the New Testament Supplement Series 293. London: T & T Clark International, 2005.

———. *Paul's Summons to Messianic Life.* Insurrections: Critical Studies in Religion, Politics, and Culture. New York: Columbia University Press, 2015.

———. "That There May Be Equality: The Context and Consequences of a Pauline Ideal." *New Testament Studies* 59 (2013) 73-90.

Wengst, Klaus. *Humility: Solidarity of the Humiliated.* Philadelphia: Fortress, 1988.

———. *Pax Romana and the Peace of Jesus Christ.* Translated by John Bowden. Minneapolis: Fortress, 1987.

Westerholm, Stephen. *Perspectives Old and New on Paul: The "Lutheran" Paul and His Critics.* Grand Rapids: Eerdmans, 2004.

White, L. Michael. "Paul and *Pater Familias.*" In *Paul in the Greco-Roman World: A Handbook,* edited by J. Paul Sampley, 457-87. Harrisburg, PA: Trinity, 2003.

White, L. Michael, and O. Larry Yarbrough, eds. *The Social World of the First Christians: Essays in Honor of Wayne A. Meeks.* Minneapolis: Fortress, 1995.

Williams, Eric. *Capitalism and Slavery.* Chapel Hill: University of North Carolina Press, 1944.

Williams, Kristian. *Our Enemies in Blue: Police and Power in America.* San Francisco: AK, 2015.

Willse, Craig. *The Value of Homelessness: Managing Surplus Life in the United States.* Minneapolis: University of Minnesota Press, 2015.

Wink, Walter. *Engaging the Powers: Discernment and Resistance in a World of Domination.* Minneapolis: Fortress, 1992.

———. *Naming the Powers: The Language of Power in the New Testament.* Philadelphia: Fortress, 1984.

———. *Unmasking the Powers: The Invisible Forces that Determine Human Existence.* Philadelphia: Fortress, 1986.

Winter, Bruce W. *After Paul Left Corinth: The Influence of Secular Ethics and Social Change.* Grand Rapids: Eerdmans, 2001.

———. "Roman Law and Society in Romans 12-15." In *Rome in the Bible and the Early Church,* edited by Peter Oakes, 67-102. Carlisle: Paternoster, 2002.

———. *Seek the Welfare of the City: Christians as Benefactors and Citizens.* First Century Christians in the Graeco-Roman World. Carlisle: Paternoster, 1994.

BIBLIOGRAPHY

Winter, Sara B. C. "Philemon and the Patriarchal Paul." In *A Feminist Companion to Paul*, edited by Amy-Jill Levine with Marrianne Blickenstaff, 122–36. Cleveland: Pilgrim, 2004.

Wire, Antoinette Clark. *The Corinthian Women Prophets: A Reconstruction of Paul's Rhetoric*. Minneapolis: Fortress, 1990.

Witherington, Ben, III. *Jesus, Paul, and the End of the World: A Comparative Study in New Testament Eschatology*. Downers Grove, IL: InterVarsity, 1992.

———. *The Paul Quest: The Renewed Search for the Jew of Tarsus*. Downers Grove, IL: InterVarsity, 1998.

Wrede, W. *Paul*. Translated by Edward Lummis. London: Elsom, 1907.

Wright, N. T. *The Climax of the Covenant: Christ and the Law in Pauline Theology*. Minneapolis: Fortress, 1993.

———. *How God Became King: The Forgotten Story of the Gospels*. New York: HarperOne, 2012.

———. *Jesus and the Victory of God*. Christian Origins and the Question of God 2. Minneapolis: Fortress, 1996.

———. *The New Testament and the People of God*. Christian Origins and the Question of God 1. Minneapolis: Fortress, 1992.

———. "On Dropping the Debt." *NTWrightPage* (blog), May 12, 2008. Online. https://ntwrightpage.com/2016/04/05/on-dropping-the-debt.

———. "Paul and Caesar: A New Reading of Romans." In *A Royal Priesthood? The Use of the Bible Ethically and Politically: A Dialogue with Oliver O'Donovan*, edited by Craig Bartholomew et al., 173–93. Grand Rapids: Zondervan, 2002.

———. *Paul: In Fresh Perspective*. Minneapolis: Fortress, 2005.

———. "Paul's Gospel and Caesar's Empire." In *Paul and Politics: Ekklesia, Israel, Imperium, Interpretation. Essays in Honor of Krister Stendahl*, edited by Richard A. Horsley, 160–83. Harrisburg, PA: Trinity, 2000.

———. *Simply Christian: Why Christianity Makes Sense*. San Francisco: HarperSanFrancisco, 2006.

———. *Surprised by Hope: Rethinking Heaven, the Resurrection, and the Mission of the Church*. New York: HarperOne, 2008.

———. *What Saint Paul Really Said: Was Paul of Tarsus the Real Founder of Christianity?* Grand Rapids: Eerdmans, 1997.

Yarbrough, O. Larry. *Not Like the Gentiles: Marriage Rules in the Letters of Paul*. SBL Dissertation Series 80. Atlanta: Scholars, 1985.

Yeo, Khiok-Khng. *Chairman Mao Meets the Apostle Paul: Christianity, Communism, and the Hope of China*. Grand Rapids: Brazos, 2002.

Ziesler, John A. *Pauline Christianity*. Oxford Bible Series. Oxford: Oxford University Press, 1983.

www.ingramcontent.com/pod-product-compliance
Lightning Source LLC
Chambersburg PA
CBHW021344300426
44114CB00012B/1068